The Power of Sexual Surrender for Christians

Thank You for Unpacking Dr. Robinson's Book

I've read Dr. Robinson's book three times. My husband was reading It, and we were discussing it weekly and praying with it. But Patsy's new book has really broken it down into a way that is easier to understand.

—Older Millennial Wife

Wow! Is All I Can Say About the Man's Orgasm!

As a man, the description of the man's orgasm got my attention. Sex is definitely a heart, not a head, issue.

—Older Millennial Reader

Chapter 17 on Pullbacks Is Awesome!

Marie Robinson is wise and insightful, but Patsy Rae comes along with her insights from the scriptures, and BAM! It gives you the confidence that you can actually make progress and come into the light (even with some pullbacks)!

—Ladies Bible Class Teacher

Patsy Made the Original *Sexual Surrender* Incredible!

This book, and all of Patsy's other books, changed my life for the better. I read the original Sexual Surrender book, and it was great. But then Patsy came along and made it incredible! I hope this book helps many, many people the way it helped me. I love the way this new edition has scriptures throughout, just like Patsy's other books. I am so thankful for Patsy and the work she has put into this book.

—Millennial Single Woman Working Through the Book

Important for Our Generation

We love this book and feel that it is extremely important for our generation.

—Young Millennial Couple Reading the Book Together

The Divorce Rate Would Be Zero

Patsy, if you can get this across to the body of Christ, the divorce rate would be zero.

—DB, Christian Counselor

We Didn't Know How Good Our Marriage Could Be

Patsy's help, understanding, and insights walked us through some of the hardest times in our marriage. We couldn't have imagined how beautiful the other side could be of what we thought would be lifelong struggles.

—Young Millennial Wife Working Through the Book

I Am so Thankful for Chapter 28!

I realized I've often taken my anger out on either the people closest to me or myself. I realize now it should have been directed toward my parents. I am thankful for the tips I learned for finding peace and releasing stored up emotions. Ephesians 4:32 spoke to me because of my anger toward my parents. I know it needs to be released so I don't sin in my anger, and so I can move on and look at my parents with compassion and kindness. I can have empty-chair conversations, journal, or do slam balls.

—Client's Thankfulness Exercise

Provides a Path to Sexual and Marital Happiness

While we are bombarded with sexual talk and imagery in our media and culture, deep discussion about the true problems and joys of sex is almost impossible to find. The truth about sex is hiding under mountains of lies and deceptions, and it is revealed in this book. Thank you to Dr. Robinson and Patsy Rae Dawson for using both clinical experience and scripture to reveal a path to sexual and marital happiness.

—Older Millennial Reader

The Way to Sexual Maturity

In this important book, a leading psychiatrist examines a problem that endangers the stability of marriage and threatens the happiness of four out of ten American husbands and wives—sexual inhibitions. Through the use of actual case histories, she considers vital aspects of the problem: its cause, degree, and treatment. She details the roles that husband and wife must play if the couple is to effect a cure and achieve sexual fulfillment through the mature power of sexual surrender.

– 1959 SIGNET BOOK Back Cover

The Power of Sexual Surrender for Christians

Awaken Orgasmic Attitudes
to Overcome Inhibited Desire and Pleasure

A Commentary on Marie N. Robinson's Book
Excerpts from The Song of Solomon and The Sexless Marriages Survey

Patsy Rae Dawson

Marriage: A Taste of Heaven Series

The two-toned ribbon starts out folded and slightly ordered with a dusty light blue interior conveying leaving childhood hang-ups to transform into a godly, loving individual. It unfurls upward with an extreme perspective to let loose as the blue smolders and heats up into uninhibited purple as the multi-faceted benefits of passionate lovemaking are realized.

MARRIAGE: A TASTE OF HEAVEN MEDIA
TRANSFORMING LIVES WITH THE POWER OF THE SCRIPTURES

Published by:
Marriage: A Taste of Heaven Media
an imprint of Patsy Rae Dawson LLC
PO Box 550427
Dallas, TX 75355-0427 USA
PatsyRaeDawson.com

Translation abbreviations: ASV (American Standard Version), CJB (Complete Jewish Bible), JB (Jewish Bible), KJV (King James Version), NASB (New American Standard Bible), NIV (New International Version), NKJV (New King James Version), and RSV (Revised Standard Version), YLT (Young's Literal Translation).

Library of Congress Cataloging in Publication Data
Dawson, Patsy Rae, Marie N. Robison, MD
The power of sexual surrender for christians, awaken orgasmic attitudes to overcome inhibited desire and pleasure, a commentary on marie n. roboinson's book, excerpts from the song of Solomon and the sexless marriages survey.
1. Marriage—United States—Religious aspects—Christianity. 2. Love. 3. Sex—Religious aspects—Christianity.

Cover Design: Phillip Gessert, visit gessertbooks.com to see his work.

ISBN-10: 0938855115
ISBN-13: 978-0938855118

Table of Contents

Dedication

To Abby and Wyatt, a young couple deeply in love and devoted to God, who let me share their journey of overcoming childhood inhibitions and embracing God's way of a man with a maid. God brought you into my life for our mutual benefit. Your transparency with each other and with me allowed me to glean many epiphanies through working on this book that increased my knowledge and love for God. Thank you.

Acknowledgments

To Janelle Perdue Hulsey and Mevanee Parmer, cherished Truth Speakers Critique partners, who worked with me over Zoom through the COVID-19 pandemic. Your comments, insights, and suggestions resulted in many style and content changes to make this book more useful. I will be eternally grateful for your friendship, support, and love.

In memory of Suzana Sandoval, my original critique partner of many years, who entered the hospital as I began work on this project. Although Suzi did not recover and rejoin our group, she called several times to offer encouragement. She called two days before she died to say, "Never give up. Keep writing." Losing Suzi left a big hole in our hearts as we still mourn her loss and celebrate her life.

To my Alpha Readers who read the unpublished manuscript and offered comments "as a reader": Jeff, Tina, Marie-Lyne, Gillian, Anita, Adele, Abby, and Wyatt, I thank you with my whole heart. I started this project expecting to make two or three passes through Dr. Robinson's book and finish in three months. I lost track of how many additional passes your individual comments generated, expanding my original plans to seven months. I thrilled many times over as I experienced each of you making at least one unique comment that changed this book. You embodied what it means to be an "Alpha Reader." Thank you so much for your participation. You helped make this book better able to guide couples through overcoming their inhibitions and pullbacks so they can experience God's amazing love.

To God be the glory forever and ever,
Patsy Rae Dawson

Warning and Disclaimer

This Book Does Not Deal with Spouse Abuse

Dr. Marie N. Robinson writes frequently about anger and its relationship to sexual inhibitions as the wife takes her anger against her parents out on her husband and children. Patsy Rae Dawson also writes about both the wife's and the husband's anger, its parental source, and the emotional damage it does. Anger, rage, and hatred can quickly become emotionally and physically abusive and dangerous. This book does not deal with those potentially life-threatening issues.

This Book Does Not Address Sexual Addiction

Certainly, sex addicts need to understand the four parts of one flesh love that is taught in this book—intellectual, emotional, spiritual, and sexual. However, this book does not deal with the addictive nature of sexual addiction. Those individuals may need professional counseling. The first six signs of a sex addict that WebMD lists are the most common:

> "(1) obsessive sexual thoughts, (2) spending excessive time on sex [several times a day past the honeymoon period], (3) feeling shame or depression, (4) excluding other activities, (5) masturbating excessively, (6) engaging in risky or inappropriate behaviors, (7) cheating on partners, and (8) committing criminal sex offenses" (Dan Brennan, MD, 12/02/2020).

This Book Is Written for Self-Examination in Two Areas

1. The Impact of One's Childhood on One's Own Inhibitions

It is written for individuals who want to understand the impact of their home of origin on their ability to love and are receptive to examining their heart and behavior.

2. The Impact of the Spouse's Childhood on Inhibitions

Readers may also seek to understand the source of the anger directed toward them by an inhibited spouse. This knowledge enables them to step back emotionally and examine their situation more clearly so they can make wise decisions to protect themselves and their children. Both Dr. Marie N. Robinson and Patsy Rae Dawson write with the goal of helping both men and women find understanding so they can grow up into love for themselves, their mates, and their children.

Legal and Disclaimer

The contents of this book are for informational purposes only. It isn't the purpose of this material to provide all the information that is otherwise available. The information provided is on an as-is basis and without warranties of any kind, either expressed or implied. This book is not a replacement for professional services such as psychiatric or medical advice, diagnosis, or treatment. Always seek the advice of a qualified health provider with any questions regarding any psychological or medical condition. Never disregard professional medical advice or delay seeking treatment or diagnosis because of something you read in this book. This book does not provide legal services or legal advice.

Patsy Rae Dawson's study and faith are not a substitute for your own study and faith. You are responsible for your own well-being, choices, and decisions, including when using this material. Reliance on any information provided by this book is undertaken at your own risk.

2 Corinthians 13:5: "Test yourselves to see if you are in the faith; examine yourselves!"

Emergency

If you think you may have a medical or safety emergency, call 911 immediately. Most of the numbers below respond 24/7.

- National Domestic Violence Hotline: 1-800-799-SAFE (7233)
- National Teen Dating Abuse Helpline: 1-866-331-9474
- National Sexual Assault Hotline: 1-800-656-HOPE (4673)
- National Suicide Prevention Lifeline: 1-800-273-TALK (8255)
- Crisis Text Line: Text "LISTEN" to 741-741

Never Argue with Your Gut Instincts!

If your gut is telling you something is wrong, probably 95% of the time, something is wrong. Don't take a chance on being in the other 5%. Many women who are murdered had a gut feeling they were in danger but talked themselves out of it. Go to a women's shelter or a qualified health professional and let a counselor help you analyze what is going on. They are trained. You and your religious leaders probably aren't. Many shelters work with abused husbands.

Half a Century Preparing to Update This Book

I started studying about marriage and the Bible when I was 25, the age at which our brains mature to begin recognizing and solving problems. In 2020, I turned 75. Thus, I've spent half a century preparing to edit and add a commentary to Dr. Robinson's original 1959 work.

When I started teaching ladies marriage classes at age 27 in 1972, I determined not to talk about the then taboo topic of sex. But I kept getting questions. So I began to read multiple books about sexuality.

Fortunately, I discovered *The Power of Sexual Surrender* in early 1973. Although Dr. Robinson's book is not Bible-based, she recommended books about religion and sex. That religious influence shows especially in Chapter 15: "The Power of Love." And she says the vaginally orgasmic woman is nearly always a woman of faith.

This Book Opened Up the Scriptures About Sex

Dr. Robinson's words brought to mind scriptures about sexuality, which I'd wondered, "Why are these verses in the Bible?" Her focus on emotions and my recognizing how the scriptures emphasize the importance of our attitudes for enjoying ecstasy changed my life. I quickly transitioned from clitoral orgasms to multiple vaginal ones. I got excited about these psychological and Biblical truths.

Before I taught these new radical and revolutionary insights concerning the scriptures, I tested my understanding. I presented the material to two older Christian women who had taught women's classes for decades. They gave me their blessing.

Next, I presented the material to the young college wives who had already completed seven weeks of my classes. But my face turned red, and I stammered when I tried to say certain words. I could barely talk.

Afterward, the preacher's wife said, "I wondered what in the world were you trying to say when you got so embarrassed. Then when you said it, I thought, 'Is that all?'" She was a surgical nurse, and I realized "clitoris" and "vagina" were only biological, medical terms to her.

The next week I asked my students, "If I beat around the bush about the vaginal orgasm, will you get it?"

They unanimously agreed, "No! We want you to be plain."

Students, readers, and clients often tell me, "We like it because you are so frank," or "blunt," as one man gave as the reason he wanted to work with me.

Dr. Robinson's teaching about how our thoughts determine the way our bodies respond sexually opened up the theme of the Song of Solomon for me—soulmate before lovemaking for a lifetime of passion. As long as *The Power of Sexual Surrender* was in print, I bought it by the case and gave copies to my students.

This Book Is Now in the Public Domain So I Updated It

It makes me almost giddy now that Dr. Robinson's book is in the public domain, and I can reproduce it and supply the scriptures for you. My experience is that God's word is often the turning point for both men and women in making major changes in their attitudes and lives. It is faith-building to see the power of the scriptures to transform people's love lives demonstrated through Dr. Robinson's experiences.

Added Details about Men's Sexual Inhibitions

In 1959, when Dr. Robinson wrote this book, psychologists thought only women had sexual inhibitions. I knew that wasn't true because three of my first students wanted help dealing with husbands who weren't interested in sex. Inhibited husbands was the #1 problem I faced. Researchers now recognize men have the same inhibitions women do.

I devoted 2014-2015 to turning my Song of Solomon chapters into a standalone book. A friend recommended Dr. Douglas Weiss's book, *Intimacy Anorexia,* about the addiction of withholding sexual intimacy. As a result, I gleaned more insights about male and female sexuality.

I spent the last four years administering the *Sexless Marriages Survey: With Self-Assessment Checklists* and discovered 31 shocking facts about sex-withholding spouses.

Seeing how similar God's sexual instructions are for men and women showed me how valuable Dr. Robinson's material is for men. Plus, she frequently encouraged husbands and wives to work together so they both become better lovers. Following the direction of her teaching, I included information for dealing with men's inhibitions and highlighted the multi-faceted benefits of couples working together as a team. I also added male nouns and pronouns to include men in her original teaching about the role of emotions in sharing vaginal orgasms.

Added Headings to Dr. Robinson's Work

I edited Dr. Robinson's text and added headings to make her wisdom more easily discernable.

Added My Commentary Between ♥*PRD: ...* ♥

You will find my commentary in italics between ♥*PRD: ...italics...*♥. I shared scriptures along with my comments and updates from science. I also provided excerpts from my books.

Updated the Words "Frigid" and "Neurosis"

Dr. Robinson frequently used the word "frigid," the accepted psychological term 60 years ago to describe a nonorgasmic woman. The label was abandoned in the 1980s after Dr. Helen Kaplan's research made "inhibited sexual desire" the standard term. Today, "frigid" has become a term of derision used against women, especially in verbal abuse. Thus to further update Dr. Robinson's work, I replaced "frigid" with "nonorgasmic," "sexually inhibited," and other suitable words.

Also, I substituted "cognitive distortion," "distorted thinking," and "disruptive" for Dr. Robinson's outdated word "neurosis."

Had Five Epiphanies This Time Through

My understanding of the teaching in the scriptures about lovemaking had grown so much since the first time I studied *The Power of Sexual Surrender* that updating it opened up five new epiphanies. The first one relates to anger in Chapter 6: "Sexual Inhibitions Linked to Cognitive Distortions." Three are in Part 2: "Radical Epiphany on Awakening Male-Female Sexuality," "Why Don't Sexless Spouses Kiss, Hug, and Touch?" and "Pullbacks and Terrified, Angry, Truth-Telling Child-Adults." The fifth is in my revised book, *Male and Female: God's Genius, Soulmate to Fall in Love All Over Again* regarding God's 6 kinds of soulmating love. Updating this book has been a labor of love and transformation for me and the clients I worked with while writing it.

Matched the Theme with the Song of Solomon

The theme of Dr. Robinson's book supports God's theme in the Song of Solomon: "soulmate before lovemaking." The theme of *The Power of Sexual Surrender* is "release your inhibited thinking from your spirit so you can soulmate to share vaginal orgasms." The two become:

Awaken your orgasmic attitudes by soulmating
to enjoy God's way of a man with a maid.

May God bless you on your journey of love,
Patsy Rae Dawson
September 23, 2021
Seagoville, Texas USA

Part 1:

The Power of Sexual Surrender by Marie N. Robinson

Preface

I believe the problem of sexual inhibitions in women is one of the gravest marriage problems of our times. Over 40 percent of married women suffer from it in various degrees or forms. And their suffering, emotionally and physically, is real indeed.

Those who are most closely related to the nonorgasmic woman—husband and children—suffer too. This is so because being sexually inhibited is an expression of cognitive distortion, a disturbance of the individual's unconscious life, and is destructive to personal relationships. No matter how much she may consciously wish to, the sexually inhibited woman cannot protect her loved ones from the effects of her problem. Thus disruptive thinking constitutes a major danger to the stability of marriage and the health and happiness of every member of the individual family.

Despite its extent and seriousness, women who suffer from sexual inhibitions generally know little about their problem. They do not know the nature or the causes nor how or where to find help for their lack of feelings and response. No adequate book for the lay reader, nor any popular magazine article that indicates a real way out, has yet been written on this enormously important subject. The problem has been surrounded by silence, and this has engendered ignorance, misinformation, and has fostered feelings of helplessness and hopelessness in the suffering individual.

I have written this book to break this unhealthy silence, to bring to the individual woman what science knows about sexual inhibitions, to show her that, no matter how much she may have despaired, her problem can almost certainly be resolved.

Marie Robinson, MD
November 1, 1958
New York, New York

1.

Paradise Lost for Men and Women

Happiness between men and women has never had such a bright outlook as in this decade [the 1950s]. Perhaps for the first time in history, the two sexes find themselves in a position to explore together the infinitely varied and rich potentials of real love.

I am not a blind optimist in making such a statement. In my profession as a psychiatrist, I see enough daily misery and destructive misunderstanding between men and women to keep a healthy skepticism alive in my mind about all human relationships, particularly those that exist, at least in part, on sexual love.

Women Have Achieved Sexual Equality with Men

I can make such a statement about the potentials of modern love for one reason—women today have achieved complete equality with men. Above all, this equality can be observed as fully operative in the realm of sexual love. In the past thirty-odd years, and particularly in the last ten, the taboos, ignorance, and misunderstanding which had obscured our visions for centuries and prevented any real knowledge of feminine sexuality have been washed away.

Women Have the Same Needs for Passion as Men Do

We have been through a sexual revolution of major proportions. In the course of that revolution, we learned through science, not hearsay, the real facts. We know that the woman has the same need for passion and the same capacity for sexual response that the man has. We know she is the equal and fitting companion for all his possible raptures down to the last detail. She can know with her entire body and mind and can share in vivid companionship the delighted storms of sexual love that were considered his province exclusively in the recent past.

♥PRD: The Bible has always taught that women have the same capacity and needs for sexual love as men do. For example, the Song of Solomon is written in a woman's voice. It records her inner thoughts as she agonizes over whom to marry. Should she choose the powerful king who has a fetish for virgin breasts

and only cares about her body? Or should she marry the humble Shepherd who loves her as a lifelong soulmate and sexual partner and values her as the future mother of his children? The Maiden speaks without shame as she promises to initiate ecstatic love with the Shepherd:

Song of Solomon 8:2-3:
"I would lead you and bring you
Into the house of my mother, who used to instruct me;
I would give you spiced wine to drink from the juice of my pomegranates.
Let his left hand be under my head
And his right hand embrace me."

This is just one small example from the Song of Solomon of feminine sexuality with all its passion and beauty. Likewise, the Apostle Paul recognized the sexual equality of husbands and wives:

> *1 Corinthians 7:3-4: "The husband must fulfill his duty to his wife, and likewise also the wife to her husband. The wife does not have authority over her own body, but the husband does; and likewise also the husband does not have authority over his own body, but the wife does."*

About 3000 years behind the Bible, science still has much to learn about speaking God's beautiful language of love™.♥

The Sexually and Emotionally Frozen Victorian Woman

Few, however, realize how recent and how revolutionary this view of womankind is. The image of the Victorian woman, the sexually frozen, emotionally withdrawn vestal virgin, has faded quickly from our minds. It is essential, for many reasons, to recall her, if only briefly. She dominated our whole view of womankind up to the beginning of the 1920s when the flappers rejected Victorian morals. By taking a quick look at her, we can see how far women have come in so short a time. And we can see why the prospect for love has brightened so considerably.

♥*PRD: The Victorian Man's and Woman's Mindsets Live On*

Unfortunately, the Victorian woman and man have not faded away—they have only dropped the religious aspects of Victorianism. When a young millennial couple read the chapters on Victorian morals in my book God's People Make the Best Lovers, they emailed me:

> *"We were reading about our parents. Only no one talks about it. The same disrespect for men and women sexually is just there in their everyday mindset, actions, and putdowns. We picked up a lot of these attitudes from our parents without knowing where they came from, or*

> *even knowing there was a different way to think."*

Both the emotionally and sexually frozen elements of the Victorian mindset are still thriving in many modern homes among husbands and wives, mothers and fathers, and their male and female children. Following are two excerpts from my book God's 11 Secrets of Sex:

The Purity Culture Replaces Victorian Morals

Young people on our college campuses are immersed in sexual extremes—neither of which brings true happiness. Those in the Purity Culture often view sex as a necessary evil that they must fight against to be pleasing to God.

Dianna E. Anderson, in her blog "Taking the Lead in Developing New Sexual Ethics," shares their typical attitude of a "God of sexual shame, a heavenly father who sits upon his throne and condemns" their sexual thoughts and desires (2/4/2015). This attitude doesn't magically disappear with marriage.

Virginity-Pledging Men Inhibited in Marriage

In 2008, Sarah Diefendorf, a doctoral candidate in sociology at the University of Washington, studied a group of 15 young evangelical Christian men. She wanted to know how they expressed their sexuality after pledging sexual abstinence until marriage. When Diefendorf reconnected with the young men in 2011 and 2012, all were married except one. She observed:

> *While sex is framed as "sacred," "wonderful," and a "gift from God" post-marriage, these married men still think of sex in its "beastly" terms. In focusing solely on the goal of abstinence until marriage, conversations on healthy sexuality within marriage were never part of the discussion for these young men.... They viewed their wives as simultaneously protected,* ***non-sexual beings, and their sexual partners. Women are given a fairly impossible and contradictory role as wives to these men****, with seemingly few resources to navigate such assumed responsibilities.*

Many churches fail their young people by refusing to discuss the benefits and joys of married lovemaking. But God doesn't fail us. The way of a man with a maid is his proudest creation, and he didn't leave us without instructions (Proverbs 30:18-19). He preserved the beautiful, sexually explicit Song of Solomon to show us the secrets for enjoying a lifetime of passionate sex.♥

The 19th Century-Prevailing Attitude Toward Women and Sex

The prevailing attitude toward the woman and her sexuality throughout the nineteenth century and up to the end of World War I was that sex, as we understand it today, did not exist for her. Virtually everybody held this belief, and it is nowhere more clearly stated than by the medical authorities of that era. Thus Acton, a leading medical specialist in the functions of reproduction, whose views were widely influential, wrote: "The majority of women (happily for society) are not very much troubled with sexual feeling of any kind."

Doctors Regarded Sexuality in Women as "Pathological"

Acton also stated that people who believed differently were making "a vile aspersion" against women. Two other doctors of the time agreed (and presumably after checking their facts). Fehling held that any appearance of sexual feeling in a young girl in love was "pathological." And Windschied stated that if a female showed any innate or spontaneous sexual attributes, "there is an abnormality."

These men were not crackpots. They were reputable and distinguished. This was the "scientific" view of the matter, and it was shared by most people, men and women alike.

Women Can Enjoy Sex Without Guilt or Inhibitions

This new sexual freedom throws into clear relief the potentials of the present woman's new and revolutionary self-awareness. The knowledge gained in the past thirty-odd years that she may function with total sexual equality with men and eager acceptance by them without guilt or inhibition makes the past seem like a nightmare. It is as though men and women had emerged from a long journey through a dreary jungle full of fear and shame to the rim of a paradisal valley where they actually may live happily ever after, as in the fairy tales.

Women Don't Know How to Enjoy Their Sexual Freedom

But now we come to the tragic flaw in this picture. For, though the possibilities lie before them, millions of women find they must stay on the verge of, never enter, the paradisal valley. They find themselves in an age where true womanhood is highly valued but sexually inhibited.

What Does Sexual Inhibition Mean?

I shall explain sexual inhibition in greater detail later, but I can give a preliminary working definition now.

1. Sexual inhibition is the inability to enjoy physical love to the limits of its potential. The inhibited woman is, to a greater or lesser degree,

blocked in her sensual capacities. Generally, she cannot experience vaginal orgasms. If she has penetrative orgasms at all, they are weak and unsatisfying.

2. However, many inhibited women not only do not have any orgasm but may also lack the capacity to feel even the beginnings of sexual excitement. Even kissing and hugging are not enjoyable for many of them.

3. To some, the sexual act is painful, and many are ashamed to go see a doctor about their sexual health.

♥*PRD: The Myth that Men Don't Have Sexual Inhibitions*

Thanks to Victorian hang-ups, men are often criticized as sexual animals. Even in 2011 and 2012, young Evangelical husbands still described their desires as "beastly." The Victorian husband didn't bother his prim-and-proper wife with his animalistic urges, except for procreation. Instead, he visited prostitutes, sometimes with his wife's blessing.

The religious moralists and doctors never entertained the thought that men might be sexually inhibited. When Victorian men were dismayed by too much sexual desire or still having sexual needs after 45, the doctors treated them for worms, constipation, and other maladies. The doctors worried that men might engage in too much sex; that men might be sexually inhibited seemed impossible.

Science Now Knows Sexual Inhibitions Also Affect Men

The myth about men's sexual inhibitions started to be seriously debunked in the late 1970s when researchers finally understood that the most powerful sexual organ is the brain. Dr. Helen Kaplan helped coin the expression "inhibited sexual desire" to refer to the psychological problems that hinder both men and women from enjoying satisfying sexual relationships.

Unfortunately, these new insights into male inhibitions happened about 20 years after Dr. Robinson wrote this book and closed her private practice to focus on drug addiction. Since she worked primarily with women who wanted help, she didn't have the opportunity to observe the same inhibitions in men.

Believing the Myth Makes the Problem Worse

The number-one marriage problem I dealt with beginning with my first classes was husbands who weren't interested in sex. They seldom initiated sex and frequently rejected their wives' attempts to seduce them.

The wives in my first classes read Dr. Robinson's book and began to enjoy vaginal orgasms. To their surprise and dismay, their husbands' sexual behavior didn't change after the wives became better lovers. Nor did the husbands stop blaming their wives for their lack of interest. The husbands just found something new to criticize to justify withholding sex.

Due to Victorian influences and Dr. Robinson's assertion that men don't have sexual inhibitions, these wives and their teacher, me, continued to believe the myth. Consequently, the wives accepted their husbands' blame and focused on earning their husbands' love.

50 Years Exposes the Harm of the Myth

Looking back over 50 years of working with sexless marriages and five years of administering the Sexless Marriages Survey: With Self-Assessment Checklists, it's easy to see the harm this myth has done to couples. The wives didn't know men have the same sexual hang-ups as women do and that they needed to hold their husbands accountable for their cold, dead bedrooms.

Every one of these sexless marriages except one ended in divorce, most taking decades for the husband's inhibitions to grow into outright hatred and sometimes open unfaithfulness. In the one marriage that didn't end in divorce, the husband woke up to his sin against his wife when she had an affair. Rather than divorce her, the husband accepted responsibility for his behavior and began responding like a loving husband.

Some of these marriages might have been saved if the wives hadn't believed this destructive myth that men don't have sexual inhibitions. Thus I feel a tremendous responsibility to correct this flaw in Dr. Robinson's original book and expose the myth that men don't have sexual problems. When both husbands and wives are held accountable for their harmful sexual attitudes and actions, couples have a chance to learn how to begin speaking *God's beautiful language of love™ that transcends mere human words.*

Men and Women Are Amazingly Alike Sexually

One of the fascinating characteristics about the way God created men and women is how alike they are in their sexual responses. Sexual arousal has a strong emotional element for both of them, although the wife may respond a few seconds behind her husband. Even during the sexual act, they are uniquely matched. Both of their bodies engorge with blood, even their earlobes and lips, which increases their physical sensations. Their orgasms are so similar that it's hard to tell from the description if it's a male or a female.

The Good News

Because of the sexual similarities between men and women, Dr. Robinson's insights apply equally to husbands and wives. Her approach to female inhibitions was revolutionary when she wrote this book. Due to humanity's continued allegiance to one extreme or the other—the Virginity Culture versus the Hookup Culture, her observations are still cutting-edge and life-changing today—for both husbands and wives.

Most importantly, her two-step process for healing sexual inhibitions mirrors God's formula in 1 Timothy 4:1-10 for solving all marriage problems. This includes both male and female sexual issues. I discuss these scriptures later when Dr. Robinson shares her method of overcoming sexual inhibitions.♥

The Inhibited Man and Woman Learned to Fear Sexual Love

The inhibited man and woman have learned to fear physical love, to run from it, and this fear has profound repercussions on their relationships with the opposite sex. The reasons for their fear are hidden from them, are locked in their unconscious mind. Consciously they may wish, above all things, to achieve real closeness with their mate, to give and receive the greatest of all mutual joys between man and woman, sexual gratification, but they have not the capacity to receive this joy.

If Men and Women Had $1M and Couldn't Spend a Cent

It is beyond the man's and the woman's will and control. It is as if they had a million dollars and could not spend a cent of it; as if they were surrounded by the finest foods and must starve. The fact of the woman's new sexual equality makes their problem even more humiliating, bitter, and frustrating.

♥*PRD: You Can't Buy Love*

Dr. Robinson's metaphor is similar to the Shulammite maiden's words to the Shepherd as they leave King Solomon's palace and head home. The following two excerpts come from God's 11 Secrets of Sex:

Song of Solomon 8:7b:
"If a man were to give
all the riches of his house for love,
it would be utterly despised."

The Shulammite laughs and says, "Wow! Did I ever learn from Solomon that we can't buy love! He offered my mother and me an expensive dowry. It would have made such a difference in our lives. Everything would be easier. But I saw firsthand how empty he is and how void of love his palace is."

Growing serious, she continues, "O my beloved, if I'd married Solomon, I would have given up a lifetime of passionate lovemaking for what? For money? How can money compare to the love we share?"

King Solomon—The Poor Rich Man

The Maiden avoided becoming trapped in marriage to the wealthiest man in the country whose palace was filled with gold objects as silver was as common as gravel to him. But he didn't know the first thing about how to love a woman. Her scorn of his proposal and offer of luxuries shows in her wedding joke:

Song of Solomon 8:11-12:
"Solomon had a vineyard at Baal-hamon;
He entrusted the vineyard to caretakers.
Each one was to bring a thousand shekels of silver for its fruit.
My very own vineyard is at my disposal;
The thousand shekels are for you, Solomon,
And two hundred are for those who take care of its fruit."

The Shulammite takes care of a multitude of vineyards, including Baal-hamon, which her family leases from Solomon. Most commentators say they don't know where Baal-hamon was, and some offer guesses. The explanation most consistent with the story comes from Professor for the Old Testament, Ellen F. Davis, who sees the humor in the expression:

> *Solomon is the butt of [her] jibe. We know of no real place named Baal-hamon, but the name itself makes the desired point. It means "master/husband of a multitude" or alternately, "owner of a lot [of wealth]." The Song throughout emphasizes the unique value of "the one" [the Shulammite]....*
>
> *This name mocks Solomon as the poor rich man, whose silver and gold are only a foil to show up the superior wealth of love.... Wisdom and real happiness lie in shunning too much wealth, too many lovers, and treasuring what is "my very own" (301).*

The Maiden doesn't address these two lines to Solomon but to the wedding guests. It's easy to visualize the Maiden, the Shepherd, and her brothers making Solomon the brunt of a family joke with a pun for the nickname of the vineyard they lease from him. Farmers often name different parcels of land. Indeed, the joke is on Solomon, the poor rich gentleman farmer who never understands that his money can't buy love.♥

Women Who Ask for Help Can Be Helped

In my fifteen years as a psychiatrist and psychoanalyst, I have treated many, many women who came to me in despair because of their partial or total inability to enjoy the sexual part of their marriage and because of the repercussions from this inability. Hundreds of other psychiatrists and I have been fortunate in helping many of them overcome their difficulties.

♥PRD: *You Can't Help Someone Who Doesn't Want Help*

The key to success is the man's or the woman's attitude toward getting help. Dr. Robinson worked with women who came to her for help. For the most part, she didn't work with women whose husbands talked or coerced them into going to a psychiatrist. An email I received from a male reader of my Embarrass the Alligator Newsletter illustrates this problem:

> *I have been married for 15 years and am in a sexless marriage. I enjoy receiving your newsletter, but I am searching for actionable steps to work towards some remediation. I am being blamed for everything that goes wrong. Even when the kids misbehave, it somehow is my fault. Our intimacy has declined to less than once every 8 weeks.*

Sadly, according to my Sexless Marriages Survey, 89% of sexless Christians refuse to talk or read about sex and refuse to learn about becoming loving. It's easy to help someone who knows they have a problem and wants help. It's impossible to help men and women who don't want to give up their unloving ways. The only actionable steps for this husband are to get his wife's attention that they have a serious marriage problem that will only worsen if ignored.♥

Must Learn About Oneself, Gender, and Inhibitions

We found that before men and women can be expected to take full responsibility for reaching true sexual maturity, they must know all about themselves, their gender, and their problem. Then and only then have they the material to start growing up, in all pleasure, to their full masculine or feminine stature.

Men and Women Who Are Willing to Work Can Be Helped

If men and women are willing to work in all seriousness, they can be helped to overcome their sexual difficulty. The information they receive, the insights they obtain into the conditions that have kept them from experiencing real love, can sweep away their ignorance, misunderstandings, and irrational fears.

♥PRD: *"Willing to Work in All Seriousness" Is the Key*

God's formula for overcoming sexual difficulties in 1 Timothy 4 concludes with the attitude of being willing to work in all seriousness:

> *1 Timothy 4:7-8: But have nothing to do with worldly fables fit only for old women. On the other hand,* ***discipline yourself*** *for the purpose of godliness; for bodily discipline is only of little profit, but godliness is profitable for all things, since it holds promise for the present life and also for the life to come."*

Regrettably, we find lots of worldly fables regarding sex, such as "the vaginal orgasm is a myth." Yes, it's a myth for women who haven't learned the power of their attitudes over their physical sensations. Dr. Robinson dispels not only that myth but also others about men and women and sex as well.

"Discipline yourself" literally means to "exercise naked." The idea is to mentally exercise without restraint as one would find in wearing tight clothing to the gym. In other words, "willingly work in all seriousness" to apply the formula for solving all sexual problems to your way of thinking and acting.♥

Working on One's Own Inhibitions May Help the Mate

Men's and women's experience with the psychiatrist may help their mate, too, for the therapist will often see their mate for periodic discussions. These talks help their mate understand the inhibited spouse's problem and see deeply into the nature of the spouse and, therefore, all mankind and womankind. This knowledge allows their mate to directly help affect the inhibited spouse's release from the immobilizing grip of sexual inhibitions.

♥PRD: *Most Successful Clients Are Couples Who Work Together*

When couples work together to learn how to love each other in the fullness of one-flesh love, they achieve an emotional and physical bond neither one could have imagined or found separately. This is true whether the sexually withholding partner is the husband or the wife.

Many couples read each of my books aloud together. They frequently stop to discuss points that touch their hearts. They share painful childhood events and misconceptions about lovemaking. They often discover that neither one of them grew up in a loving home, and both need to learn how to love each other.

Or it may be that they grew up in healthy homes but picked up society's harmful myths about men and women. Sometimes both men and women read erotic scenes in romance novels and draw erroneous conclusions about sex. The Sexless Marriage Survey indicates they get much harmful information from their teenage peers.

The couple who reads and studies together soulmates and cleanses their minds of myths about sexual love. As a result, they report more physical and emotional pleasure during lovemaking. One husband and wife team said, "We're enjoying sensations we didn't know were possible."♥

The Mate Isn't to Blame for the Spouse's Inhibitions

Learning about the spouse's problem helps sexually deprived mates be patient when they might have been irritable and tender when they might have been demanding. It keeps them from the error of believing they are to blame for their spouse's inhibitions and thus complicating the relationship by becoming defensive, as one unjustly accused would become—indeed, should.

Inhibitions Begin in Childhood and Adolescence

Sexual inhibitions are always rooted in incomplete knowledge gained in childhood and adolescence.

♥PRD: I frequently tell men and women who are married to someone who withholds sex, "This is not about you. This is a problem your mate brought to the marriage from his or her childhood. When you can step back emotionally from your sex-withholding spouse's blaming you, then you can more clearly see options for solving the problem."♥

Destructive Misinformation from the Victorian Age

We are not, as I have pointed out, far from the Victorian age. Any man or woman of thirty or more had, in all probability, parents who were reared in the traditions of Victorianism, which denied the sexuality of women, connived with every available force to deny it, repress it, and stop it at its source. These efforts were extraordinarily successful.

♥PRD: Destructive Misinformation from the Virginity Culture

Sixty years after Dr. Robinson wrote this book, many men and women in their 20s also have parents affected by the Victorian mindset. Only the prejudices against the opposite sex and one's own masculinity or femininity have lost the Victorian label. This same Victorian era's ignorance is freely promoted in encouraging or forcing virginity pledges on both young boys and girls.

A millennial client emailed me. "After reading your discussion of Victorian morals in God's People Make the Best Lovers, I recognized these attitudes in both of my parents and my grandmother. I just accepted them without discussion and without knowing where they came from."♥

Destructive Misinformation from the Roaring Twenties

Any woman now in her twenties [in 1959] probably had parents who were deeply affected by the equally mindless and vicious protest against Victorianism, which characterized this country from, roughly, 1920 to 1930—the period we call the Roaring Twenties or the Jazz Age.

This era was full of destructive misinformation about sex and love. Sexual promiscuity for women was openly advocated and found far too many adherents in the younger generation after World War I. The moral climate created in the Jazz Age was alien to the very nature of truly masculine and feminine love. It led to serious sexual conflicts in millions of individuals, which affected their offspring.

♥*PRD: Destructive Misinformation from the Hookup Culture*

The Roaring Twenties and the Jazz Age live on in today's Hookup Culture. Young women drink alcohol to numb their brains so they can give their bodies without guilt. Although it makes their hearts race, young men take VIAGRA to enhance their performance with the available young women. Many participants in my Sexless Marriages Survey check that their sex-depriving spouses were part of the Hookup Culture.

Yes! Destructive information from the two extremes—the Purity and the Hookup Cultures—can damage relationships for a lifetime until the person decides to learn better. God's 11 Secrets of Sex discuss these cultures in detail.♥

Widely Held, Incorrect Beliefs About Inhibitions

Before we advance into the subject itself, I should like to dispose of a few widely held and thoroughly incorrect beliefs about the inability to share orgasms. I do this to clear away some of the underbrush that can impede those who are seriously seeking a resolution to inhibitions.

The Inhibited Man and Woman Need Information

Let us begin by looking at the problem of a woman's sexual "responsibility," as it has been called. Much has been written about it, and much of what I have read is pure nonsense, based on a sort of mechanical conception of what love is and what the act of love means. I fear that such books encourage men and women to approach the problem from the wrong direction and before they understand the real nature of their difficulties. Such an approach leads them to attempt futile "solutions," which can only discourage and disillusion them. The fundamental error is in trying to make the individual man and woman "responsible" without giving them any real information about their condition.

Men and Women Don't Consciously Desire to Be Inhibited

The fact is that no man or woman who suffers from sexual inhibitions consciously desires to. Nor can they be, for a single second, held accountable for the fact that the problem developed. The word "blame" cannot be used in connection with their problem. I strongly urge you to let that point sink deeply into your heart and mind.

Problems Develop from Family and Historical Influences

How could it be that they had any responsibility in the matter? This problem always develops in childhood or infancy. It is partly a product of early family and historical influences over which they had no control. And it is partly a matter of the biological heritage of all men and women everywhere. They certainly can't be held responsible for that.

♥PRD: *Song of Solomon Teaches Sex Education Begins in Infancy*

The Shulammite maiden in the Song of Solomon recognized that being prepared for a wonderful love life began in infancy with the Shepherd's mother and her mother nursing them—letting them experience that skin touching skin is pleasurable. She gave her mother credit for teaching her how to enjoy lovemaking for herself and to give love to her future husband:

Song of Solomon 8:1, 3:
"Oh that you were like a brother to me
Who nursed at my mother's breasts.
If I found you outdoors, I would kiss you;
No one would despise me, either....
Let his left hand be under my head
And his right hand embrace me."

God's 11 Secrets of Sex, a modern study of the Song of Solomon, discusses these verses in detail and contrasts them with Solomon's dysfunctional home of origin and his inability to find sexual love in his harem of 1000 wives.

A male reader said: "I doubt many mothers today or in the past were as bold as the Shulammite's mother to actually teach their daughters. I had ZERO teaching from my parents. And after talking with my wife and separately with her father, she had little to no teaching. When something sexual came up, her mother always said, 'That's gross!' Even though my wife knows better, that 'sex is gross' is in her subconscious and has damaged our marriage."♥

Men and Women Are Responsible for Defeating Inhibitions

Here is the attitude I have found most helpful to take toward this matter of sexual responsibility: Men and women are not responsible for developing a difficulty any more than the stutterer is accountable for his stutter. However, once men and women realize their sexual inhibitions are a problem and have repercussions on them and those dear to them, they are responsible for finding out everything they can about the issue. Then, based on that information, they are responsible for taking whatever action is necessary.

♥PRD: *The Inhibited Person Is Responsible for Growing Up*

At the end of 1 Corinthians 13, the famous chapter about the qualities of love, the Apostle Paul concluded with the personal responsibility husbands and wives share to overcome their childhood upbringing and to put on love:

> *1 Corinthians 13:11: "When I was a child, I used to speak like a child, think like a child, reason like a child; when I became a man, I did away with childish things."*

Ideally, marriage forces one to grow up emotionally as the person learns how to live with the mate lovingly. Unfortunately, too many people choose to stay locked in childhood inhibitions instead of daring to choose to grow up sexually. Lovemaking is a lifelong journey that gets better with practice.♥

The Myth of "No Such Thing as an Inhibited Wife, Only Clumsy Husbands"

A vast body of published information blames the husband for the wife's sexual inhibitions. Beginning in the 1930s, book after book appeared that showed conclusively that a happily married sexual life depended on the male's drill in arousing the woman. Such books instructed the husband to manipulate or caress his wife for X minutes in Y number of erotic zones. Presumably, by then, she would have reached such a state of excitement that true sexual satisfaction could not possibly fail her. A woman's failure to respond adequately in the marital bed was always supposed to be due to a faulty technique on the husband's part.

♥PRD: *The "Clitoral Orgasm" Defined*

The "clitoral orgasm" requires the husband to fondle his wife's clitoris and/or G-spot in specific ways for a certain length of time to bring her to orgasm. For these wives, orgasm is limited to their clitoris or G-spot as they don't move on to vaginal orgasms. The myth asserts that "if the wife doesn't experience an orgasm, it's all her husband's fault for not caressing her properly."♥

Practicing This Myth Can Make the Problem Worse

The myth is not true. Caressing or manipulating the genitalia or secondary erotic zones of certain types of inhibited women would only result in exacerbated nerves or a condition of inwardly screaming protest.

In other types, caressing might give temporary satisfaction. But in the long run, it could be harmful from a psychological standpoint and deepen or encourage immature methods of gratification.

♥PRD: *Authors and Bloggers Keep the Myth Alive*

Today, the majority of bloggers and authors on sex for women still promote this same myth. Even though they try to help women enjoy their sexual freedom, for the most part, they are clueless about the emotional foundation of lovemaking. As a result, they often teach techniques and blame the husbands for not learning how to give their wives manual pleasure. They don't know how a woman mentally takes charge of her own enjoyment of lovemaking with her husband. If the husband can have an erection for penetration sex, the wife possesses the power to respond with vaginal orgasms with cervical kisses.

The Common Argument for the Clitoral Orgasm

A negative reviewer on Amazon for The Power of Sexual Surrender wrote:

> *The theory this book is positing, the basis of the book is not understanding female anatomy. I have no idea if the psychological ideas have been debunked. This book was given to me as a joke a few birthdays ago. You can say "the reason your sex is bad is because you've lost your feminine role" and that could be 100% correct, but a big chunk of this book ignores where the nerve endings are located. In the 40 years since this was published, I think someone went ahead and talked to some women, maybe even did some science-y stuff, and decided 80+% of women weren't just orgasming wrong.*

Science Debunks the Clitoral Orgasm Myth

Excerpt from God's 11 Secrets of Sex gives the science for the vaginal orgasm:

*God designed the clitoris as an important organ that increases the woman's pleasure as **it works with the vagina—not in place of the vagina.** Dr. David Rueben reveals in Any Woman Can that the clitoris' roots are filled with super-sensitive nerve endings and reach deep into the walls of the vagina. The husband's movements and the woman's contractions all stimulate the clitoris and heighten the woman's pleasure (37-38).*

The clitoris connects to the labia minora, the small lips on either side of it. Respected medical writer Ronald M. Deutsch describes in The Key to Feminine Response in Marriage how during lovemaking, the small lips engorge with blood and increase two to three times their normal thickness. At the same time, the area in between the lips becomes engorged. This effectively adds one or more inches to the length of the vagina. The swollen lips help support and hold the penis during lovemaking (42-3).

In his book Everything You Always Wanted to Know About Sex But Were Afraid to Ask, Dr. Rueben explains that the clitoris is extremely sensitive to any tugging or pulling in this whole area, which normally takes place during sexual intercourse. Instead of needing a specific position to stimulate the clitoris as the books promoting clitoral orgasms recommend, just the back and forth thrusts of the male member within the woman's vagina stimulate this whole region as the clitoral area is pulled toward the vagina (43).

The woman who discovers the secret of her thoughts over a vaginal orgasm finds that her clitoris becomes even more sensitive than before. Just her husband brushing against her pelvic region standing in the kitchen sends waves of desire through the vaginal area. She doesn't require manual stimulation.

For the woman who has learned how to respond vaginally, when she and her husband are sitting beside each other, he can reach over and touch her leg and her vagina will jump with exciting memories of lovemaking. Likewise, if her husband uses the same tone of voice that he frequently uses during sex, her nipples will tingle pleasantly. If loving thoughts can cause these sexual sensations outside of the sexual act, imagine what they do during lovemaking.

However, if the woman is over-tired or out-of-sorts, a brief touch to that region causes memories of past unions to flood her being. Even if she wants to stay mad at him, these intense feelings cause her body and emotions to yield to his caresses. This all takes place within a few moments for the woman who has learned to respond vaginally. Thus frequent lovemaking helps keep emotional barriers at bay and impedes them from gaining a foothold in a marriage.♥

The Husband Can't Cure His Wife with Mechanical Means

In short, through tenderness and understanding, a husband may help his wife face the true nature of her problem. But he is never responsible for the existence of her inhibitions. He cannot, through any mechanical means, get her over it.

♥*PRD: The Wife Can't Cure Her Husband with Mechanical Means*

Many loving men and women who participated in my Sexless Marriages Survey worked at learning better techniques to help their spouses enjoy lovemaking more. It didn't work. Why? Because more than a physical problem, sexual inhibitions are the result of attitude problems that developed during the inhibited person's childhood.♥

The Myth of a Glandular Problem

Another misconception about inhibitions: Women who suffer from a greater or lesser degree of an inability to enjoy orgasms often believe that something is wrong with them glandularly. Misunderstanding something they've read or heard, they get the idea that somewhere, somehow, a drug will cure them.

A gynecologist told me that at least three women each week ask him to give them hormones to step up their sexual responses. I checked with several other gynecologists and five obstetricians. They all said that the request for hormonal injections from women is a daily constant.

♥PRD: Following are excerpts from God's 11 Secrets of Sex, which show that sexual inhibitions are generally a heart problem rather than a medical one:

Can VIAGRA Cure a Sexless Marriage?

Can a visit to the doctor for VIAGRA restore romance to a sexless marriage? It depends on why the marriage doesn't have enough sex to keep both the husband and the wife satisfied. If it's a medical problem, then perhaps the little blue pill can revive the passion of yesteryear. But if the problem originates between the man's ears instead of between his legs, then VIAGRA probably can't offer much help....

The miracle drug for erectile dysfunction can't miraculously turn an unloving or unloved male organ into a pulsating love machine. Pfizer's "Patient Information" insert warns that "VIAGRA...helps a man get and keep an erection only when he is sexually excited (stimulated)" (3/2015). In other words, VIAGRA "has little effect" on men who aren't emotionally tuned into their wife....

Can Addyi Bring Passion into a Dead Bedroom?

Addyi, the first commercial drug to improve female libido, bypasses the woman's genitals and acts on her brain chemicals. The drug was originally studied as an antidepressant. Like Pfizer states about VIAGRA, the FDA News Release says Addyi is ineffective in dealing with inhibited sexual desire and pleasure in regard to "problems within the relationship."

Many doctors still don't understand male and female sexuality. To solve the problem of low libido in both men and women, the couple needs to work on their attitudes to free their bodies for powerful orgasms of love. That's the same truth Dr. Robinson teaches.♥

Sexual Inhibitions Are Basically a Psychological Problem

Inhibitions are rarely a problem of glandular malfunction. Much work has been done in this area and, unless your case is relatively unusual, you may rest assured that your problem is a personal and psychological one. How can I be so certain of that last statement? *Because real inhibitions react to psychological treatment.* They can generally be cured in a psychiatrist's office without the use of any drugs.

If you reply: "Well, perhaps the mind has caused a glandular shutdown with an orgasm problem," we would answer: "Even if that were true, the mind would still be the 'cause,' and a real cure can be effected only by getting at the cause."

Male and Female Inhibitions Are a Psychological Problem

Let me make myself clear. *Sexual inhibitions are, in the vast majority of cases, essentially a psychological problem. The only way to approach it with any hope of resolving it is through the mind, by understanding it.* Anybody who tells you differently is, to put it plainly, wrong. If you have a real inhibition problem and try to ascribe other than psychological reasons for it (such as that your mate is the cause of it), you are doing your cause (that of getting over the problem) a grave disservice.

Sexuality and Personality Develop Side-by-Side

When I say that the problem of sexual inhibitions is a psychological one, I am not overstating the case. I am, to simplify matters, rather understating it. The greatest contribution of psychiatry in the past sixty years has been the discovery of the central importance of sexuality in the development of the individual.

In her classic work *Psychosexual Functions in Women*, Dr. Therese Benedek states the whole matter succinctly: "The sexual drive...is the axis around which the organization of the personality takes place."

Both Personality and Sexuality Can Become Frozen

When all goes well in the development of the young boy and girl, both their personality and their sexual passions develop naturally. They achieve a beautiful and integrated maturity.

But if, as so often happens, thwarting or blighting experiences take place, the development of their personality and their sexuality will become frozen at their sources. Maturity will remain a never-never land whose existence they will come to doubt. I will explain more in a later chapter.

Success Is Waiting on the Other Side of Fear

If men and women wish to resume their growth, they must be fearless. They must find and face the events that block their advancement, the misunderstandings and ignorance that prevent them from reaping the rewards of adulthood. They must insist, deep within themselves, on achieving that honest and passionate relatedness with their mate for which nothing can substitute in their journey through life.

The bridge to emotional and sexual maturity is built of many facts—hard, scientific facts. Master these facts, gain information on this subject, and you can pass from a land of bitter deprivation to the richness that is your due, your heritage. It is waiting for you on the other side of fear.

♥PRD: *The Title of This Book Is About Growing Up Emotionally*

The remainder of this book develops the point Dr. Robinson just made: "sexual inhibitions are a psychological problem." And as you finish this book, you'll realize that the title, "The Power of Sexual Surrender," is only secondarily about surrendering sexually in your mate's arms.

The title refers primarily to surrendering emotionally to your own masculinity or femininity as you heal from your childhood traumas. When you rectify your past, you embrace the ability to love yourself, your mate, your children, and your fellow citizens. At the same time, your soul surrenders to coupling with your mate's masculinity or femininity in all the glory God built within the creation of the male and the female—his soulmating genius. The importance of surrendering to your authentic self is the subject of the rest of this book. Sexual surrender to ecstasy is the result of your intellectual, emotional, and spiritual surrender.♥

Memories of When You First Fell in Love Can Help

We have found that at such a juncture, husbands and wives are often helped to alter their defensive attitudes by seriously reflecting on the picture of marriage and love they had when they first fell in love. They should then compare that image with the defeated feelings they have now, compare their first hopes of creatively shared lives with the empty realities of the present, the loveless activities they engage in now.

♥PRD: *First Duty of Marriage Is Growing a Loving Sexual Relationship*

God makes it clear he wants newlyweds to engage in a lot of sex. In fact, he wants them to get drunk on sex. Notice God's command to the Shulammite:

Song of Solomon 5:1b:
"Eat, friends;
Drink and imbibe deeply, O lovers
[and drink, until you are drunk with love!—CJB]"

God used the metaphor of wine to tell the Shulammite and the Shepherd to get married and get drunk on lovemaking. It takes a lot of wine to get drunk. God said the first duty of marriage is to engage in sex until you're tipsy and giddy with love to establish a healthy sexual relationship.

God Commands Husbands and Wives to Become Great Lovers

Couples don't get married automatically knowing how to be great lovers. It takes practice and experimenting. It takes getting drunk on love. This is so important that we need to notice what God commanded the Israelites:

Deuteronomy 24:5: "When a man takes a new wife, he shall not go out

> *with the army, nor be charged with any duty; he shall be free at home one year and shall give happiness [cheer up-KJV] to his wife whom he has taken."*

God told the Israelites to take one-year honeymoons having sex until they were sore, resting up, and going at it again. Nearly every time I've taught this verse in a ladies' class, a woman has spoken up saying, "I got cheated!"

An active, enjoyable sexual relationship that gives the bride "happiness" requires both the groom and the bride to grow up emotionally—learn what it takes to enjoy a successful sexual relationship with another human. If you're not growing emotionally, then sex is going to be miserable—like it is in sexless marriages. Dr. Robinson emphasizes that point over and over in this book.

God Wants Older Couples to Be Lifelong Lovers

God created the wife as a lifelong sexual companion for ravishing her husband:

Proverbs 5:18-19:
"Let your fountain be blessed,
And rejoice in the wife of your youth.
As a loving hind and a graceful doe,
Let her breasts satisfy you at all times;
Be exhilarated [ravished—KJV] always with her love."

This is the woman he married in his youth. Not only have they grown old together, but they've also become experienced lovers. Their "exhilaration" or "intoxication" is better than when they were newlyweds.

Deeply Inhibited Spouses Inhibit Their Mates

With most of the clients I've worked with, it's not just her or just him who has a problem. They both usually do, but one of them is more deeply inhibited than the other. The one who has the worst problem either limits or cuts off sex. Consequently, neither of them learns and grows emotionally and sexually as God intends. The deprived one can't relax and practice becoming a great lover.

Not enjoying enough sex affects deprived mates in every part of their lives. On the Sexless Marriages Survey, 81% of the participants checked one or more of the following areas, with the sex-deprived mates checking "most" of the areas:

- ✓ *You never rise to your full potential as a spouse*
- ✓ *You never rise to your full potential as a parent*
- ✓ *You never rise to your full potential as a Christian*
- ✓ *You never rise to your full potential as a worker*

By the time the couple contacts me, the uninhibited mate is trying to be perfect to win the inhibited spouse's love. Neither of them is enjoying sex. They both are just trying to survive emotionally. That's not healthy for anyone.♥

Patience to Work and Learn Together Is Important

Patience is essential. Husbands and wives need all of it they can muster for a time. At certain points, they may have to remind themselves of the rewards at the end of the journey.

♥PRD: *Soulmate to Build Intimacy for Sexual Ecstasy*

The best and safest way to start soulmating and sharing emotionally is by reading and discussing books about God, love, and marriage together. The rule is, you can't say anything negative about your spouse. You can only make negative comments about yourself.

For example, you can't say, "You never do...." Or "You always do...." Once you start criticizing your spouse, it won't be long before he or she is no longer interested in reading and discussing the book with you. Besides, the constant criticism and blame that the inhibited spouse indulges in is destroying the marriage and must stop.

However, you can say, "Wow! I didn't know that. I can see where I've been making a mistake doing...." Or "I don't know if I agree with that. What about a situation where...."

At this point in your marriage, neither you nor your mate knows enough about God's word regarding marriage, lovemaking, and solving problems. You need to fine-tune your understanding of God's standards before you start gripping about your expectations.

Listening to your spouse talk about his or her views and feelings regarding God's teaching about sex is a great way to begin soulmating—to begin building intellectual, emotional, and spiritual intimacy. Without this all-encompassing mental intimacy, you may do all the physical things precisely right, but your body will deny you the greatest of sexual thrills and intimacy.

Working Together Produces Amazing Rewards

Husbands and wives working through this book together allows them to practice and grow together in a safe, loving environment. I've witnessed that the couples who study God's word together, not to criticize the other, but to fine-tune their understanding and behavior, are the couples who reap the rewards. In the formula for solving all marriage problems, the Apostle Paul said:

> *1 Timothy 4:8b: "...godliness is profitable for all things, since it holds promise for* ***the present life*** *and also for* ***the life to come****."*

Applying God's formula for solving sexual problems rewards husbands and wives in two areas: (1) their love life on earth and (2) their life to come with the God of heaven in whose mind sexual ecstasy originated.

Case History: Young Millennial Couple Found Success Together

A young millennial couple I worked with exemplifies the above verse and the value of working together, and how each affects the other's sexuality. They read all their assignments aloud and discussed the homework. The husband, who was the deprived one, emailed me their reaction to one of the chapters:

> *Reading this chapter caused us to relive the start of our marriage and our sexual journey. I felt regret and conviction while reading the pages. So much we didn't know. I wish we knew sooner the importance of our attitudes (instead of just focusing on sex). We had a rocky start that could have been avoided by some simple instruction.*
>
> *When the sexual connection would start getting strong, one of us (including me) unknowingly/subconsciously would pull back, and then we would try and find what caused the pullback. That took about 5 days to work through, and then we would start the cycle over again.*
>
> *When I look back over the journey of our intimacy, I see a few pivotal times where one of us didn't handle a situation properly, and it caused a deeper reaction in both of us. I see that we are healing. I do believe that the more we work on our attitudes and love, we can be restored.*

It's time to start reaping God's promises for this present life as this young couple did—the promises for a passionate love life that brings joy to you both and prepares you for the life to come with an amazing and loving God.

The Thankfulness Exercise

In Chapter 16: "The Steps to Freedom from Sexual Inhibitions," you'll learn that developing gratitude is part of God's formula for solving all sexual problems. Developing a spirit of gratitude makes the journey to embrace love easier and is required for lovemaking success. Once thankfulness begins to become a habit, it can transform a person's whole life as it helps chase away negativity, anger, and bitterness and replaces it with love.

Keeping a grateful heart is so powerful that one of the first things I ask my clients to do is "The Thankfulness Exercise" for each chapter they read in my books. So I strongly recommend you start a "Thankfulness Notebook" and answer the following four questions for each chapter in this book:

1. *What Bible verse especially spoke to your needs now? Why?*
2. *What things did you learn about to thank God for as gifts from him?*
3. *What do you need to ask God to help you with in your life?*
4. *How can you change your routine to make it happen?*♥

Section 1:

The Normal Man and Woman

2.

Vaginal Orgasms with Cervical Kisses

The first thing I will do on this journey with you is give you a view of your destination. I am going to describe a vaginal orgasm in detail.

We occasionally do this in psychiatry when dealing with a nonorgasmic problem, and sometimes it has astonishing results. Some women almost immediately break through to their sensual goal after hearing for the first time a complete description of what to expect of themselves in the act of love.

Case History:
Woman Learns How to Orgasm from Sister's Success

A patient, who over months worked through a severe nonorgasmic problem, detailed to her younger sister the wonderful sexual experience she was now enjoying. The younger sister had been married only two months and had not once reached sexual climax. She seriously contemplated consulting a psychiatrist about her "problem." The night her older sister described an orgasm to her, she achieved her first complete satisfaction with her husband.

Sudden Cures Come from Lightly Rooted Inhibitions

My chief motive in describing the normal vaginal orgasm is not to try to bring about a quick cure. In cases where the release of enlightened sexuality is achieved, and thaw comes like a sudden spring, even though the nonorgasmic problem may appear to be deep-seated, it is generally a superficial one, lightly rooted in the personality.

We Need to Understand Health to Grasp Disease

I start with the orgasm because a picture of the normal is necessary if you are to understand deviations from it clearly. It is a truism that to understand illness in the body, it is first necessary to understand health. Every doctor knows this, and so do his teachers. In medical school, he first learns through classes in anatomy and physiology the structure and functions of the healthy body.

You will understand sexual inhibitions more thoroughly if we pursue the same technique by first explaining the genital anatomy of women. Then, I will describe the normal orgasm, its function in healthy men and women, and other pertinent material.

The Woman's External and Internal Genitalia

Both men and women are often ignorant of the woman's genitalia and how it functions during the act of love. Following is a brief discussion of the major organs involved in lovemaking.

The Clitoris Is the Most Misunderstood Organ

The clitoris is the most misunderstood part of the woman's external genitalia. It lies immediately above the top fold of the labia minora and is a little piece of tissue slightly less thick than a pencil. This organ is enormously crucial to the whole psychological and sexual development of the woman. It is often called the "homologue of the male penis." This means that the embryo cells which form the penis in the male are the same cells that form the clitoris in the female. Thus the penis and the clitoris share the same cellular derivation.

The Clitoris and the Penis Are Similar

The clitoris, like the penis, is made up of erectile tissue. When a woman is sexually excited, the clitoris becomes erect in the same manner that the penis does. It also has a head and a foreskin covering it. The head of the clitoris, at least in children and adolescents, is generally extremely sensitive to stimulation.

Sensitivity of the Clitoris Gives Way to Vaginal Sensitivity

In the fully mature female, this sensitivity often diminishes, giving way to the vagina as the primary source of the greatest sexual pleasure. However, many women who become fully mature sexually maintain much of the original sexual responsiveness of the clitoris.

Entrance to the Vagina Is Susceptible to Sexual Excitation

The remainder of the external genitalia is contained within the vestibule, which is the entrance to the vagina and is highly susceptible to sexual excitation. The vestibule lies between the minor lips and is directly beneath the clitoris. It contains the hymen, the urethral opening, and the opening of the Bartholin's glands.

The Bartholin's Glands Lubricate the Vaginal Opening

The Bartholin's glands are essential to the act of love. These glands discharge a thin colorless mucus in sexual excitation that lubricates the vaginal opening and canal during intercourse. The amount of secretion varies with each individual. Sexual inhibitions often affect these glands adversely, causing the secretions to be inadequate or nonexistent. However, the amount of secretion varies rather dramatically at times in individuals who have no basic sexual blocking. Therefore, Bartholin's glands cannot be taken as a final criterion of sexual adequacy or inadequacy.

"Vagina" Means "A Sheath for a Sword"

The vagina is a passageway of some three to three and a half inches that extends from the vestibule on the outside to the cervix, which is the bottom end of the uterus. It is the canal that accepts the penis, and it may interest you to know that in Latin the word means "a sheath for a sword." The sexual act in its purest form expresses the female's passivity and the male's aggressiveness, the actor and the acted upon. The Romans understood this difference at least linguistically.

The Vagina Is Short But Extremely Elastic

It may have surprised you to learn of the relatively short length of the vagina. The tissue of its walls is exceptionally elastic, however. Not only can it contain a penis of virtually any thickness or length, but it can stretch enough to allow the newborn infant to pass through it.

Cervical Kisses Occur When the Penis Goes Deep

The penis presses against the cervical end of the uterus, which may be forced upward until the penis gains full entrance. *Contact with the soft tissue of the cervix is a source of great pleasure for the male, and the pressure can be an equal pleasure for the woman.*

The vaginal walls are lined with soft skin, not unlike mucous membrane, but it does not secrete as mucous tissue will. A secretion is, however, released from the cervix, and this also helps to lubricate the vaginal canal during intercourse.

♥PRD: Although Dr. Robinson doesn't use the expression "cervical kiss," this description describes that experience, a "delightful" sensation unlike any other for both the male and the female. But if sexual inhibitions have numbed a wife's

vagina to her husband's presence, her cervix will be dead to sensations too.♥

Vagina Orgasms Give a Woman Her Greatest Pleasure

I have said that the vagina is the most important part of a woman's sexual equipment. This is because it is within the vagina that the orgasm of the truly mature and emotionally uninhibited woman takes place. Upon it and within it, she receives the most incredible sensual pleasure possible for a woman to experience.

Description of the Male and the Female Orgasm

This brings us to the subject of orgasm. You will understand it more fully if I describe it in the context of the sexual experience as a whole.

The Sexual Instinct Encompasses Both Body and Mind

The sexual instinct in both men and women is marvelously complex. When unencumbered by inhibitions and cognitive distortions, the sexual instinct gives color, shape, brightness, charm, vividness, and direction to the entire personality. The mechanisms by which the sexual instinct operates encompass both body and mind.

♥*PRD: This physical phenomenon was observed by Belgian researchers in the following excerpt from God's 11 Secrets of Sex:*

Vaginal Orgasms Affect the Way the Wife Walks

In 2012, Rob Waugh wrote the article "You Can Instantly Know a Woman's Sex History From Her Stride, Claims Study." He shared details from Belgian researchers at the Universiti Catholique de Louvain. The academics demonstrated with a blind study that just by watching videos of how women walked, sexologists could determine if the women regularly enjoyed vaginal orgasms. The catch? The orgasm had to come from "penile-vaginal intercourse" to affect the woman's gait.

The researchers videotaped two groups of "healthy young Belgian women." The first group had a history of vaginal orgasms with a man. The second group was unable to orgasm vaginally through sex. Just any orgasm didn't affect the way a woman walked. For example, a clitoral orgasm didn't produce the same walking results as a vaginal orgasm.

A group of sexologists viewed the videos to see if the way the women walked revealed their sexual history. The results of the blind study showed that vaginal orgasms improve a woman's walk when other types of orgasms don't because of the way it exercises her muscles, vertebrae, and pelvic floor. The sexologists observed the spring-in-her step as "a gait that comprises fluidity, energy, sensuality, freedom, and absence of both flaccid and locked muscles" (5/2012).

Medical journalist Colette Bouchez clarified that the women's walk wasn't "the old Marilyn Monroe hip-swinging, or the obviously provocative Madonna-esque stances" (9/12/2008). Their walk exhibited energetic freedom and confidence. The women radiated innate sexual satisfaction.♥

A Woman Responds Chiefly to Tenderness in Words or Acts

Desire can be cut off in a woman either in response to a touch or by some act, sight, or thought to which she has been exposed. One of the main things an orgasmic woman responds to is cumulative tenderness expressed in words or acts.

♥PRD: *Men Also Respond to Tenderness in Words or Acts*

Some sexually inhibited wives know they can thwart having sex by saying derogatory things to their husband that will cause him to immediately lose his erection. One husband said, "I no longer have the self-confidence to initiate sex because of my wife's verbal attacks on my sexuality. Now we only have sex when she initiates, which seldom happens. I am more lonely than ever."♥

Men Can Be Ready for Intercourse in Three Seconds

Whatever the stimulus, the brain receives the signal and, through the nervous system, sends out preparatory reactions throughout the body. The response of men to stimuli perceived by the brain as sexual is amazingly fast. Some men arrive at full sexual preparedness for intercourse within three seconds—that is, their penis becomes fully erect and ready to enter the vagina within that time.

Women Take a Few Seconds Longer than Men to React

Women react somewhat more slowly. However, under the best of conditions, her full preparation for intercourse is often only a few more seconds than the man.

Changes Could Be Frightening In Other Circumstances

As the sexual excitement increases, tremendous changes occur throughout the body, changes that might frighten you if they occurred under other circumstances.

Pulse and Blood Pressure Rise Significantly

The pulse rate goes up astonishingly. Records show it reaching 150 and more as the individual approaches and then reaches the sexual climax. Such pulse rates generally occur, in health, only in athletes who perform prodigious tasks of speed or endurance.

The blood pressure, too, goes up precipitately. In a few seconds, it can rise well over 100 points.

Breathing Changes as if the Person Has Been in a Race

Breathing also becomes much deeper and swifter. With the approach of orgasm, the breathing becomes interrupted, inspiration comes in forced gasps, and expiration occurs with a heavy collapse of the lungs. It is as though the sexually excited person had been in a race. As the sexual activity continues, a general shortage of oxygen throughout the body accounts for the unusual breathing. This gives rise to a tortured expression on the face as if the person were undergoing severe pain.

♥*PRD: Allowing Yourself to Breathe During Sex Works Wonders*

One of the first things I suggest husbands and wives do is give themselves and each other permission to experience all the different ways sexual intercourse makes them breathe. Holding back their breathing hampers all sensations for both men and women. Rapid, heavy, and gasping breathing are all natural parts of male and female orgasms. Audible breathing communicates personal pleasure to the mate. For many people, hearing their spouse's sounds of love increases their own sensations. This one activity of allowing oneself to breathe naturally can start a couple on the road to success.♥

Women Fake Orgasms by Trying to Look Happy

Faking orgasms was observed by Kinsey in his famous study of female sexuality, and I quote here an interesting paragraph on the phenomenon:

> Prostitutes who attempt to deceive (jive) their patrons, or unresponsive wives who similarly attempt to make their husbands believe that they are enjoying coitus, fall into an error because they assume that an erotically aroused person should look happy and pleased and should smile and become increasingly alert as he or she approaches the culmination of the act. On the contrary, an individual who is really responding is as incapable of looking happy as the individual who is being tortured.

♥*PRD: Men Also Fake Orgasms*

Below is a short excerpt from God's People Make the Best Lovers. More of the excerpt is included in Chapter 5: "Five Common Types of Sexual Inhibitions."

Lorna and Philip Sarrel's 1977 article "What Men Need from the Women Who Love Them" revealed that men fake many aspects of their sexuality just as women do. They explained that the male is as complex a sexual being as the female regarding feelings, thoughts, guilt, physical sensations, and what they fake (115).♥

The Body Flushes and the Temperature Rises

Within seconds after sexual arousal, the blood supply in the veins and arteries lying close to the skin increases, causing the body to become flushed and the temperature to rise slightly.

♥PRD: Orgasms vary in intensity for both males and females. During incredibly passionate times, the mate's body may feel extremely hot to the touch. The heat can be another turn on for the other in soaring to the heights of passion.♥

Blood Engorgement of the Whole Body Occurs

Certain areas of the body engorge with this blood and become swollen and erect, notably the penis of the man, which often swells to twice its size. In women, this also happens to the clitoris, which becomes firm, and to the nipples of both sexes. The firmness of these organs increases as the sexual climax approaches.

♥*PRD: Science Knows More About Engorgement Arousal*

Following is an excerpt from "Secret 7: Turn on Double-Dose #10 Orgasms" in God's 11 Secrets of Sex that explains the engorgement process:

Science now knows that emotional arousal plus physical arousal leads to engorgement arousal. The whole body is affected by engorgement along with mounting muscular tension during sexual stimulation. Even the ear lobes and the mouth may become thickened and swollen with blood. And nearly all of a person's muscles are affected.

Both men and women experience whole-body orgasms. For women, "from head to toe, the muscles contract and relax, in steady or more convulsive rhythms." For men, "the primitive pain nerves throughout their body become sexual triggers ready and waiting" for their wife's passionate touches and nibbles.

The engorgement sensations are "accurately detected and enjoyed" as tingling and other intense responses. The sensations increase the man's and the woman's readiness for sexual activity and pleasure. "Only men with chronic situation erectile dysfunction typically under-rate their physical response." Many women don't recognize these sensations at all, perhaps because they don't expect them or know they are theirs to claim.♥

Muscles Tense Throughout the Body and Secretions Flow

Muscles throughout the body begin to tense at the onset of sexual excitement, and the tension increases as the excitement grows. Certain glands and tissues also increase their secretions as the sexual act commences and moves closer to completion. The salivary glands and the nasal mucosa flow freely. This latter fact causes, in conjunction with the engorgement of the surface blood vessels, the characteristic nasal stuffiness so many people notice after intercourse.

The Woman May Falsely Think She's Having an Ejaculation

In some women, the secretions of Bartholin's glands and the mucus from the cervix become amazingly copious as sexual excitement rises, particularly during orgasm itself. This profuse flow may have given rise to the widely held but mistaken idea that women have an ejaculation similar to males. Women have no such ejaculation—nor any female organ that could make ejaculation possible.

All Five Senses Become Extremely Dulled

One of the amazing aspects of sexual intercourse is the fact that all five senses become extremely dulled as the activity increases in intensity. The ability to feel hot and cold, to feel pain, or to hear sounds becomes almost nonexistent. The eyes take on a characteristic trance-like stare, as vision becomes constricted. The entire mind and body are concentrated fully on the mounting sexual feelings and exclude all else. In orgasm itself, the anesthesia of the senses is almost total. Indeed, many people experience a temporary loss of consciousness for a matter of seconds.

To Understand Sexual Inhibitions, Need to Grasp the Nature of a Vaginal Orgasm

This brings us to an examination of the experience of orgasm itself. If you are to understand sexual inhibitions in women, it is essential to grasp the nature of orgasm and what it means physically and psychologically. The importance of such understanding is due to the fact that the type of orgasm described here is the very thing the nonorgasmic woman is unable to have. Its absence from her experience is the usual definition of a woman's sexual inhibitions.

Inhibited Women Can Stop Short of a Vaginal Orgasm

Certain kinds of sexually inhibited women may experience one, two, or all of the physical and psychological reactions described above, which normally would terminate with orgasm. But the final experience eludes them. Despite an agonizing need to come to a climax, at the vital juncture the body refuses to respond. It draws back and goes dead.

♥*PRD: Inhibited Men Can Stop Short of Ejaculation*

The wife of a sexually inhibited man may stop feeling his ejaculations as his bitterness and resentment toward her grows. Questioning him about the enjoyable sensation's disappearance may only lead to lies about it and placing the blame on her.♥

Orgasm Is Preceded by an Increase in All the Above

Orgasm is the physiological response for both men and women, which brings sexual intercourse to its natural and beautiful conclusion. It is preceded by a dramatic increase in all of the phenomena noted above. At the moment just before orgasm, muscular tension suddenly rises to the point where, if the sexual instinct were not in operation, it would become physically unendurable. The man's pelvic motions and thrust of his penis back and forth within the vagina increase in speed and intensity. The woman's pelvic movements also increase as her whole body attempts to heighten the exquisite sensations she experiences within her vagina.

♥*PRD: The Power of the Surrendered Male's #10 Orgasm*

A male client shared that he was experiencing sensations he didn't know were possible. I asked him to describe how his orgasms had changed to help other men glimpse the power of their emotions over their bodies. He wrote:

> *As the sensation grows, it feels like I completely lose control, and my body takes over. It feels extremely strong, first in the genitals, then through my core, chest, and head. It feels deeply internal and ends being on the verge of passing out, but I never actually do. Pure ecstasy! These types of orgasm are rarer, though not elusive. Every other orgasm is felt solely in the genitals (which are still incredibly intense and pleasurable).*
>
> *The key with the most intense orgasm is it happens when my mind is completely uninhibited.* ***My attitude ultimately determines my level of pleasure.*** *My mind used to be messy with dishonesty, secrecy, doubt, and all the little things not communicated. Even when I wouldn't be conscious of situations/problems, my subconscious was aware, which kept me from experiencing supreme pleasure.*
>
> *Whether we are aware of it or not, we owe the truth it's due, which is*

radical honesty and responsibility. Once that fell into place, my sexual sensations changed drastically. And my refractory period significantly shortened.

For the husband and wife who overcome their inhibitions and begin speaking God's beautiful language of love™, God reserves ecstasy that defies description for them.♥

Cervical Kisses Give Great Pleasure to Men and Women

According to many women with whom I have discussed this experience, the greatest pleasure is caused by the sensation of fullness within the vagina and the pressure and friction upon its posterior surface.

♥*PRD: These women described cervical kisses—a words-defying sensation unlike any other that the male and the female share during deep penetration. A simple biological feature explains why this sensation is so delicious and unlike any other, especially for the woman.*

The Science Behind Cervical Kisses

David Linden, professor of neuroscience at the John Hopkins University School of Medicine, says in <u>Touch: The Science of Hand, Heart, and Mind</u> that some of the nerves in the woman's cervix and uterus and the man's testicles and prostate bypass their spinal columns. These nerves send erotic sensations to the brain via the vagus nerve that travels through the chest cavity to the base of the neck and on to the brain. This is significant because recent research shows that men and women with spinal cord injuries often can continue to enjoy orgasms. Yes, the cervical kiss is real and delightfully pleasurable (98).♥

Strong Muscular Tension Turns into Spasms of Pleasure

At the moment of greatest muscular tension, all sensations seem to take one further rise upward. The woman tenses beyond the point where it seems it would be possible to maintain such tension for a moment longer. Indeed it is not possible. Now her whole body suddenly plunges into a series of muscular spasms. These spasms take place within the vagina itself, shaking the body with waves of pleasure. They are felt simultaneously throughout the body: in the torso, face, arms, and legs—down to the soles of her feet.

These Spasms Represent True Orgasm

These spasms, which shake the entire body and converge upon the vagina, represent and define true vaginal orgasm. At this moment, the woman's head is thrown back, and her pelvis tips upward to obtain as much penetration from the penis as possible. The spasms continue for several seconds in most women, though the time varies with every individual. In some women, they may continue through with decreasing intensity, for a minute or even more.

Many Women Can Repeat This Orgasm Two or More Times

Many women can repeat this performance two or more times before their partner has his orgasm. The pathway, neurologically and psychologically, has been set for the vaginal orgasm and, if her partner continues, she can respond. I have had women say that the last orgasm is sometimes more intense and satisfying than the first.

♥PRD: My experience, as a woman and as a mentor to other women, is that once a woman has her first orgasm, as long as her husband maintains his erection, she can continue to enjoy orgasm after orgasm of varying degrees of intensity with perhaps brief rests of a few seconds in between.

And yes, the last one is often the most intense with pulling her upper body forward into a powerful Kegel hug of his organ of love. Her body then falls back in delightful exhaustion. As they rest for a few seconds in each other's arms, her breathing may involuntarily increase as her vagina goes into a couple of small orgasms. Even though her husband has lost some of his "oomph," he has enough remaining erection for his wife's vagina to continue to give them both pleasure. He may even laugh out loud in delight as she gives him several final hugs. Such is the wonder and the power of her emotions and her mind.♥

Orgasm Releases All Neurological and Muscular Tension

If the man and the woman are satisfied by their orgasmic experience, they will discharge the neurological and muscular tension developed in the sexual build-up. When satisfaction has been achieved, their strenuous movements cease. Within a short period, blood pressure, pulse, glandular secretion, muscular tension, and all the other gross physical changes of sexual excitement return to normal, or even to subnormal, limits.

♥PRD: The appendix chapter "Orgasms of Love with Cervical Kisses" in God's 11 Secrets of Sex gives a composite description by many authors of how husbands and wives share vaginal orgasms with cervical kisses. It goes into a little different detail than Dr. Robinson does.♥

Managing the Other's Pleasure Hinders Your Own

In sex, one's body can feel only its own raptures. Even the exquisite sensation of giving the partner pleasure is psychological and, by definition, important only when it heightens one's pleasure, not when it decreases it.

Over Concern Robs Sex of Its Lusty Spontaneity

Therefore, it is important for the husband and wife to drop their self-consciousness about the other's pleasures or lack of them during intercourse. Both must start with a clean slate on this score, take the healthy natural view that sexual sensations are a self-centered, even selfish, matter. Over-concern for the other can rob it of its lusty spontaneity entirely.

Forget Mutuality and Be Present in the Moment

Enjoying sex for yourself may strike you as a new concept. In most books on married sexuality, the mutuality of the act is the point emphasized. Such books always speak glowingly about the pleasure one experiences in the other's reactions. When sexual inhibitions are present, this "mutuality" can become a mockery.

♥*PRD: Tip: Micromanaging the Other's Responses Hampers Your Own*

Here is a tip I gave some new clients who filled out the Sexless Marriages Survey:

What I'm going to say will sound counterproductive and selfish, but it isn't. From your survey answers, it's apparent that you both are trying too hard to please the other sexually. Consequently, you both are holding back and letting the other dictate your response.

The greatest compliment and show of love you can give the other is to enjoy lovemaking for yourself regardless of whether the other is in the moment. You are using your ecstasy to show how much you love the other. The love language of your body transcends your spoken word.

When you are so in tune with the other's mood, that hampers both of your moods and holds you both back, which in turn holds the other one back even more. It's a self-defeating cycle.

I don't expect you to overcome this immediately. You both come from sexually hostile homes of origin. We will work on the negativity. The personality study will help. I just want you to be aware and start to give yourself permission to enjoy lovemaking even if the other one doesn't seem to be getting the most out of it. One mate enjoying the embrace of love can become a huge turn-on for the other.

You both committed to learning how to enjoy lovemaking to the fullest for yourself and the other. Let the other one make this journey at his or her own pace—as long as your mate is moving forward. The best way you can help the other is to clear the garbage from your own mind to free your own body to respond in glorious ecstasy. Going down the path of enjoying lovemaking for yourself will help the other one more than holding back until you see them enjoying sex.

Work on Your Journey of Love Together

I'm happy to report that both the husband and the wife say they never knew sex could be so fantastic. The wife worked for four months to conquer her pullbacks. Although she got discouraged from time to time, she was transparent with her husband and worked her way through them.

A big part of this couple's success was that they read the assigned chapters in my books aloud together. They stopped at various points to discuss what they were reading. They talked about their homes of origin and the attitudes they brought into their marriage. Then the wife did the homework exercises and emailed them to me for accountability.

Ecstatic lovemaking is the ultimate expression of total intimacy. When you figure out intellectual, emotional, and spiritual intimacy; sexual intimacy will take care of itself.♥

Male and Female Orgasms Parallel Each Other

There have been detailed studies made of the physical reactions of both men and women during intercourse. It is important to realize that in almost every detail, including orgasm, these reactions and the subjective experience of pleasure parallel each other in the sexes. The major differences are that the woman is slightly slower to respond at the outset than the man, and the man's orgasm is characterized by the ejaculation of sperm into the vagina.

Calmness Follows Full Sexual Satisfaction

A state of utter calm follows full sexual satisfaction. The body feels quiescent. Psychologically the person feels completely satisfied, at peace with the world and all things in it.

♥*PRD: Too Tired for Sex? That's When to Say, "Yes."*

The Shulammite maiden uses the metaphor of wine "going down smoothly" to explain the effects of lovemaking on falling asleep:

Song of Solomon 7:9b:
"It [sex] goes down smoothly [sweetly—KJV] for my beloved,

Flowing gently through the lips of those who fall asleep."

The saying, "Sex puts a man to sleep, but it leaves a woman wide awake," simply isn't true. When a woman learns the art of welcoming her husband's presence deep within her, she may fall asleep before he does. Robust lovemaking expends energy and releases hormones that "flow gently through the lips of those who fall asleep."

So the next time you think you're too tired and just want to roll over and go to sleep, don't say, "No." Soften your lips into a sly smile as you say, "Yes." Allow your mate to stir up your desire with deep kisses that deposit arousing hormones into your mouth. Then share love for the best night of sleep ever. (Excerpt from God's 11 Secrets of Sex.)♥

The Wife Feels Extremely Loving Toward Her Husband

The woman, in particular, feels extremely loving toward the partner who has given her so much joy, such a transport of ecstasy. Often she wishes to hold him close for a while, to linger tenderly in the now subdued glow of their passion.

♥*PRD: A beautiful way for the wife to "hold her husband close for a while, to linger tenderly" is to wrap her legs around him while they are still joined together. Then they can roll over onto their sides, still connected. As they lay together in shared afterglow, her husband's penis will slowly return to its normal size through a series of spasms. The sensations are intensely pleasurable for the wife both emotionally and physically. She loves the feeling and the knowledge that she is enjoying every bit of him.*♥

Some See the Vaginal Orgasm as a Foretaste of Heaven

As you can see from this description, orgasm is a tremendous experience. No physiological or psychological experience parallels its sweeping intensity or its excruciating pleasure. It is unique.

Many lovers take a mystical view of this ecstatic coupling of man and woman in love. They think of it as a symbol of a lost unity between the sexes that strives to reassert itself in the act of love. Others see in it a foretaste of heaven, the carnal representation of endless spiritual delights for humanity. Many who experience orgasm in intercourse find it difficult not to ascribe some purposive intent on the part of the Creator; the experience is that profound.

Orgasm Creates an Unbreakable Bond Between Lovers

The individual perceives orgasm as a reward equal to none. It puts the sacrifices and compromises necessary to an enduring marriage into their proper perspectives. It makes the constant giving and sacrifice done by both the man and the woman seem worthwhile and highly desirable. Orgasm is the strongest link in the unbreakable bond between two who love.

♥PRD: The Hormones of Love Glue the Couple Together

Although science didn't know much about the hormones of love released through lovemaking when Dr. Robinson wrote her book, she did a beautiful job describing their effect. One example of the hormones of orgasm bonding a couple together occurs in the account of Adam and Eve's creation. God said he designed a special relationship for only husbands and wives to share:

> *Genesis 2:24: "For this cause a man shall leave his father and mother, and shall cleave to his wife; and they shall become one flesh."*

The significance of "cleaving" wasn't known to Adam and Eve or the following generations. It wasn't until recently that science revealed God's marvelous plan for cleaving. It's much more than leaving one's parents and cozying up with one's spouse. The definition of cleave, "to glue together, cement, join or fasten firmly together," ***is more literal than poetic.***

In Hooked, New Science on How Casual Sex Is Affecting Our Children, Doctors McIlhaney and Bush state that bonding hormones released during sex bathe both the man's and the woman's brains. The hormones of love act "almost like the adhesive-effect of glue—a powerful connection that cannot be undone without great emotional pain" (37).

The couple's bond grows stronger over the years with frequent lovemaking as the hormones continue to glue the couple together. Science has shown that God doesn't use super glue on a husband and wife—he uses oxytocin on the woman and vasopressin on the man, which hold better than Gorilla Super Glue does.

For more information on the hormones of love and how they affect husbands and wives, see "Secret 4: Grow the 4 Parts of Intimacy and Love" in God's 11 Secrets of Sex.♥

Sharing the Vaginal Orgasm Is the Hallmark of Emotional Surrender

The ability to share a full vaginal orgasm is, in most cases, the hallmark of the psychologically mature man and woman. It is the sign that they have successfully weathered the storms of childhood and youth. They have come, unscathed, into full manhood and womanhood with all that it implies. Sharing orgasms is the hallmark of total emotional surrender to their mate.

♥*PRD: The following excerpt from "Secret 7: Turn on Double-Dose #10 Orgasms" in God's 11 Secrets of Sex shows how emotions turn orgasms into relationship barometers:*

Male and Female Orgasms Are Relationship Barometers

A woman's orgasms change from day to day, along with the daily stresses of life. Although she continues to experience orgasms, sometimes her internal sensations are more robust than at other times. She doesn't always enjoy the hot glow of a #10. The key is to relax and enjoy the orgasm your body gives you for where you are intellectually, emotionally, physically, and spiritually in that moment.

Once a woman experiences firsthand how her attitudes affect her sexual reflexes, it becomes a powerful motivation to keep communication lines open and solve problems quickly. She gladly works to build an emotional bond filled with love and esteem for her husband.

Dr. Zilbergeld in Male Sexuality and the Sarrels in "What Men Need from the Women Who Love Them" state that the same is true for men. A husband's attitudes toward his wife, himself, children, home, and work determine how intense his physical pleasure is. His sensations can range from monotony and a total lack of pleasure to an explosion of ecstasy.

God regulates the husband's and the wife's bodies by designing them to respond wonderfully to the right attitudes toward each other. Being able to share vaginal orgasms is a barometer of the relationship. A woman's healthy attitudes that allow her to enjoy lovemaking is the highest compliment she can pay her husband. Likewise, a man's ability to love his wife intellectually, emotionally, sexually, and spiritually is the highest compliment he can pay her. Frequent lovemaking keeps a couple in tune with each other and strengthens their bonds of love.

Christianity is about growing our ability to love others, especially our mate and children. Thus the better Christian you are, the better lover you will become to your mate, and the more your body will respond in the act of love with glorious #10s. The sexual joy God gives us testifies to his great love for both men and women. Truly, God's people serve a wonderful Creator!♥

3.

The Female Sex: The Not Impossible She

What is the mature woman? Who is she? What are her characteristics? Her personality? Her role in life? It is vital to understand the sexually inhibited woman to answer these questions. For again, only by understanding what health is can we truly grasp the meaning of any departure from it.

Beware of Society's Definition of Normal for Women

Great arguments have been presented about what the word "normal" means. Millions of words have been written about it. I fear that most of them have only clouded the issue. Odd definitions of normalcy have led millions of women down strange and unhappy paths.

Victorians Viewed Sexual Inhibitions as Normal

For example, you will recall that Victorianism elevated sexual inhibitions to the position of the normal for all womankind—with disastrous results.

The Feminist Movement Promoted Inhibitions and Divorce

At the start of my practice, I encountered another peculiar and tragic view of the normal that has had a powerful influence on American women. This view still has wide repercussions and is intimately bound with the subject of inhibitions and divorce—the feminist movement.

Case History: Woman Angry About Being Raised as a Feminist

In my introduction to the feminist movement, a lovely woman of forty came to consult me. She could hardly speak as she wept so emotionally.

I felt at once that she hid a deep rage behind her tears. I recognized her name when she was able to get it out; she was a successful lawyer whose name many would still recognize.

(1) In her thirty-ninth year, she fell in love for the first time with a fine man, another successful lawyer. Her dormant sexuality and true femininity were awakened completely since their marriage a year before. Now they both wanted children. Unhappily, as it so often is for women who postpone pregnancy too long, an examination indicated she needed a hysterectomy.

(2) She felt cruelly deprived, and I saw her for several sessions. During these periods, she told me about her background. Her father died when she was an infant, and her mother was a militant leader of the movement for women's "rights." The emphasis in her early upbringing was on achievement in the male world, in the male sense of the word. She was taught to be competitive with men, to look upon them as basically hostile to women. Women were portrayed as an exploited and a badly put upon minority class. Marriage, childbearing, and love were traps that placed one in the hands of the enemy, a man whose chief desire was to take advantage of the woman.

(3) Her mother profoundly instilled in her the belief that women were to work in the market place at all cost, to be aggressive, to take love (*à la Russe*) where they found it, and "to be tied down by nothing, no one; no more," as her mother put it, "than a man is."

(4) Such a definition of the "normal" made her fearful of a deep or enduring relationship with a man. For years she sedulously avoided men entirely. Gradually, through her grownup experiences, she learned of other values. But by the time the right man came along, it was too late to have children.

To Heal, She Vented Tears of Rage Toward Her Mother

I was right that her tears were tears of rage. She directed her anger at her mother's authoritarian but mistaken view of the feminine role in life and was, to my mind, justified.

♥*PRD: In the case history above, she cried and raged over the following:*

1. *Love awoke her femininity and sexuality.*
2. *Her mother was a militant leader of the feminist movement.*
3. *Her mother taught her to act like men in work and sex.*
4. *The feminist definition of normal made her afraid of men.*♥

Revising Feminist Values Allowed Her to Love Her Family

When my patient had sufficiently vented her righteous anger, but not until then, we were able to move on to more practical matters. Her marriage was happy, and finally, she adopted two children. With some of her values revised, she made a wonderful mother for them. I visited this family recently, and it seems to be one of the happiest and healthiest, psychologically speaking, I have ever seen.

Women Raised by a Feminist Have Two Choices

However, most women, who are reared with such ideas of normal, are not as fortunate as this patient. They have two choices to make in life.

1. Can Cling to Self-Destructive Values to the Bitter End

Many of these daughters cling to their defensive and self-destructive values to the end, which is often bitter. And they are passionately convinced and often eloquent purveyors of these ideas. Their foggy contours remind me of the glamorous-sounding but fleeting and mist-enshrouded goals that many of the sexually inhibited and lonely women I treat have when they first come for help.

After reading the bestseller, *The Second Sex*, by Simone de Beauvoir, the French authoress, I was saddened to see such clarity and brilliance in the service of such a mistaken cause. Her tacit conclusions seem to be that the woman's historical role of wife and mother is degrading and has kept the woman from her true destiny. As she describes what that true destiny is, her clarity departs, and the role and function of this woman of the future become more than merely vague.

2. Or Can Enjoy a Loving Mental and Sexual Life

The normal woman has no vagueness about her goals, functions, and needs. Science in recent years has thrown a bright light on her, and that is why we can be certain of many fundamental details about her. She is a mature, fully functioning woman who has realized the better part of her potentials, who knows how to achieve and handle love and happiness, and who enjoys a fully satisfying mental and sexual life.

Feminist Reactions to the Description of Femininity

I frequently draw a word portrait of such a woman for patients who consult me about their sexual problems. The description often makes them angry, and they deeply resent some of the characteristics of this idealized woman. They call her all sorts of names:

1. "A victim of the male."
2. "An impossible ideal."
3. One eloquent younger woman called her "a faceless tramp."
4. Older women, brought up under a more inhibited code than exists now, call her "a shameless hussy."

Yet They Yearn for the Possibility of Femininity

Despite the hostility my portrait receives, my troubled listeners are often touched deeply by the idea that such a picture of womanhood might be a possibility for them. "Do you think I could ever get to be anything like that?" The yearning question, phrased in any number of wistful ways, inevitably comes, despite the apparent resentment, the bristling defenses, and the fact that the speaker is scared blue of sex, motherhood, and all they mean.

You see, women want to find themselves, desperately want to. And in this portrait, they get a hint, often the first they have ever had, of what to aim for, of the real potential inside themselves.

♥PRD: One client, who believed the vaginal orgasm was a myth, contacted me because the descriptions of a woman's orgasms in a book she read caught her attention. For the first time, she began to hope that perhaps women really could enjoy sex for themselves. She wanted to learn if lovemaking offered more for a woman than just doing her duty and finding some consolation in her husband's obvious pleasure in being with her. Next, she read The Power of Sexual Surrender but had problems applying it. She found me when she googled "Power of Sexual Surrender counselor" and my name came up with several articles I'd written quoting Dr. Robinson.♥

The "Idealized" Woman's Description

I call this subject of my sketch "idealized," and she is. But I want to emphasize that she is not a personal idle daydream of my own, based on airy nothingness; much to the contrary.

She's Based on Psychological and Biological Facts

Her characteristics are based on exact and thoroughly checked psychological and biological facts, facts upon which the leading scientists in this field are in general agreement.

She's a Composite of Observations of Women

And she is a composite based on observations of women I have known, and not always clinically. If you stop to think as you read about her, you may realize that you have known such women too.

We Don't Know What She Looks Like

What, then, is she like? To give us a frame for our portrait so we can see what we do know more clearly, let me state what we cannot know about her; what is irrelevant. We don't know what she looks like. She may be tall or short, red-haired, blond, or brunette. She may have large breasts and round hips and sloping shoulders, or she may be small-breasted (or even flat-chested), have wide shoulders and narrow hips.

Things We Don't Know Are Unimportant

She may have a career or not have a career. She may be more intelligent or less intelligent, be better educated or less well educated than her husband. She may have children or be unable to have children. She may be rich or poor, come from New York society or the slums. She may be a bit shy or at ease socially. She may be athletic or unathletic. These things we don't know about her and, for our purposes, they do not matter. Here are some of the things we do know.

The Description of the Mature Orgasmic Feminine Woman

♥PRD: The Bible contains two portraits of women that Dr. Robinson's profile mirrors. I refer to these women in my comments about the orgasmic woman, so here's a little bit of their background:

The Woman of Great Price in Proverbs 31:10-31

Women have loved this portrait of a loving, industrious wife, mother, and citizen since King Lemuel's mother taught him how to choose a wife. We know she is an older woman because her husband sits with the elders at the gate to the city. Also, her daughters are old enough to assume household duties. She is a successful entrepreneur. Her husband praises her saying, "In contrast to many young wives who are doing a great job with their families, you—my gray-haired jewel—are the best of all."

The Shulammite Heroine of the Song of Solomon

The Maiden credits her mother with teaching her how to satisfy a husband and how to enjoy sex for herself. Her mother told her to look at the mating habits of the gazelles and the hinds of the field for an example of successful courtship. Learning that a passionate marriage requires soulmating before lovemaking protected the young woman from being fooled by King Solomon's polished proposals to add her to his harem. She is also an entrepreneur who looks forward to motherhood. The Shulammite is one of the young women the Woman of Great Price's husband spoke about as doing well. She is on course to grow into a Proverbs-31 woman.♥

The Ideal Woman Is Glad to Be Born a Woman

She is totally "at home" in the world. Deep inside herself, she feels profoundly secure, safe, both with herself and with her husband. She is glad to be a woman, with all the duties, responsibilities, and joys it entails. She can't imagine what it would be like to be a man and has no interest in imagining it as a possible role for herself.

She Has a Deep Understanding of World Reality

She feels that her husband makes the world safe for her. This feeling of safety may seem unrealistic, given the insecurities in the world today. However, as you will discover, it is based on a far more profound understanding of reality than the one reflected in the alarms published in the media.

♥PRD: The Woman of Great Price has gained a wise world view from her time spent taking care of her family and being a merchant:

Proverbs 31:25-26:
"Strength and dignity are her clothing,
And she smiles at the future.
She opens her mouth in wisdom,
And the teaching of kindness is on her tongue."

Wallowing in bitterness or self-pity is not her choice. Instead, she displays the strength, dignity, and happiness of a woman who understands life and her place in it. Her wisdom and kindness bless everyone she comes in contact with.♥

She Selects a Husband Who Appears to Be Good for Her

This sense of reality almost invariably leads her to select a husband who is good for her. He might not be perfect for another woman, nor perfect in any ultimate sense, but he is near perfect for her. He loves her and intends to go on loving her. He may be a carpenter or an architect, a lawyer, a dockhand, or a poet, but with her, he is passionate and loyal, a good companion, and a good father for her children. She has an infallible sense about this matter, and though she may have had an adolescent or college crush on a no-gooder, she never will marry him.

♥PRD: Sexless Christians Often Use "Bait and Switch" in Courtship

Respondents to my Sexless Marriages Survey disagree with Dr. Robinson's statement that sexually healthy individuals always marry someone good for them. Unfortunately, many men and women grew up in homes where one parent didn't emotionally and sexually love the other. Consequently, they failed to learn what healthy love looks, sounds, feels, tastes, smells, and acts like. As a result, they are easily fooled.

The survey reveals that 87% of sex-withholding Christians used bait and switch in courtship by feigning desire for married passion. One frequent statement is, "She couldn't keep her hands off me in courtship. Now she won't kiss, hug, or touch me."

Thus many Christians who are searching for a sexually healthy marriage partner so they can do better than their parents are tricked into an unhealthy marriage. One sexless wife told her husband, "When we were dating, I told you what I knew you wanted to hear to make you marry me." After they had all the children she wanted, she made it clear that she considered his approaches for sex "marital rape."

Men fool women the same way. One boyfriend wrote his girlfriend several years' worth of love letters claiming he couldn't wait to show her how much he loved her. He promised, "When we get married, I'm going to kiss you 100 times." After marriage, when she told him French kissing made her instantly ready for sex, he refused the Frenchies claiming they were germy. He never showed her how much he loved her or kissed her 100 times.

The Difference Between Those Who Stay and Those Who Divorce

The difference between men and women who grew up with loving parents and those who grew up with a cold, indifferent parent is their self-images. If the sex-withholding spouse refuses to get help, the ones who observed love between their parents and felt loved by them often divorce their inhibited spouse somewhat quickly. The ones who never observed healthy love between their parents often stay married for decades and become co-dependent as they suffer emotional and sexual neglect and harm in their unloving marriage.♥

She Exhibits Genuine Feminine Concern for Others

Of course, marrying a good husband adds to her sense of "at-homeness" in the world. Related to her sense of security, seeming almost to spring from it, is a profound delight in giving to those she loves. Psychiatrists consider this characteristic the hallmark, the *sine qua non*, of the truly feminine character. They call it "essential feminine altruism."

♥PRD: Not only does the Woman of Great Price care about her family, but she also shows concern for others in the community as well:

Proverbs 31:20:
"She extends her hand to the poor,
And she stretches out her hands to the needy."

The more loving husbands and wives are to each other, the more caring they become for people in the community and the world. When they close their hearts to loving each other, they become selfish and calloused toward others.♥

She Enjoys Giving Herself to Her Husband and Children

As you will see, giving of herself has its roots in the woman's biology, and on its deepest level, it is a need in her that must have expression. The finest flower of this altruism blossoms in her joy in giving *the best of herself* to her husband and children. She never resents this need in herself to give; she never interprets its manifestations as a burden or an imposition. It pervades her nature as the color green saturates the countryside in the spring. She is proudly delights in it.

♥PRD: *The Woman of Great Price Exhibits These Qualities*

Proverbs 31:11-12:
"The heart of her husband trusts in her,
And he will have no lack of gain.
She does him good and not evil
All the days of her life."

Proverbs 31:28-29:
"Her children rise up and bless her;
Her husband also, and he praises her,
'Many daughters have done nobly,
But you excel them all.'"♥

Lack of a Giving Spirit Leads to Rage and Self-Pity

It is this altruism, this givingness, that motivates her to keep her equilibrium, to hold onto her *joie de vivre* despite whatever may befall. It stands her in marvelous stead for all the demands that life is going to make on her—and they will be considerable. When a woman does not have this instinctually based altruism available to her, or when she denies that it is a desirable trait, life's continuous small misfortunes leave her in a glowering rage, helpless, and beside herself with self-pity.

♥*PRD: Dr. Robinson goes into detail about the woman's rage, helplessness, and self-pity in Chapter 6: "Sexual Inhibitions Linked to Cognitive Distortions."*♥

She Is Deeply Religious

Another fact about her which you may be surprised to learn is that she is deeply religious—though not necessarily officially or even consciously. If her husband's background has been antagonistic to formal religion and he is still reflecting his upbringing, she may pay lip service to his agnosticism or atheism. But that doesn't mean a thing. Beneath the surface is a steadfast belief in the existence of a Creator and some form of heaven. She's not so clear about hell.

♥PRD: Dr. Robinson's belief in God shows in her choice of some words from the Bible, such as "one flesh." She also demonstrates a respect for male and female and masculinity and femininity that is absent in books written by evolutionists. They often theorize how we've evolved into this state of love and are moving toward a better one.

Dr. Robinson's faith allows her to speak with authority that recognizes eternal truths about men and women. These truths make her book timeless even though it needs to be updated with scientific discoveries, such as those about hormones and the way the brain works.

The Shulammite Prayed to God to Bless Her Marriage

The Maiden addressed the different winds as ancient Hebrew symbols for appealing to God for help:

Song of Solomon 4:16:
"Awake, O north wind,
And come, wind of the south;
Make my garden breathe out fragrance,
Let its spices be wafted abroad.
May my beloved come into his garden
And eat its choice fruits!"

God answered her prayer by telling her to marry the Shepherd and to get drunk on passionate lovemaking:

Song of Solomon 5:1b:
"Eat, friends;
Drink and imbibe deeply, O lovers."

God gives a 3-step formula that contains the keys for a couple to delight in an ecstatic lifelong sexual relationship. It's simple: (1) eat, (2) drink, and (3) get tipsy on love. The Song of Solomon has preserved this wine-based formula for over 3000 years. It gives the Divine answer to the Shulammite's prayer.

Unfortunately, most Christian teetotalers don't know enough about healthy wine sipping to understand God's formula. You can read the details in "Secret 5: Sip the Divine Wine of Passion" in God's 11 Secrets of Sex, a verse-by-verse study of the Song of Solomon.♥

She Is the Carrier of Immortality Biologically

She also believes firmly in the fact that marriage is a sacrament, binding forever. Given the slightest encouragement or support, she will formalize these beliefs, join a church, or develop a personal view of God in nature. Why? Biologically speaking, she is the carrier of immortality, of the generations of man.

She Exhibits a Wonderment at the Awesome Creation

This gives her a close affinity to and appreciation of the awesome and creative mysteries of the universe: moon-rise, tidal flow, along with the growth, death, and rebirth of things.

She Nearly Always Enjoys Vaginal Orgasms

Sexually, she almost always reaches a climax during the act of love. Sometimes she reaches two or, if she and her husband are feeling particularly lusty, even three. But the number of times is unimportant, despite the Kinsey report.

What is important is the *kind* of orgasm she has. It is the type described in the previous chapter, which starts deep within her vagina and extends to all parts of her body.

♥PRD: Once a woman learns the power of her emotions over her physical sensations, when her husband enters her private garden, she can refresh him in multiple ways from her life-giving spring. The Shepherd looked forward to the Shulammite's sexual charms in marriage:

Song of Solomon 4:12:
"A garden locked is my sister, my bride,
A rock-garden locked, a spring sealed up."

The older wife delights her older husband with her many talents perfected over a lifetime of loving each other:

Proverbs 5:15-19:
"Drink water from your own cistern
And fresh water from your own well.
Should your springs be dispersed abroad,
Streams of water in the streets?
Let them be yours alone
And not for strangers with you.
Let your fountain be blessed,
And rejoice in the wife of your youth.
As a loving hind and a graceful doe,
Let her breasts satisfy you at all times;
Be exhilarated always with her love."♥

She Describes Her Orgasms Poetically

The orgasmic woman doesn't talk about lovemaking often, but when she does, it is always poetically.

1. I have heard one woman refer to it as "a sensation of such beauty and

intensity that I can hardly think of it without weeping."

2. Another said, "It's like a mounting symphony, rising in tremendous and irresistible rhythms till your whole being feels as though it has been swept away."
3. One woman, less lyrical but still exact, said, "It's like going over Niagara Falls in a barrel."
4. Nobody can ever quite evoke the exact sensations in words, but, as one woman told me, "Nobody who has ever had it will doubt whether her experience is the real thing."

She's Not Modest in the Bedroom

What else characterizes her sexually? Well, she's not modest, I'm afraid. She's quite a show-off and likes sexual compliments from her husband, dressed or undressed, verbal or otherwise. Her nineteenth-century sister would have been vastly shocked by her whole attitude in the bedroom.

She Doesn't Hesitate to Initiate Lovemaking

She's not sexually shy at all. She wouldn't demur a moment at initiating love with her husband. However, she will immediately change her amorous direction if she finds he is too tired or is preoccupied, without feeling the least bit rejected. Don't forget that just under the surface (and sometimes on it), she considers her marriage a heaven-made arrangement that will last forever, and she need not look upon any single experience as too important in itself.

♥PRD: *The Shulammite Maiden Promises to Initiate Lovemaking*

Song of Solomon 7:12:
"Let us rise early and go to the vineyards;
Let us see whether the vine has budded
And its blossoms have opened,
And whether the pomegranates have bloomed.
There I will give you my love."

"My love" literally refers to "her breasts as the seat of love." The Maiden tells the Shepherd, "We'll get married in the fall. And then I want to experience the full sweetness of loving you. There I will initiate lovemaking by giving you my breasts as an expression of my love."

The Shulammite looked forward to initiating sex. She was not timid about expressing emotional and sexual love for her Shepherd.♥

She Takes Her Cue From Her Husband

However, there is another important point. I have indicated that sexually she takes her cue from her husband. What does she know, do you suppose—know deeply and instinctively—that makes her do this, while other women refuse to?

If the Husband Can't Respond, Lovemaking Won't Happen

She knows this: that it is the man who, from the purely physical viewpoint, has to be ready before sexual intercourse can take place. No matter how many books ignore the fact, it is nevertheless true that, if the man does not have an erection, lovemaking cannot occur.

Just think about it for a moment A woman can make love at any time; a man only when he is ready. There may be psychologically preferential circumstances for a woman, but there is no physical prerequisite.

That is why (by virtue of that deeper sense of reality we spoke of) when her husband is ready to make love, our lady is nearly always willing, barring sickness or certain difficulties that may come up during pregnancy. That is why she is always willing to forgo lovemaking if he is not ready. Her deep altruism makes her extremely sensitive to his moods, and she will not find it in herself to treat him as if he were a robot, become angry, or feel rejected when, if she pushes the button, he doesn't respond.

♥PRD: The physical natures of the male and the female bodies fit perfectly together. God designed a woman as the guardian of both mental and physical love. She can make love nearly any time—whether she's tired or energetic, though she can become so fatigued or preoccupied that her body doesn't respond as fully as she would like.

Likewise, the woman can forgo lovemaking even when she greatly desires it if her husband isn't physically able. A loving woman understands that her husband is made differently from her, and she isn't hurt when he is ***temporarily*** *unable to engage in the sexual embrace. At such times she channels her love into other avenues of expression such as hugging, patting, kissing, or even cooking her husband's favorite meal. She knows that when they must postpone lovemaking, anticipation makes it just that much better the next time.*

A Loving Wife Can Make Love to a Tired Husband

The man, however, is more limited by his physical abilities. If he's overworked or preoccupied, he may desire lovemaking but lack the physical stamina necessary. When a couple joins emotionally and shares genuine concern for each other, the woman possesses the ability to always satisfy her husband by her gentle sexual makeup. She takes her cue from him by either stimulating his tired body into action with her skilled foreplay or by waiting for a more energetic time.

A Loving Wife Cannot Awaken a Sexually Inhibited Husband

However, the sexually inhibited husband won't allow his wife to touch him intimately because he doesn't want to be aroused by her charms. He prefers to satisfy himself with masturbation. It's important to keep in mind that Dr. Robinson is portraying a loving woman married to a sexually healthy man.♥

She Knows How Important Her Husband's Sexuality Is to Him

On this same point, she knows how much store men put on their potency, how vulnerable they can become if they are made to feel inadequate to a wife's needs. She would die a thousand deaths rather than have her husband gain any such inference from her actions. It's her altruism again.

♥PRD: The Wife Determines What Happens to Her Husband's Sexuality

God created the woman as the guardian of love, and the husband depends on her to fulfill her role. In The Sexual Responsibility of Woman, Dr. Maxine Davis says the wife's attitude toward lovemaking determines what happens to her husband's sexual capacities in his later years. When the wife passively does her duty, she may cause her husband to become "impotent with her" long before age takes away his abilities. The wife, more than the husband, keeps sexual interest and activity going throughout a long marriage (Davis 38).

The Shulammite shares Davis' view. She promises to do her part to keep the Shepherd sexually healthy throughout their marriage:

Song of Solomon 8:1b-3:
"If I found you outdoors, I would kiss you;
No one would despise me, either.
I would lead you and bring you
Into the house of my mother, who used to instruct me;
I would give you spiced wine to drink from the juice of my pomegranates.
Let his left hand be under my head
And his right hand embrace me."

She would flirt with kisses as she brought him pomegranate juice—an aphrodisiac that helps keep a man's sexual organs healthy way unto old age. Both the Maiden and the Shepherd often refer to aphrodisiacs as they prepare to enter a lifetime of passion. Throughout the Song of Solomon, it's the Shulammite who continually mentions looking forward to frequent lovemaking, not the Shepherd.♥

She Knows the Power of Emotions Over Sensations

Her eternal acceptance, her ever-readiness, never lets her in for a painful sexual experience, however. She knows that ninety-nine times out of one hundred even negative sexual feelings in herself will soon return to eagerness and eagerness to desire. Even if that once in a hundred times occurs, she still gets profound satisfaction from the obvious pleasure she gives her husband, once more her deep altruism.

She Loves to Follow Her Husband's Lead in Lovemaking

But she not only follows her husband's lead about whether they are going to make love—the kind of love they are going to make is also usually his decision and, in pure delight, she follows him completely.

1. If he feels *purely lusty*, soon she does too.
2. Does he feel *gentle and tender*, then she picks up that mood.
3. *Experimental?* Let's, by all means, experiment.
4. *Passive?* She'll be active.

A Geisha's Techniques Can't Compare with a Wife's Love

It takes her little time to find out that a geisha has the tremendous disadvantage of believing that techniques are more important than love and the love of following one's partner.

♥*PRD: "Breasts of Love" Contrast with "Bosoms"*

The wife of his youth is the older man's bride who has grown older along with him. The wife who has practiced the art of enjoying vaginal orgasms and cervical kisses for a lifetime doesn't have to fear her husband being attracted to a "sweet young thing":

Proverbs 5:18-20:
"Let your fountain be blessed,
And rejoice in the wife of your youth.
As a loving hind and a graceful doe,
Let her breasts satisfy you at all times;
Be exhilarated always with her love.
For why should you, my son, be exhilarated with an adulteress
And embrace the bosom of a foreigner?

"Love" is the same word the Shulammite uses. The older wife's "breasts as the seat of her love" contrast with the "bosom" of the young adulteress. "Bosom" is strictly a biological term, offered to the man without emotion. A wife who has spent a lifetime loving her husband offers him thrills he can't find with anyone else.♥

She Doesn't Fantasize About Other Men

Despite her pronounced wantonness with her husband, she has no promiscuous urges whatsoever. She is realistic about other men and finds them attractive or unattractive, as the case may be. But she neither desires them nor has any fantasies of a sexual nature about them.

One woman put it this way: "I like other men if they're attractive." She said, "Their attractiveness does honor to the sex my husband belongs to."

♥*PRD: Fantasizing About Other Men Is Mental Adultery*

Fantasizing about someone other than one's spouse is mental adultery when accompanied with self-masturbation. Lustful thoughts coupled with self-masturbation exert a powerfully negative effect on the brain. They interfere with both the wife's and the husband's ability to share vaginal orgasms. Mental adultery is more harmful than a dysfunctional upbringing.

In the context of divorce, Jesus condemned mental adultery accompanied with self-masturbation as grounds for divorce:

> *Matthew 5:27-30: "You have heard that it was said, 'You shall not commit adultery'; but I say to you that everyone who looks at a woman with lust for her has already committed adultery with her in his heart. If your right eye makes you stumble [the eye you lust with], tear it out and throw it from you; for it is better for you to lose one of the parts of your body, than for your whole body to be thrown into hell. If your right hand makes you stumble [the hand you masturbate with], cut it off and throw it from you; for it is better for you to lose one of the parts of your body, than for your whole body to go into hell."*

Husbands and wives whose spouses masturbate to images of other people easily recognize that their spouses are unfaithful. They know they are being sinned against.

This lesson was brought home when a husband and wife talked to me about the husband's sexual addiction. He revealed that he had a problem lusting after women he was teaching how to become a Christian.

His wife blurted out, "But I didn't know you were masturbating to them!"

He turned bright red, hung his head, and whispered, "That's part of lust."

Thanks to MRI and SPECT scans, scientists now know that masturbation causes changes in the brain just as sexual intercourse does. Certainly, Jesus' words are true, "Everyone who looks at a woman with lust for her has already committed adultery with her in his heart."

Guarding Your Heart Leads to Life and Health for the Body

Proverbs 4 elaborates on the benefits of pursuing wisdom and understanding. Notice the two benefits you receive when you guard your heart:

Proverbs 4:20-23:
"My son, give attention to my words;
Incline your ear to my sayings.
Do not let them depart from your sight;
Keep them in the midst of your heart.
For (1) they are life to those who find them
And (2) health to all their body.
Watch over your heart with all diligence,
For from it flow the springs of life."

You are to "watch over your heart" because "from it flow the springs of life." God's words of wisdom and understanding about his proudest creation—the way of a man with a maid—gives (1) life and (2) health to your body—to your sexual body (Proverbs 30:18-19). Dr. Robinson makes this point over and over: Take care of your attitudes so your body can ravish you with ecstasy.

Science recognizes this principle by promoting sports visualization techniques for training and competition. Athletes are encouraged to visualize themselves participating and excelling in their chosen sports. Visualization is called "the secret weapon" for winning at sports.

This same kind of visualization is reinforced with self-masturbation and can be called "the secret weapon" for losing physical sensations with one's mate. It works in the bedroom the same way it works in the sports arena. Masturbation, the manifestation of mental adultery, numbs the husband's and the wife's physical sensations with their spouse. It brings the growth of their marriage to a halt because it "trains" their body to respond apart from their spouse.

God Doesn't Trap Anyone in Sexless Marriages

The purpose of this book is not to teach about divorcing a sexless spouse. You can read articles about God's teaching regarding sexless marriages and divorce at my website PatsyRaeDawson.com. For now, notice that God doesn't trap anyone in a loveless, sexless marriage, but provides many ways of escape.

> *1 Corinthians 10:13: "No temptation has overtaken you but such as is common to man; and God is faithful, who will not allow you to be tempted beyond what you are able, but with the temptation will provide the way of escape also, so that you will be able to endure it."*

One way of escape is to recognize the sinfulness of lustful masturbation and to begin to appreciate that men and women who share vaginal orgasms with cervical kisses don't masturbate. This topic is so important, Dr. Robinson talks about it in several chapters, and I'll expand on the Bible's teaching as she gives more information.♥

Self-Masturbation Doesn't Satisfy Loving Wives

Nor is the loving woman ever tempted to indulge in self-masturbation, at least not after one or two tasteless and pointless experiments she may make during her first absence from her husband. To her, sexuality is devoid of any meaning if mutuality is not shared.

♥PRD: *Solo Sex Is Distasteful to Loving Men and Women*

Solo sex numbs the man's and the woman's sensations for the next time lovemaking occurs. The loving wife would never tell her husband, "Go take care of yourself." Nor would she ever consider taking care of herself with a vibrator.

Each time a woman pushes her husband to masturbate, or she self-masturbates, they teach their bodies how to respond apart from each other. In effect, they numb their physical sensations and deny themselves ecstasy in each other's arms.

Since Dr. Robinson wrote this book, vibrators are now heavily recommended for women. Some husbands resort to a vibrator to try to bring their wife to an orgasm. In one dysfunctional marriage, the husband threw the vibrator at his wife and hollered, "Go take care of yourself!"

The Vibrator Was Invented to Relieve Victorian Sexual Hysteria

Unbelievable, a British physician invented the vibrator to help doctors deal with the "hysteria pandemic" among Victorian women. Since initiating sex with their husbands was not a moral option for these frustrated women, they made appointments with their doctors. The doctors used "manual genital massage" to bring these women to orgasm and thus relieve their hysteria. The vibrator helped the doctors shorten the time required to perform this "chore" (Berman and Berman 25, 249).♥

The Orgasmic Woman Enjoys Everything About Her Sexuality

Lest you think that our paragon's altruism could end up by making her a martyr, a person without any real regard for herself, I must hasten to dismiss that idea. In her quiet way, she is quite self-centered. She's contented with her body, all the details of female anatomy that give her so much pleasure. If her cultural background tended to instill disgust with certain natural functions, she finds herself rejecting them.

She Rejects the Idea of "The Curse" for Menstruation

For example, several patients ruminated on the word "curse" during therapy as it is used to describe the menstrual flow. Reflection almost always made them drop the word from their vocabulary entirely. In the end, they were more likely to call it a blessing.

♥*PRD: The Blessing in the Woman's Menstruation*

Interestingly, since perhaps the beginning of time, many people refer to a woman's menstrual functions as the "curse" as part of God's punishment of Eve after she ate the forbidden fruit. Yet God nowhere cursed Eve in this manner.

On the other hand, God told the serpent, "Cursed are you more than all cattle," and he told Adam, "Cursed is the ground because of you." God didn't punish the woman by causing her to menstruate, but by increasing her pain in childbirth. Labeling a woman's reproductive functions as a curse ignores the facts, for God cursed only the serpent and the ground. God didn't curse the woman or anything about her.

The woman's punishment of pain centers on her unique difference from the man—her womb—her ability to bear and nurture children. Thus a woman's menstrual functions serve as a monthly reminder that she is different from the man and focuses her attention on bearing children. This time of the month is the most likely time for a woman to become depressed over an inability to conceive as it reminds her of her motherly role.

When a woman goes into menopause and loses her monthly menstrual functions, she may welcome it with joy as she embraces her new freedom. However, it won't be long before she realizes all those monthly hormonal events were a blessing. She would welcome them back with nary a complaint to embrace their benefits once again. Too late, she realizes they moisturized her soft, beautiful skin. They made her hair thick and luxurious. They protected her heart and bones. Instead of a curse, they were a gift of health and beauty.♥

She Likes the Way She Looks in Youth and Old Age

This self-love, her pride in and love of her body, is reflected in her outward appearance. She likes to be as clean as a cat and as neat as a pin. She enjoys dressing well. She is aware of the things that bring out her special attractiveness. She also knows how to make herself up to the best advantage. But she does not spend hours daily on grooming in front of the mirror. She is far too confident of herself, has too much self-love, to feel that such a production is necessary.

♥*PRD: The Shulammite repeatedly expresses satisfaction with her appearance even when Solomon's virgins in waiting were disgusted with her dark skin that was burned by the sun from working in the vineyard. Later when Solomon makes a sensuous proposal, the Maiden tells him she is the rose of Sharon, the lily of the valleys. She can be particular about whom she marries. Even when it comes to the king.*

Song of Solomon 2:1-2:
"'I am the rose of Sharon,
The lily of the valleys.'
'Like a lily among the thorns,
So is my darling among the maidens.'"

Solomon agrees and says all the other maidens are like thorns compared to her. The Shulammite's healthy self-image helps protect her from making a disastrous marriage choice with a man incapable of loving any woman.♥

She's Getting Older, and She's Getting Better

The loving woman accepts and is pleased with the way she is and the way, as time passes, she is going to be. This is true of her mental capacities as well as of her physical attributes, but we can see it most clearly in her attitude toward her physical self. As I said at the beginning, we don't know whether she has small breasts or large breasts, rounded hips or narrow hips. We only know that, whatever she's got, she enjoys.

♥PRD: The Woman of Great Price's husband praised her as being an older woman whom good young wives can't compete with:

Proverbs 31:28-29:
"Her children rise up and bless her;
Her husband also, and he praises her, saying:
'Many daughters have done nobly,
But you excel them all.'"

The young women are doing nobly, but they still have some life to live and some lessons to learn before taking their place among the amazing feminine women. They are Women of Great Price in training.♥

She Enjoys Loving Her Husband Passionately

You see, she knows perfectly well that it is passion and response which spin the plot of love and not, ever, fetish or fashion. She feels sorry for women who worry about what they haven't got or the effect of growing older. If she were small-breasted, she would never disguise that fact, and you can be confident that her husband, at least after the relationship got underway and he had a chance to experience her pleasures, would soon drop any adolescent preferences he possessed.

The husband of one such woman said to me: "When I was in college, I had a conviction that beautiful women had to be redheads. I can't imagine now what made me believe such a thing." I know his wife well; she's a brunette, and you and I might not be the least bit impressed by her looks. But he knows better; he knows her real beauty. And, I happen to know, so does she.

♥*PRD: The Woman of Great Price's Husband Said It Best*

Proverbs 31:30:
"Beauty is vain and charm is deceitful.
But a woman who fears the Lord, she shall be praised."

A man will not marry a woman he is not attracted to physically. But physical beauty does not last. If that's all his wife has to offer, he'll be sorely disappointed.

Neither will a man marry a woman who lacks charm. He chooses a woman who praises him and tells him he's the most wonderful man around. But charm is deceitful. Too many men discover that their bride's praise was only temporary when her admiration turns to complaints and blame.

The husband of Proverbs 31 found a feminine woman who truly loved him and did him good and not evil all the days of her life (Proverbs 31:12).♥

Her Self-Love Leads to Putting Her Family First

Our fair lady's confidence and pleasure in her person and her other attributes (her self-love) have one odd quality. And it is an all-important one. This self-love is detachable.

With a flick of her psyche, she can project practically all of it onto her children, take as much joy from their beauty, achievements, and pleasures as she ever got from her own. She detaches it, too, on behalf of her husband, often will exaggerate his good qualities and minimize any weakness he might have, as long as the weakness is not a danger to family and home.

♥*PRD: The Shepherd said the Maiden possessed excellent qualities for becoming a loving mother, and he asked her to become the mother of his children. He used the metaphors of henna, nard plants, saffron, calamus, cinnamon, and trees of frankincense, myrrh, aloes, along with the finest balsam to describe their future children (Song 4:13-14).*

The Shepherd's words are similar to the husband's compliment of the Woman of Great Price. At the end of their lives, the Proverb writer wrote, "Her children rise up and bless her; her husband also, and he praises her, saying: 'Many daughters have done nobly, but you excel them all.'" Instead of looking back over a life well-lived, the Shepherd looked into the future to praise the Shulammite.

One student remarked, "It sounds like the Shepherd wants to have a lot of children!"

Yes, it does, and that brings up an important premarital question. In our modern age, it's not a given that either the man or the woman will want children. Many divorces occur because the husband or the wife discovered after marriage that the mate didn't want children. The desire or lack of desire for children is a crucial premarital discussion.

Another important premarital question involving children: Is having children the main reason the person wants to get married? For example, many husbands learned to their sorrow that the only reason their wives married them and engaged in sex was to have children. After the right number of children were born, the wife refused to make love with her husband. These men thought they were getting a life companion. Instead, they were used to fertilize the woman's eggs and to provide for her offspring.

This is somewhat like the female praying mantis who bites off the head of the male after mating. If you think this simile is overdramatic, talk to a couple of these husbands. The ones who talk to me fight bitterness at being tricked into marrying their wife just to give her children.♥

She Enjoys Fantasies About Becoming Pregnant

Her detachable self-love and her need to give unrestrainedly are two chief components of the maternal instinct. Perhaps you noticed, this instinct permeates her. The fulfillment of it is the most central and all-important function of her life. It colors, deepens, and enriches her sexual energy.

Her unconscious fantasy with every intercourse is that he might make her with child. Her psychological and biological gratitude to him for this richest of all potential gifts is boundless. Her fantasies about becoming pregnant may excite her directly.

Overcoming Fear of Pregnancy Enhances Lovemaking

I have paid particular attention to this connection between the sexual instinct and the maternal instinct in many patients who have come to therapy because they were afraid of childbirth. When they were able to rid themselves of such fears, they are almost always struck by the new dimension that is added to their sexual life. The things they say about it are often poetic or even mystical.

Case Histories: Women's Poetic and Mystic Views of Lovemaking

Because of childhood experiences, one woman's fear of bearing a child was causing partial inhibitions. She said to me of her new sexual experience: "I was living in one room of a whole mansion, and now I have the whole mansion for my own."

Another woman thought her love life was complete despite her deep fear of pregnancy. She said of the change in her feelings during lovemaking: "Oh, it was fun before, but now the idea that I might become pregnant makes me feel at one with the whole universe. It's strange. There are almost no words to express it."

The Orgasmic Woman's Attitudes Toward Motherhood

Our ideal woman carries this characteristic feeling of a deep identification with nature and all things that grow, bud, and blossom through her pregnancy and long after that.

Her Attitude Toward Childbirth

Childbirth has no real terrors for her; she sails through it proudly, like a clipper made especially for such weather. She usually wants to nurse her child at her breast. She does, too, unless a breast abscess or some other unforeseen difficulty arises. Though I have no statistics to prove it, I would bet that her milk is both plentiful and good.

Her Attitude Toward Children Versus a Career

Today, society emphasizes the importance of careers for women, but I am afraid our mature woman cannot get excited about the subject. I do not mean that she is antagonistic to this whole women-working movement. She may be a career woman herself, a nurse, a doctor, a lawyer, a fashion designer, whatever. But now, happily married and with children in the offering or already here, she cannot feel that it is of central importance. If it is necessary for the family welfare, she will keep her job. However, any career drive she had after high school or college is sacrificed, if necessary, to her lovemaking and homemaking instincts.

Her Attitude Toward Her Husband's Career

She is not the least bit jealous of her husband's work. She may be smarter than her husband or may have a much higher intelligence quotient, or she may be far more thoroughly educated than he is. Or she may be highly talented in writing, music, painting, or sculpture.

However, you will never hear her complain that she gave up a career for her family or angrily envy her man's daily adventures in the marketplace. Her joy and satisfaction in fulfilling her biological destiny make all other personal achievements pale for her. Any other considerable use for her energies is almost a waste.

♥PRD: Two Female Entrepreneurs in the Bible Show How to Do It

The Shulammite and the Woman of Proverbs 31 were entrepreneurs. But neither of them sacrificed their family or made a career their life goal.

The Shulammite Oversaw the Orchards

The Shulammite wanted to marry the Shepherd in the spring, but her brothers needed her to oversee the vineyards while they were forced to work on Solomon's building projects. She not only supervised the workers, but she also handled the money. She paid the most powerful man in the land, King Solomon, the rent they owed him on the land and the workers their wages.

Song of Solomon 8:11-12:
"Solomon had a vineyard at Baal-hamon;
He entrusted the vineyard to caretakers.
Each one was to bring a thousand shekels of silver for its fruit.
My very own vineyard is at my disposal;
The thousand shekels are for you, Solomon,
And two hundred are for those who take care of its fruit."

As a young 13-year-old farm girl, the Maiden rose to the occasion when she was needed. Her brothers depended on her skills to save their vineyards.

The Woman of Great Price Balanced Her Duties

Proverbs 31:13-19:
"She looks for wool and flax
And works with her hands in delight.
She is like merchant ships;
She brings her food from afar.
She rises also while it is still night
And gives food to her household
And portions to her maidens.
She considers a field and buys it;
From her earnings she plants a vineyard.
She girds herself with strength
And makes her arms strong.
She senses that her gain is good;
Her lamp does not go out at night.

She stretches out her hands to the distaff,
And her hands grasp the spindle."

Verse 24:
"She makes linen garments and sells them,
And supplies belts to the tradesmen."

This description sounds overwhelming, but notice, her daughters are old enough to be given "portions" or household duties. "Her lamp does not go out at night" doesn't refer to working all night while the family sleeps. Instead, it reveals that she keeps a lamp filled with oil burning in the window as an ancient street light for people who must be out in the night. As a small-business woman, she invests in property and makes garments and belts to sell.

Women of the Bible Worked in the Fields

Many women during Bible times worked in the fields alongside their husbands. However, several generations of families lived together, sometimes in different compartments of the same tent. When the young women went to work with their husbands, the grandmothers took care of the children.

From the moment a woman becomes pregnant, the milk-duct glands in her breasts begin to enlarge. Thus any woman who has given birth can produce ample milk for a baby as the sucking stimulates her glands to make the right amount of milk. As the baby grows and sucks harder and more, the glands produce sufficient nourishment for the babe. This phenomenon allowed grandmothers to serve as wet nurses for their grandchildren while the mothers worked in the fields.♥

Her Attitude Toward Her Empty Nest

As the woman grows older as her family grows up, and the children learn to stand on their own feet and use their wings, she may return to work. Even then, interest in her grown children and grandchildren will be far greater than any she can summon up for her job.

She ages gracefully. The instincts that led her to successful love in marriage and rearing her children stand her in good stead now. She still loves to give, and she perceives the right time to give her children up, let them stand on their own, and learn the problematic uses of freedom. This is a great sacrifice for a mother, but she is pleased to make it. And in doing so without fuss, she wins her children's regard and love forever.

♥PRD: Older Women Make Excellent Teachers of Young Women

At this stage of life, the mature woman makes an excellent teacher of young women as the Apostle Paul advised the young evangelist Titus:

> *Titus 2:3-5: "Older women likewise are to be reverent in their behavior, not malicious gossips nor enslaved to much wine, teaching what is good, so that they may encourage the young women to love their husbands, to love their children, to be sensible, pure, workers at home, kind, being subject to their own husbands, so that the word of God will not be dishonored."*

The older woman's good and bad experiences have honed her insights in ways young women cannot look into the future and foresee. Indeed, one of the primary ways God develops human wisdom is through hindsight—reflecting on how a person could have done things differently.

Many young women begin marriage without the most basic knowledge of how to love their husbands or care for their homes. Then children come along and compound the problems. The young women long for answers and ache for someone to teach them what their mothers neglected to tell them.

Young women often need an older woman to adopt them, to bring them up to full maturity. Fortunately, when a woman's children leave home, it gives her time to devote to re-raising young women. She can teach them how to cook, love and discipline their children, and conquer bitter and resentful feelings toward men in general and their husbands in particular.

Sharing their hindsight and being transparent with these wives about their own marital and childrearing successes and failures turns older women into teachers and role models young women love and admire.♥

Menopause Doesn't Diminish Her Sexuality

I am pleased to say that menopause brings no diminution in her ability to enjoy her husband sexually. Contrary to what many people think, her orgasm does not decrease in intensity or kind. Increasing age and the absence of children in the home now bring her and her husband closer together. As great companions, they develop a whole series of shared pleasures consistent with their years.

♥PRD: *Women in Their 70s Can Out Orgasm Women in Their 20s*

Dr. Bernie Zilbergeld sheds light on an amazing statement about an older wife's sexual love and appeal to her husband in Proverbs 5:15-20. In 2004 he published Better Than Ever: Time for Love and Sex. He interviewed 145 men and women aged 45 to 87. He called the ones enjoying great sex "Lovers." He noticed that women in their 70s who had figured out the emotional and physical part of sex could out orgasm the average 20-something woman. He also learned that older couples can still enjoy fantastic lovemaking even when dealing with age-related medical problems.

Interestingly, while working on the book for two years, Dr. Zilbergeld shared copies of the manuscript with his older patients. They gave him great reviews on his work. Then he decided to share chapters with clients in their 20s. He thought they could learn something about love from the older couples. While they did, the younger ones reported that the best benefit they got was discovering that great sex was possible throughout life (xi-xvi).♥

She's Not Afraid of Death

As the feminine woman goes to the other side of her middle years, she is not troubled with regrets for things left undone. She has a deep sense of fulfillment, of her life lived rightly. Whether she has become consciously religious or not, she is still a believer in immortality, for she has served it with her whole being. She looks on death unafraid, wondering perhaps what the Creator who has made her life such a marvel is like on an even closer view.

The Idealized Feminine Woman

This is the idealized picture of the truly feminine woman. While the plane of maturity she has achieved is perhaps too exalted for most women to attain, I have given her to you for some concrete reasons.

Seeing New Horizons Helps the Woman Move Forward

With merely this ideal to follow, I have seen many women reap immediate rewards sometimes before they were able to come to grips with their sexual inhibitions, per se. The characteristics and cognitive distorted goals that accompany sexual inhibitions often cause obvious domestic frictions that can be greatly reduced when the woman begins to see new horizons for herself—that she need not blame others. Her grateful husband will reward her at once for her change, with renewed affection and tenderness, a new solicitude, a new caring.

When a New Goal Is Clearly Defined, Half the Battle Is Won

Our idealized portrait can help you, too, to grasp more thoroughly the rest of this book. In psychiatry, we have found that half the battle has been won when a goal is clearly defined. In the chapters on sexual inhibitions, their whys and wherefores, their kinds and causes, and cures, you will find a picture of the potentials of men and women. You will discover a landmark to show you how far men and women can stray from real masculinity and femininity and a guide to keep you from confusion. You will never subscribe again to false and destructive ideas of what it is that constitutes real adulthood.

4.

The Male Sex: A New Horizon

The next most helpful step to take, I have found, is a reevaluation of the male sex. The woman who suffers from sexual inhibitions has, by definition, little knowledge of what men are truly like.

Parents Form Attitudes Toward Men

Since a woman's attitudes toward men were formed in her distant past and have altered little through the years, she has a child's view of men. To her, men are powers as parents to a child, not people. Projecting her own childhood fears and hopes and needs upon men, she calls that reality and acts accordingly.

Need to Learn How the Male Differs from the Female

The conscious reevaluation of men can be achieved by learning what the male sex is like—how men differ from the female sex, what makes them think, act, and feel the way they do in everyday life. By contrasting this knowledge with the negative attitudes and feelings from her childhood, the wife will soon learn to understand her husband as he is, and thus achieve the ability to love him in all his uniqueness and individuality.

♥PRD: Healing for the female means accepting and enjoying her own femininity and loving her husband's masculinity. Healing for the male means accepting and enjoying his own masculinity and loving his wife's femininity.♥

Aggressiveness Differentiates the Male from the Female

The male's central characteristic, and the one that most clearly differentiates him from the female, is his aggressiveness.

♥PRD: God Created the Differences Between Men and Women

In the creation, God gave the man the primary job of subduing the earth. The word "subdue" implies in Genesis 1:28 that the creation will not do man's bidding gladly or easily, and that man must bring the creation into submission by his strength (TWOT 430). When man sinned, God punished him by making the earth even harder to subdue.

God built within the man the brute strength and aggression necessary to subdue the earth to provide food, clothing, and shelter for his family. Essentially, the man's strength and aggression help him serve his family.

The loving woman balances him with her tranquility and peace as she nurtures the family. Together they make an amazing one-flesh team for subduing the earth, filling it with people, and glorifying God. This proverb reflects these differences in men and women:

Proverbs 11:16:
"A gracious woman retaineth honour:
and strong men retain riches" (KJV).

The word "strong" means "mighty and awe-inspiring" and describes God's power for protecting his people as that of a "dread champion" in Jeremiah 20:11 (Strong 92). It's the kind of strength men need to subdue the earth and make a living.

Men quickly recognize graciousness in women. Gladly, they honor such women who create a home environment of comfort and splendor. Likewise, men understand how the graciousness of women balances their aggression. Although strong men require assertive natures to subdue the resisting earth, they especially enjoy the pleasant kindness and favor of gracious women.♥

The Male in the Sexual Sphere

In the sexual sphere, this shows itself most clearly in the fact that the man takes, for the most part, the initiative in wooing. He is the pursuer, the woman is the pursued. He is the one who proposes, and he is the one who initiates sex.

♥*PRD:* God Unites the Male and the Female in Perfect Harmony

Twenty years after Dr. Robinson wrote The Power of Sexual Surrender, a 1978 Redbook article gave a more complete picture of the man's sexuality over time. The following explanation comes from God's People Make the Best Lovers:

As the husband's body slows down, he sometimes needs more physical stimulation from his wife than before—not the pretty body of a mistress parading before him, but the loving mind and body of the wife of his youth beside him. And as his body slows down, the sexual union takes on new characteristics that, according to many older couples, make for the best sexual delights ever. The Redbook questionnaire of 40,000 men states that while teenage boys tend to want a passive woman, mature men find their wives' passiveness unappealing (Tavris, "40,000 Men" 176.)

The Victorian Mindset Gets in the Way

Unfortunately, Victorian morals took away many an older wife's freedom to enjoy her husband's body. Such a woman views her husband's penis as something she shouldn't talk about, let alone look at or touch. But it is part of him—part of the man she loves. It is his organ of pleasure both for her and for him. As the man ages and his penis calms down from his youth, her caresses stimulate both him and her.

Now, the husband occasionally gets too tired to do all the work of initiating sex. At the same time, he still deeply desires to make love with his wife. It gives the wife great joy to bypass his tiredness and speak the language of love directly to his organ of pleasure. She's glad for his years of adolescence and puberty when this organ worked at knowing its job apart from the man's brain. Now his penis listens to her tender expressions of love and adoration. Great joy swells in her heart as her husband's body comes to life in response to her love.

The Key Is Relaxation Coupled with Joy

The key to success is relaxation with a total absence of pressure to perform. If it happens, great; if not, tomorrow will be even better. For the moment, the husband simply relaxes and lets his wife play her charms of love upon his receptive body. And a tired masculine body finds energy and desire throbbing for union with the wife of his youth who gives him so much joy.

Experiencing great rapture in the arms of a loving husband stirs a wife to pleasure him in any way she can—it becomes her delight rather than her duty. As the husband and wife grow older, their sexual natures change and continue to conform to each other. The husband seeks a stronger mental involvement with her while she enjoys the physical union more than ever. God makes them blend into perfect harmony in their golden years as well as the earlier ones.♥

The Aggressive Sperm Expresses the Aggressive Man

An analogy to the male's fundamentally aggressive activity is seen, in a primordial biological form, by the function of his sperm. As you may know, the spermatozoon is an individual cell that is propelled by a microscopic tail. After the deposit of spermatozoa in the vagina, the individual sperm actively seeks out and joins the ova, which has been passively waiting for it. According to certain leading theoreticians, this physiological metaphor well expresses the fundamentally aggressive nature of man in relationship to woman, psychologically and sexually.

♥*PRD: God's Gift to Men Is Their Sexuality*

In Sex, Men and God, Dr. Douglas Weiss, who specializes in sexual addiction and sexless marriages, says "God's gift to men is our sexuality." He continues:

> *Understanding that male sexuality is God's great design can motivate every man to exert whatever effort is required to complete his personal journey to sexual success.... I have studied the Scriptures for almost 20 years and have clearly seen that God's Word addresses what I call the two sides of sexuality. By this, I mean that He clearly communicates the reality of external sexuality as well as our internal sexuality (2).*

"Our external sexuality, as well as our internal sexuality" is precisely the topic of The Power of Sexual Surrender.

Both men and women must take care of their internal sexuality first so their external sexuality can flow uninhibited.

My article in Part 2 "Radical Epiphany on Awakening Male-Female Sexuality" explores God's amazing gift to men and women of the man's sexuality.♥

Accepting the Husband's Uniqueness Is to Love Him

In general, the male directs his aggressiveness toward everyday life. When a woman learns to understand her husband *as he is*, she thus achieves the ability to love him in all of his uniqueness and individuality.

♥PRD: A Redbook survey of 40,000 men found that the best sexual times for husbands occurred when the woman thoroughly enjoyed lovemaking. The woman's obvious enjoyment of the embrace of love played a vital role in the man's sexual pleasure (Tavris 195).

The same is true for women. When her husband lets her see his delight in her sexual charms, it thrills her and increases her pleasure.♥

The Male in the World's Sphere

The male's aggressiveness is also directed to mastery of the outside world. It shows in him from his earliest years.

The Male Selects Sports that Reflect Physical Aggression

The sports that the man selects have to do with physical aggression almost exclusively (of course, some girls also like certain aggressive sports at an early age, but most give them up in puberty). He enjoys sports where he has to run, charge, tackle, throw, and hit. In his adolescence, he will spend years mastering skills that concern such aggressive activity.

In Adolescence, the Male Competes with Other Boys

A component of this aggressive desire for mastery is his

competitiveness with other boys. He wishes to be as good or better than they are, to make his mastery known to the outside world.

The Male in the Mental Sphere

The male also displays this aggressiveness in the mental sphere. His chief passion is in mastering the outward environment that surrounds him, as in to use a phrase from football, "throwing it for a loss."

♥PRD: Two significant sources of a man's self-confidence come directly from God to help him subdue the earth and provide for his family:

Proverbs 20:29:
"The glory of young men is their strength,
and the honor of old men is their gray hair."

Young men glory in their strength. They take pride in their physical abilities to work hard day after day, to lift heavy objects, and perform feats women find physically hard to do.

As a man grows older and loses the strength of his youth, his honor becomes his gray hair, a symbol of his wisdom. As a man solves the problems of life, his insights develop over the years and become much greater than in his youth.♥

The Male's Aggressiveness Influences His Career

The man's desires lead him to become a scientist, controlling through knowledge some aspect of the world or the universe. Or he may become a businessman, wresting a living from the competitive market place. Or he may become a philosopher, probing the "why" of the world. Whatever role he plays in life, he must use his aggression to master the environment he selects as his province.

♥PRD: Excerpt from <u>Male and Female: God's Genius</u> discusses how a man aggressively working reflects God's image:

One Way Man Reflects God's Image Is by Working

> *John 5:17: "But He answered them, 'My Father is working until now, and I Myself am working.'"*

God worked during the creation of the world and continues to work even now. At the same time, Jesus the Savior works. A man who refuses to work does not share anything in common with God and Jesus who created man in God's image. As a result, God doesn't show sympathy for the hunger of men who avoid working. Work is so important to God's plan for man, he commands his followers not to feed those who refuse to work:

> *2 Thessalonians 3:10: "For even when we were with you, we used to*

give you this order: If anyone will not work, neither let him eat."

God said in Genesis 3:19, "By the sweat of your face you shall eat bread." No sweat—no bread. God did not create man to be an idle loafer but an active breadwinner.♥

The Woman Prepares for Motherhood

In comparison to men, women have a much smaller store of aggression directed toward the outside world. They largely focus their activity inward. Psychologically speaking, a woman is conditioned by her final biological function.

The Woman's Psychic Energy Prepares Her for Motherhood

At the center of her nature, she is preparing herself for motherhood, which determines the main direction of her psychic energy. Her childhood interests show this clearly. She plays with dolls, she plays house, loves to be around Mother, and fantasies about marriage. She is enormously curious about all of her internal functions.

The Woman Can Summon Aggression If Life Demands It

However, the woman has a certain store of interest and aggression, which she can direct outward. But this characteristic becomes secondary to her when life circumstances do not force her to use it.

The Woman Is Inward Intellectually

Intellectually, the woman is also basically inward. Her most potent faculty is her great intuition, her almost magical ability to understand another person by consulting her inward nature. This contrasts with the man's objective "intellectual" type of understanding.

♥*PRD: God Blesses the Man with Fatherhood*

Psalms 127:3-5:
"Behold, children are a gift of the Lord,
The fruit of the womb is a reward.
Like arrows in the hand of a warrior,
So are the children of one's youth.
How blessed is the man whose quiver is full of them;
They will not be ashamed
When they speak with their enemies in the gate."

One husband said, "I used to think my job of providing for my family was more important than my wife's job of caring for the home and our children. One day I realized that if my wife neglected our children and they grew up mentally deficient, all my work to provide for them would be in vain. Now I consider my job as a necessary means of enabling my wife to do life's most important work—properly caring for our children."

Mothers Influence Their Children's Emotional and Sexual Health

This husband was half right. Dr. Robinson's case histories show over and over how important the mother's job is in helping both her sons and daughters grow up to be emotionally and sexually healthy marriage partners and parents to the grandchildren. Indeed, the wife's attitudes toward her own motherhood profoundly affect her daughter's view of being a mother. And they affect her son's ability to function as a loving father.

Fathers Influence Their Children's Emotional and Sexual Health

The same is true for the man as a father. Dr. Robinson's case histories illustrating the three types of sexual inhibitions show that the father is his young daughter's first love. He's the model for her future husband. The attention he gives her at each stage of maturity affects her ability to love and enjoy her husband. And when she is unable to love her husband, her children are damaged as she was.

Dr. Douglas Weiss in Sex, Men and God says that "the way we men role-model male sexuality is impacting our sons." He says fathers are the best protection sons have for avoiding the disastrous influences of our sex-saturated society that leaves emotional bonding out of sexual experiences. He explains:

> *The positive role model is one who is deliberate about communicating healthy sexuality to his son. He gets informed and looks for opportunities to talk about girls with his son in a positive way. He is behaviorally pure himself from pornography and adultery, and he teaches his son to respect his mother and sisters....*
>
> *Regardless of the kind of role model your father was for you, it is possible for you to become sexually successful and become a good role model for your sons. They will catch more of your sexuality from your life than they will learn from any book they read or video they watch (198-199).*

Fathers are extremely important to the healthy development of both their sons and daughters.

God's Gift to Parents Is Their Gift to Their Children

> *Ecclesiastes 9:9: "Enjoy life with the woman whom you love all the days of your fleeting life which He has given to you under the sun; for*

> *this is your reward in life and in your toil in which you have labored under the sun."*

God's gift to man for working so hard to subdue the earth and fill it with people is to enjoy life with the woman he loves. "Love" means to "love sexually or otherwise." A great sex life floods both the father's and the mother's bodies with hormones that bind them to each other and their children. The affection between the parents naturally spills over onto nurturing their children. The whole family enjoys peace and love that influences their everyday lives. Best of all, the father and mother model healthy sexual love to help their sons and daughters experience wonderful marriages of their own.♥

These Descriptions Are Absolute Types

In describing the male's essential characterological structure and contrasting it with the female, I am defining absolute types, not people as they are.

Men and Women Share Both Passivity and Aggression

In actuality, most men have a certain store of passivity, of inwardness. And normal women have a certain amount of aggression. However, the normal male will be preponderantly outgoing and aggressive; the normal female's psychic energies will be generally focused inward.

Inhibited Women View the Man's Attributes Negatively

As a direct or indirect result of man's aggression and his commitment to the outside world, in maturity, he develops certain behavioristic patterns that are diametrically opposite to female characteristics. Inevitably, the sexually inhibited woman uses her husband's attributes to show that her man:

- Has no interest in her
- Is weak
- Is withdrawn
- Is cruel
- Wishes to exploit her

Having no objectivity about men, she finds his inherent differences cause for estrangement, fear, and hostility.

♥*PRD: Inhibited Men View the Wife's Attributes Negatively*

The Sexless Marriages Survey reveals that many inhibited men believe the same negative attributes about their wives that women harbor against their husbands:

- *Has no interest in him*
- *Is weak*
- *Is withdrawn*
- *Is cruel*
- *Wishes to exploit him*

Both inhibited men and women conceal distorted views of the opposite sex. Interestingly, their attitudes of rejection and exploitation are similar.♥

The Woman's Home Is All-Important to Her

Let me give some instances of these behavioristic differences in everyday life. To the woman, the bearer of children and the nest-maker, the home and everything in it is all-important. She invests her home with a great deal of pride. She loves clean sinks, windows, and floors. She wants things in her nest to be neat and orderly. She has made them that way, and she wants them to stay that way.

The Man's Work Is All-Important to Him

It is easy for the woman to misunderstand the fact that her husband invests a significant portion of his pride elsewhere: his work and achievements in the outside world.

♥*PRD: Excerpt from Male and Female: God's Genius concerning God's punishment of the man for his sin in the Garden of Eden:*

God Made Man to Toil for a Living

> *Genesis 3:17-19: "...in toil [sorrow—KJV, painful toil--NIV] you shall eat of it all the days of your life. Both thorns and thistles it shall grow for you; and you shall eat the plants of the field; by the sweat of your face you shall eat bread,..."*

"Toil" is the same Hebrew word ('issābôn) translated "pain" twice in Genesis 3:16 to describe Eve's punishment of "pain" in conception and "pain" in childbirth. Both Adam and Eve would suffer "physical pain as well as emotional sorrow" as their punishment centered around the unique purposes in their creation (TWOT 687-688).

Man must work harder at surviving than any other living creature. In nearly every climate, man needs clothes for protection from either sunburns or frostbite. All other creatures are provided clothing. Fur-bearing animals shed fur in the summer to keep cool and grow extra-thick coats for hard winters. Animals don't have to work as hard as a man does for shelter. Most just dig a hole or move into a cave.♥

The Inhibited Woman Is Disturbed by Her Husband's Habits

The man takes the cleanliness and neatness of his home for granted. He may even be, "by his wife's standards," seemingly antagonistic to neatness, actually sloppy, throwing his clothes around, leaving the sink cluttered, and whatnot. These things are not in themselves pleasant traits, but the sexually inhibited woman will generalize about them, use them to indicate her man's essential indifference to her.

♥PRD: *This Does Not Endorse the Husband Acting Like a Slob*

Dr. Robinson sounds like she is saying, "Every husband of an inhibited woman is not only a slob, but also an intentional slob, and the loving wife should not care." That's not the case. Dr. Robinson is addressing the same problem I've observed multiple times with sexually inhibited clients. The key phrase is "by his wife's standards." In other words, the wife's impossible-to-please perfectionism is the real problem. Living in the weaknesses of perfectionism is destructive to all relationships.

Inhibited Individuals Often Freeze Wearing a Perfectionist Mask

Dr. Robinson observed in her patients what I also deal with in my clients. Our personalities are 60% genetic and are 40% learned. But toxic nurturing can be so bad as to mask or hide a child's genetic leanings. The inhibited men and women whose personality profiles I've done, most of them were masked to the perfectionist square to survive an unloving home. As a child, to stay out of trouble or earn the parent's love, they hid their genetic personality by working hard to wear the uncomfortable mask of a perfectionist.

In the first chapter, "Paradise Lost for Men and Women," Dr. Robinson explains how a person's personality and sexuality develop side by side:

> *When all goes well in the development of the young boy and girl, their personalities and their sexual passions will develop naturally. They will achieve a beautiful and integrated maturity. But if, as so often happens, thwarting or blighting experiences take place, the development of their personality and their sexuality will be frozen at their sources, and maturity will remain a never-never land whose existence they will come to doubt.*

Putting on rigid perfectionism is often how the inhibited person's personality and sexuality freeze and stop maturing.

Unfortunately, getting married doesn't automatically restart the maturing process. Instead, many inhibited men and women carry over their perfectionist way of surviving to demand rigid perfection in their mates and children. They often go to extremes. Here are a few examples:

1. *Baseboards must be dusted regularly.*
2. *Dishes must be washed and put away nightly.*
3. *Beds must be made perfectly.*
4. *Children are on tight schedules for eating and bedtimes.*
5. *Rigid standards for the children's behavior are enforced.*
6. *Other people's homes are ridiculed to justify perfectionism.*
7. *Demands are policed with anger and putdowns.*

For many sexually inhibited individuals, perfectionism is how their mates and children must earn their love. But the family's efforts are seldom enough. The emotionally frozen men and women don't know how to give love freely or spontaneously. Everyone in the family walks on eggshells as codependents trying not to incur the perfectionist's wrath. See my article in Part 2, "The Connection Between Personality and Sexuality" for more information on how toxic parenting damages a child's personality.♥

The Inhibited Woman Views the Man as Not Caring

The husband may also not notice a new rug or even a new chair in the house. He may be impatient with any household duties he is forced to undertake: replacing a broken step or even a burned-out bulb. These attitudes can be quite confusing to a woman. If she has any motive to do so, she can interpret this kind of male behavior as further evidence of her husband's indifference to her and the family.

♥PRD: Once husbands and wives go down the road of being offended, the mate can't do anything to please them.

Proverbs 18:19:
"A brother offended is harder to be won than a strong city,
And contentions are like the bars of a citadel."

I tell clients not to answer "extreme accusations." The more you try to answer them, the more you perpetuate the argument. More extremes can spew out than you can answer in a week. Besides, it is not about you and the accusations against you. Answering them won't change anything.

The anger is about the spouse's childhood reaction to the parents' neglect and abuse. You can't win the argument because you're not arguing about the right thing. And the sexually inhibited person is not arguing with the right people—the parents.

I also tell the inhibited person, "Your anger is not about you. It is about your parents and their lack of parenting skills. It's frightening to be so angry at one's parents. It's safer to blow up at your spouse than at your mother or your father."

One woman said, "We were never allowed to express any kind of disapproval for anything our mother did. If we did, we got slapped or ridiculed. I have buried so much pain and resentment. My anger toward my mother scares me because I'm afraid I'm going to lose my soul over it. I know it's wrong, but I don't know how to get rid of it."

I have two recommendations:

1. *Go through my "How to Fight Fair and Face Anger" classes in Challenges in Marriage so your arguments with your mate can become productive instead of destroying your marriage. You can find the handouts on my website in the Book Shelf.*
2. *Take Dr. Karyl McBride's Healing the Daughters of Narcissistic Mothers Virtual Workshop. This course is also good for men who are the sons of narcissistic mothers or fathers. Dr. McBride is the author of Will I Ever Be Good Enough? She guides participants through coming to terms with harmful parenting and how to continue to deal with that parent in a less stressful way.*♥

The Husband's Habits Are Not Indicative of a Lack of Love

When objectionable behavior occurs, it is usually just male. It may be helpful to the wife to try to imagine how long her interest in the details of his business life holds her attention. The house is her business, and it is not surprising that he behaves the way he does in it, nor is it indicative of any lack of love in him.

The Sexually Inhibited Woman Resents Sex

Of course, sex itself remains one of the most fruitful sources for resentment and misunderstanding in the inhibited woman. Here male aggression can be most clearly seen.

The Man Is Aroused by Things that Don't Excite the Woman

The man is stimulated easily by things that would not excite his woman in the least. He is susceptible erotically to all sorts of sights, sounds, and odors. His wife undressing may excite him; her perfume may excite him; he may become aroused if she is looking wan or bright-eyed. The sexually inhibited woman, not comprehending male reactions or their plural causes, generally feels that his desires are unselective and impersonal. She takes his ardor as an affront for that reason.

♥*PRD: Excerpt from God's People Make the Best Lovers:*

The Man's #1 Need Is Love

Many a wife mistakenly views the sexual union as a purely physical act for a man. That simply isn't true but a holdover from Victorian thinking that equates men with animals. God created the man's emotional needs as strong as the woman's. If a wife truly satisfies her husband's physical needs, she satisfies his emotional needs first. A wife satisfies her husband by giving her body as an instrument of love with a desire to please him. Love keeps a woman's body looking attractive to her husband even as it grows older through the years.

The Redbook questionnaire "40,000 Men Tell About...Their Ideal Woman and Their Wives" confirmed this as 81% of them listed a wife's love as her most important characteristic. Only 5% of the men didn't consider her love important at all. Yet only 16% of the men considered large breasts important. They ranked a woman's love, sense of humor, self-confidence, and intelligence at the top of the list of important characteristics. Body features made up the bottom of the list with shapely legs ranking sixth while a pretty face came in eighth. The report explained that as a man ages, a pretty face becomes even less important to him (Tavris 112-3, 176).♥

The Thrusting Penis Offends the Inhibited Woman

During the sexual act, the aggressive thrusting of the man's penis offends too. As passion increases, the strength of the thrust increases, sometimes becoming a formidable series of pushes (one of the slang expressions men use for intercourse is "a bang"). This sometimes strong thrusting is a perfectly normal aspect of male sexuality, and to the normal woman, it is highly desirable. Sexually inhibited women are frightened of it, experience it as an invasion of their integrity, and an act of hostility against them.

♥PRD: Excerpt from the first chapter of God's 11 Secrets of Sex:

God Loves Passionate Sex

God openly boasts about lovemaking being his proudest, most brilliant accomplishment in the creation:

Proverbs 30:18-19:
There are three things which are too wonderful for me,
Four which I do not understand:
The way of an eagle in the sky,
The way of a serpent on a rock,
The way of a ship in the middle of the sea,
And the way of a man with a maid.

This is not God's empty locker-room brag. It's God's genius for husbands and wives to enjoy! Proverbs says the first three things are too wonderful to understand: an eagle soaring in the sky, a snake slithering across the mountain, or a ship sailing in the sea. But four amazing things are hidden from man's understanding.

Interestingly, these first three wonders not only testify to God's genius in creating them, but also to the man's aggressive and adventurous nature. For example, ancient men have frequently attempted to fly like the eagle. Finally, the Wright Brothers solved the puzzle. Yet, men continue to improve on their brilliance from airplanes, to rocket ships, to drones.

To climb a mountain, men must strap on cleats and use safety lines to imitate the agile snake. Centuries ago, they explored the highest mountain tops. Now with airplanes flying mountaineers all over the world, the "peak baggers" scale fourteeners (mountain peaks of at least 14,000 feet) because they can.

Matthew Maury said, "If God said paths are in the sea, I'm going to find them" (Psalms 8:8). He spent eighteen years charting the ocean's currents. Today men who compete in worldwide commerce and travel depend on these paths to make a living from the sea.

The eagle, the snake, and the paths in the sea testify to God's superior intelligence in creating the world as men seek to replicate his divine creations. But the fourth is the most profound and difficult for men to figure out—the way of a man with a maid.

Even in the bedroom, men attempt to improve on God's creation. They invent sex tools, make porn more easily accessible, and promote bondage.

Yet none of God's creations, nor any of man's imitations can compare to God's design for a man's touch to stir up a maid's emotions and powerful sensations. It's God's proudest invention.

Read more about the way of a man with a maid in Part 2: "Radical Epiphany on Awakening Male-Female Sexuality."♥

The Man's Thrusts of Love Join Him to His Beloved

Nothing could be farther from the fact than thinking that the man's thrusting penis is an "act of hostility against women." In his aggressive movements, a man shows his love in his particular way, his passionate need to lose his isolation, rid himself of it, and join with his beloved. To misunderstand this is to misunderstand all.

♥*PRD: Society Gets Male Sexuality All Wrong*

Excerpt from "Secret 9: Layer Your Hormones to Intensify Emotional Ecstasy" in God's 11 Secrets of Sex shows how we get male sexuality precisely backward:

Sex Is More Emotional for Men than It Is for Women

Based on 46 years of working with both men and women when I launched my Sexless Marriages Survey in 2016, I knew that sex is emotional for men. Many of the husbands I worked with shared their emotional pain of being rejected by their wives. They struggled with feeling like a beggar and being unloved. The husbands longed for affectionate touching, lingering playful kisses, and back-rubbing hugs.

Instead, their wives accused them of being sexual addicts because they weren't content to live in celibacy or to "go take care of themselves."

Thus when I started the survey, I knew it takes more than the physical act of sex or a wife lying there doing her duty to satisfy a man's masculine hormones. Even so, I was shocked to learn something I could never have guessed apart from the survey:

Husbands Suffer More Emotionally from Rejection than Wives Do

For a loving husband, sex is not an "animalistic" action as the Victorian moralists and doctors insisted. Likewise, sex is not a "beastly" activity as the young evangelical men claimed in the University of Washington study regarding the effect of virginity pledges on boys. And sex is not just a "release of pent up semen" as our modern society asserts.

In contrast to these false assumptions, I was surprised at how millennial and baby-boomer husbands answered the survey questions about emotional pain from sexual rejection. They checked nearly double the number of painful emotions that women participants marked. Notice their anguish:

- ✓ *Your masculine spirit is crushed.*
- ✓ *Your soul has been killed.*
- ✓ *You're drowning.*
- ✓ *You're fighting for emotional survival.*
- ✓ *You can't think straight.*
- ✓ *You don't know what's true anymore.*
- ✓ *You never rise to your full potential as a spouse.*
- ✓ *You never rise to your full potential as a parent.*
- ✓ *You never rise to your full potential as a Christian.*
- ✓ *You never rise to your full potential as a worker.*

This isn't to discount the wives' emotional pain, because they checked plenty of negative points too. But the husbands checked more items! Society gets male sexuality all wrong, and both husbands and wives suffer because of it.♥

The Things that Anger the Sexually Inhibited Woman

Doubtlessly, we could make a longer list of the characteristic things men do that anger or are misunderstood by sexually inhibited women. I wish to emphasize that the majority of these negative emotions are caused directly or indirectly by man's underlying and most distinguishing characteristic—his aggression. This trait most clearly defines him, and it is this trait that is at the root of the inhibited woman's anger, fear of, and feeling of rejection by men.

Women Don't Understand Masculinity or Femininity

The inhibited woman is antagonistic to the man's aggression because she does not understand it. Since she cannot understand or accept her feminine nature, she feels that male aggression is opposed to her, and she takes every opportunity to prove to herself that this is so. His strength, his ability to master the outside environment make her feel personally nullified and exploited. She endlessly contrasts his essential quality of aggression with her essential traits, to her detriment.

This Single Point Can Help Inhibited Women

A reexamination of this single point can put the inhibited woman's attitude back into proper perspective to correct her fundamentally distorted view of all men, and her husband in particular. She can do this by looking at the most important thing men do with their aggression in our society.

The Man Uses His Strength and Aggression for His Family

Far from seeking to exploit women, to misuse them through his strength and aggression, man has put these two great attributes entirely at his wife's service. It is (and always has been) this fact that makes it safe to be a woman, to bear his children with a sense of security, and rear them, knowing that he is there, always and forever, earning their bread, watching over them ceaselessly.

♥PRD: Over and over, Dr. Robinson emphasizes that the man's masculine force serves the woman's nurturing femininity. At the same time, she stresses that the woman's feminine nature values the man's aggressive masculinity. God's genius prevails in how he designed the male and the female to work together, complement each other, and support the other's deepest needs.♥

Section 2:

The Psychology of Sexual Inhibitions

5.

Five Common Types of Sexual Inhibitions

Now that we have seen the real potential of men and women, how they can flower and blossom in the climate of love, what they can be like when they embrace their true destiny, we turn to an examination of inhibited sexual desire and pleasure with some perspective. This section deals with what sexual inhibitions are, specifically, why they can and do occur in men and women, blighting their capacities, stunting their personality, and chilling and killing their ability to love at their heart's deepest core. Only when men and women get a clear picture of such matters can they find their way back to the high road of real adult love.

"Sexual Inhibitions" Defined

If we take "sexual inhibitions" in its most general sense, it means, as I have already stated, an inability to enjoy sexual love to its fullest potential. This means, purely and simply, the inability to have an orgasm of the type described in Chapter 2, being able to share vaginal orgasms with cervical kisses. But it is more complicated than that, for there are degrees of inhibitions. It is essential to understand what this means.

1. Totally Sexually Inhibited Men and Women

Perhaps I can make this idea clearest by describing the symptoms of a totally sexually inhibited woman who came to see me recently.

Case History: Wife Had No Sexual Reactions

(1) In our first interview, she described herself as having no sexual reactions whatsoever. She did not respond to her husband's caresses in any way at all. Her clitoris, vagina, and labia were incapable of the slightest sexual response.

(2) She received no stimulation from kissing or physical closeness.

Her breasts and all secondary erotic regions were, from the standpoint of sensual response, dead.

(3) Her vaginal passage never became lubricated before or during intercourse. The act of love was excruciating for her. An examination by a competent gynecologist showed no physical condition which would explain her pain. Her external genitalia were all fully developed. Her reproductive organs—the vaginal tract, cervix, uterus, tubes, and ovaries—also were normally developed and showed no pathology.

(4) Her sexual unresponsiveness was entirely psychological. On a scale showing the degrees of inhibitions, she would represent "absolute zero."

(5) This is no longer true of her, incidentally. She has made progress in therapy in a relatively short time, considering the extent of her difficulty. Her final prognosis promises to be excellent.

♥PRD: This woman's symptoms demonstrate "total sexual inhibitions":

1. *Wife had no sexual reactions.*
2. *Kissing and physical closeness gave her no stimulation.*
3. *The act of love was painful.*
4. *Her psychological sexual responsiveness would register zero.*
5. *She made progress in a relatively short time.*

This case history and the one in chapter 12 demonstrate that Dr. Robinson was able to help women overcome sexual anesthesia.♥

Overview of Sexual Anesthesia

A subnormal degree of sensation in the entire genital area and weak and infrequent orgasms characterize sexual anesthesia. This form of inhibitions is called "sexual anesthesia" in textbooks, and I will use that phrase here when I refer to it. The word "anesthesia," as you probably know, simply means the absence, or relative absence, of sensation.

♥PRD: The Male Version of Being Totally Sexually Inhibited

Sex is as emotional for men as it is for women and was in Dr. Robinson's case history of the totally inhibited woman. We can see this by studying what happens with wet dreams when a man is medically impotent.

Wet Dreams and Erectile Dysfunction (ED)

Wet dreams are the body's way of getting rid of old sperm to make room for the man's body to produce newer, healthier sperm. Young boys and men who don't masturbate experience these nocturnal emissions without any conscious effort. The wet dreams are not necessarily accompanied with sexual fantasies as in the case of masturbation. (Chapter 9 contains more information.)

Dr. Alice G. Walton, a biopsychology and behavioral neuroscience expert, states in "Male Sexuality: Not so Simple":

> *Men, who have had surgery to remove the prostate gland, can experience orgasm even without an ejaculation or even an erection. On the other hand, ejaculation during nocturnal emissions (a.k.a. "wet dreams") often happens in the absence of any kind of physical stimulation, which implies that there is a purely cerebral component to orgasm.*

This mental connection to the man's ability to orgasm through wet dreams even after removal of his prostate gland corresponds with observations by Dr. Rosemary Basson, Director of the University of British Columbia Sexual Medicine Program. She discusses how both men and women send signals from two distinct areas in their brains directly to their genitals for an explosion of ecstasy. (I discuss Dr. Basson's research in "Secret 7: Turn on Double-Dose #10 Orgasms" in God's 11 Secrets of Sex. I also review wet dreams and the harm of masturbation in the appendix.)

Male Sexual Inhibitions and Erectile Dysfunction (ED)

What's the point about wet dreams and ED? The man's sexual organs are connected directly to his emotions in the same way as the woman's sexual organs are connected to her emotions. Therefore, Dr. Robinson's applications of sexual inhibitions to the female can be made to the male and his difficulties in enjoying rapture in the arms of his wife.

Husbands and Wives Can Block Their Daily Sensual Twinges

In the article "Why Women [or Men] Lose Interest in Sex," Linda Murray explains how the normal man or woman experiences hundreds of erotic thoughts and feelings during the day. Many of these impulses pass by so fleetingly that the person fails to consciously notice them. But this "psychological priming" keeps both men and women in a "constant state of emotional readiness for sexual activity."

Husbands and wives deal with their daily impulses in several ways. Here is the uninhibited way to increase ecstasy:

1. *They choose purity by channeling their sensations toward their mate to enhance desire. This turns into daytime flirting and planning for lovemaking, which intensifies their individual passion and pleasure.*

Here are the inhibited options that numb sensations with the mate:

2. *They can direct their sexual urges toward any person of the opposite sex within their vicinity. They may refrain from planning how to get together with that person but simply wonder what sexual contact would be like.*

3. *They can direct their thoughts toward a pornographic picture or video.*
4. *They may block these romantic signals for just their mate or all persons of the opposite sex. Some men and women block their desires all their lives because of feelings of disgust and shame.*
5. *Prescriptions can interfere with sensual twinges. Drugs may act so subtly that the person doesn't realize what is happening until the mate says something. It pays to read about side effects and to discuss them with the doctor or pharmacist. (Excerpt from God's People Make the Best Lovers).♥*

2. Partially Sexually Inhibited Men and Women

At the opposite end on this inhibitions scale are men and women, who tremble on the verge of sexual maturity but cannot completely step over the line.

They Have All the Responses but Don't Come to Orgasm

In the act of love, these men and women have all the responses that take place in normal sexual intercourse, but they cannot come to an enjoyable orgasm. Or at least orgasm happens quite rarely—only once in ten or twenty times. And it is generally a mild and unsatisfactory one.

♥*PRD: Men Can and Do Fake Orgasms*

This excerpt from my book God's People Make the Best Lovers shows a surprising fact about men:

In 1967, Dr. Philip M. Sarrel, a member of the Department of Obstetrics and Gynecology at Yale, set up a course on human sexuality for medical students. He and his wife Lorna, a psychiatric social worker, eventually set up a sex counseling service at Yale after the college began accepting female students.

The Sarrels revealed in a 1977 article "What Men Need from the Women Who Love Them," that men fake many aspects of their sexuality just as women do. They explained that the male is as complex a sexual being as the female regarding feelings, thoughts, guilt, physical sensations, and what they fake.

An orgasm isn't always a great experience for a man. Just as the woman experiences degrees of pleasure based on her attitudes, so does the man. While a man may ejaculate, an effortless feat for most men, pleasurable physical and emotional sensations may be nearly non-existent. At other times his physical and mental sensations create intense sexual rapture (115).

In 1978, Dr. Bernie Zilbergeld, a psychologist who treats sexual disorders of men, helped bring male sexual inhibitions out into the open with his ground-breaking book Male Sexuality, A Guide to Sexual Fulfillment. A widely quoted expert, he was the first to offer self-help for male sexual problems (O'Connor 6/21/2002).

Zilbergeld debunked society's assumption that men automatically know all about sex, which places great pressure on many a man to perform with prowess. Admitting that a sexual problem might be his fault or stem from his lack of knowledge takes away from his feelings of manliness. While a man's ability to have an erection is obvious and he seldom becomes impotent, he can fake an orgasm along with interest in sex (Zilbergeld 4).

Case History: Older Couple Soulmated to Overcome ED

An older couple, who met on a dating site, committed to avoiding both kissing and sex during courtship. This practice allowed them to soulmate without being distracted by the hormones of kissing and sexual activity that could fool them into thinking they were in love. The man had part of his prostate gland removed and could no longer ejaculate, although he had erections. After marriage, the wife said, "We connected strongly on an emotional level before marriage. And we are both so excited—his ED is nearly gone!"♥

Partial Sexual Inhibitions Are Relatively Easy to Solve

You will be interested to know that partial inhibitions are relatively easy to resolve.

1. This is the kind of inhibitions that may disappear entirely after the birth of a child.
2. It may be dispelled by a single conversation with a wise counselor or with just time and a minimum of insightful understanding.
3. Sometimes one can obtain healing by taking thought or learning more about the nature of the problem.

All solutions involve correcting certain misunderstandings about the nature of sex, marriage, the mate, and love.

3. In-Between Sexually Inhibited Men and Women

In between sexual anesthesia and being on the verge of enjoying wonderful orgasms are all degrees of inhibitions.

Three Things Determine the Severity of Inhibitions

The severity of a sexual problem, or the lack of it, can be calculated in terms of the degree of inhibitions by three things:

1. The response to the mate's caresses

2. The frequency of satisfaction in intercourse
3. The quality of the orgasm itself

The Degree of Inhibitions Is a Subjective Matter

Determining the degree of inhibitions is purely a subjective matter that can be judged only by the individual. If the orgasm is weak and chronically leaves one with a feeling of dissatisfaction, a certain degree of inhibitions is present.

♥*PRD: Most Totally and In-Between Inhibited Spouses Reject Touching*

On the Sexless Marriages Survey, the respondents indicated that both inhibited husbands and wives frequently rejected all forms of touching:

Ways your companion withholds demonstrations of love:

50% Doesn't initiate hugs
53% Hugs are stiff, not caressing
18% Doesn't return hugs
68% Doesn't initiate kisses
56% Kisses are stiff-lipped
39% Doesn't return kisses
76% Doesn't initiate touching
46% Doesn't return touching
19% Calls touching groping

Here are some of the comments:

- *There are SO many facets of his withholding that I could be here typing an answer to this one query for the next two hours. If you can name it, it's probably one of his withholding modalities.*
- *I have to initiate EVERYTHING...she never just comes up to me and kisses me...WILL NOT kiss me during sex...seriously...turns her head...she will...but only if I pretty much make her...then she turns her head again...she will give me a peck goodbye in the morning, etc...but that's just because I gripe at her if she doesn't.*
- *Subtly pushes my hand away when I try to touch him. Rarely says I love you first. Won't touch me around friends or family.*
- *Withheld his body. On a rare occasion, when I pushed for sex he told me not to touch private areas, that he didn't like it. When I tried to kiss him, anything beyond a peck, he would get annoyed, push me away, and ask why I was jumping him.*

The above answers indicate that many husbands and wives were trying to survive marriage to a spouse with a high degree of sexual inhibitions. See "Why

Don't Sexless Spouses Kiss, Hug, and Touch" in Part 2 for more information.♥

4. Masturbating Sexually Inhibited Men and Women

♥PRD: Dr. Robinson introduces masturbation in this chapter. She goes into detail in Chapter 9: "Masturbation Leads to Sexual Inhibitions."♥

Female "Clitoral-Type" Sexual Inhibitions

In addition to the degrees of inhibited desire and pleasure, another type of sexual inhibitions is essential to understand. We call a woman suffering from this form of inhibitions a "clitoral" type. To make her problem clear to you, I shall describe her typical sexual reaction.

She Is Passionate During Foreplay

This woman's responses to sexual stimulation are usually quite passionate. In the foreplay preceding sexual intercourse and even in the first part of intercourse, her reactions parallel the normal to a greater or lesser extent. This type of woman, however, can always be identified by the kind of orgasm she has.

She Has Clitoral Orgasms

Her orgasm takes place on her clitoris exclusively. She does not feel the orgasm in her vagina, nor do the sexual sensations spread strongly to the other parts of her body. The sensual experience is primarily localized at climax.

She May Defend Her Orgasm as Adequate

Though, owing to her lack of experience with the emotional nature of orgasm, she may defend her orgasm as normal and adequate. It is not. Therapy has helped many women with this constricted reaction to sexual intercourse, and once they experience the profound pleasure of the vaginal orgasm, they admit quite freely their former deprivation.

She May Need Masturbation to Orgasm

The clitoral woman seeks to obtain her typical orgasm in two ways:

1. In intercourse, she will sometimes strive to bring her clitoris into direct contact with the penis, thus obtaining the stimulation necessary to achieve climax. Most women, however, are not able to gratify themselves in this way. Intercourse seems to deaden their sexual feelings, even their clitoral feelings. It is as though the male penis in the vagina represents a dangerous and hostile presence.

2. Such women can come to a clitoral climax only by masturbating themselves or having their husbands do so before or after intercourse.

♥PRD: It is now common for clitoral women to bring vibrators to bed for their husbands to use on them. Other women self-masturbate with their vibrators to learn what they would like their husbands to do to them. The irony is that a vibrator isn't even a good simulator for a loving husband.♥

Clitoral Orgasms Alone Are Widespread

The clitoral woman—that is, the woman who experiences orgasm on her clitoris alone—is suffering from a form of sexual inhibitions. Indeed this form of inhibitions is prevalent, and we will devote much space to it in Chapter 9: "Masturbation Leads to Sexual Inhibitions," tracing the origin of the difficulty and the need for treatment.

♥PRD: Some inhibited men and women pursue their own unique form of masturbation over the enjoyment of shared penetration.

Clitoral and G-Spot Orgasms Are Promoted Today

Clitoral and G-spot orgasms are promoted in most books, blogs, and podcasts on female sexuality. Women are encouraged to teach their husbands what kind of manipulations they need to enjoy sex. Many of these authors talk about attitudes as being important. Indeed, a woman's attitudes are what distinguish the clitoral woman from the totally inhibited woman whose clitoris is unresponsive.

Sadly, most of these teachers don't seem to know about the vaginal orgasm or how to take their fans to the next level of vaginal orgasms with cervical kisses. Many authors who promote the Song of Solomon see all kinds of techniques in the book and fail to recognize the emphasis on orgasmic attitudes toward oneself, the opposite sex, and God's desire for his people to enjoy passionate sex. Unfortunately, most of the conservative books, blogs, and podcasts on sex celebrate clitoral inhibitions.

Male "Oral-Sex-Type" Sexual Inhibitions

One of the first questions I got about sex nearly 50 years ago came from two wives at different times. They both asked, "What about a husband who insists on oral sex and deprives his wife of a vaginal orgasm?"

Undoubtedly, requiring oral masturbation is the male version of a wife requiring clitoral masturbation to come to orgasm. Additionally, the male probably likes oral sex only when he is the recipient. In other words, he does not enjoy performing oral sex on his wife.

Oral Sex Can Prepare Both the Male and Female for Vaginal Play

In contrast to requiring oral sex to orgasm, a wife's loving oral attention to her husband's penis is a wonderful way to bring a tired male member to life and ready it for sharing vaginal orgasms with cervical kisses. Oral kisses can also turn on the wife as she allows her rapid breathing to begin, which helps ready her vagina for entry. However, I suspect insisting on oral sex is as inhibiting and widespread among men as experiencing only clitoral orgasms is among women.♥

5. Psychically Promiscuously Inhibited Men and Women

I have now described the basic degrees and the psychological consequences of sexual inhibitions. However, I have reserved another class of inhibitions until now to explain because it has certain confusing elements in it. Psychologically and sexually, these inhibitions seem to run counter to the generalities I made about sexual inhibitions so far. Though we consider this man and woman inhibited in the broad sense of the word, *this type can enjoy full and complete orgasms practically every time they have intercourse.* This is quite an astonishing fact, considering the usual close connection between emotions and sexuality.

Unable to Build a Relationship with Any Person

However, this kind of man and woman cannot build a lasting relationship with the opposite sex. Thus they generally become sexually promiscuous in the end. Somehow, a wedge was driven between their sexuality and ability to relate psychologically in a love relationship for any length of time. *Their sexuality has come to apparent maturity while their character has remained infantile. We call this psychic inhibition.*

Not to Be Confused with the Nymphomaniac and Satyriasis

This type of man and woman is not to be confused with the hyper-sexual nymphomaniac woman and satyriasis man. In my experience, the nymphomaniac and satyriasis are generally seriously mentally disturbed. For that reason, they are not included in this book.

Psychic Inhibitions Often Based on Childhood Molestation

Men and women with psychic inhibitions usually have sexual affairs with one person at a time. Their cognitive distortions are generally based on sexual seduction in early childhood. In section 3, I discuss this further with a case history.

♥PRD: In Chapter 14: "Promiscuous Sexual Inhibitions," Dr. Robinson contrasts

people who are psychically promiscuously inhibited ***(1) due to childhood seduction*** *with those who are promiscuously inhibited* ***(2) due to looking for sexual awakening****. Neither (1) the seduced individual nor (2) the one looking for sexual awakening is able to build a lasting bond. They both go from partner to partner. Dr. Robinson devoted only this one paragraph to the promiscuously inhibited person:*

> *The problem of* ***sexual promiscuity*** *in men and women suffering from inhibited sexual desire and pleasure is a common one. Speaking in general terms, it* ***can be said to emanate from a desire to be sexually awakened.*** *Women who seek a solution of this type feel that the next man will somehow break through the barrier that separates them from true sexual satisfaction, true relatedness, restore them to their erotic birthright. They are doomed to disappointment, for an exterior solution of any permanent kind of this interior problem does not exist.*

It's important to distinguish between the two types of promiscuously inhibited men and women here and again in chapter 14 to avoid drawing false conclusions about the causes of promiscuous inhibitions.

Overview of the Types of Sexually Inhibited Men and Women

1. ***Totally sexually inhibited men and women*** *have no sexual reactions whatsoever, sometimes called "sexual anesthesia."*
2. ***Partially sexually inhibited men and women*** *are on the verge of sharing vaginal orgasms with cervical kisses but are not quite there.*
3. ***In-between sexually inhibited men and women*** *range between sexual anesthesia and partial sexual ecstasy.*
4. ***Masturbating sexually inhibited men and women*** *prefer manual stimulation of their private parts over penetration with their mates.*
5. ***Psychically sexually inhibited men and women*** *enjoy full orgasms at first, then develop inhibitions as they are unable to form a lasting emotional bond with anyone.*
6. ***Men and women with no sexual inhibitions*** *are ready to enjoy frequent and passionate lovemaking as described in Chapter 2: "Vaginal Orgasms with Cervical Kisses."*♥

Sexual Inhibitions Are Complicated

I wish inhibitions were as uncomplicated as the descriptions make them sound. If they were, we would simply have a large number of men and women who aren't getting all the pleasure out of life that is possible. But there is far more to it than this, as the next chapter demonstrates.

6.

Sexual Inhibitions Linked to Cognitive Distortions

The sad fact is that being sexually inhibited usually has profound psychological repercussions on the individual. Male and female inadequacy is rooted in:

1. Childhood or adolescence
2. Early fears and misunderstandings
3. Largely forgotten events

Sexual Inhibitions Lead to Negative Character Traits

As crystals on a string around these early experiences cluster a whole series of negative character traits that make life hard for inhibited men and women. And often, they also make life unbearable for those nearest and dearest to them—their spouses and children.

The More Inhibited, the More Cognitive Distortions

To put it plainly, sexual inhibitions are generally a product of cognitive distortions. And importantly, the inhibited man's and woman's disruptive behavior is directly proportional to the degree of their inhibitions. *I have found it to be true that the more inhibited they are, the more troublesome their behavior becomes, and the more detrimental to their own good and the good of their family.*

Sexual Inhibitions Lead to Maladjustment in All Areas

These psychological repercussions make the problem of sexual inhibitions a serious one for the individuals and society. The inhibited man's and woman's often grossly distorted psychological traits raise havoc with our marital institution in the form of:

1. Unhappiness
2. Divorce
3. Maladjusted children

♥*PRD: Many Christians Want to Divorce the Sexless Spouse*

The Sexless Marriages Survey shows that 61% of sex-deprived Christians consider divorce. They've tried everything they know to get help for their sex-withholding spouse. They feel trapped in an unloving marriage that is getting worse. However, most state that they would gladly stay married if their spouse would only get help. Dr. Robinson's concerns about divorce in sexless marriages are very real indeed. If you want more information about divorce, you can read articles on my website at PatsyRaeDawson.com.♥

Men and Women Rarely Face Their Psychological Issues

Women will usually face the fact that they are sexually inhibited. Generally, they have to as the knowledge is forced upon them. But they will rarely face the fact that they have psychological and character issues that are directly related to their obvious sexual difficulty.

♥*PRD: Men are often better at denying they are sexually inhibited than women are. That's because their orgasms can be observed externally. Getting men to admit to a sexually related psychological or emotional problem is as difficult as getting women to.*♥

Case History: Psychological Inhibitions with Sexual Anesthesia

Let me give you an illustration. Last year an intelligent woman came to see me who was an associate professor of history at a leading university. According to her, her only complaint was that she could not have an orgasm during intercourse. She was unusually frank in describing the sexual aspect of her problem in her first interview. When she finished detailing her reactions and lack of them, she had depicted a woman with a rather severe sexual anesthesia. She had neither clitoral nor vaginal sensations. She claimed only some vague pleasant feelings on her labia, but nothing approximated an orgasm.

(1) She was a fine woman, but she was confused about this area. "If I could break through this silly little block," she told me, "our marriage would be ideal." I could get no further real facts from her. She insisted that she and her husband had "a whole community of shared interests" and two "wonderfully normal" children. I asked to see her husband.

(2) I got the real story from him. He told me, he was quite worried about his wife and their marriage. He had been for a long time. He said his wife had always been an extremely competitive woman. But since his promotion from associate professor to full professor four years earlier, while she remained an associate professor, this characteristic had become almost unendurable. "I hardly dare to open my mouth anymore," he told

me, "because I know she's going to contradict me."

(3) Quarrels had become extremely frequent, and their oldest child was showing signs of emotional damage.

(4) I inquired about her reactions during her pregnancies. Her husband said she was frequently ill physically and was deeply frightened by the whole experience, although she would not admit it. Indeed, after the birth of the second child, she became severely depressed for over two months. He told me that yes, indeed, they shared a community of interests for the first couple of years of their marriage. However, her competitiveness with him became so pronounced that any mutuality, from his viewpoint, was now almost impossible.

(5) Any knowledgeable psychiatrist could have guessed from the woman's description of her sexual problem what I learned about her from her husband. As I have pointed out, the kind and degree of inhibitions a woman may confess to are also an open statement of the kind and degree of cognitive distortion she is subject to.

(6) As one might guess, this patient was not easy to treat. She had developed a powerful tendency to handle her fears by denying their existence. However, when she was finally able to see through this self-deceiving trait, she came to grips with her problem. She recognized that she had been in a ten-year competition with her husband instead of a marriage. When she realized this, she gained control of her competitive actions. She received immediate rewards in the form of renewed affection and companionship from her grateful husband, which motivated her to find out more and more about herself.

♥PRD: Overview of the above psychological inhibitions leading to sexual anesthesia:

1. *Claimed she had a good marriage with wonderful children.*
2. *Her husband said she was quarrelsome and competitive.*
3. *The oldest child was showing signs of emotional damage.*
4. *Her marriage suffered as she was frightened by pregnancies.*
5. *Degree of sexual inhibitions equal cognitive distortion.*
6. *She was hard to treat as she handled fears by denying them.*

The number-one problem people married to a sexual withholder have is the same as the inhibited spouse has. Neither one realizes that withholding sex is a physical manifestation of an emotionally cold heart. Warming up the heart frees the body to heat up gloriously in the arms of the mate and creates a loving, nurturing environment for the whole family.

Sexually Inhibited Men Are Competitive with Their Wives

Men who don't have confidence in their masculinity or cherish their wives' femininity can be competitive with their wives—sometimes secretively. One husband, who never initiated lovemaking, ran a business with his wife. He kept secret spreadsheets that compared her accomplishments in the industry to his successes. The wife didn't learn they had a contest going until she found his secret records spanning several decades.

Denial of Attitude Problems Is Hard to Overcome

The denial of attitude problems is the most challenging issue to overcome with an inhibited spouse. According to my Sexless Marriages Survey, 89% of sex-withholding Christians refuse to talk or read about sex. They deny responsibility for overcoming their inhibitions by wallowing in their addiction of blaming their mates for everything, although the problem usually existed before marriage.

The difference between the woman in Dr. Robinson's case study and the survey respondents' sexless spouses is that the woman took the first step toward healing by asking for help. Although she resisted accepting responsibility, she finally did and reaped the benefits. In many sexless marriages, the withholding spouse rejects accountability to the bitter end of the marriage.♥

Through Insight, She Learned to Give and Take Love

This intelligent but dreadfully insecure person became a real feminine woman able to give and take in every aspect of the love relationship through understanding and insight.

♥*PRD: The Dream of Every Person Married to an Inhibited Spouse*

This is the dream of every husband and wife who is married to a sex-denying spouse—that the mate will finally be "able to give and take in every aspect of the love relationship."♥

Sexual Inhibitions Cause Cognitive Distortions

I wish to impress this on you deeply. Sexual inhibitions cause cognitive distortions and character issues. It means that the person:

1. Misunderstands reality
2. Denies their distortions
3. Blames others for their miseries and failures

♥*PRD: Sex-Denying Spouses Commonly Blame the Mate*

Dr. Douglas Weiss says in Intimacy Anorexia that blaming the spouse for whatever is going wrong is an almost universal characteristic of husbands and wives who withhold sex. You see all three of the above distortions and character issues in Dr. Weiss's discussion of blaming:

> *Blame, as a characteristic, is when an issue or problem comes up in the marriage; the anorexic* ***[3] [sex withholder] blames or puts the responsibility on the spouse for the issue*** *before they [the spouse] can see* ***[1] their [the sex-withholder's] contribution to the problem or issue....*** *Blaming is almost reflexive for many anorexics....* ***[2] Blame is mentally manipulating to stay hidden from yourself or being exposed*** *[emphasis added for clarity] (36-37).*

The Sexless Marriages Survey Shows Blaming Is Common

The characteristic of blaming others is rampant in sexless marriages. The Sexless Marriages Survey reveals that 83% of sexless Christians blame their spouses, although their sexual issues existed before the marriage. As Dr. Robinson emphasizes, sexual inhibitions always have their origin in childhood.

Blaming is a destructive defense mechanism found in both male and female sexual withholders. But it isn't only blaming for a lack of the withholder's interest in sex. Dr. Robinson said, "The characteristics and distorted cognitive goals that accompany sexual inhibitions cause obvious domestic frictions." The longer the blaming goes on, the more likely it is to turn into hatred.

One husband said, "She blames me for everything, even when the children misbehave. I can't please her on anything."♥

Case History:
Woman's Distorted Thinking Leads to Poor Decisions

One woman who was cured of a severe inhibition problem phrased it this way: "I was looking at life and people through a distorting glass. No wonder I made such poor decisions." She was right too. Her problem had driven her to promiscuity, then to marriage with an alcoholic.

Sexually Based Distortions Can Ruin Children

When she first came for treatment, I was glad she had not yet had children. With her deeply seated, sexually based personality problem, she might have ruined them. I am even more pleased that she remarried a fine man, and she has two children now. A later section examines in detail these personality problems that accompany sexual inhibitions.

♥PRD: Children Are Harmed by the Sex-Withholding Parent

The last checklist in the Sexless Marriages Survey addresses the harm done to children. The older the children, the more noticeable the harm is. And the older the children, the more difficult it is to help the children overcome that damage.

One mother said, "My greatest regret is that I didn't recognize how much my husband's sexless behavior affected his character and his parenting. Because I didn't understand what was going on, I wasn't able to protect my children when and how I should have."

I advise the sex-starved spouse, "Step out of your pain into your children's pain so you can see how to protect them." Then I tell them, "You are too young to put up with this problem because you have a lot of life left. But your children are too old to suffer through it because they are already being damaged." Shortened, it becomes:

"You are too young, and your children are too old to endure this problem."

Sexless Marriages Are Solvable

Fortunately, Dr. Robinson makes it clear that the problem of a sexless marriage is a solvable one. The first step is recognizing the damage that closing up one's heart to intellectual, emotional, sexual, and spiritual intimacy does to everyone in the family. The second step is to determine to put in the work necessary to release the heart to love one's family. The one who closes his or her heart to love is the one who is harmed the most. That's what this chapter is about—the damage to the sexual withholder.♥

Problems from Lack of Sexual Satisfaction

I would like to go into some more immediate symptoms that result from sexual failure. You will recall in the description of sexual intercourse leading to orgasm how thoroughly the body becomes mobilized: heartbeat, pulse, and blood pressure rise precipitately, tissues become engorged with blood, glands secrete freely, and muscular tension mounts to a pitch, which would be unendurable if the sexual instinct were not demanding expression.

Sexual Failure Causes Physical and Cognitive Problems

Complete satisfaction brings an end to all the above processes. The energy discharged through normal channels and in a normal manner leaves the person in a relaxed condition with a sense of well-being. When orgasm does not take place, and no release occurs of the intensely mobilized energy, the individual experiences immediate physical and psychological repercussions.

Sexual Failure Causes Anger at Self and Partner

The person who has been brought to such a pitch suffers a feeling of acute psychological frustration that consciously or unconsciously turns to anger at oneself and one's partner.

Sexual Failure Causes Physiological Symptoms

If the anger is unconscious, a person may undergo physiological symptoms—headache, nausea, throat constrictions, heart palpitations, or difficulty breathing. The person may also weep uncontrollably, vomit, or have tremors throughout the body.

The Depriver Heaps Anger on the Mate and the Children

This unconscious anger at one's frustration may also cause the person to quarrel with the mate or to take out one's rage on the children.

♥PRD: Unfortunately, we just don't realize the great harm done to children by sexually inhibited fathers and mothers. Many times people who contact me say, "My sexless spouse is a great father or mother."

It's not emotionally possible for a person to withhold emotional and sexual affection from the mate and turn around and show healthy emotional, nurturing love to the children. What is usually true in these marriages is that the inhibited person delights in the cute baby who is easy to take care of. But as the child grows and requires more thought and skill, the inhibited parent tends to resent the child and becomes overwhelmed with parenting.

The sexless spouse may take the children places and play with them. But the warmth of touch and affection that unconsciously bubbles out of a sexually satisfied person is missing. The children grow up never observing what love looks, smells, tastes, sounds, feels, and acts like. Consequently, they often make disastrous marriage choices or become sexually inhibited themselves.♥

The Depriver Blames the Mate for Lack of Ecstasy

I want to emphasize that the sexually inhibited person usually does not see any connection between these symptoms and his or her unsatisfying sexual experiences. When the anger at one's disappointment becomes conscious, the person usually blames the mate for the lack of satisfaction. However, the mate is rarely to blame.

Repressed Anger Can Lead to Physical Symptoms

Purely physical symptoms not connected with repressed anger may also follow upon sexual excitement, which has not been released through orgasm. These physical problems can probably be traced to undischarged neuro-muscular and glandular energy. Such symptoms include low back pain, general restlessness, and often acute insomnia. Several of my patients complained of severe vaginal pains, which lasted several hours. Gynecologists report that abdominal cramps, probably emanating from contractions of the uterus, are frequent.

No Other Health or Social Problem of This Magnitude

Conservative estimates indicate that 40 percent of all American women suffer from some degree or kind of sexual inhibitions. No other public health or social problem even approaches this magnitude.

♥PRD: *Male and Female Sexual Inhibitions Is the #1 Marriage Problem*

Fifty-six years after Dr. Robinson wrote the above words, we know that both male and female sexual inhibitions are the number-one marriage problem worldwide. In God's 11 Secrets of Sex, I give the following statistics:

Dr. Seth Stephens-Davidowitz is an economist and former quantitative analyst at Google. As a Harvard graduate student, he began writing about how Google searches can give "us fresh insights into socially sensitive topics." In response to numerous requests, he ran the numbers on sex. In his article "Searching for Sex," his statistics show that between a quarter and a third of a million people google each month for one of these key phrases in this order of frequency:

- *Sexless marriage*
- *Sexless relationship*
- *Sex starved marriage*
- *No sex marriage*
- *Won't have sex with me*

That means that every month, between 250,000 and 333,000 men and women search the Internet to find answers for dealing with a sex-denying spouse who refuses to get help. The numbers don't reflect the people who looked last month,r don't know to look for help, or have already given up on finding help.

Dr. Stephens-Davidowitz's figures reveal that a nearly equal number of husbands as wives suffer in dead-bedroom marriages. These sexless-marriage statistics are much higher than searches for "unhap

Looking back over 50 years of being the confidante of both husbands and wives in unloving marriages, I've observed this: If the sexual relationship is defective, then the marriage is flawed on all levels. Without a doubt, such a home environment is harmful for nurturing children. The family lives in an emotional vacuum in which the couple and their children are starved for love.♥

Inhibitions and Cognitive Issues Are Common and Serious

As you can see from this recital of symptoms and my preliminary descriptions of cognitive distortions manifested through unreasonable anger, men and women may pay a high price for their sexual inhibitions. If the condition were relatively rare, we could take some comfort from that fact, at least. But inhibitions are not rare. They are one of the most common and serious chronic problems that beset society today.

♥*PRD:* *Anger Leads to Withholding Kissing and Touching*

My Sexless Marriages Survey verifies that kissing and touching are dead in most sexless marriages as all forms of physical affection are withheld.

In working through Dr. Robinson's material, it's easy to see why withholding touch is common with sexless spouses. It's nearly impossible to make yourself touch someone you are angry with or hate. Here are the statistics of how often Dr. Robinson used critical words that describe character faults:

- *Bitter—9 times*
- *Anger—25 times*
- *Rage—15 times*
- *Hostile—25 times*
- *Hate—4 times*
- *Quarrel, quarrelsome—13 times*
- *Argue—2 times*
- *Frustration—14 times*
- *Frightened—33 times*
- *Distortion—3 times*
- *Kill ability to love—3 times*
- *Anxiety—22 times*
- *Neurosis, neurotic, and neurological (changed to cognitive distortions and distortive)—43 times*

In 192 pages, Dr. Robinson used emotionally negative words 211 times. Notice one more statistic:

- *Frigid, frigidity (changed to sexual inhibitions)—323 times*

In 192 pages, 65% of the time, Dr. Robinson connected frigidity or sexual inhibitions directly to negative emotions—cognitive distortions.

The point? Bitterness, anger, rage, and all the other negative emotions that go with it were a major issue in the inhibited patients Dr. Robinson treated.

Some Withholders Use Anger and the Silent Treatment

Dr. Douglas Weiss says in Intimacy Anorexia that some withholders use anger or silence to push away, punish, or control their spouses. If anorexics use either of these extremes against their mates, he stressed that they will use those tools of avoidance often and with a vengeance.

Two of his case histories illustrate the connection between anger and the silent treatment: Todd said, "I will do this whenever she is getting too close to me. I will start playing the blame game and get angry at her or stop talking to her."

Helen said, "He uses intentional aggression or shutting down verbally to push away" (51-52).

Dr. Weiss emphasized, "If the anorexic chooses recovery, this behavior will need consequences and boundaries to conquer it." Pick up my free handout, "How to Fight Fair and Face Anger," at PatsyRaeDawson.com to get started.

Review of This Chapter from the Scriptures

From a Christian standpoint, what Dr. Robinson calls personality or psychological difficulties are character issues and leftover childhood survival techniques. The Apostle Paul teaches in 2 Timothy 3:1-5 that 18 character sins cluster around number 9—being without natural affection for family, including the mate and children. These 19 sins find fertile ground to grow and thrive in sexless marriages. They frequently surround both male and female withholders:

> *2 Timothy 3:1-5: "But mark this: There will be terrible times in the last days. People will be lovers of themselves, lovers of money, boastful, proud, abusive, disobedient to their parents, ungrateful, unholy, without love [for family], unforgiving, slanderous, without self-control, brutal, not lovers of the good, treacherous, rash, conceited, lovers of pleasure rather than lovers of God—having a form of godliness but denying its power. Have nothing to do with such people" (NIV).*

The above scriptures form the basis of my Sexless Marriages Survey. The following information comes from that survey.

Bitterness and Anger Thrive in Sex-Withholding Spouses

The survey reveals that the full spectrum of bitterness to anger to hatred is experienced in sexless marriages. It corresponds to the age of the marriage and the degree of damage done to the inhibited spouse in their home of origin.

Sometimes in courtship and at the beginning of the marriage, the sex-withholding spouse permits a certain amount of hugging, kissing, and sex. As the marriage progresses without healing, the inhibitions, bitterness, and anger increase as the touching decreases. Eventually, if the marriage endures despite the sexual problems, the caustic emotions cause all touching to cease. Sexual inhibitions can't be ignored. They will get much worse!

Bitterness and Anger Lead to Marriage-Destroying Sin

Below is a list of the 19 sins in 2 Timothy 3:1-5 and how they relate to being "without natural love for family" with special emphasis on bitterness and anger. They are given in escalating order as they appear in the scriptures:

1. *Lovers of themselves (lacks sacrificial love and empathy for the mate)*
2. *Lovers of money (withholds financial blessings, loves things)*
3. *Boastful (competitive with the mate, perhaps secretively)*
4. *Proud (shows contempt for the mate and the opposite sex)*
5. *Abusive (judges the mate's motives as evil and blames for everything)*
6. *Disobedient to parents (dysfunctional reaction to unloving home of origin)*
7. *Ungrateful (criticizes and minimizes the mate and the opposite sex)*
8. *Unholy (blames and judges the mate for own inability to love)*
9. *Without love (perpetuates dysfunctional, unloving home of origin)*
10. *Unforgiving (withholds forgiveness, holds grudges, and judges motives)*
11. *Sanderous (slanders and judges the mate's motives as evil)*
12. *Without self-control (gives in to anger and rage, perhaps secretively)*
13. *Brutal (fights dirty and enjoys besting the mate)*
14. *Not lovers of the good (grows to hate the mate who prays love will triumph)*
15. *Treacherous (takes vengeance against the mate, perhaps secretively)*
16. *Rash (throws temper tantrums and lobs outrageous accusations)*
17. *Conceited (denies personal responsibility in withholding love)*
18. *Lovers of pleasure rather than lovers of God (pleasures self sexually)*
19. *Denies the power of godliness (rejects God's plan for sexual love)*
20. *Have nothing to do with such people (get away from people like this)*

Judging motives amplifies every one of the above sins. See Chapter 25: "The Sin of Judging Motives to Be 'Bad' or 'Good'" for more information.

The Growth of Bitterness and Anger Defiles a Person

For Christians who withhold intellectual, emotional, sexual, and spiritual love from their mate, the above sins in 2 Timothy 3:1-5 ought to cause you to stop and contemplate the disastrous path you are heading down. Not only are you jeopardizing your relationship with God, but how can your marriage possibly survive such an onslaught of distorted thinking and character flaws that get worse over time and refuse to be reasoned with?

Likewise, for the mates of the husbands and wives who withhold sexual love, this is evidence that it isn't about you. Step out of your pain and into your children's pain so you can make healthy decisions for everyone in your family.

The 19 sins of 2 Timothy 3:1-5 can be summed up in one verse:

> *Hebrews 12:15: "See to it that no one comes short of the grace of God; that no root of bitterness springing up causes trouble, and by it many become defiled;...."*

The Greek language reveals a metaphor of a poisonous plant to describe bitterness that isn't easily recognized in our English translations. Note the plant aspect in the definitions of the following words:

*"Root" means "**a root**; metaphor: cause, origin, source" (Thayer 563).*

*"Bitterness" means "bitter gall, extreme wickedness, **a bitter root, (and so producing bitter fruit; bitterness, i.e. bitter hatred**, of speech" (Thayer 509).*

*"Springing" means "1. to beget, bring forth, produce; pass. to be born, **to spring up, to grow**, 2. **to shoot forth, spring up**" (Thayer 661).*

*"Cause trouble" means "to excite disturbance, to trouble, annoy (**absolutely of the growth of a poisonous plant, figuratively representing the man** who corrupts the faith, piety, hater of the Christian church, etc.)" (Thayer 217).*

*"Defiled" means "1. **to dye with another color, to stain**, 2. to defile, pollute, sully, contaminate, soil; to defile with sin" (Thayer 414).*

Now read the verse while emphasizing the metaphor of bitterness and bitter hatred as a poisonous plant that destroys a person's life:

> *See to it that no one comes short of the grace of God; that no root producing bitter fruit begins to grow into a poisonous plant that destroys many people as if they were dyed with a contaminating stain.*

If you allow the bitterness of distorted thinking and acting into your life, it will take over your emotions and continue to grow over time. It'll destroy your ability to think clearly. You'll change so much that you'll lose touch with reality as you become contaminated with bitter hatred.

Unless you pull this poisonous plant out of your heart by its roots, it'll continue to grow until it destroys your ability to love your spouse, your children, and your neighbor. Unfortunately, some of your children will welcome this poisonous plant of bitterness and hatred into their hearts as well and will mistreat their mates and your grandchildren.

Dr. Robinson, in the remaining pages of this book, addresses overcoming distorted thinking from psychology. The blessing is that her techniques mirror God's formula for growing marital love and creating a nurturing environment for your children. When you combine Dr. Robinson's worldly wisdom with God's divine instructions, you can pull up this root of bitterness and allow amazing love to grow and flourish in your previously bitter heart.♥

7.

Various Traumas Lead to Sexual Inhibitions

Some time ago, a young husband sat in my office. His wife had come to me for help with sexual inhibitions, and after the first session, he asked her if he might see me. I usually assume that's a good omen for a relationship, and I was not disappointed when I met him.

Case History:
Inhibited Wife's Husband Offered Help

He quickly told me that he did not care how long it took for his wife to overcome her difficulty. "I'd stay with her even if she didn't," he said in a low voice. "I don't love her problem, but I love her, and I want you to know I didn't marry her for better only but for worse as well."

No matter how much a psychiatrist hears about love, its difficulties, and its triumphs, a statement like that always moves one, makes one feel that tasks and problems have been lightened. In short, I liked him, and this encouraged me to ask him about himself.

"That's what I came to tell you about," he said. "There's something I thought may help."

The Husband and Wife Grew Up in Similar Homes

He wanted to tell me the amazing similarity between his background and his wife's, and as he talked, I could see some of the reasons for his broad sympathy with her problem. They were both children of farm people and were reared in the strictest of Puritan disciplines.

The Mothers Were Unloving and the Fathers Were Punitive

Their mothers hated and feared sexuality and communicated freely to the children that sex was dirty and wicked. Their fathers were punitive on the one hand and withdrawn on the other.

This young man broke away from home as early as possible, and so did his wife. They came to the city, got jobs in the same business, and there they met.

The Wife Overcame Her Inhibitions and Cognitive Distortions

I will take leave of our young husband now because the above facts illustrate the question I want you to ask yourself. However, I can tell you his marriage had a happy outcome. Through the sense of security his love gave her, his wife resolved her sexual inhibitions and the other disruptive cognitive problems, which invariably accompany it.

Why Are Inhibitions Common Among Women, But Impotence Is Rare Among Men?

But to the question: With almost identical backgrounds, why had the wife developed a rather severe inhibition problem, and the husband remained perfectly normal sexually? If you wish to extend that question, you may ask yourself: Why are sexual inhibitions so widespread among women and sexual impotence rare among men?

♥*PRD: Emotionally Caused Impotence May Strike in the Man's 40s*

We've seen that sexual inhibitions aren't rare among men. But Dr. Robinson's use of the word "impotence" is flawed, even for the year she wrote this book. Eight years earlier, in 1950 in The Illustrated Encyclopedia of Sex, Drs. Willy, Vander, and Fisher explained that even back then, many doctors recognized that impotence due to sexual inhibitions was not as rare as Dr. Robinson thought.

The doctors wrote that 90 percent of all impotence is due to "psychological causes":

> *Fortunately, the masculine genital glands are composed of cells capable of regeneration for a very long time, and the cells of the erection apparatus are also long-lived. Experience shows that **in an otherwise healthy man, the capacity for erection and impregnation continues far into old age**.*
>
> *In view of this, the question poses itself: How is it that diminution of potency is so frequent in men during their forties? The explanation is simple. This diminution of potency is not a typical phenomenon of the "aging" of the masculine germinal glands. It should be noted that **90 percent of all cases of impotence are due not to physical but to psychological causes** (Willy, et al. 347).*

In 1950—Impotence Linked to Low Sexual Desire

The description Doctors Willy, Vander, and Fisher give below of the "psychological causes" in men sounds similar to the sexual inhibitions Dr. Robinson previously assigned to women. The Encyclopedia of Sex states:

> *Twenty-five years of experience as a specialist has taught the author of the present chapter that men in their forties who consult a doctor about potency troubles, always admit, after careful interrogation, that* ***their potency was not particularly strong even in former years****.... Now if the specialist interrogates his patient expertly, it will be found that the latter's* ***sexual appetite was not particularly keen even in his youth****, or if it was, then he was unable to enjoy intercourse without certain disturbances. And if the patient is further interrogated, he will admit that* ***he had never attached too much importance to sexual intercourse****.*
>
> *...When such men are interrogated, they inevitably realize that their* ***sexual appetite in relationship to their wives has been almost extinct for years****, and that they only continue to engage in sexual intercourse with them because the woman wanted it or out of "masculine pride."*
>
> *"Masculine pride" plays a curious role in the sexual life of such men. It happens far more frequently than it might be assumed that the sexual act is carried out to save this "pride," and without any genuine libido (Willy, et. al. 348-349).*

Impotence Linked to Childhood Experiences

The doctors gave examples of childhood experiences that cause young boys to develop unhealthy attitudes toward their sexuality. They listed being threatened with "hellfire" and with "doing irreparable damage to their health by masturbating." Other childhood events can also burden many men with fear and a sense of guilt regarding their masculinity (349-350). Failing to deal with their childhood inhibitions puts these men on a collision course with impotence in their forties.

27 Years Later—Impotence Linked to "Inhibited Sexual Desire"

Men's inhibitions were mostly overlooked until 1977 when Dr. Helen Kaplan's research was published in *Disorders of Sexual Desire**. She coined the expression "inhibited sexual desire" to describe the number-one problem researchers saw in men and women.*

She said ***most of their failures in previous treatments were due to looking for a medical cause****. She explained, "These patients had developed impotence or orgasmic disorders mainly because* ***they had tried to make love without feeling lust or desire****, and we had been trying to treat these secondary genital dysfunctions* ***without being aware of the underlying desire disorders****" (The Sexual Desire Disorders, Kindle). Today most researchers recognize that men have the same inhibitions women do.*

64 Years Later—Impotence Linked to Obesity

Doctors still recognize relationship problems as causing ED. *However, the increase in "obesity" has changed the ED percentage recognized as due to sexual inhibitions. Honor Whiteman wrote for MedicalNewsToday that "62% of the world's obese lived in developed countries." The US "had the highest increases in the prevalence of adult obesity—a third of the population is now obese" (May 29, 2014).*

In a March 2020 Healthline article, Daniel Yetman reveals the devastating effect of obesity on impotence: "Men who are overweight have a significant risk of developing ED. As many as ***79 percent of people with ED have a body mass index (BMI) over 25****." Most of the medical issues he lists as contributing to impotence are directly related to obesity, such as diabetes, heart disease, high cholesterol, and metabolic syndrome.*

69 Years Later—Impotence Still Linked to Low Sexual Desire

A July 2019 German study of 12,646 men observed that "premature ejaculation, erectile dysfunction, and lower urinary tract symptoms were ***associated with low sexual desire****." The researchers concluded, "Our study revealed that* ***low sexual desire among 45-year-old men is a common sexual dysfunction****, with a prevalence of nearly 5% and might be affected by various factors, including sociodemographic and lifestyle factors, as well as comorbidities [simultaneous presence of two or more diseases or medical conditions in a patient]* ***and sexual behavior****."*

70 Years Later—Impotence Linked to Childhood and the Relationship

Putting all this research over the last 70 years together, we see that ***impotence is primarily a psychological issue that centers around a low sexual desire for one's partner****. The national increase in obesity adds major medical problems to the mix that can cloud the emotional difficulties. Obesity-related diseases make it easy for both doctors and men to assume a pill will fix the problem when* ***it's primarily an issue with the man's childhood and his relationship with his wife****. This review of impotence shows why Dr. Robinson's book about the role of emotions in sexual inhibitions is as relevant for men as it is for women.*♥

The Victorian Era Convinced Women They Were Asexual

We saw that under the adverse conditions caused by the Victorian era that women could, by the millions, abandon sexual gratification and convince the world, doctors, and themselves that, biologically speaking, they were asexual beings. There was never the faintest suspicion that man, on the other hand, would or could abandon his sexual nature, no matter how difficult the going became.

Men Might Develop Sexual Inhibitions, But Not Abandon Sex

Men might develop inhibitions, and they might even take odd sexual directions or pursue perversions if their parents were sufficiently emotionally inhibited. But abandon sexual gratification en masse, they could not.

♥*PRD: Dr. Douglas Weiss Agrees by Disagreeing*

The husband's sexual hang-ups and how they affect the marriage were revealed 36 years after Dr. Robinson wrote this book. In 1995, Dr. Douglas Weiss met in Dallas, Texas, with other sexual addiction experts to discuss a puzzling observation about some recovering male sex addicts. Although these men gave up sex with themselves (solo-masturbation) and stopped looking at porn or having sex outside of marriage, they still weren't having sex with their wives. They avoided sex with their wives for weeks, months, and even years after overcoming sexual addiction. (At that time, psychiatrists didn't recognize female sexual addiction.)

Dr. Weiss continued to work with both male and female sex addicts for 15 years before writing Intimacy Anorexia in 2010. He stated:

> *Over time, it was clear to me that this dynamic [sexlessness] had a whole lot more to do with avoiding intimacy than it had to do with avoiding sex. Now, much later in my career of treating anorexics, very few men and only some women avoid sex. However, both the men and the women were actively avoiding intimacy (8).*

Interestingly, in discussing intimacy anorexia (withholding sex from the mate), Dr. Weiss agrees that few men give up on sex. But he disagrees by stating that one way they frequently don't give up on sex is by becoming masturbators.

Dr. Weiss also discovered that "only some women avoid sex." Today's modern women are almost as likely as men to engage in secret sex with themselves instead of giving up on sex.

Rather than Avoiding Sex, Men and Women Are Avoiding Intimacy

Dr. Weiss concluded, "However, both the men and the women were actively avoiding intimacy." Establishing intimacy is the topic that Dr. Robinson deals with in this book. Intimacy is also the theme of the Song of Solomon: Don't have sex until you establish intellectual, emotional, and spiritual intimacy. Only then will sexual intimacy lead to emotional and physical ecstasy.♥

Psychological Inhibitions Can Be Overcome

You will be able to see why the problem of sexual inhibitions is so psychological in nature. Therefore, when a woman's chief complaint is being nonorgasmic, we feel that if she means business, she can get over it.

♥PRD: *Male Psychological Inhibitions Can Be Overcome*

Happily, Drs. Willy, Vander, and Fisher ended the chapter on impotence with this encouragement: "Men in their forties have no reason to despair. An efficient specialist [psychoanalyst] and the will to understand is all they require" to heal and enjoy God's wonderful sexual blessings (351).

Passionate Sex Was God's Plan in the Creation and Still Is

In the account of the creation and fall of Adam and Eve in Male and Female: God's Genius, I show how passionate lovemaking was God's design from the beginning as he declared:

> *Genesis 2:24: "For this reason a man shall leave his father and his mother, and be joined to his wife; and they shall become one flesh."*

The one-flesh relationship is so meaningful that Jesus and the apostles quoted Genesis 2:24 four times in the New Testament, each time revealing a different aspect of "one-flesh" intimacy—intellectual, emotional, sexual, and spiritual. The Song of Solomon teaches these four parts of one-flesh love in detail. For more information, see "Secret 4: Grow the 4 Parts of Intimacy and Love" and the appendix chapter, "The 4 Parts of One Flesh, Love, and Intimacy" in God's 11 Secrets of Sex.

God states that a beautiful sexual life is one of the tools he gave men and women to help them subdue the earth, fill it with people, and glorify him:

> *Ecclesiastes 9:9: "Enjoy life with the woman whom you love [literally sexually or otherwise] all the days of your fleeting life which He has given to you under the sun; for this is your reward in life, and in your toil in which you have labored under the sun."*

Thus passionate sex is a specially designed blessing that God gives men and women to help them enjoy life and serve him.♥

Reason 1:
Various Traumas Lead to Sexual Inhibitions

Three primary reasons can lead to sexual inhibitions in men and women. I am going to treat them separately in different chapters. I begin with the first one—the effect of various traumas on the sexual drive.

Case History: Actress Tells About Discovering Her Sexuality

A lovely actress I was treating for a rather severe sexual-inhibition problem came for her regular hour one day and paused on the threshold of my office. She appeared different—her face was softer, her motions slower—she was elated. I felt at once that she had experienced the first reward for her hard work on her problem.

"We Can Cast It Aside; We Can Put It on Again"

I was right. I shall never forget her method of telling it. She wore a lovely pink cape; its flowing lines and delicate color seemed to express the very essence of the feminine.

As she stood smiling, she unbuttoned the cape and threw it on the floor between us with a beautiful gesture. "Thus we can cast it away," she said. Then, stooping, she picked it up. "And thus we can put it on again," and with a flourish, she put it back on her shoulders. That hour was a celebration of her new-found capacity.

Her histrionic gesture, expressive of so much happiness in her, was not only graceful but was deeply symbolic of a woman's sexual nature. To see why this is so, let us first turn our attention to the biological meaning of the sexual drive.

The Biological Meaning of the Sexual Drive

You perhaps know that every animal is motivated by a profound instinctual need to preserve his species. His nature has developed those characteristics that ensure the continuation of his kind; lemmings excepted, perhaps. We know that characteristics that ensure the species are more deeply rooted in the biology of a given animal than ones that are not necessary to the preservation of a species.

♥PRD: The "instinctual need to preserve the species" is found in both the young man and the young woman.♥

Sex Is the Method to Preserve the Species

In the human-animal and many other species, sexual intercourse is how the species is preserved. In this elemental instinctual activity, the male deposits his sperm in the respective female, who then, within her body, nurtures and protects the fetus until it is ready for birth.

For Pregnancy to Occur, the Male Must Have an Orgasm

But here's the critical point: To deposit his sperm, the male must have an orgasm. If he did not, the sperm could not be released inside the female. Thus the male orgasm is absolutely necessary to the continuation of the species. If the male had ever lost his orgasmic ability, the species would have disappeared from the earth.

Sexually Inhibited Women Can and Do Bear Children

However, it is not a biological necessity for a woman to have an orgasm to fulfill her sexual role. It is only necessary for her to receive the sperm. The mere reception of it, no matter how unresponsive she may be to the ardors of the male, fully discharges her duty to the species of humankind. Maternity, not orgasm, is her biological duty. She can be as sexually cold as the polar cap, and it will not necessarily affect her ability to have children to the slightest degree.

♥PRD: *Pregnancy Doesn't "Fully Discharge" Duty to Humankind*

I disagree strongly with Dr. Robinson's conclusion about the "duty" of orgasm and pregnancy. Yes, orgasm isn't required for a woman to get pregnant and give birth. However, her "duty to the species" is not "fully discharged" with her pregnancy and childbirth. Her duty to the species has just begun. The woman's biological duty continues as she nurtures and protects her children until they are ready to go out into the world. Although orgasm is not necessary for a woman to conceive, her orgasms play an essential role in her pregnancy and rearing her children as the following discussion shows.♥

Male Orgasm Is a Necessity; Female Orgasm Is a Luxury

Can you see the implications? One of my colleagues summed up the difference in this way: "To express it in a purely biological sense [for propagating the species], the male orgasm is a necessity. The female orgasm is a luxury."

♥PRD: *Women Need Great Sex to Be Wonderful Mothers*

According to the Bible's teachings, this summary statement by Dr. Robinson's colleague is not only short-sighted but also potentially harmful. Such thinking can cause both men and women to discount the importance of the female's orgasm. Sexual enjoyment is necessary for both the male and the female according to God's design for the sexual relationship.

I have taught for over a decade that women need great sex to be wonderful mothers. Modern science supports the Bible's emphasis that good sex is a requirement for women as the guardians of love and for the family's emotional health. So I disagree with the colleague's statement. However, thinking about his and Dr. Robinson's comments led to an important epiphany that I would never have recognized apart from working on this book. For detailed discussion, see my two chapters in Part 2: "Radical Epiphany on Awakening Male-Female Sexuality" and "The Wife Needs Passion to Be a Wonderful Mother."♥

Bad Homes of Origin Rarely Shut Down the Man's Orgasm

This "necessary" aspect of the male orgasm explains why men, no matter how deeply disturbing their childhood experiences were, rarely lose their ability to have an orgasm and why women so frequently do.

♥PRD: *The Man's Orgasm Is External*

I suspect one reason men rarely lose their ability to have an orgasm is that their orgasms can be viewed and accessed outside their bodies. Puberty activates this ability at a young age. Additionally, nocturnal discharges or wet dreams draw men's attention to their orgasmic abilities. In the Old Testament cleanliness laws, God declared wet dreams "unclean," which discouraged self-masturbation and pushed men toward marriage. For more information, see the appendix chapter on this topic in God's 11 Secrets of Sex.

The Woman's Orgasm Is Internal

In contrast, a woman's sexual response is internal and out of sight. As a young woman, she dreams about becoming a mother. Her sexuality is not awakened until marriage when she begins to have vaginal intercourse with her husband. See my article in Part 2: "Radical Epiphany on Awakening Male-Female Sexuality" for more information on "awakening" in the Song of Solomon.

Sexually Inhibited Men Are at Risk for Mid-Life Impotence

In The Encyclopedia of Sex, the doctors stated that biologically men retain their "capacity for erection and impregnation into old age." However, sexually inhibited men are at risk of impotence in their forties due to "psychological causes" (347). Protection of the man's orgasmic abilities for preserving the species can only be depended upon for his first forty years.

Ironically, the man's protected erection time equals the woman's fertility period. *To ensure old-age potency, a man must soulmate with his wife and engage in frequent passionate sex to keep his and her sexual organs healthy.*♥

Orgasm Is Subject to Trauma in Men and Women

Please understand me. I am not saying that the orgasm a woman has when she can achieve it is any less intense than a man's. Nor am I saying that it is not necessary to her psychological well-being and maturity to achieve it. I am saying that a woman's ability to have an orgasm is far more subject to outside influences than a man's ability is. In many ways, the woman's orgasm is more subject to the psychological experiences, the mental and moral traumas of growing up than the man's is.

♥*PRD: Women Need Orgasms Because of Outside Influences*

The fact that a woman's orgasm is subject to outside influences is precisely why her orgasm is necessary to the family's emotional health. She is the guardian of love. The emotional nature of her orgasms makes them a barometer of the emotional state of the marriage and the nurturing environment for the children.

Cecil Murphey Documents Sexual Trauma for Men

In When a Man You Love Was Abused: A Woman's Guide to Helping Him Overcome Childhood Sexual Molestation, New York Times Best-Selling Author Cecil Murphey describes his abuse:

> *The female relative who abused my two younger brothers and I wasn't someone I could have accused. It happened when we were so young, how did we know it was abuse? I don't want to go into details but it included her fondling us and forcing us to do the same to her. Even after I was in my early teens, that female relative used to tell me explicitly sexual jokes. When I was as old as fifteen, she embraced me with her whole body—and I detested myself for evil thoughts. Perhaps that's one reason some of us didn't talk: we assumed something was wrong with us.*
>
> *Those who should have been the best confidants, such as relatives, Sunday school teachers, pastors, and guidance counselors, have often been the abusers. They are authority figures, individuals we trusted, those who should have encouraged us and taken care of us (78).*

Murphey says, "One in every six males has experienced unwanted or abusive sexual experiences before the age of sixteen." In his chapter, "If His Abuser Was a Woman," he says:

> *When the perpetrator is a woman, the effects of the abuse on the victim often are more acute. It's difficult enough for a boy to understand what is happening when a male touches him inappropriately or forces himself on the boy. But it's far worse for the victim to face the reality that his sister or aunt involved him in sexual acts. When the abuser is the mother, the situation seems even more horrendous.... Many men say that the abuse by their mothers was the most shameful and damaging form of childhood victimization they experienced (70-71).*

Indeed, this kind of abuse is damaging to a man's self-image and ability to love himself and his wife. Even his children are affected.

When Dr. Robinson wrote this book, she worked with women, and society promoted many Victorian-era stereotypes about men. That men were abused was a dark, dirty secret. More similarities exist between men and women sexually than differences.♥

Sexual Inhibitions Have an Element of Being "Chosen"

The fact that sexual inhibitions are so psychological, so subject to the mind, gives them an almost "willful" character. It is as if a man or a woman had "chosen" to be inhibited. I don't mean consciously chosen to be, generally speaking. It's an unconscious choice. But the fact that sexual inhibitions have the element of "choosing" in them make inhibitions a poignant condition.

Case History: Female Doctor Chooses Inhibitions

I know one case where the "choice" was, in part at least, conscious, and I am going to tell it briefly to emphasize the fact that sexual inhibitions have a high element of the mental as opposed to the biological. Years ago, on a vacation with my husband, I met an older woman with whom, until her death, I had a close friendship. She was a wonderful woman. She was a doctor, but this had not prevented her from having five children, two of whom have since become famous.

The Doctor, Who Married in 1904, Had Victorian Inhibitions

One day, after our friendship had deepened and we had begun to exchange confidences, she told me the following story. She was deeply in love with her husband but was totally sexually inhibited. This did not seem strange at the time since she married in 1904, and the traditions of Victorianism were still adhered to.

She Began Having Orgasms After Giving Birth

However, after her third child's birth, she began to experience feelings of pleasure during intercourse, and these gradually increased. At this point, she had her fourth child, and intercourse was interrupted for several months. When it resumed, her feelings of pleasure increased enormously, and on the second time, she had a profound orgasm.

Her Training Made Her Frightened and Ashamed

But the doctor was not, like my actress, delighted with the new horizons the experience opened up for her. She was consciously frightened and ashamed. All her background and training was against it.

She Decided Never to Let the Experience Repeat Itself

She consciously decided never to let the experience repeat itself. She was entirely successful in her resolution. Unlike my actress, she threw off the lovely pink cloak of her feminine potential and never donned it again. Her husband died after the birth of their last child, and it was not until a few years afterward, with the new information science had developed on the subject, that she realized the tragedy of her decision.

♥*PRD: Nursing a Baby Releases Hormones of Love*

The doctor's trauma was common during the Victorian era. Women often began experiencing orgasms while nursing a baby because of all the hormones of love being released. Like this doctor, their pleasure frightened them because of the false religious and medical teaching about women being asexual.

This is what happened to the doctor. The reason it happened after her third and fourth pregnancies was probably due to breastfeeding changes. She may have had trouble getting her milk established with her first pregnancy. Women usually have better luck with succeeding babies because each time a woman gets pregnant, her milk-duct glands immediately start enlarging. Thus with each pregnancy, the mother produces more milk. Breastfeeding releases hormones that make the mother more loving toward her infant. The copious amounts of hormones naturally spill over onto her husband and other children.

Scientists have injected these hormones into roosters. To their surprise, the roosters gathered up the baby chicks under their wings just as the hens did. Jesus compared his love for people to that of a mother hen:

> *Matthew 23:37: "Jerusalem, Jerusalem, who kills the prophets and stones those who are sent to her! How often I wanted to gather your children together, the way a hen gathers her chicks under her wings, and you were unwilling."*

Due to religious teaching and medical opinion that godly women didn't enjoy sex, many Victorian women were horrified when nursing a baby released their sexual love for their husbands. They went to their doctors for medical help. Unfortunately, the standard treatment was to remove the clitoris. Physically, that wouldn't have prevented the woman from enjoying vaginal orgasms. But the trauma of the surgery was enough to prevent future orgasms.♥

Sexuality Is Subject to Outside Influences

The doctor's story is poignant, but I did not tell it for that reason. I told it because it illustrates how subject to the mind, to outside cultural and moral influences, feminine sexuality can be.

♥*PRD: Cultural and moral influences also influence the male's expression of his masculine sexuality.♥*

If Inhibitions Can Be Chosen, Sexuality Is Fragile

If a grown woman can choose to destroy her mature and flowering sexuality at the height of its strength, just think of the fragility of this sexuality in the bud.

♥PRD: *Case History: Man's Wife Chose Sexual Inhibitions*

One of the first participants to my Sexless Marriages Survey in 2016 was a man in his 60s married 41 years. He was a non-denominational preacher, song leader, and elder. He grew up with an abusive father and suffered from self-image problems. His sex-withholding wife was a children's Bible class teacher. Prior to marriage, she was part of the hookup culture. She pushed for marriage and indicated she would be an eager lover. That changed quickly after marriage. Following are some of his survey answers:

List other ways your companion withholds feelings:

She said that soon after our marriage, I said something that hurt her feelings and vowed there would be no tenderness or affection in our marriage and has held true to that vow. She would not tell me what I said when I asked to make restitution or at least apologize.

Do you withhold feelings? If yes, explain:

I used to share feelings, but they were soon used to belittle or ridicule me – I no longer tell or show how I feel or react to any verbal attack.

Do you withhold sex? Review the above list, and if yes, explain:

I don't know. Her rejections have been so emphatic and emotional I haven't tried to initiate since March of 2000 [16 years, 7 months before the survey].

Are you without natural affection? If yes, explain:

I don't know. I tried for years to find out how to please her – going through all of Patsy's materials, read articles in my wife's magazines. When she told me about the vow never to have tenderness or affection in our marriage (after 30 years of marriage) I just gave up.

His answers on other questions show his wife regularly engages in cognitive distortions. She fights dirty by judging his motives, ridiculing him, putting words in his mouth, comparing him to despicable people, and giving him the silent treatment.

Case History: Wife's Husband Chose Sexual Inhibitions

It's as common for men to choose sexual inhibitions as it is for women. A survey participant's husband chose to neglect her sexually for several reasons, including something she said years ago: "We never had children in 13 years because of a lack of sex. Now endometriosis was discovered in my body, and I had surgery. It's another argument for him to say I cannot have children—even if it is not exactly what the doctors said—so there is no point trying. He also said because I make little income and participate less in the home finances, ***and because I hurt him verbally a long time ago,*** *he doesn't want to engage. Even though it has been like this since our first year of marriage."*

Case History: How I Chose to Turn Off My Desires for My Husband

I learned firsthand how a wife has tremendous power to turn off her sexual desires and enjoyment. After about twenty years of marriage and trying to earn my sexless husband's love, I was frustrated with constantly having my initiations of lovemaking rejected.

I loved my husband and our spiritual life together as he worked as a preacher, and I taught ladies classes. I reasoned, "If I can become like him and not need sex, then we will have a perfect marriage." Yes, I know. Stupid!

I set out to turn off my sexual desires by distracting myself from the little daily twinges of desire—to not allow myself to enjoy those feelings of anticipating sexual love. Before long, I began to have some success. But instead of getting a perfect marriage, I realized that as I was clamping down on my sexual desires, I was also losing my ability to love my children. I was making myself be without natural affection for my whole family.

I was horrified! I immediately began to work at restoring my love for my husband and my children. And I had to work at it. I learned the hard way that a woman cannot close up her heart to the natural sexual expression of love for her husband without hindering her ability to love others—even her own precious children.

Reason 1: Various Traumas Lead to Sexual Inhibitions

The first reason Dr. Robinson gives for why women often experience sexual inhibitions is their reactions to childhood traumas. She asserts men aren't bothered as much by dysfunctional homes of origin. However, eight years before her book, doctors recognized that men's sexuality is also fragile; their problems just don't always show up as quickly as women's do. Orgasm is fragile for both men and women who can choose to turn off their sexuality.♥

8.

Fear of Parenthood Leads to Sexual Inhibitions

♥PRD: In this section, Dr. Robinson explains the second reason women might become sexually inhibited—fear of childbirth and motherhood. Since she wrote this book, research shows that men react to fatherhood in similar ways as women. Both men and women who fear and resent parenthood inhibit themselves sexually. At the end of this chapter, I discuss similarities between men and women.♥

Case History: Woman Terrified of Having Children

Recently a woman of thirty-five came to my office. She called me twice to make appointments and twice broke them at the last moment. When this happens, a psychiatrist generally assumes the patient has become frightened of her decision to face whatever problem is troubling her and has gone into a last-minute flight. I expected to encounter a reticent, scared, perhaps terrified person if I ever did see her.

Instead, the person who sat opposite me was a pretty woman of thirty-five, well dressed, clear-eyed, and straightforward. She came right to the point. "I'm here because I'm terrified of having children," she told me. "I must find out what's at the root of my fear."

"Was your fear the reason you canceled the two appointments?" I asked sympathetically.

"Oh no," she answered quickly, "the children were ill. We've had flu for a month. The first one came down with it, and then another."

"Children?" I asked in puzzlement. "What children?"

"Mine, of course," she said.

"How many do you have?" I asked.

"Four," she said, "but John and I want six, and I thought...." She paused; then, catching my smile, she looked down at the floor for a moment and back at me, and then we both burst into laughter.

However, she did have a fear of childbirth, dating from certain traumatic experiences in her childhood, and we were able to resolve it. It was a marked fear, but the point is that even with it, she had gone right on and had four children.

The Maternal Instinct Equals the Paternal Instinct

The maternal instinct is as deep and indestructible in women as the instinct to plant the seed of his species is in man. They both achieve the same result, the continuation of the race. Even if a woman's childhood is sown with cognitive distortions and fears by unhappy parents—yes, even distorted fears of childbirth—her desire to have children survives relatively intact.

A Woman's Body and Femininity Point Toward Children

Thank heavens this is so. The bearing and rearing of children is the beautiful destiny toward which a woman's whole body and personality point from their earliest childhood. If this profound goal cannot be achieved, the result is often a shriveling of the woman's femininity.

Even the Feminists Couldn't Overcome the Maternal Instinct

Thank heavens this is so, too, for the good of the race. One of my colleagues neatly expressed the whole thing in a paper given to a private psychiatric group. "If the feminists had been able to injure the maternal instinct of the nineteenth-century woman to the same degree they injured her sexual instinct, the Western world would by now be well on its way to being depopulated."

A Mother Can Impart Fear and Inhibitions to Her Daughter

No, the maternal instinct cannot be fundamentally affected by adverse circumstances. However, the proper handling of information about the maternal instinct by a mother is crucial to the healthy sexual development of her daughter. Misunderstandings about maternity and what it means can scare a young child badly—so severely that the fear of it can be a direct cause of later inhibitions.

A Mother Must Be Willing and Ready to Die for Her Children

Here's why the maternal instinct can cause trouble to a young girl's developing sexuality. Most women know this, even if they have never phrased it in this manner. To gratify the maternal instinct, a woman has to put her life on the line. In a real sense, she has to be willing to say, and to keep on saying: "I am willing and ready to die for the sake of or the safety of my child."

I'm not only speaking of the slim chance that she might die in childbirth, though I should like to point out that until recently, that possibility also had to be faced by every mother-to-be. And the enormously high mortality rate in childbirth throughout history and in every civilization shows clearly that women were willing to face death to have their child. They have not changed.

A Mother Puts Her Child's Welfare Before Her Own

What I mean is that the maternal instinct demands of the woman in every situation an ever-readiness to put her child before herself, before her safety, before her personal needs, before everything.

Case History: Mother Rescued Children from Fire

Yesterday, I read of a woman who saved two of her children from their burning home. The place went up like tinder, and she snatched them up, one seven and one ten, and, holding them under her arms, brought them to safety down a flaming stairway.

She thought her 12-year-old had gotten out by himself but discovered he had not. She started back at once, without a moment's hesitation, to rescue him, but the building was now about to collapse, and several firefighters restrained her.

So powerful was her drive to save her child that she broke away from their grasp and entered the building. She found her son on the kitchen floor, overcome by smoke, and somehow got him out. She was badly burned, though she will live. But the child was all right! The child was alright! That was all that mattered.

Protection of a Child Is More Powerful than Self-Preservation

And her child is all that matters to every mother, unless she is dreadfully ill mentally—psychotic, in fact. Just think of it; this aspect of the maternal instinct is more powerful than the instinct for self-preservation, which is known to be one of the basic instincts of all life. It supersedes self-preservation, annuls it; there are no reservations about it. It will never whisper: "You've done all you can; three powerful men are holding you down, and you can't get to him anyway." The maternal instinct will fight powerfully and to the end for the mother's right, her indomitable need, to save her child.

Childrearing Involves Everyday Sacrifices

Of course, most mothers never have to face physically dangerous situations for their children. In most lives, this aspect of the mother's instinct expresses itself in everyday sacrifices. Mothers give up (and, in the healthy woman, with pleasure, by preference) their time, intellectual pursuits, careers, first to have the child, and then to see him safely to maturity. Everything else a woman could call her own becomes secondary to this impulse in the maternal woman.

Pregnancy and Motherhood Misrepresentations Cause Harm

As you saw in the normal woman, there are checks and balances within the female personality, which prevent her from making a psychological martyr of herself to the point where she would be a detriment to her children. However, at this time, I should like to make a different point.

I have said that the maternal instinct is more powerful than the instinct for self-preservation. I ask you to imagine for a moment how easily this characteristic of women could frighten a young girl if the experience of pregnancy or the role of the mother is improperly presented to her. She will react with acute anxiety and fear rather than with joyful anticipation. This anxiety will color in dark hues, though it will not overwhelm her desire and determination to have babies. *However, it will tend to take all the pleasure out of her sex life. It will tend strongly to make her sexually inhibited. And it will tend to make her a less effective mother, even a very poor mother indeed.*

The Maternal Role Is a Great and Beautiful One

The biological role of the woman is motherhood. If a woman cannot dare to accept this aspect of her destiny, she will be deeply defeated in life. From any standpoint one wishes to look at the maternal role, it is a great and beautiful one, embodying in it, and giving expression to qualities that are universally admired and cultivated: nobility, the sacrifice of self, fortitude, and "love that passeth understanding."

Filling a Young Girl with Fears Cuts Off Her Femininity

Depreciating motherhood in any sense in the mind of a young girl is a crime against her if one is in a position to be influential. To fill her with fears, misunderstandings, resentments, and reservations about her historic role is to cut her off from full flowering as a woman.

Teaching Fear of Motherhood Promotes Sexual Inhibitions

A woman's ability to have an orgasm, her most profound form of relatedness to a man, is tightly interwoven with her psychological experiences at every stage of her development. The quickest and most effective way to force her into sexual inhibitions is to teach her to be frightened of the maternal aspects of her personality.

Case History:
Woman Afraid to Get Pregnant

I should like to give the contents of a letter that came into my hands recently. It is a beautiful letter. It describes in a simple way the reactions of Margaret, a woman who was caught in a maze of misunderstanding and fear. But she found her way out and learned the power and joy she could receive by surrendering to her true destiny.

Fear of Pregnancy Ruined Her Sexual Relationship

Six months earlier, this young woman was sick with anguish at her joyless marriage. She was unable to enjoy any aspect of her sexual relationship because of constant and acute fear of becoming pregnant. She consulted her church pastor, having heard that her church offered psychiatric services.

She Joined a Group-Therapy Project for Troubled Marriages

The pastor got her admitted to a group-therapy project run by a psychologist. The group consisted of women who had encountered some difficulty in their lives with their husbands and children.

The patient attended the group for four months and then had to leave, for her husband's job was transferred to another part of the state. The letter to the members of the group arrived three months after she moved. I received special permission from this ex-patient to reproduce her letter on the understanding that the names originally mentioned in it be changed.

She Became Pregnant and Sounded Like a Honeymooner

Dear, dear Friends:

(1) I will leave out all the details of our move here except to say that we are all settled down and in our wonderful new home. Anyway, I can't wait to tell you that I am going to have a baby. It is a constant astonishment to me, for it is so different from my expectations. It all happened so easily. I don't quite know how, but my fears and worries have left entirely. I didn't know life could be like this. I must be a new person. If the doctor hadn't told me to stay relatively quiet, I would be dancing in the streets. Sam says I sound like a honeymooner, but he's delighted. To think about what I deprived both of us of because of a lot of nonsense!

(2) The strangest thing is that I can't remember the things I used to talk about in the group. I wonder if this happens to everybody. I keep asking myself: What was so painful? What was it that made me always angry with Sam?

(3) And I've found a new deep love for my mother. I am not angry with her, only sorry that she had to miss so much. You probably won't remember, but when I asked my mother how she had felt when she was pregnant, she had said quite sharply to me: "Put such thought out of your mind. You're young, so enjoy yourself. You'll know all about it soon enough, too soon."

(4) The reply seemed so ominous and foreboding to me. Plus the fact that she was constantly complaining about all things female. I guess I had picked up her attitude as a child without realizing it until I aired the effects on me for the first time with all of you.

(5) I tell you this to let you know the fears do go when you get them out and see them for what they are. I love you all, and I am deeply grateful to you, and I shall never, never forget the help my talk with all of you has given me.

With love and deep gratitude,
Margaret

♥PRD: Review of the above letter from the wife who was afraid of pregnancy:

1. *After going to classes for four months, she is excited to be pregnant.*
2. *She can't imagine why she was always angry with her husband.*
3. *She found love and forgiveness for her complaining mother.*
4. *As a child, she picked up her mother's unhappy attitude.*
5. *She discovered that the fears go away when you let them out.*

The mother's negative attitude toward pregnancy was probably passed down to her from her mother. Fortunately, her daughter was able to feel sympathy for what her mother missed in life. Her forgiving spirit reflects the daughter's newfound ability to love her husband and forgive her mother for instilling in her a spirit of negativity about femininity and masculinity:

> *Luke 6:37: "Do not judge, and you will not be judged. Do not condemn, and you will not be condemned. Forgive, and you will be forgiven" (NIV).*

Forgiveness is powerful for both the one who forgives and the forgiven. Best of all, it preserves our relationship with God who forgives us of our ignorance of his wonderful design for male and female and the way of speaking God's beautiful language of love™.♥

Loving Femininity Is a Wonderful and Privileged Condition

If a woman is to find true happiness once again, she must return to her real and joyful self. She must relearn that surrender to her biological destiny is not a trap, not misuse of her uterus, or exploitation by man and nature, but rather a wonderful and privileged condition.

♥PRD: *Similarities in Men's and Women's Fear of Parenthood*

Here are some of the negative mental and physical aspects of childbirth and parenting that some mothers and fathers deal with that can affect their ability to relate to each other sexually:

- *Postpartum depression affects men as well as women.*
- *A lack of sleep is detrimental to the mental health of mothers and fathers.*
- *Responsibility for someone else's life creates an identity crisis.*
- *Men experience "dad's bias" by being ignored at doctor's visits.*
- *Negative health issues can occur within one year of birth.*
- *Both may feel like they've lost their best friend and companion (mate).*
- *Men are especially at risk of increasing drinking alcohol.*
- *Both men and women can simmer with anger and rage over the changes.*
- *Spouse abuse against the wife often increases during pregnancy.*

Brain scans show some amazing changes in fathers that correspond to the same changes in the mother. Google search on "daddy brain" to learn more about the following discoveries in neuroscience:

- *Hormones change for both men and women during pregnancy.*
- *The man's testosterone decreases after birth, which probably makes him more patient as he waits for his wife's body to heal so that sex can resume.*
- *A biochemical bond is quickly established between the father and child after birth.*
- *Skin-to-skin contact with the baby releases the love hormone—oxytocin—also a bonding hormone in both the father and mother.*
- *Men's brains grow new neurons as priorities change in the first four months after a baby is born.*
- *"Daddy brains" are hardwired after birth to respond to any threat to their children.*

A Mother Is to Learn to Love Her Children

God instructs older women to teach young mothers to love their children:

> *Titus 2:3-4: "Older women likewise are to be reverent in their behavior, not malicious gossips nor enslaved to much wine, teaching what is good, so that they may encourage the young women to love their husbands, to love their children."*

"Love" comes from the Greek word phileo and expresses an affectionate, emotional, and physical love. A woman manifests it by patting, hugging, squeezing, and kissing her loved one.

In a presentation on this verse, I gave the most extreme example I could think of to illustrate phileo love. I said, "This is the kind of love a mother has for her child if he's failed the first grade three times. To her, he's the most wonderful son she could have. She readily hugs, pats, and kisses him."

After class, a woman said, "Thank you so much for your example of the little boy. My son failed the first grade three times. Plus he has a bladder problem, so he always smells bad. I've had a hard time resenting him. Thank you for teaching me how to love him."

A Father Is to Imitate God's Love and Delight in His Children

God doesn't leave fathers out. He refers to a father who delights in his child to describe his own love for us. Notice the balance of affectionate love with discipline in God's relationship with us and a father's bond with his children:

Proverbs 3:12:
"For whom the Lord loves He reproves,
Even as a father corrects the son in whom he delights."

"Delights" frequently describes "God's pleasure with his servants, particularly referred to the Messiah [or Jesus] (Isaiah 42:1)" (TWOT 859).

> *Isaiah 42:1: "Behold, My Servant, whom I uphold; My chosen one in whom My soul delights. I have put My Spirit upon Him; He will bring forth justice to the nations."*

Ironically, the Apostle Paul tells men to love their wives as Christ loves the church, to nourish and cherish them (Ephesians 5:25-33). Then Proverbs 3:12 tells fathers to love and delight in their children, the fruit of his sexual love, the way God delights in Jesus, his son and model for the husband's love of his wife.

God sets a high standard for men as both husbands and fathers—to imitate him and his son in the man's love for his wife and children.

Reason 2: Fear of Parenthood Leads to Sexual Inhibitions

Both men and women can become sexually inhibited through their fear of parenthood. In contrast to this, God describes his own love for us by referring to a loving father in Proverbs 3:12. Then in Isaiah 66:10-13, God uses a nursing mother who carries her child on her hip and plays with him on her knee to describe his love for Israel. God wants our homes to be refuges of physical demonstrations of emotional love and delight in our children—even if they failed the first grade three times and have a smelly bladder problem.♥

9.

Masturbation Leads to Sexual Inhibitions

I have already described the so-called clitoral woman to you, but now I must tell you more about the implications of her problem. You will remember that in the female genitalia, both the clitoris and the vagina are capable of experiencing orgasm. This fact is of decisive importance to the problem of sexual inhibitions in women.

Why Is It Important that Women Have Two Sexual Organs?

In effect, women have two distinct sexual organs, both capable of bringing her release from sexual tension. That's important because, in the unconscious sense, many women can "choose" one type of sexual satisfaction in preference to another. This ability to choose often spells disaster, for one of these methods of gratification represents incomplete satisfaction and is connected to cognitive distortions.

Men Become Impotent When They Block Sexual Feelings

A man has only one organ: his penis. He has been given no anatomical alternative. If, as happens in relatively rare cases, upsetting early experiences cause him to block off his sexual feelings, he simply becomes impotent. He will experience this impotence as a tremendous and tragic deprivation and will be powerfully motivated to overcome it. Those who have witnessed a man's sufferings with such a problem know just how powerful his drive back to health is.

♥*PRD: The Man's Version Is Oral Sex and Impotence in His 40s*

As we saw in Chapter 5, "Five Common Types of Sexual Inhibitions," the man's requirement for oral sex with his wife corresponds to the woman's need for clitoral orgasms with her husband. Then in Chapter 7, "Various Traumas Lead to Sexual Inhibitions," we learned that male impotence is much more frequent than Dr. Robinson was aware of as a psychiatrist for women. Additionally, specialists at the time believed that 90% of all cases of impotence were psychologically based. A man may suffer for decades with sexual inhibitions before impotence hits him in his 40s.

Science now knows that men have as many sexual hang-ups as women do, which also lead to cognitive distortions in the male.

Men Have Two Orgasms as Well: Masturbation and Penetration

If a man chooses masturbation, he inhibits himself just as much as the woman inhibits herself with masturbation of her clitoris. The woman who masturbates conditions her clitoris to respond to a hand or a vibrator rather than to a man awakening her vagina with his warm velvet-tipped penis. The man who chooses masturbation conditions his penis to respond only to a hand or a mouth instead of his wife's passionate vaginal hugs and soft cervical kisses.

Masturbation Leads to Low Sex Drive in Men

In 1976, 18 years after Dr. Robinson wrote her book, Tim LaHaye said in The Act of Marriage that a man's heavy use of masturbation is the most common cause of a low sex drive in a husband for his wife. He explained that a man often gets into the habit in his youth and carries it over into his marriage. When a couple comes to him for counseling because of a husband's low sexual interest, the first question he always asks is if the man masturbates (169).♥

A Woman's Vaginal Orgasms Reveal a Loving Personality

The loving female's orgasm takes place within the vagina. The fact that a woman can experience this kind of orgasm generally marks her as a fully developed woman in all aspects of her femininity.

♥PRD: The loving husband's orgasm also takes place within his wife's vagina. The fact that he can thrill to a penetration orgasm generally marks him as a fully developed man in all aspects of his masculinity.♥

Clitoral Orgasms Numb the Vagina and Reject the Penis

The clitoral orgasm takes place on the clitoris only. It numbs the vagina for enjoying sensual participation, and it is often independent of the male penis. This kind of orgasm is possible at an early stage in female development. If in growing up, the young girl becomes for any number of reasons frightened of mature vaginal sexuality, she can block that pathway. She can keep it blocked permanently without consciously experiencing any strong feelings of being deprived. She can do this because she is already having, as far as she knows, an amply satisfying experience through her clitoral orgasm. Since she has never experienced a sexual awakening, she doesn't know what she is missing. Consequently, she doesn't miss a vaginal orgasm.

♥PRD: Not only does the clitoral orgasm not require a penis, but the woman

doesn't even need to know the man's name that she is having sex with to enjoy it. This fact allows feminists to promote one-night stands for women to imitate their Victorian concept of male sexuality. They falsely assume sex is an unemotional, animalistic event for men and pursue the same for women.♥

The Clitoral Woman Isn't Motivated to Seek Loving Sex

You can see then that the woman who experiences only clitoral orgasms has no strong motive for moving on to the next stage of sexual maturity. Her developing sexuality was channeled off into a sensual cul-de-sac, and unless bold and conscious steps are taken, it tends to remain there. As the early years of growth move on into adolescence and further, the direction of her sexuality will not change, for she feels no reason to change it. Indeed, the channel grows deeper as the earlier method of sexual response becomes more ingrained. In the end, she can respond in no other way unless she determines to change her focus.

♥PRD: The Masturbating Man Isn't Motivated to Seek Loving Sex

Likewise, the man who orgasms through self-masturbation has no strong motive for moving on to the next stage of sexual development of vaginal intercourse. He can easily become a sexual addict who prefers fantasies and porn over learning how to make love with a real, live woman.

Such sex-withholding husbands often tell their wives, "Sex with you is too much trouble." Sure it is! Sharing vaginal orgasms requires emotional bonding with the wife. It takes time, thought, and work to maintain a loving relationship.

The Song of Solomon teaches soulmating before lovemaking for a lifetime of passion in each other's arms. King Solomon spurned putting in the effort to soulmate with any of his 1000 wives. When the Shulammite maiden told him she wouldn't marry him until after they soulmated, he refused. He never got the message that he could enjoy better sex with one wife than the porn-quality sex he had with 1000 women. He needed only to put in the emotional work.

Before Dr. Douglas Weiss coined the phrase "intimacy anorexic," Solomon exhibited all the classic characteristics of someone who thought putting the effort into enjoying sex emotionally was too much work. See my chapter "Solomon Never Had Great Sex with 1000 Virgins" in God's 11 Secrets of Sex.♥

The Lack of Sexual Love Leads to Two New Problems

1. Since such men and women are not advancing sexually, they tend to remain static emotionally.
2. If their fears of real masculinity and femininity are not resolved, they will begin to build up defenses of their childish emotional needs and

their childish methods of gratification.

♥PRD: Masturbation Stunts Emotional Growth

Masturbating to orgasm, whether done by oneself or with a partner, is addictive and can get in the way of the emotional bonding necessary for sharing vaginal intercourse. In contrast, sharing vaginal orgasms requires that a person keeps healthy attitudes toward the mate, oneself, and the sexual relationship.

Vaginal orgasms also demand that the man and the woman take care of the normal problems of life when they arise and refuse to let them fester. Having frequent sex pushes husbands and wives to grow up emotionally and to maintain orgasmic attitudes that promote ecstasy in each other's arms.

Masturbation, on the other hand, allows both men and women to stay locked within themselves with limited with immature ways of dealing with problems. Just as psychologists recognize that overuse of alcohol stunts the emotional growth of teenagers and adults, getting hooked on masturbation also stunts a person's emotional growth. Then instead of growing and working toward embracing one's masculinity or femininity, the person becomes defensive and protective of their dysfunctional way of relating sexually, and nothing changes.

Three Types of Masturbation in the Bible

Habitual self-masturbation is different than wet dreams that God designed to replace old semen with fresh when a man doesn't have a wife. It is different than a man masturbating when his wife is sick or out of town to drain off semen. Habitual solo-masturbation is often an inhibiting act of lust, not love. The Bible teaches three types of masturbation:

1. *Wet dreams (regulated in the Old Testament)*
2. *Spouse driven (temporary activity as when the mate is sick)*
3. *Lust driven (condemned by Jesus as mental adultery)*

I devote seven pages to these three types of masturbation in the Appendix: "Wet Dreams, Laws of Cleanness, and Masturbation" in God's 11 Secrets of Sex.

Masturbating to Images of the Husband or the Wife

One husband tried to nullify the harm of self-masturbation by asking, "What if the husband is thinking about his wife while he masturbates?"

Dr. Douglas Weiss says on his podcast "#43 To Masturbate or Not to Masturbate" that both husbands and wives assume if they're thinking about their mate, then no harm is done by solo-masturbation. He explains that even if they're thinking about their mate, they're not thinking about their husband or wife as they really are. They've turned their mate into a fantasy lover who may have different hair color, body build, and personality. Their redesigned mate may even act differently, perhaps more aggressively or passively. And the fantasy mate is always ready for sex.

When they engage in sex with their flesh-and-blood mate, they keep their eyes closed so they can make love to their fantasy partner instead of the person they're naked with. This is an example of "3. Lust driven" masturbation (condemned by Jesus as mental adultery) on the previous page.♥

Masturbation Accompanies Cognitive Distortions to Marriage

By the time the young man and woman are ready for marriage, they may already harbor full-blown cognitive distortions that work against the success of any close relationship.

This is how biology can represent destiny, with a helping hand from psychology. In a real sense, this dual potential of the man's and the woman's anatomy contains the seeds of sexual and personal tragedy.

♥*PRD: Anger and Cognitive Distortions Connected to Sexual Inhibitions*

It took reading Dr. Douglas Weiss's 2010 book Intimacy Anorexia and five years of analyzing participants' answers to the Sexless Marriages Survey for me to recognize that "cognitive distortions" are a significant part of the sexually inhibited man's and woman's character. Rather than being unusual, their angry, disruptive actions are to be expected and are directly related to their sexual inhibitions and frustrations.

Dr. Robinson had this information in this book for 60 years, and I missed it. I suspect part of the reason was her use of the word "neurosis" that is not specific enough for her lay readership. Also, at the time, most authors on sex thought as Dr. Robinson did, that if sexual difficulties existed, the wife was the primary one with the problem. Sex was supposed to be so natural for men that their wives often didn't recognize their husbands' sexual sins against them.

In looking back over 50 years as the confidante of both men and women, I can easily detect the signs of distorted thinking and anger in many of the inhibited men and women I worked with either directly or with their mate. I wish the connection of sexual inhibitions to anger and cognitive distortions had jumped out at me when I read this book in 1973. I would have taught comprehensively on the subject and known better how to hold others accountable.♥

The Inhibited Woman Is Confined to Clitoral Orgasms

Remember that the woman who is confined to clitoral orgasms is inhibited. Statistics on the prevalence of this sexual problem are not available, but most psychoanalysts agree it is widespread. It may even be the dominant form of sexual inhibitions in our society.

The Kinsey Report
Ignores the Different Kinds of Orgasms

Unhappily many women who suffer from this form of inhibitions have not been helped in past years by widely published and thoroughly erroneous views concerning sexual behavior in the human female. The Kinsey report, above all, has erred in this respect. It makes no distinction between vaginal and clitoral orgasms. Indeed, its authors passionately defend the view that all orgasms are clitoral. How trained observers could come to this conclusion is difficult to say.

♥*PRD: How the Myth of the Vaginal Orgasm Is Perpetuated*

Unfortunately, it's easy to understand how trained observers can conclude that the vaginal orgasm is a myth. In the introductory chapter to my book God's People Make the Best Lovers, I share information about the Kinsey report and Masters and Johnson's work on sexuality, plus other early researchers. The material shows how their work is flawed by the nature of their test subjects, many of whom had their partners supplied by the researchers. Without the emotional environment of love, it's impossible for a woman to experience a vaginal orgasm. Thus the assertion that the vaginal orgasm is a myth continues.

God's People Make the Best Lovers contains two chapters based on the sexually frustrated wife of Proverbs 7—an ancient version of the modern-day "cougar" who only had clitoral orgasms. One chapter examines the attitudes of the self-righteous wife who is addicted to techniques. The other chapter looks at the young man who visits her and is also addicted to different sexual practices. Both the emotionally hardened wife and the naive young man could have been some of Kinsey's test subjects.

Two chapters teach the power of orgasmic attitudes that lead to a ravishing love life. They examine the personality and character of husbands and wive who understand the emotional elements of a satisfying sexual relationship.♥

Women Quote Kinsey to Defend Cognitive Distortions

The sad thing, however, is that the Kinsey report is often used to bolster the defensive attitude of women who are able to achieve only clitoral orgasms. They can say to themselves that their method of gratification is perfectly normal; do they not have a tremendous body of "scientific" data to support their view? And somehow women with this difficulty find the Kinsey "results." Several women suffering from the kind of problem I have just described quoted Kinsey to me in defense of their method of gratification. And, having checked with several of my colleagues, I find that they all report similar experiences.

♥PRD: The Kinsey report and similar works still serve as the basis of many sex-education classes in schools and universities today, which help trap both men and women into emotionless methods of sexual gratification.♥

Clitoral Women Are Not Motivated to Seek Ecstasy

Women who suffer from any other form of sexual inhibitions are frequently motivated to face their problems by feelings of sexual frustration. Sooner or later, driven by natural hunger and desire, they will take steps to throw off the yoke of their difficulty.

Unfortunately, the woman who can have a clitoral orgasm has no such strong motivation. She can ruin her life and never be the wiser, never realize the reason why.

♥PRD: It doesn't help that many authors, bloggers, and speakers about female sexuality also promote clitoral and G-spot orgasms. They take their fans to the edge of sexual liberation by teaching somewhat about attitudes. But they stop short of victory by promoting self-masturbation and shaming husbands who don't manipulate their wives to orgasm.♥

Men and Women Must Face Their Dilemma

Therefore, I strongly advise that men and women who insist on masturbation, either by themselves or by their mate, be more than usually wary about their tendency to be complacent and that they become insistent about finding a way out of their *dilemma*. Above all, they must recognize their life situation as a *dilemma*, a serious *dilemma* that can be rationalized far too easily.

Men and Women Are Not to Blame for the Past

At this point, I wish to emphasize once more the role of the man's and the woman's responsibility in this matter of sexual response. They often feel a stronger-than-usual underlying irrational fear. Even when they admit they have a problem, this fear makes them hesitate to face up to their problem in any effective way. *Therefore, I wish to reiterate that nobody who suffers from this problem should feel shame or blame for it.*

1. You did not choose in any conscious sense to remain on this earlier and less "dangerous" plane of sexual development.

2. Your body made the choice, and you had nothing to say about that.

3. The strange dual sexuality of men and women is at the base of the matter.

4. It all happened because you misunderstood or misinterpreted "early"

experiences.

5. Or a grownup responsible for your early training was ignorant or misinformed.

♥PRD: See my article "Pullbacks and Terrified, Angry, Truth-Telling Child-Adults" in Part 2 for more information about why the inhibited man and woman are not to blame for their sexual inhibitions.♥

Men and Women Are Responsible for the Future

Now it is the better part of wisdom and valor for you to face up to the fact that your method of gratification is an expression of immaturity. Even if that immaturity was forced on you when you were too young to know the difference, don't fall back onto feelings of guilt and inferiority about the problem.

♥PRD: "Sexual Immaturity" Defined

*Dr. Robinson defines "sexual immaturity" in Chapter 20, "The Lore of Love and Sexual Positions" this way: "As a rule of thumb, I would say that any practice that does not culminate in vaginal intercourse tends to be regressive and infantile **if it becomes a chief method of sexual expression**." This definition fits both men and women. See Chapter 20 for more information.*

God Commands Christians to Learn About Sexual Love

The Bible teaches that both men and women can overcome their emotional hang-ups about sexual love if they "mean business." God commands them to put in the effort to learn how to enjoy ecstasy in their mate's arms:

> *1 Thessalonians 4:3-8: "For this is the will of God, your sanctification; that is, that you abstain from sexual immorality; that each of you know how to possess his own vessel in sanctification and honor, not in lustful passion, like the Gentiles who do not know God; and that no man transgress and defraud his brother in the matter because the Lord is the avenger in all these things, just as we also told you before and solemnly warned you. For God has not called us for the purpose of impurity, but in sanctification. So, he who rejects this is not rejecting man but the God who gives His Holy Spirit to you."*

God doesn't hold a person responsible for developing unhealthy attitudes toward sex as a child and during puberty while still under the authority of the parents. However, God expects that person to grow up emotionally and move beyond parental ignorance and superstition. Sexuality is learned—first in the home and then perfected as an adult. God commands Christians to learn and do better than their parents did.

God Condemns Christians Sexually Mistreating Their Mates

God takes it personally when Christians ignore their adult responsibilities and fail to learn how to love their mates sexually. Paul states, "He who rejects this is not rejecting man [the mate] but the God who gives His Holy Spirit to you [through his inspired words]." This passage (1 Thessalonians 4:3-8) is so important that I teach it verse-by-verse in God's People Make the Best Lovers.♥

It's Time to Move Forward into a Life of Indescribable Joy

Remember that you are not alone. Millions of men and women have the same problem. You can be the one who achieves the joys that lie just beyond this. They are real and solid delights, and they contain none of the terrors you thought they do. Not one.

Husbands Don't Like the Limitations of Clitoral Orgasms

One of the things I found helpful in motivating a woman with a clitoral problem is to present her with its effect on her husband. Women with this fixation have a curious inability to see these effects or to face them realistically. Even when such women know their form of gratification prevents them from enjoying greater sensations, they insist that their husbands do not mind the manual manipulation necessary to bring them to climax. They also claim their husbands prefer this method of sexual contact to intercourse. Such has never been the case in my years of clinical experience. Husbands do mind very much indeed.

Case Histories: Husbands Who Don't Like Clitoral Orgasms

One husband, whose wife was able to move on from her clitoral fixation, told me, "I feel like a man again. No matter what anybody says, your wife's response is the most important thing, and it's got to be a response in intercourse. If she doesn't respond that way, you gradually lose faith in yourself, and then you lose interest in making love."

Another man, whose wife has just come to me and who has only clitoral orgasms, said, "I may sound unsympathetic and petty, but if I felt there was no end in sight to this kid's stuff, I mean this form of having to stroke endlessly, I think I'd give up on the sex part. It's lost all its fun."

He'll get his fun back, for his wife, knowing a lot more than she did when she started, is intent on helping herself. And the husband is not unsympathetic or petty in his complaints. He is merely human, and there's a limit to human endurance.

♥*PRD: For the woman who has learned to enjoy vaginal intercourse, clitoral stroking and manipulations are annoying, a waste of time, and a hindrance to the real pleasure and emotional connection of penetration.♥*

Inhibited Spouses Ask for Help When Fearing Divorce

The wife's denial that the husband is bothered by a clitoral problem, I have found, is based on a deeper fear—the fear that her problem is endangering the marriage. Both of the women mentioned above (and many others I have treated) admitted that they came for help because they feared their marriage was headed for trouble, that their husbands were close to leaving them.

Husbands Are Not the Problem

The fact is, many men seem to have a high tolerance for this problem in their wives. I have yet to find any man who has broken up his marriage for that reason. Indeed, both the men I quoted above reassured me they could and would go on enduring their frustrations. They just strongly preferred not to.

♥PRD: The two case histories above involve wives with "partial sexual inhibitions." More than likely, the wife is not refusing sex and may even enjoy it. She simply has not learned how to respond to vaginal intercourse. Instead, she is insisting on clitoral manipulation by her husband. A husband's tolerance may be very different for a wife who is "totally sexually inhibited" or "in-between sexually inhibited." Please see Chapter 21: "31 Surprises About Sex from the Sexless Marriages Survey" in Part 2 to get a more accurate picture of how most husbands and wives feel about divorce and deeply inhibited spouses who withhold sex.♥

The Sexually Inhibited Woman Rejects Her Husband

No, the danger is not from the husband. The threat is from the woman herself. Because of her immaturity in not knowing how to enjoy and seek penetration, she will reject and blame her husband rather than face her problem. The real danger is that she will force the man away from her without even realizing she has done so.

♥PRD: Unfortunately, some of the promoters of clitoral orgasms tell women it's okay to refuse sex when their husbands deny them "clitoral" orgasms. These "authorities" have no understanding that the wives are cheating their husbands out of the joy of sharing vaginal orgasms and cervical kisses with them—different experiences and sensations for both the husbands and the wives than shared clitoral orgasms. This ill-conceived advice also deprives the wife of opportunities for activating and surrendering to vaginal passion.♥

Sexually Inhibited Women Are Evasive and Hide Facts

You can begin to see that the chief characteristic of women with this type of problem is evasiveness and hiding from the facts. It is as if they feared what they would find if they faced things. I can only tell them that they are not going to find a single thing that is frightening, not a single thing they cannot handle.

♥PRD: *Both Inhibited Men and Women Are Evasive and Hide Facts*

My experience is that the above paragraph is true about both men and women. However, getting the evasive spouse's attention to begin seriously working on the problem is extremely difficult. Dr. Weiss in Intimacy Anorexia says if the marriage goes on long enough, the sex-depriving spouse will become addicted to enjoying causing emotional and sexual pain to the mate. This so-called pleasure is also characteristic of spouse abusers who have progressed from "I'm so sorry and ashamed" into enjoying hurting their mates and children.♥

Inhibited Men and Women Look to Techniques for Solutions

I wish to cover one more attribute of the men and women whose sexual feelings have become fixed on masturbation, which, if they are forewarned, they should be suspicious of. It is the tendency to look for solutions for their problem in directions where no answers lie. I have treated women who have tried everything in their search for an easy resolution of their clitoral issue—drugs, surgery, even yoga.

One of the most widely used evasions can be found in the many popular manuals written, ostensibly, to tell one how to achieve a happy marriage. Such books, published in good faith, almost invariably counsel married partners to diversify their sexual positions during intercourse. Many of these books contain illustrations to drive their lesson home.

Variety Helps Only When Sex Is Good to Start With

Nothing is wrong with this advice in and of itself. Anybody with a little experience knows variety is one of the finest spices of love. However, the books generally neglect to say that such variety is only relevant to a sex life in which the partners have no deep-seated sexual problem to start with. By omitting that piece of information, these books give the strong tacit impression that various sexual positions will solve an already well-established sexual difficulty.

Variety Will Not Undo a Fixation on Masturbation

The desperate man and woman will seize on these implications as upon a panacea for their ills. I must state that the innumerable positions of love described in the Hindu Kamasutra (from which so many of our marriage manuals derive much of their information) will not undo a fixation on masturbation. The man and woman are asking for just one more emotional defeat if they insist that a solution lies in this direction.

The Three Things that Lead to Sexual Inhibitions

We have now seen the three things that make sexual inhibitions possible in both men and women. I will repeat them briefly so you will remember them later.

Reason 1: Orgasm Is Subject to Various Traumas

The man's and the woman's ability to enjoy wonderfully satisfying orgasms is affected by childhood traumas. Both major and minor traumas can lead them to unconsciously turn off their sexuality and ability to love their mate fully. To protect the propagation of the species, sometimes the sexual inhibitions do not show up until midlife in both men and women.

Reason 2: Orgasm Disappears with Fear of Parenthood

Parenthood calls for psychological and sometimes physical sacrifices for both mothers and fathers. It means parents must reverse the natural law of self-preservation and put their children's welfare ahead of their own. The woman's fear of pregnancy and childbirth and the man's adverse reaction to fatherhood hinders their orgasm sensations.

Reason 3: Orgasm Is Harmed by Masturbation

In effect, both the man and the woman have two choices for sexual contact—masturbation or penetration. The husband chooses either oral or vaginal sex, and the wife chooses either clitoral or vaginal sex. Both the husband and the wife can turn off their desires for their mate through solo-masturbation. Choosing masturbation is immature, evades true masculinity and femininity, and is considered a form of sexual inhibition. However, millions of men and women find this method of gratification so satisfying that they are not motivated to move up to the mature level of sharing vaginal orgasms with cervical kisses.

10.

The Awakening of Orgasmic Love

One of our medical school courses studied the psychological stages of development man goes through from infancy to maturity. It included the various pitfalls people encounter during these stages, the biological and psychological experiences that can prevent them from reaching psychological maturity.

The Body and the Mind Gravitate Toward Health and Maturity

During one class in which we reviewed the psychological hazards of adolescence, a student raised his hand and was recognized by the professor. "How does anyone ever really grow up?" the student asked.

The class laughed. But the professor took the question seriously and complimented the student for his acuity. He then addressed us for a half-hour on the indomitable and surging drive of the human body and mind toward health and pleasure.

This Drive Can Overcome Many Obstacles

This drive can often overcome seemingly insurmountable obstacles. However, it may pause at times, apparently defeated, only to revive its original energy and to resume its move toward the goal of health and maturity.

We see this drive daily in people who come for psychiatric help, and we know that it is the most critical element in psychological healing. As soon as the difficulty holding the person back has been resolved, his whole mind and body tend once again to resume their move toward health and happiness. It is well to keep this factor in mind as we explore the stages of development women go through on their way to adulthood.

The Feminine Woman Is a Delightful Sexual Partner

We have seen the grownup, truly feminine woman in operation. You will remember that she is a delightful partner in that closest and most perfect expression of love, the sexual act. A great part of her personality is organized around her maternal instinct. The chief characteristic of that instinct is her pleasure in giving, her unappeasable altruism that always puts husband and child before herself, even to the point of risking her own life and welfare.

Her central activities revolve around her nest building and childrearing. Her personality reflects deep intuitiveness about others. She devotes her energies to that deepest of all needs, the procreation of the race of man through her own body.

How Did the Feminine Woman Get This Way?

By contrast, the feminine woman's husband is aggressive, occupied with his struggles in the outside world. Her stage and focus of her main interest is the home, its preservation, and its happiness.

How did she get this way? Or, in the case of women who fail to achieve a truly feminine personality, what actually happens, how do they get that way?

Women Go Through Development Stages

To answer these questions, one must first understand the stages of development that all women go through in growing up. These phases have been under the closest scientific scrutiny for several decades. The realization of their importance for psychological health and illness has been one of modern psychiatry's major achievements. They have been thoroughly explored, and if we do not yet know all that we can learn about the subject, we still know a great deal.

Problems Rooted in Infancy, Childhood, or Adolescence

The material I am about to go into is a scientific fact, not an opinion. If the information seems new or strange or even irritating to you, do not be surprised or upset. It is new and strange to most people. At first, it may not seem applicable to you. But if you will stay with it, use it to understand the case histories that I will discuss afterward, you will gradually see why understanding these phases is so necessary and helpful to the individual who has not yet achieved her full femininity.

All psychological problems are rooted in infancy, childhood, or in adolescence. To uproot these problems, we must return to those stages of development with new tools, new ideas, and a new master plan.

Two Stages of Growth and Development

Every individual must go through two basic stages of biological and psychological development. The first stage lasts from birth to about ten years of age. In turn, this stage is divided into two phases. We call the first phase infancy, and it lasts roughly for the first five years of life. We call the second phase the latency period, and it occupies the second five years of life.

♥PRD: *Overview of a Girl's Sexual Development*

The following is an overview of Dr. Robinson's discussion of the two stages of a girl's sexual development that lead her toward a successful marriage:

1. *The first stage has two 5-year parts:*
    1) *Infantile Period—Ages 1 to 5—Sexuality develops alongside personality*
    2) *Latency Period—Ages 6 to 10—Sexuality goes underground*
2. *The second stage has two parts:*
    1) *Puberty Period—ages 10 to 13, 14, or 15—Sexuality is awakened as the body begins to change, and the preteen learns about sex.*
    2) *Adolescence Period—ages 13, 14, or 15 to Maturity—Sexuality goes back underground as the girl enters the Daydreaming Stage to prepare for motherhood.*
3. *Marriage—The husband awakens the mature woman's desire for vaginal lovemaking.*

A boy's sexual development follows a similar path with some notable variations. For more information on the boy's road to maturity, see my chapter "Radical Epiphany on Awakening Male-Female Sexuality" in Part 2.♥

The Infantile Period: The Child's Personality Develops for the Rest of Her Life

The first five years of growth, the infantile period, is of enormous importance for later development. In this phase, the whole personality takes shape and develops the characteristics that will distinguish it from that time on.

The Child's Sexuality Develops Alongside Her Personality

At this point, I have to note a scientific fact that may surprise or disconcert you. I ask you to withhold any prejudices of a personal or a moral kind you may have about this fact, for they will only obscure the issue and make it difficult for you to understand a critical contribution science has made to the understanding of the human mind.

The decisive fact about the infantile period is that the little creature is heavily endowed with intense sexual feelings. The students of this subject are in absolute agreement on this point. There is no longer the slightest inkling of a doubt about it. All scientific methods of checking the fact have been employed. These range from direct observation of children to the recovery of childhood memories through hypnosis or while subjects are under the influence of hypnotic drugs, direct reports from children, and several other sources.

First Three Years: Child Is Primarily Attached to Her Mother

For the first three years, the little girl is deeply and primarily attached to her mother. In the sense that infants "realize" things, the little girl knows that her mother is the source of all her security. These feelings have a clear sensual nature.

♥*PRD: Boys and Girls Learn to Love Through the Mother's Touch*

Dr. Robinson wrote The Power of Sexual Surrender in 1959. Dr. Ashley Montagu wrote Touching: The Human Significance of the Skin in 1971. He was regarded as "one of the few experts on just about everything to do with people." He had written over 60 books on varied subjects such as anatomy and physiology, psychology, anthropology, race, love, aggression and touching, and human development. In the 1986 third edition of his book, Dr. Montagu added the chapter "Skin and Sex." He explained how the child begins to learn about sex:

> *By being stroked, and caressed, and carried, and cuddled, comforted, and cooed to, by being loved, the child learns to stroke and caress and cuddle, comfort and coo, and to love others. In this sense, love is sexual in the healthiest sense of that word. It implies involvement, concern, responsibility, tenderness, and awareness of the needs, sensibilities, and vulnerabilities of the other. All this is communicated to the infant through the skin in the early months of his life and gradually reinforced by feeding, sound, and visual cues as the infant develops. The primacy of the infant's first perceptions of reality through the skin can no longer be doubted. The messages he receives through that organ must be security-giving, assuring, and pleasurable if the infant is to thrive. Even in food intake, as Brody has shown in her excellent study of mothering, "save under conditions of body security and comfort no infant, however hungry, appeared to enjoy his feeding" (217).*

Dr. Montagu's views correspond with the Maiden saying she had observed that the Shepherd grew up in the same kind of loving home she and her brothers did:

Song of Solomon 8:1:
"Oh that you were like a brother to me
Who nursed at my mother's breasts.

If I found you outdoors, I would kiss you;
No one would despise me, either."

The Shulammite knows they will enjoy a sexually happy marriage because they both began to learn how to love at their mothers' breasts—skin on skin.♥

The Little Girl May Start to Masturbate

The little girl loves to be close to the mother, be stroked by her, and to have her mother clean her genitalia. She associates her masturbation with the pleasant sensations she receives, psychologically and physically, from her mother.

♥*PRD: Masturbation Is Often a Sign of Not Enough Parental Touching*

Dr. Montagu warned that masturbation is usually the result of not enough parental tactile love during the early years:

> *Early deprivations of tactile experience may lead to behavior calculated to provide substitutes for such tactile deprivations in the form of self-manipulation of various kinds, masturbation and toe-, finger-, or thumb-sucking, pulling or fingering the ears, nose, or hair. It is an interesting fact that among nonliterate peoples who generally give their children all the tactile stimulation they require, finger-sucking or thumb-sucking seldom occurs. Moloney, for example, writes: "My observations in Africa, Tahiti, and the islands around Tahiti, the Fiji Islands, Islands in the Caribbean, Japan, Mexico and Okinawa confirmed for me the fact that most babies in these areas are breastfed and carried on the person of the mother. In these areas I noted that thumb sucking was practically non-existent" (221-222).*

Parents Can Protect Their Children From the Need to Masturbate

To avoid a problem with masturbation, Dr. Mantagu offered suggestions on how parents can protect their children under the heading "Tactile Deprivation and Excessive Masturbation in Children":

> *The relationship between tactile deprivation in infancy and childhood and sex is clearly evident in the many reported cases of early excessive masturbation in children. In the absence or withdrawal of warm tactile stimulation, the child sometimes turns to its own body for gratification. Dr. Glen McCray, in a report of five cases, four girls and one boy, found that excessive masturbation may be produced by actual or fantasized withdrawal of parental affection and may also appear with the birth of a new sibling, prolonged absence of a parent, or actual loss by divorce or death. In each of Dr. McCray's cases, excessive masturbation ceased when parental attitudes changed, and the parents were able to*

reinstitute appropriate tactile stimulation. Touching, holding, patting, wrestling, or any other game which involved a good deal of body contact was encouraged and carried out by those parents able to subdue their own erotic feelings in deference to the child's need for physical contact (224).

God Uses the Example of a Loving Mother to Describe His Love

Notice how God uses the example of a loving mother touching her child in various ways to describe his love for his people:

Isaiah 66:10-13:
"Be joyful with Jerusalem and rejoice for her, all you who love her;
Be exceedingly glad with her, all you who mourn over her,
That you may nurse and be satisfied with her comforting breasts,
That you may suck and be delighted with her bountiful bosom."
For thus says the Lord, "Behold, I extend peace to her like a river,
And the glory of the nations like an overflowing stream;
And you will be nursed, you will be carried on the hip and fondled on the knees.
"As one whom his mother comforts, so I will comfort you;
And you will be comforted in Jerusalem."

Dr. Montagu's whole chapter discusses the effect of childhood touching versus the lack of touching on the husband's and the wife's sexual responses.

Dr. Robinson's Observations Made Close to the Victorian Era

Dr. Robinson wrote in the first chapter "Paradise Lost for Men and Women" that people in their thirties probably had "parents who were reared in the traditions of Victorianism, which denied the sexuality of women. They connived with every available force to deny a woman's sexuality, repress it, and stop it at its source. These efforts were extraordinarily successful."

Generally, the Victorians were cold emotionally and unloving toward their children. So probably most of the women Dr. Robinson worked with grew up without sufficient touching from their mothers and fathers. Masturbation would have been their way of trying to replace the missing parental touch of love. No wonder they had trouble relating to their husbands with warm sexual passion.

Today with many mothers working to help pay bills, many children will continue to be denied enough parental touch to grow up into loving sexual beings. Indeed, masturbation during childhood may continue to be a characteristic of women with sexual inhibitions.♥

Around 3 Years Old Girl's Attachment Grows for Her Father

Around three years of age, the little girl becomes aware of her growing attachment to her father. His tenderness and play with her stimulate her whole being, and her sensuality becomes increasingly attached to him. At first, she is not aware of the conflict in this attachment. However, as her little mind becomes a bit more aware of reality, she vaguely and incompletely senses that her increasingly sensual response to her father puts her into competition with her mother. Her mother is another woman who has a prior claim on her first man!

The Girl Begins to Compete with Her Mother

At this point, she begins to develop hostile feelings toward her mother. The whole thing seems too fantastic! A little child competing with her mother for her father's love? Impossible!

♥*PRD: The Boy's Attachment Grows for His Mother*

This same scenario happens for the young boy, only his attachment grows for his mother, the model for his future wife. He may also develop hostile feelings toward his father.♥

Case History: At Age 5 Girl Dreamed of Marrying Her Father

Let me give you a clear example of a typical dream my women patients have. An inhibited woman had several consultations with me. In one of them, she suddenly remembered that at the age of five, she was convinced her father would marry her when she grew up. She had buried that memory in her mind, only to resurrect it in therapy.

That night she dreamed she was lying in a crib. A tall thin man with glasses and a mustache was lying on a bed nearby. A stout, florid-faced woman lay next to him. Suddenly this woman had a convulsive seizure and, after a few moments of writhing, became still. The man then looked at her and smiled as if pleased. "She's dead," he said. Then he rose from the bed, went to the crib, and picked my patient up. "We will have four," he said to her, and she felt immeasurably excited and pleased.

My patient woke up in a state of anxiety. In our session, she told me her father was tall, thin, and sometimes wore glasses to read in bed. Her mother was stout and high-colored. My patient suddenly recalled that in the childhood fantasy of marriage to her father, she decided to have four children with him. Her logic was this: her mother had three children; she would go her mother one better!

Patients Confirm the Childhood Love Triangle

I cannot tell you how often we psychiatrists get, directly from our patients, confirmation of the existence of an early triangle between mother, father, and child. It naturally causes a conflict in the child. This early conflict in the little girl takes place so subtlely that its existence escaped the conscious notice of mankind from the dawn of history until the end of the nineteenth century.

♥PRD: One client's 4-year-old daughter told him, "Daddy, I'm going to marry you."

A grandmother asked her 3-year-old granddaughter who brought the flowers sitting in a vase on the kitchen bar. She glowed, "My daddy brought them to me! I love him! But I share the flowers with Mommy."

My youngest brother was 3 when I started dating my future husband. He happened to see my boyfriend kiss me. Mom told me later that my baby brother had kissed her in a way he never had before and said, "I'm Toots!" which is what he called my boyfriend.♥

Nature Set Up the Conflict Between Mother and Daughter

I described this early source of conflict to a woman patient recently in much the same way I described it here. After pondering for a moment, she asked a question that goes to the heart of the matter. "If this early situation causes a conflict in the child, which can lead to cognitive distortions later, why did nature design things that way? I thought nature set things up to foster growth, not to hinder it."

The Conflict Pushes the Child to Grow

The observation raised a point that is generally ignored. Nature designed this early sexual conflict for a special reason. The competition with her mother fosters the little girl's growth and pushes her on to the next step in developing her femininity and a little farther along the path to her ultimate role of wife and mother.

Girl Focuses on Her Mother as Sexual Feelings Develop

Let me explain this a bit further. For the first few years, by the very nature of family life, all the little girl's feelings are focused on her mother. Her mother is the center, the fountain of life itself. The little one looks to her for food, security on all levels, and "love." This love soon becomes tinged with a strong erotic feeling connected with the little one's growing sensuality, which is centered on her mother.

Erotic Feelings for Her Father Make Her "Man-Centered"

It is necessary for humans to love and to have erotic feelings centered on others. But if this early love situation did not change at some point, the little girl would grow up to have women as her erotic centers of interest. Nature intends no such result. She intends these erotic feelings to become ultimately very much man-centered.

Thus nature makes the role of the father in the child's development all-important. He becomes the first bridge from the infantile erotic and dependent relationship with the mother to mature relationships with members of the opposite sex. The growing girl will have to traverse several other bridges on her journey to maturity, but this first one is of central importance.

Girl's Father Remains a Role Model for Her Future Husband

Ultimately, she will give up her father as the center of erotic interest. But he will remain in her unconscious life as the model of all that she wants from the male in her life.

Girl's Infantile Sexuality Ends at About 5 Years Old

At the end of this early development phase is the first big step in preparing the little girl for her destiny as wife and mother. But since she is nowhere near ready for such functions, we might wonder how nature ends this early period and enters the second stage of growth.

The Latency Period: Consists of 5 Years of Non-Sexuality

The end of the first stage and the beginning of the second (which will last to about 10 years of age) commences with a remarkable psychological event: the early infantile sexuality goes completely underground. The little girl "forgets" that she ever went through such sensual experiences and that she faced anything the least bit erotic in her former attachments. Her masturbation stops under normal circumstances, and she enters into approximately a five-year period of total non-sexuality.

Forgotten Sexual Memories Continue to Influence Her

When I use the word "forget," I do not mean it literally. In psychiatry, we use the word "repression" to describe this kind of forgetting. It refers to the human mind's ability to push anything it does not wish to recall out of awareness into a part of the mind called the unconscious. When we repress a memory or experience, we do not remember that it ever happened with our conscious mind. However, it remains intact in our unconscious mind and can and does exert an influence on us that we are not aware of. It can be revived in the conscious mind by later experiences, or, even if it does not revive, later experiences can be influenced by the "forgotten" memory.

The Latency Period Is for Physical and Mental Growth

The new stage into which the young girl now enters is called the "latency period" because the sexual feelings of the earlier period have become repressed or latent. The latency period is chiefly characterized by an attempt on the little girl's part to understand and master her environment. Tremendous physical and mental growth marks this period. She is interested in everything that gives her a chance to advance herself physically: rope-jumping, doll-playing, ball-playing, swimming, climbing, and running.

♥PRD: "Latency" means "the state of existing but not yet being developed or manifest; concealment."♥

Sometimes the Girl Is a Tomboy

Sometimes, almost nothing that she does, feels, or thinks in this period distinguishes her in any critical manner from a little boy of the same age. She may be a bit more obedient, a bit better about doing her homework than a boy, but not dramatically so.

The Child Grows Up Mentally and Physically

We may ask what nature's intention is in bringing on this latency period. Let me put it this way. Nature simply wishes to give the child a chance to grow a little mentally, learn to master her body and mind, and integrate her earlier development phase. She learns how to form personal relationships so that when she comes to the next phase marked by menstruation and female maturation, she will be ready.

Sexuality Continues to Develop Alongside the Personality

Think about what would happen if the little girl were plunged from the stresses and strains of infantile sexuality directly into full sexual readiness. Her body might be ready, but psychologically she would have no understanding of her environment, no idea of personal relationships, and no sense of herself or her abilities.

♥PRD: The Child May Mask His or Her Personality to Survive

The fact that sexuality develops alongside the personality is one reason working to take off the dysfunctional survival personality mask can help overcome adult sexual issues. However, the young child is not intellectually equipped to be a fully functioning sexual person. Her sexuality goes underground to blossom when it's appropriate.

See "The Connection Between Personality and Sexuality" in Part 2 for more information on how the boy's and the girl's sexuality and personality develop side by side. If the personality is thwarted, their sexuality will also be affected.♥

Nature Tries to Avoid "A Child's Mind in a Woman's Body"

With too early sexual activity, the young girl would have, as the actress Elizabeth Taylor noted of herself and her reaction to a too-early plunge into grownup experiences, "a child's mind in a woman's body." Nature intends no such dilemma for women. If the parents co-operate, nature's step-by-step plan leads the woman safely to the haven of physical and psychological maturity.

♥*PRD: Song of Solomon Instructs Parents to Protect Their Children*

A major takeaway from the Song of Solomon is the answer to the wedding riddle at the end of the story:

Song of Solomon 8:8:
"We have a little sister,
And she has no breasts;
What shall we do for our sister
On the day when she is spoken for?"

The little sister has not reached the puberty stage of personality and sexual development—she has no breasts yet. How does the family protect her from getting into a disastrous marriage? The Shulammite answered that each child needs to be protected individually. The child needs teaching and dating privileges according to his or her personality, character, and self-control.♥

The Girl Still Needs Her Father's Admiration

The latency period marks a close relationship with the parents, especially the father. However, now the girl feels no conscious sexual feelings attached to him. She admires and values her father above all others and wants his admiration and high regard. Most fathers instinctively give their daughters a great deal of love and reassurance during this phase. The child basks in her father's attention as a flower in the sun.

She Tries to Please Her Father and Make Him Notice Her

She strives to do the things that will please her father, make him notice her, and make him love her. She studies his responses assiduously, and in this way, she receives her first real experience with the all-important feminine need to "please her man." The feelings of joy she gets from his pleasure in her accomplishments, physical and mental, are the precursors of the rewards she will later prize so highly when bestowed on her by a loving husband.

Her Father Helps Develop Her Femininity

As you might suspect, this period is essential to her development into full womanhood with its varied psychological give-and-take. If the father seriously fails in his role during this period, he can do irreparable harm to the growing girl.

Her Mother Emerges as a Model for Her to Imitate

The mother's role continues to be important too. The little girl has repressed her guilt feelings toward her mother, along with all of her directly sensual feelings. During the latency period, her mother emerges as a model to imitate. In effect, the little girl says something like this to herself: "Mom, after all, got the man I prize most highly in the whole world. Therefore, she must have something desirable. Therefore, I'll imitate it." She proceeds to do just that.

Of course, I do not mean that this is all there is to her feelings about her mother. She loves her mother deeply and abidingly, and without her would feel and be grief-stricken. Her imitation of her mother is a tribute to those feelings too. However, I am selecting those aspects of the child's relationships that directly impact her later sexual maturity.

♥*PRD: The Shulammite's Mother Taught Her About Sex*

The Shulammite maiden in the Song of Solomon credits her mother with teaching her about sex, not only how to please her husband, but also how to enjoy lovemaking herself. Her mother began this teaching by nursing her and teaching her that touching feels good and shows love:

Song of Solomon 8:1-3:
"Oh that you were like a brother to me
Who nursed at my mother's breasts.
If I found you outdoors, I would kiss you;
No one would despise me, either.
I would lead you and bring you
Into the house of my mother, who used to instruct me;
I would give you spiced wine to drink from the juice of my pomegranates.
Let his left hand be under my head
And his right hand embrace me."

Then the maiden repeated the theme of the Song of Solomon—soulmate before lovemaking—take time to create a strong emotional bond before marriage and engaging in sex:

Song of Solomon 8:4:
"I want you to swear, O daughters of Jerusalem,
Do not arouse or awaken my love
Until she pleases."

This premarital theme of emotional bonding corresponds with Dr. Robinson's theme throughout this book. She states in chapter 18 that sharing orgasms is the result of psychological health and proper attitudes in the following four areas for both men and women:

1. *The opposite sex*
2. *Lovemaking*
3. *Parenthood*
4. *The mate*

Healthy, loving attitudes in the above four areas comprise the orgasmic attitudes that free the man's and the woman's bodies for sharing ecstasy.♥

The Puberty Period: Starts at About Age 10 and Ends with Complete Maturation

The next development stage starts at approximately the age of ten and ends with the individual woman's complete psychological and biological maturation. It is often divided into two phases; the first phase, which lasts until thirteen, fourteen, or fifteen, we call puberty; the second, by that much-misunderstood word "adolescence."

Puberty Ushers in Great Glandular Changes

Through great glandular changes in the child, the young body begins to take on the semblance of womanhood. Breasts begin to grow; pubic hair appears. Gradually the uterus, or womb, stirs, begins to expand, readies itself to hold the child, which will ultimately grow there. In the midst of this preparatory growth, menstruation starts in earnest with the cyclical ebb and flow of fertility. In a few months, the child stands just within the portal of physical maturity.

Puberty Releases Rather Strong Sexual Feelings

The little girl now again (for the first time since infancy) begins to experience relatively strong sexual feelings, and she reacts to them with some anxiety.

The Girl May Start to Masturbate Clitorally

She may start once more to masturbate clitorally, although this time the act is accompanied by feelings of guilt and apprehension. As I pointed out, these feelings of anxiety can be thought of as justified.

♥PRD: Review earlier comments about masturbation, that it's a sign of not enough parental touching when boys and girls were an infant and young child.

Boys Have Nocturnal Wet Dreams

During puberty, boys begin to experience wet dreams as their penis begins to have a mind of its own. Parents need to teach their boys about God's purpose for wet dreams and talk to them about how their body is preparing them to be a husband and a father.

Unfortunately, due to Kinsey interviewing sex offenders for his research, he failed to recognize the role masturbation plays in perversions and how it can easily become compulsive. Today schools teach masturbation as a safe outlet for draining off sexual energies. Some programs encourage masturbation as a way to avoid AIDS and other sexually transmitted diseases. Without their parents teaching them otherwise, young boys may take up masturbation instead of allowing wet dreams to occur naturally. They don't understand the risks of addiction that accompany self-stimulation. They are dangerously naive.

Review my chapter "Radical Epiphany on Awakening Male-Female Sexuality" in Part 2 for more information on the boy's sexual development. Also see my appendices chapter "Wet Dreams, Laws of Cleanness, and Masturbation" in God's 11 Secrets of Sex for additional teaching on wet dreams and masturbation. Alert your son to the epic way God created the male body for sharing love.

Survey of Junior and High School Boys on Watching Porn

Until his death, Oscar Miles, a licensed Christian family therapist and gospel preacher, worked with young men and their fathers and taught sex-education classes at teen retreats. His classes helped the young men avoid and overcome sexual addiction. Oscar conducted the following survey in 2008 with junior and high school boys to assess the damage Internet porn does to our young men whose parents are Christians:

9-10th Graders (age 14-16)

20% Never viewed Internet porn
33% Viewed on accident
47% Viewed on purpose
20% Still viewing occasionally or somewhat regularly
13% Admitted viewing homosexual porn on the Internet

11-12th Graders (age 16-19)

90% Viewed Internet porn "on purpose"
67% Still viewing occasionally or somewhat regularly
22% Viewing it "somewhat regularly"
22% Admitted to viewing homosexual porn
11% Admitted to having an interest in homosexual porn

When Oscar taught plain sexual material to high-school boys, they often asked, "Why didn't someone tell us these things when we were in junior high before we developed these bad habits (compulsive masturbation and addiction to pornography) that require so much hard work to overcome?" Upon learning Oscar would give them honest help, many of these young men drove long distances to counsel with him.♥

The Girl Knows Her Sexuality Will Lead to Motherhood

The girl's sexuality will lead to motherhood, which means she will have to face the dangers of pregnancy and childbirth, the biological need to put her child's welfare ahead of her own. In effect, she will need to suspend the law of self-preservation as it applies to her own person.

Prudish Preteens Seem to Find Out the Facts of Life

The little girl knows this. She knows it with her body and mind, for even the most prudish child cannot be prevented from finding out the facts of life. If her parents have not told her, she will soon find out all about life from her girlfriends.

♥PRD: Preteens is the perfect age for teaching young girls and boys the Song of Solomon. I was privileged to teach "The Song of Solomon for Teenagers, Their Mothers and Grandmothers, Ages 11 to 99" at a couple of congregations.

I observed a difference in the body language between preteens and teenagers. The preteens listened with smiles on their faces and sometimes leaned forward. In contrast, the teenage girls often sat back in their seats with their arms folded across their chests as if to say, "You're not going to teach me anything."

The Song of Solomon is God's answer to the problem of sex education in schools and homes. It's written as poetry, so you can teach the basic story to young children. Then as your children mature and ask questions, you can supply details without embarrassment. Helping your children fall in love with the Song of Solomon protects them from many of the pitfalls of dating.♥

She Functions Between Anxiety and Pleasure

The new changes in her cause apprehension. They also produce feelings of joy, excitement, and intense curiosity. Throughout her entire puberty, she will run between the two emotions of anxiety and pleasure.

The Girl May Love-Hate the Changes in Her Body

At times she will look back in envy at the blissful latency period when she was not bothered by these powerful indications of her biological destiny, which lies immediately ahead. She will hate her developing breasts, her menstrual period, and the hair growing under her arms and around her genitalia. At other moments she will rapturously embrace these same changes.

Withdraws from Parental Love to Prepare for Romantic Love

At this point, she withdraws from her parents to a large extent. As we saw in the latency period, nature must prepare her biologically and psychologically for womanhood. If the little girl were to maintain the total dependency on her parents that she has had up to this point, she would not be able to develop the fullness of her personality, strength, and individuality necessary for successful wifehood and motherhood.

But she is not a woman yet by any means. Do not get that impression, for she must take some vital steps first. The attempt some girls make to embrace full sexuality and femininity around the age of 14 or 15 is generally disastrous.

Flutters Between Dependency on Parents and Rebellion

In normal development, she will flutter between strong feelings of dependency on her parents and rebellion against them, or rather rebellion against her intense desire to be a little girl with them again. The success of this phase is marked by achieving the feeling that she has the "potentiality," not the "actuality," of freedom from her parents.

The Girl Shares Secrets with a Special Girlfriend

At some point during this period, the girl will become dramatically attached to a girlfriend. This fact is so unalterable in normal development that the whole period of puberty is often referred to as "the chum stage." This friendship buttresses her feelings of separateness and independence from her parents. The two share secrets constantly and pool their information on all matters pertaining to sex, boys, women, and childbirth. Their friendship provides a liberal education for both and should be encouraged for the most part. The girlfriend is sometimes older by a year or two or three, and the younger one's worship of her is clearly a substitute for her feelings toward her mother. If the older girl is not too precocious sexually, good can come from this relationship.

Puberty Merges Gradually into Adolescence—The Daydreaming Stage

Gradually, puberty merges into adolescence. This is the last stage before maturity. I call this whole period the "daydream stage." It is a period of almost literal waking dreams on the part of the young woman. She is still held lightly by the long preparatory sleep of childhood and early youth, but she is ready to wake.

Young Woman Makes Maternal and Humanitarian Life Plans

The young woman's head is filled with tremendous plans for herself. These plans usually have a high maternal and humanitarian character about them. She will become a great doctor and serve suffering humanity in darkest Africa. Or she will become a lawyer and defend the poor free of charge. Or she will become a nurse and, under fire that would daunt a lesser creature, she will tend the wounded among our boys at the front. She has scores of great loves with boys or men whom she considers wonderful—all in her head.

The Young Woman's Dreams Ready Her for Real Love

The satisfaction of her now nearly mature maternal and sexual impulses through such dreams is clear. But they serve another function, which is perhaps obscure. She is not ready for real love yet. She still has one foot in childhood and one foot in adulthood. She still is reluctant to give herself wholly to the realities of adulthood. She needs to hang upon the tree for a few more years to ripen a bit. In most cases, the great roles she plays in her daydreams are not achievable. By the impossibility of their fruition, they allow her to have her cake and eat it too.

Man Is an Aggressive Doer; Woman Is a Romantic Dreamer

Yes, the dream of young love is a long and lovely one, and it readies the dreamer for real love. The woman will always be a romantic dreamer, a weaver of inner reflections, of tapestries of thought that give her personality its richness and flavor. In love, as in life, the man is a doer, an aggressive achiever. The woman is the passive one. She is the dreamer who values the man's achievements, who creates the need for his achievement and gives color and glory to it through her appreciation of it. The dreams of adolescence ready her for this role with her man.

May Be a Lot of Petting with the Opposite Sex

Adolescence is a gradual preparation for true sexuality and love. In it, the young girl conquers her impulse to masturbate, though in certain rather "free" communities, a great deal of petting with the opposite sex may go on. If the girl puts the high value on herself that is characteristic of this period, she will not have sexual intercourse until she falls in love seriously.

♥*PRD: Petting Can Set a Young Girl Up for Sexual Inhibitions*

The impression Dr. Robinson gives that petting is okay as long as it doesn't lead to sexual penetration is a dangerous one. The Sexless Marriages Survey reveals that wives, who were sexually active growing up and engaged in petting, often entered marriage with severe sexual inhibitions. They accused their husbands of groping their breasts, gave quick pecks instead of real kisses, and avoided sex as much as possible. They never flirted with their husbands.

No doubt, these experiences harmed these wives. Following are some scriptures that apply to petting for both boys and girls:

A Girl's Breasts Are Part of Her Virginity

When God addressed the Israelites as his wife, he chastised them for their unfaithfulness with Egyptian idols. The scene God described in common with petting, fondling of the girl's or woman's breasts:

> *Ezekiel 23:3: "...and they played the harlot in Egypt. They played the harlot in their youth; there their **breasts** were pressed, and there their **virgin bosom** was handled."*

Interestingly, the words translated "breasts" and "bosom" come from two different Hebrew words. The first word means "the breasts of a woman or animal (as bulging)" (Strong 112). It's a plain biological term for labeling body parts. The second word means "the breasts (as the seat of love)" (Strong 24). It refers to giving the breasts as a reflection of love.

Proverbs 5:19-20 contrasts the two types of breasts as Solomon compares the benefits of an older wife with a harlot. The word for the older wife's "breasts" includes love. But the word for the foreigner's "bosom" is another biological term that refers to the hollow between the breasts—it involves no emotion at all. A wife's attitude of love captures her husband's heart and satisfies him and her in the giving of her body.

The two words for "breasts" in Ezekiel show that it doesn't matter why a woman gives her breasts to a man—whether she gives them to him just as a warm body, the biological term, for a physical thrill, or if she gives her breasts to him because she loves him. The woman's motives and feelings don't matter when she gives her breasts to someone who has no right to touch or kiss them. Fondling the breasts outside marriage is still part of sexual immorality or fornication. (This excerpt comes from God's People Make the Best Lovers.)

Kissing Can Fool a Girl into Thinking She's in Love

To be clear about dating, the Song of Solomon begins with the Shulammite maiden longing for her shepherd boyfriend's kiss:

Song of Solomon 1:2:
"May he kiss me with the kisses of his mouth!
For your love is sweeter than wine."

God doesn't condemn kissing in courtship, but kissing is also part of married foreplay. Following is an excerpt from God's 11 Secrets of Sex to highlight the dangers of kissing in courtship:

Jack Schafer, Ph.D., in "Odd Facts About Kissing," sheds light on the Shulammite's craving her Shepherd's kisses of love. It seems that the moist mucus membranes inside the mouth are perfect for absorbing the man's hormones. "Through open-mouth kissing, men introduce testosterone into a woman's mouth." Testosterone increases a woman's libido and arouses her for sex. Schafer says, "Men prefer open-mouth kissing with tongue contact when kissing short-term partners to increase the probability of mating" (12/2012).

Since deep kissing releases hormones, which stir up sexual feelings, it's not a safe practice for beginning a relationship. Kissing can fool a woman into thinking she loves a man when she's just reacting to the dose of testosterone he injects into her system. The moist mucus membranes may make it even more effective than if he used a hypodermic needle to inject his drug of choice.

Case History: Kissing Fooled Woman into Thinking She Was in Love

Upon learning this, one woman said, "When I started dating my husband, I didn't even like him. I only went out with him to have someone to hang out with. We dated for three months before I let him kiss me. That night I lay awake for a long time thinking over and over, I love him. I know I love him. I never, ever thought I might love him until I let him kiss me."

She paused, "We dated for three years, and it never occurred to me that I might not really love him, or he might not really love me.... Our marriage was a disaster. I learned the hard way I should never have dated a boy I wasn't attracted to, and I certainly should never have let him kiss me. Everything changed after our first night of kissing. From then on, I was blind to his faults and character."

Petting Teaches Girl's and Boy's Bodies a Limited Way to Respond

Petting is not a safe activity for girls or boys. They are teaching their bodies how to respond sexually in an artificial environment apart from marriage.

Girls

Girls are teaching their bodies how to respond sexually with a clitoral orgasm instead of a vaginal orgasm even if all the petting is above the waist. I suspect the frequency of this courtship activity is one reason many women believe, "There is no such thing as a sexually inhibited woman, only clumsy husbands."

When a mother talks to her daughter about sex, she should tell her something to the effect, "The reason petting is not a good idea is because you're training your body how to enjoy sex after you get married. Although it feels good for a boy you like to touch your breasts and clitoris, those body parts are just the warm-up for the most exciting event."

The mother can explain, "If those body parts start to respond like they're what sex is all about, they can block your more thrilling sensations when you get married. That's the way God created your body—the more you love your husband and take care of little problems, the more the inside of your body will welcome him. You wait because God has reserved something much better for you that's a lot more fun than petting."

One mother blessed her daughter by saying, "You be a lady while you're dating. Then when you get married, you be a lady during the day. But you turn into a tiger at night!"

The daughter said, "My mother is so straight-laced that you can't imagine her telling me something like this."

Boys

If a boy is getting blow jobs or hand jobs, he runs the risk of oral sex becoming his preferred method of gratification. He'll have a hard time sharing vaginal orgasms and cervical kisses with his wife. Additionally, if he's hurrying sex out of fear of getting caught, he's teaching his body to respond with premature ejaculations.

God didn't design the female and male bodies for petting in courtship. He created their bodies for passionate married sex and speaking God's beautiful language of love™ that transcends human words.♥

Young Woman Remains a Sleeping Beauty Until Marriage Awakens Her Love

It is essential to know that it is the man who ultimately *awakens* the sleeping beauty sexually. Until she is ready for intercourse and all that it implies in a relationship, she is conscious of no particularly urgent vaginal sensations of a sexual nature. The man *awakens* these for the first time in the act of love.

♥*PRD: Dr. Robinson and the Bible Use the Same Word "Awaken"*

Dr. Robinson used the same word "awaken" that the Bible used 3000 years ago to describe how a man awakens a woman in courtship for passionate sex in marriage. This concept is so important that the following verse is repeated three times in the Song of Solomon as the theme:

Song of Solomon 2:7:
"I adjure you, O daughters of Jerusalem,
By the gazelles [male] or by the hinds [female] of the field,
*That you will not **arouse** [form of awaken] or **awaken** my love,*
Until she [it—NASB footnote] pleases."

Gary Martin, a Hebrew scholar, explains the Shulammite's play on words in the theme by using two similar ones of different intensities. "Arouse" carries the idea of waking from sleep either mentally or physically. "Awaken" also indicates to "stir up," but is probably more intense than the first word. He concludes:

> *Both words carry the idea of "arouse" in the sense of inciting to (some kind of) action. Thus, to "arouse" or "stir up" love would mean to incite it to action, to "wake it up" from its sleeping, resting state, and set it into motion (72-73).*

The Song of Solomon Uses Forms of "Awake" Nine Times

Each of the nine times a form of "awake" is used in the story shows an adolescent 13-year-old maiden being "aroused" emotionally as she prepares to be "awakened" sexually in marriage. The story reveals that her mother guided her successfully through the infantile, latency, and puberty stages. Now she stands on the edge of full maturity, ready to embrace a lifetime of passionate lovemaking when she marries. Chapter 24: "Radical Epiphany on Awakening Male-Female Sexuality" explores the nine times "awake" occurs.♥

Marriage Does Not Sexually Disappoint the Wife

With her first intercourse, the wife finds a whole continent of sensations whose existence she had only heard about secondhand. Her clitoral sensations may still be quite pleasurable in the period of foreplay. But now her whole body, in excitement, soon learns to yearn for the penetration of her lover's penis and the unspeakable delight of the vaginally centered sensations he can give her.

She has little or no blockage to these sensations. She may experience a period of adjustment for a few weeks or months until her sensations become unfettered from childhood inhibitions and fears, but the months will be short. At last, true orgasm is hers at every sexual encounter with her husband. Their relationship will prosper and deepen in mutual joy.

♥*PRD: The Wife Taps into God's Hormones of Intimacy and Love*

Excerpt from "Secret 4: Grow the 4 Parts of Intimacy and Love" in God's 11 Secrets of Sex explains how hormones promote passionate love:

*Both men and women have the hormone **oxytocin**, but it's primarily a female hormone necessary for healthy sexual activity and bonding. It's released into the woman's brain by warm, intimate touch. Oxytocin has two roles:*

1. *It increases the woman's desire for more touching.*
2. *It bonds the woman to the man who is touching her.*

***Oxytocin and touching often lead to sexual contact and bonding.** Intimate touching and orgasm bathe the woman's brain with oxytocin. This creates a cycle of desiring more touching and lovemaking, which leads to more desire for touching and sex. At the same time, the woman becomes more and more bonded to the man.*

***Older couples get the most benefits from oxytocin, touching, and sex.** Regular lovemaking and oxytocin create long-term connectedness and happiness. A wife in such a relationship rarely seeks sexual activity outside her marriage. She is firmly bonded to her husband, who gives her so much pleasure.*

***Oxytocin bonding is more than an emotional connection for older wives.** The bonding takes place in the brain. Doctors McIlhaney and Bush state in Hooked, "It is almost like the adhesive-effect of glue—a powerful connection that cannot be undone without great emotional pain" (37). Reacting with brain cells, oxytocin physically binds the wife to her husband.*

***God didn't overlook men when he passed out hormones.** Men also bond to the woman during sex. Vasopressin controls the man's soulmating. This masculine hormone has two major roles in relationships:*

1. *It glues or bonds the man to the woman.*
2. *It also bonds the man to his children.*

Vasopressin is the "monogamy molecule" or the "commitment chemical."

***God glued Adam and Eve together with the hormones of love.** Interestingly, the doctors' description of oxytocin and vasopressin bonding sounds similar to God's declaration after he created Adam and Eve that a man would leave his parents and cleave to his wife (Genesis 2:22-24). "Cleave" means "glue together, cement, join or fasten firmly together, join oneself to, cleave (Thayer 353). God doesn't use super glue on a husband and wife—he uses oxytocin and vasopressin, which hold better than even Gorilla Super Glue.*

***Oxytocin and vasopressin affect the female and male brains similarly.** They bond the husband and wife to each other. This bond becomes stronger over the years with frequent lovemaking. Thus these hormones help love continue to grow over a lifetime spent in each other's arms.*♥

11.

Dangers on the Road to Adulthood

I have taken you through the stages the normal woman goes through on her way to sexual and psychological maturity, the step-by-step process of her growth. But we must ask what might happen to impede this growth? What pitfalls lie along the way into which she may stumble or be pushed? What might cause her to develop sexual inhibitions and cognitive distortions?

I should like to list these pitfalls in the same manner that I showed the normal and unhindered growth of a woman: by taking the stages of development in the order of their appearance. If you can see the specific dangers along the path to adulthood, you may avoid repeating them with your own child. And you may learn much about the origins of your own problem, particularly as I show their application in the specific case histories that follow this chapter.

♥PRD: These same developmental dangers affect young boys and influence their self-image, masculinity, and expression of their sexuality. Note the similarities between boys and girls as you follow the stages of growth.♥

Infantile Period (1 to 5 Years Old): The Parents' Ignorance Is the Greatest Danger

In the first or infantile stage, the child's greatest danger comes from the parents' ignorance. In the past, parents did not know that newborns have sensual feelings that become quite specific by the time they are three years old and continue until the child is about six. I am afraid many parents have not heard of this fact or do not believe it is true.

Moral Horror of Masturbation

A lack of knowledge often accompanies a moral horror of masturbation or, at the very least, intense feelings of moral disapproval. This can lead the parent to restrain the child from such sensual activity. Many parents slap the infant's hands, and some systematically remove the child's hands when they see the child playing with him or herself. When the child learns to speak, others will reprove her for her activities.

Child Can Hinder Personality and Sexuality Development

Such an attitude could not be more mistaken and can have a disastrous effect on the child. The infant is extremely responsive to even the subtlest disapproval of the parents. In this important area, the child will react violently to punishment and even to verbal warnings. She will often attempt to prevent her own masturbatory activity and try to repress the whole of her sexual nature to keep her mother's love. She may be quite successful in doing this, killing all of her natural budding impulses. First experiences are of great importance in development. This early inhibition of her sexual nature can often lay the groundwork for sexual inhibitions and an inhibited and circumscribed personality.

♥PRD: As explained in the previous chapter, "The Growth of Love," masturbation is often a sign of not enough loving parental touching. Failure to teach healthy attitudes toward the body's sexual functions and the purpose of wet dreams causes problems for both boys and girls. Two participants answered the essay question, "List other ways your parents taught you about sex," this way:

- *These are things my mother and grandmother said: Masturbation means you're gay. All men are pigs. Erections, when you are alone, are a sign of an evil spirit. The female body is beautiful, but don't look at it. Train your eyes not to look at women lustfully. Lust and natural desire are the same.*
- *My mother shared detailed information about her feelings toward sex with our father. She made us sit down (with friends and company) and watch religious speeches about sex and God not approving of masturbation.♥*

Excessive Amount of Overt Love from the Father

Another danger in this period can come from an excessive amount of overt love from the father. This is difficult for certain men to understand fully. They argue quite cogently that the young need a great deal of love, demonstrative love. That is indeed so. But it must also be remembered that children at this age are extremely erotic. They can be overstimulated sensually if the father does not bestow his loving caresses in reasonable amounts. The result can be a strong fixation of erotic feelings on the father with a consequent overload of guilt feelings.

These guilt feelings can lead to total sexual inhibition in later life and indeed may be the leading cause of this symptom. I am not saying a father should not caress and bounce his little daughter; that would be against nature. However, he should dole out his physical expressions of love in amounts that are not too stimulating to the child.

♥PRD: This is also true for boys and their mothers.♥

Seduction by an Older Child or an Adult

Another pitfall the child can encounter at this stage is the opposite in nature. Luckily, it happens infrequently, but it does happen and can affect the child's development. I am speaking of seduction by an older child or an adult. Some nursemaids or even older brothers and sisters may stroke the young child's genitals. German and Austrian maids used to do this as a matter of course, rubbing the little boy's testicles and penis or the little girl's vulva to put the child to sleep. However, this is harmful to the child, causing an over-excitation that can permanently affect the child's sexuality. Masturbation is normal for this age, and in this form of narcissistic sexual activity, the child can control the amount of sexual excitation. Under normal circumstances, the child will not exceed this amount. However, stimuli from the outside are not self-regulating, and the child's ego is not sufficiently mature to handle this over-excitation.

The result of seduction on a child at this age can be disastrous. It can lead to any of the major forms or degrees of inhibitions. In my experience, it most frequently seems to lead to the condition known as "psychic inhibitions," which is an inability to form a lasting relationship.

♥PRD: In When a Man You Love Was Abused, Cecil Murphey tells the stories of men who were abused in their youth by various men and women, including siblings, relatives, parents, neighbors, and religious workers. Most were people they trusted. This book is suitable for any man dealing with childhood sexual abuse or his wife to help her understand and support her husband.♥

The Mother Either Neglects or Overprotects the Child

The last major danger of this early period stems from any deep-seated emotional problems the mother may have. Due to problems created in her childhood, the mother may either neglect or overprotect the child over a long time. She can do serious harm to the development of the little one. Over-protection can destroy the child's self-reliance, keep her from passing into the rewarding and growth-provoking relationship with her father that moves her into the next natural step in development. On the other hand, neglect can thrust her into too close an association with the father and have equally dire results.

♥PRD: A Family Tragedy Can Stunt Personality and Sexual Growth

I've completed personality workups on two sets of siblings who experienced family tragedies. The first was two brothers whose father died in a work accident. Their mother remarried a man who was a perfectionist.

One of the exercises we do evaluates the person's personality at three stages—baby, child, and teen. When possible, we ask the parents and grandparents to fill out the chart for the client based on their characteristics at the different ages. The younger brother showed a definite shift as he masked to melancholy between child and teen, when his father died. The older brother also masked to melancholy, but he didn't show as strong of a change as the younger brother.

The brothers realized they had inherited their mother's personality, and that she had also masked to perfectionist with her new marriage. They shared with her that she was not a perfectionist. She reacted with joy and relief.

The second siblings were a brother and a sister. The older brother and his dad were both genetic melancholies. The father was injured in an accident and was in therapy for several years. When the mother rose to the challenge of becoming the breadwinner, her personality changed from the creative, fun sanguine as her take-charge choleric became more perfectionist. The 5-year-old brother then masked to sanguine to get more attention from his mother, whose creative, fun side he still remembered.

His sister was 3 years old when the accident occurred. She essentially lost the attention of her father at this critical stage. And then her mother, who was to serve as a model for a wife, suppressed her nurturing sanguine. This presented a confusing role model for the sister. The little girl masked to a perfect melancholy and a peaceful phlegmatic to please everyone in the family. The sister's genetics are the same as her mother—choleric/sanguine.

The two sets of siblings had to overcome various levels of sexual inhibitions in their adult relationships. Both families demonstrate that outside life forces can so change the parents' personalities and the families' dynamics that problems arise around the children's developing personality and sexuality. See Chapter 26: "The Connection Between Personality and Sexuality" for more information on this phenomenon.♥

Latency Period (6 to 10 Years Old): Danger Is Failure of Their Relationship with Their Father

Failure of the little girl's relationship with her father is the chief danger she faces during her latency period. She has transferred many of the feelings of love and dependency that a few years before she felt for her mother, to this new idol. Forever after, her father will be the model male in her life, though she will seek her ideal in other men. For the present, she worships him, and his approval means more to her than anything else in the world.

♥*PRD: For boys, the danger is a failure of their relationship with their mother.*♥

When the Father Is Disapproving and Critical

If the father is disapproving and critical and directs such attitudes toward his daughter, she may develop strong inferiority thoughts. These can lead her to feel that men are virtually impossible to please. Thus, she can become fearful of them, feeling that if a man finds out her true nature, he will disapprove of her. No reality or later acceptance by a man will overcome this irrational conviction unless, when she is grown, she examines herself deeply and eradicates this mistaken conception of the male. Her feelings of inferiority extend to her sexual drive, which she is apt to repress, as if it were discreditable, like the rest of her personality.

♥*PRD: A Screaming Parent Can Stunt Personality and Sexual Growth*

The Sexless Marriages Survey reveals that growing up with a screaming mother or father is extremely damaging to the personality and sexuality of both boys and girls. The children often grow up to become either codependents or screamers themselves. The sexually inhibited screamers use verbal abuse to push their family away and avoid emotional intimacy. The codependents crave emotional connection and become peacemakers as they try to create the "perfect" environment for love to flourish.

Both codependents and screamers often wear personality masks of perfection. The screamers try to enforce rigid perfection on their mates and children to the degree that it stifles joy and love. At the same time, the hateful words hide the screamers' imperfections. The codependents accept the demand for perfection because they don't recognize it as abnormal and emotionally unloving.

Below are the survey statistics which show that many of the respondents and their sexually inhibited spouses grew up with a screaming parent:

The sex-deprived respondents
77% said a parent screamed at them
70% said their mother screamed at them
63% said their father screamed at them
8% said a grandparent screamed at them
62% were screamed at during their childhood
58% were screamed at as a teenager
25% were screamed at as an adult
11% are still being screamed at

Their parents
50% of their parents screamed at each other
26% of their parents called each other names

The sex withholders
50% were screamed at by a parent
36% saw their parents fighting

*One male respondent's answer to the question, **"How did the screaming make you feel?"** demonstrates the cognitive distortions that Dr. Robinson describes in* *chapter 6, "Sexual Inhibitions Linked to Cognitive Distortions":*

- *I felt hurt at the time. My older 2 stepbrothers and 1 stepsister all left home as early as they could. The girl got married, the oldest brother joined the Navy, and the youngest brother was forced to join the Navy when he was only 16. That left me for my mother to yell at. One time, she came home at about 2 am and woke me up screaming about what an ungrateful person I was. I had given the 3 girls their baths, read them stories, got them to bed, had done the dishes from dinner and put them away, did some laundry, took the trash out, vacuumed, and probably more. So I couldn't figure what she was so upset about. Finally, I realized I had a dish of ice cream before going to bed. I had rinsed the dish and spoon but forgot and left them in the sink. Everything else was spotless. She must have ranted at me for 20 minutes, calling me every name in the book. She finally called me an SOB. I looked at her and calmly said, "That's right! I'm your son." She still called me many names again after that incident, but she never called me an SOB again.*

Screamers distort reality as the above example shows. *Of the survey respondents,* ***78% said that their sex-withholding spouses fight dirty****. They engage in name-calling, break things, scream, and get right up in their targets' faces to intimidate them. It's not unusual for screamers to turn red with rage. Reinventing the truth is common among sex-withholders, which is called gaslighting. They twist what their targets say to use against them. They put words in their targets' mouths to create straw arguments for an attack. Many withholders know how to push their spouses' buttons.*

Being screamed at damages the children's future marriages. *During the first development stage of 1-5 years old, the children are attracted to the opposite-sex parent as they prepare for romantic love. If the opposite-sex parent is the screamer or is also screamed at, which the survey shows happens in 50% of the families, the children develop a distorted view of the opposite sex.*

During the second stage, 6-10 years old, the children begin to view the same-sex parent as a model of how to love their future mates. Whether that parent is the screamer or one of the targets, the children are deprived of a loving model to imitate and learn from.

Thus screaming parents cause their children to mask to perfectionism as a survival technique. They damage their children's perception of their own personality and sexuality. The children grow up with a warped view of both masculinity and femininity. The adult children of screamers must actively seek to replace the verbal abuse trapped in their heads with God's truths.

The survey reveals an ugly irony. *The codependent adult children often marry sexually inhibited people who are like their screaming and emotionally withholding parents. Being screamed at, not only damages the children's self-images, but it also damages their perception of normal. They don't know how* *to recognize and reject their spouses' cognitively distorted views of perfection. They fail to hold the sex-denying spouses accountable for their abuse.*♥

When the Father Prefers His Male Children

Some fathers have a closer identification with their sons than with their daughters. Men who are not aware of this tendency can wreak havoc with their daughters' personalities at this stage of growth. Since she adores her father and wishes to become what he will admire, she will quickly detect her father's preference for the male. This often causes her to attempt to cultivate male characteristics and pursuits and to depreciate typically feminine goals, which one day she must achieve if she is to become a true woman.

Little Difference Between Boys and Girls at This Stage

The latency period is a non-sexual time for both boys and girls. Aside from their anatomical structure, there is little difference between boys and girls at this juncture. Their glands function roughly the same way; none of the typical characteristics that will differentiate them later have yet appeared.

They are both interested in mastering the world about them and the world inside them. They are both roughly equal as far as their innate store of aggressiveness is concerned. Indeed, many scientists call this whole period the bisexual period of development.

Girls Can Fantasize About Becoming a Boy

For these reasons, a father who implants male goals into his daughter's psyche at this point finds a ready audience. Psychoanalysis shows us that the little girl often can develop fantasies of an extremely odd kind at this juncture. For example, in some girls, the idea that they can magically grow a penis and turn into a boy is often quite conscious.

But even if such ideas do not become conscious, the little girl's yearning to become a boy to win her father's esteem can remain part of her unconscious mind. Later, although hidden and disguised, this wish can be at the root of much of her sexual problems, causing her to be unreasonably competitive and to reject her own female role.

Girls Need to Accept and Love the Role of a Woman

We saw that the girl in puberty and adolescence had a formidable task to achieve. She must learn to accept and to love the "dangerous" role of the woman. She must, in effect, be willing to reverse the natural law of self-preservation and put childbirth and the welfare of the child ahead of her own needs and safety.

If she is not encouraged to believe that the feminine role is a worthy one, if she is taught that the male's role is superior, she will be highly motivated to reject her femininity and, almost literally, try to be a boy. It is frequently exactly this that occurs when a woman's fear and rejection of femininity result in an inability to respond vaginally in sexual intercourse. Curiously and unconsciously, she may hold onto the sensual responses of her clitoris but feel unable to allow the sensual feelings to be experienced within her vagina.

Failure of the Relationship with Her Mother

The young girl may be influenced to reject her feminine role by the mother as well as by the father. If the mother has a strong resentment of her own femininity and, like so many women, has been reared to feel that the role of wife and mother is degraded and worthless, she can pass this attitude on to her daughter without speaking a word. The child sees it in her mother's reactions to her father in everyday life, hears it in her complaints, and sometimes feels it in the resigned and hopeless attitude with which she may face her life.

Girls Pass Through a Natural Tomboy Stage

When I emphasize this early "masculine" direction in which a little girl's values may be given, I do not wish to confuse the reader. Many a girl passes through a "tomboy" stage. This is a perfectly natural phase in her development and has nothing to do with the problem unless the child holds onto her tomboyism until well after twelve years of age.

Tomboy Stage Is the First Friendly Interaction with Males

This natural emulation of little boys is a feminine gesture on the little girl's part. She is trying to learn more about what that wonderful opposite sex does, thinks, and feels. In this way, she enters into her first friendly relationships with males other than her father.

♥*PRD: Children Are Damaged by Alcoholic and Narcissistic Homes*

A major surprise in the Sexless Marriages Survey was that alcohol played a major role in most of the homes of origin of both the depriver and the one being deprived of sex. The survey shows that 70% of the sex-withholding spouses grew up in an alcoholic home, primarily with an alcoholic father. Likewise, 50% of the sex-starved mates also grew up in alcoholic homes. They checked multiple areas where the alcoholic parent abused the other parent and them.

Additionally, 77% of the sexless spouses grew up in narcissistic homes. They suffered cruel criticism that attacked their self-image. The unloving parent often screamed at, ridiculed, and manipulated them. As powerless children, they had to find a way to survive by becoming either codependent or narcissistic.

I have yet to find a single sexless spouse on the survey who grew up in a loving home. Many grew up in a home with both narcissism and alcoholism. Others suppressed memories of their home life.

Since alcoholism turned into a major issue, I added questions to the survey to explore it more thoroughly. Participants often indicate that alcoholism goes back at least one generation with multiple family members having an addiction.

Dr. Robinson Didn't Address Alcoholism

Alcoholics Anonymous began in 1935 in Akron, Ohio, 25 years before Dr. Robinson wrote this book. Why didn't she observe that some of the parents were alcoholics and draw the connection between that toxic environment and the child growing up with sexual inhibitions?

Perhaps it was because Dr. Robinson got her information about her clients from two sources: the woman who asked for help and some of the husbands. At that time, alcohol problems in the family were a taboo topic and probably wouldn't have been disclosed unless Dr. Robinson asked about it, as I do on the survey.

According to the survey, only a small number of sexless spouses had an addiction problem even though they grew up in an alcoholic home. That is probably for the same reason a friend, whose mother was a third-generation alcoholic, never drank. She experienced firsthand the damage it did. A fair number of the respondents indicated other relatives and siblings had addiction problems of various kinds.

Alcoholics of both sexes use drink as an escape. But women alcoholics are trying to escape shame, usually based on some kind of trauma. They choose to numb themselves rather than seek help for their trauma. Consequently, the women who contacted Dr. Robinson were probably not alcoholics. But according to the survey, many of them had to be keeping the "family secret."

The positive of all this is that Dr. Robinson had a high success rate for helping women overcome their upbringing to become passionate lovers and wonderful mothers. Undoubtedly, her patients included a significant percentage of women raised by an alcoholic parent, probably the father.

Case History: Husband and Wife Both Raised in Alcoholic Homes

A 28-year-old man said on the Sexless Marriages Survey that both he and his wife grew up in alcoholic homes. He shared that he was never relaxed at school because he was terrified someone would find out about his family issues.

He said, "Almost everyone I was surrounded by was an alcoholic," including both parents, his grandparents, aunts and uncles, and cousins.

He suffered verbal, physical, and emotional abuse from his parents. He said, "My entire life revolved around substance abuse disorders within my family." His mother was the main instigator of fights with his father. He wrote, "I cried in the bathroom by myself a lot. I begged God to make it stop."

On the question "What are other ways your family of origin affected you?" he wrote, "Chaos. I don't know what a healthy home life looks like." He answered the question, "What have you learned about your marriage?" this way, "Our marriage is still feeling the impact of our childhoods."♥

Puberty Period (10 to 13 or 15 Years Old): Chum Stage Dangerous If the Chum Is Sexually Active

Remember that we called puberty "the chum stage." The young girl takes to herself a bosom companion of the same sex with whom she shares her "secrets." One of the chief dangers to arise during this part of the growing-up process comes from this relationship, which is a normal one under optimum circumstances. However, suppose the selected chum turns out to be precocious as far as sexual experimentation with the opposite sex is concerned. In that case, the friendship can lead to harmful experiences for the more innocent member of the duo.

A girl entering puberty is often attracted to a girl a year or two older than she is and will idealize this new friend, feeling that any action she performs is entirely acceptable and defensible. Neither of these children is ready for any truly heterosexual experience, but the younger one may imitate the older one and attempt to follow through in a sexual relationship with a boy or older man.

♥*PRD: Sometimes the Chum Is an Older Sibling*

A grade-school counselor noticed that children who had much older siblings tended to mature sexually earlier than children whose siblings were closer in age. Children often idealize their older siblings. Being aware of sisters' and brothers' dating activities can educate young children in an unhealthy way. One man had his first sexual experience at age 9 with a cousin after he watched his teenage brother having sex in their bedroom while their mother was gone.♥

Being Sexually Active Can Traumatize the Girl

Without mentioning the possible disaster of pregnancy at this early juncture, I should like to emphasize that sexual intercourse at this age can cause a permanent aversion for the experience. It can produce a trauma of such severity that the young person may withdraw from the opposite sex entirely and remain withdrawn.

Or it may encourage her to believe that she has attained maturity. As a result, she may act out this joyless and premature experience over and over with many different members of the opposite sex.

♥*PRD: Being in the Hookup Culture Can Lead to Inhibitions*

The respondents to the Sexless Marriages Survey indicate that many of their sex-withholding spouses were active in the Hookup Culture. Often their parents had "the talk" once and left sex education up to the schools. They learned about sex from their friends, porn, and sexual experimentation. Most were sexually active with their wife or husband before marriage, only to avoid sex after marriage or after the children were born.

Both boys and girls need their parents to teach them the Song of Solomon long before they reach this age. Even more so, teenagers need to live in a home where their parents actively love each other. In that case, the parents' marital love naturally spills over onto the children to help protect them from becoming sexually active because they aren't starved for love at home.♥

Adolescence Period (13 or 15 Years Old to Maturity): Girls Must Pass Through the Dreaming Stage Before Sex

The simple fact is that a girl is not ready for lovemaking until she falls in love with a specific individual. For this to happen in a meaningful manner, she must first pass through the daydream stage of adolescence. Boys do not go through this phase and, indeed, do not have to. They are ready for intercourse at a much younger age than girls are.

Even if we confine our observations to the purely biological aspects of sexual intercourse, girls have much to risk in love. Psychologically they must be sure that it is indeed Prince Charming who leans over them. Until it is, they must dream and sleep. If it is a rude stranger, he can shatter the dream forever and rob the young girl of any chance of ever bringing her dream to fulfillment.

♥PRD: Here are the answers of some participants in the Sexless Marriages Survey about seduction by older kids and teenage sexual experiences:

List other ways you learned about sex:

- *As a pre-teen, older girls touched me, undressed in front of me, and propositioned me. As a teenager, a few older women (late 20s, early 30s) who wanted to have sex with me kind of seduced me. One, in particular, got close to taking my virginity, but I wouldn't let her take it that far. However, we did almost everything else.*

How did your first sexual experience make you feel?:

- *At first, I felt liberated, like I no longer had the burden of my virginity, but after I continued to hook up with different guys, I slowly started to hate myself for it and the fact that I can never get that back.*

- *Uncomfortable and scared. An older boy around the age of 16 touched my vagina with my clothes on. He tricked me and told me he knew of a way to tell how much I weighed. He then started touching me.*
- *A millennial man said he had his first sexual experience at age 6. He answered the question about how it made him feel this way: Confused. Intimidated. Anxious.*♥

Overprotective Parents Can Push the Girl Out too Early

Another danger of both puberty and adolescence is that the parents will be overly strict, interpreting the young one's move toward independence as a danger to her. I have seen many cases of young girls who might have stayed within the home until their adolescence was safely over had it not been for a somewhat thin-skinned mother or father, or both. They alienated their daughters with accusations that their early dating must inevitably be immoral. This assumption by a parent can activate a highly hostile reaction in a young girl.

It is as if the parent were saying to her, "You will never be independent of us, never have a life of your own. Why don't you give up trying?" The fact that the parents do not intend their watchfulness to imply this at all is not relevant. That's the way the young one too often interprets it. And in defiance, she may do something that will injure her.

Submitting to Parents Out of Fear Is Worse than Rebelling

Equally seriously affected, if not more so, is the young girl who feels extremely rebellious but who submits to over-zealous parental authority out of fear. I have seen several girls with this problem. It generally happens that they pull back, because of undue parental influences, from indulging the personality-enrichening dreams of adolescence.

This causes them to remain on the threshold of womanhood, lost in an emotional dependency that belongs to an earlier development phase. By and large, such girls' problems when they come to womanhood tend to be more severe than those of the girls who rebelled.

♥*PRD: Case History: Virginity Pledge Effects Man's Adolescence*

This is one of my client's account of how his parents negatively affected his sexuality:

My dad had a friend who encouraged him to initiate me into manhood on my 13th birthday. So for my 13th birthday, he invited lots of people to initiate me into manhood. He wrote out a document for my virginity pledge, and I had to read it aloud in front of everybody. Then he read his portion aloud in front of everybody. He wrote something for my mom to read too. It was humiliating and extremely awkward.

Though my dad's intentions were right, it was overly showy for all of his friends who came. The words he used in the document and the poetic writing were to try to sound impressive. It was riddled with Victorian morals. I was mocked badly by my peer group during that day. There was a girl at my birthday party who I had a crush on. I was mortified.

About four months later, my folks got into some financial troubles, and we had to move and go live with a relative for a while. Through my parents' heavy condemnation of sexuality and men, I was convinced that my "sexual struggles" of masturbation, looking at the nudity in my mom's medical books, and even simple erections caused our family's misfortune. I would hear things like, "sin keeps you from prospering."

I let my wife read my virginity pledge and shared my humiliation and my blaming our family's misfortune on my masturbation. She had some good insights on this, and one thing she said, which I thought about all night, was this: "You can't hold your younger self responsible for all this." For some reason, her words brought a lot of freedom.♥

Need Moral Attitudes Taught and Interpreted with Love

In making these observations on parental strictness, I am in no way advocating a laissez-faire attitude. Every child needs to feel the force of the parents' moral teachings as they give guidance and security. The child will generally react more normally and healthfully if the moral attitudes are expressed with love rather than dogmatic commands.

♥*PRD: Case History: Parents' Moral Extremes Ruined Man's Marriage*

A 60-year-old male client was raised in a hell-fire-and-brimstone church. His parents insisted that any sex outside of procreation was sinful. When he was 14, he had his first wet dream. He was very embarrassed because of the mess it made in his bed. His father told him, "If you ever do that again, I will have to hook you up to electricity to put a stop to it."

To avoid his father's punishment, he learned to identify the buildup of semen and to release it regularly when he peed. He could not understand how God could give him such intense sexual desires, and it be such a grievous sin.

When he married, he enjoyed his wife and didn't need to masturbate. He continued to have sex with her even after all their children were born. However, in his 40s, he began to experience some business problems. He told his wife, "We're going to have to stop having sex because God is punishing us by causing my business failures."

His wife didn't say anything but looked very sad. Several years later, she divorced him and told him it was because of a lack of sex.

Some years later, he made friends with an 80-year-old retired preacher. The older man told him to lay aside what his parents told him about sex and to read the scriptures without prejudice. He was shocked to learn that God created sex to be enjoyed by Christians apart from procreation.

Even so, he continued to struggle with wanting to get married, but saying, "I will never be able not to feel guilty about having sex with my wife." I recommended additional counseling to help him stop filtering everything through his parents' Victorian hang-ups and start living for God and himself.

Masturbation Is Like Driving a Civic Instead of a Porsche

Since he is spouseless, he continues to relieve the buildup of sexual tension and semen when peeing. He says it is strictly a biological function, and he doesn't need or use porn to get relief. He described it this way, "Masturbation is like driving a Honda Civic whereas sex with my wife was akin to driving a Porsche.... I have had two Civics (a '21 top of the line) and three Porsches, and of course, there is no comparison. Driving a Civic is not a sin—it just isn't the best! I really want to be married and driving a Porsche again."

God's 11 Secrets of Sex for a Lifetime of Passion includes a bonus chapter, "Wet Dreams, Laws of Cleanness, and Masturbation." In it, I share Dr. Douglas Weiss's descriptions of the three types of masturbation, two are not sinful, but one is. The type of masturbation my client describes is not sinful and is not part of lust or sexual addiction. Please review the bonus chapter to distinguish between the different types of masturbation.

Male clients who are not sexual addicts are offended by their wives telling them to take care of themselves. They know the difference between driving a Civic and a Porsche. In Ecclesiastes 9:9, God said that one of the rewards he gives men for having to work so hard on the earth is to "enjoy life with the woman whom you love [literally sexually or otherwise]."♥

Next: The Kinds and Degrees of Sexual Inhibitions

We have now seen the stages of development that lead to maturity and the pitfalls men and women may encounter on the way. With this final information in hand, we are at last ready to look at sexual inhibitions themselves. Therefore, the next section will address the sexually inhibited man and woman. Specific case histories will show you how the kinds and degrees of inhibitions develop and what concrete problems they bring in their train. With such models in mind, we will then be prepared to examine the constructive steps individuals who suffer from inhibitions must take to win their freedom and cross the bridge to manhood and womanhood.

Section 3:

The Fear of Love—Case Histories

12.

Total Sexual Inhibitions

Although we discussed the various types of sexual inhibitions in a former chapter, I think it will be helpful now to go into greater detail. I am going to illustrate the major types of sexual inhibitions with case histories. In this way, you can get a living picture of each problem.

Hard to See Your Own Distortive Actions and Reactions

I think the case-history method of presentation is helpful to grasp sexual inhibitions. Those who are caught up in the problem usually lose their objectivity about themselves. They are unable to see with any real clarity just how their actions and reactions are cognitively distorted and just how they are affecting those around them.

The true story of another person who suffered from the same affliction mirrors the problem faithfully and allows one to achieve a clear view of oneself, perhaps for the first time. Each kind of sexual inhibitions has its own distinctive characteristics and its own unique causes.

Case Histories Help You Diagnose Yourself

But as you read these cases, you will be struck by the differences in each kind of an inability to enjoy orgasms, which will allow you to see your own image—to diagnose yourself. You will see, too, that certain characteristics are common to all the inhibitions in both men and women. Knowledge of these facts is important to the cure of the inability to experience physical love.

In giving these stories, I cannot include examples of all the pitfalls that are encountered from childhood to adulthood. That would require much more space than I have here. I will attempt, rather, to select cases of inhibited desire and pleasure that are caused by experiences most common to men and women.

Case History—Part 1: Total Sexual Inhibitions Lead to Bitterness and Blaming

The first case, then, is one of total sexual inhibitions. As you may recall from our earlier description of it, this kind is one of the most severe forms of sexual disorder in men and women and is widely prevalent. For example, I give you the case of a woman we shall call Patricia Agnew.

(1) When Patricia Agnew came to my office for her first interview, she had not come to consult me about inhibited sexual desire and pleasure or to discuss the results of such a problem on her marriage. She came because she was having, in her words, "another nervous breakdown." She was not a good-looking woman, though she had nice teeth and large blue eyes. It was her figure that was striking. In direct contrast to her inner attitude, her figure was round and voluptuous, almost the American ideal of "sexy." Her lips were full and sensual, but she held them tightly together, which gave her a judgmental, critical look. She was thirty-six years old.

(2) Her "nervous breakdowns" (she persisted in using the expression, though it was clearly inapplicable in her case), she told me, were recurrent. She had them for three successive years. Each of them started with a marked increase in inner tension. She felt panic as she was unable to cope with the manifold social and family demands of her life; a great sense of inadequacy set in gradually, and she became listless and depressed. Finally, the slightest task seemed too much, and she started to have day-long bouts of weeping. During such periods, she suffered from chronic insomnia. When she could snatch a few hours of sleep, she often had repetitive, nightmarish dreams in which criminals pursued her.

(3) At the beginning of our talks, Patricia became guarded whenever I attempted to open any discussion of a personal nature. She had come for help with the express conviction that I, the doctor, should find a quick and easy solution to her periods of acute anxiety: drugs, a sea voyage, anything that did not entail looking inward, taking responsibility for her condition.

This evasiveness, this desire to find easy solutions, is characteristic of all forms of inhibitions in women. But it is sometimes extremely pronounced in the type of sexual inhibitions this patient suffered from.

(4) As Patricia developed confidence and trust in me, the real facts gradually emerged. She had been married for ten years and had two children, six and eight. Her husband was socially prominent, financially successful, and strikingly handsome, a slender, tall, dark-haired man with a gentle and charming manner.

(5) This patient finally told me that she never had "one solid hour of

happiness" during her entire marriage. From the beginning, she quarreled with her husband. The domestic strife on her part had become genuinely bitter after the birth of their first son. She felt that her husband was becoming increasingly cruel, selfish, demanding, and insensitive to her needs. She believed he was trying to impose his will on her in all situations and that it was necessary to struggle against his domination.

"I feel as if he will shatter my integrity if I don't put up a fight," she told me. "It is as though he wishes to exploit me, nothing less; it will be either he or me."

(6) The quarrels were generally over petty matters. Although her husband almost invariably tried to make up within a few hours, she would rebuff him. Consequently, bitter feelings often endured for a week or more at a time. Her power struggles terminated only when she felt he had been sufficiently punished for his transgressions. She confessed that she often forgot what the original quarrel was about by the time she was ready to forgive him.

(7) She felt, too that her husband was extremely critical of her and that he never really gave her full approval for anything. She believed he did not like the way she dressed, the way she conducted herself socially, or how she managed the children. When I asked her to give an example of how he showed his disapproval, she could not think of anything specific. She concluded lamely: "Well, he usually praises me to my face, but I can tell by his expression that he doesn't mean it."

(8) In the areas she specifically mentioned, I later checked with her husband on his attitudes. He told me that he felt initially and still felt that his wife dressed beautifully and that she was perfect at any kind of social function. "She has a remarkable gift for conversation of any kind with practically any person," he said. On the other hand, he sometimes felt that she tended to be too permissive with the children and she worried about them excessively. However, he learned early that he could not help her in this matter and only prayed that the children would have no adverse effects from her tendency to pamper them. I should like to report that, as she recovered, Patricia gradually became aware of the fact that this "critical" attitude she had ascribed to her husband was almost entirely a product of her cognitive distortions.

(9) Another powerful conviction she possessed was that her husband did not really love her. She felt that he was mainly interested in exploiting her for his "selfish" sexual needs and advancing his business. At the beginning of their marriage, her husband entered his father's engineering firm. At once, he faced the necessity of doing a great deal of entertaining. His wife, he soon found out, was an excellent hostess, and he came to depend on her gracious parties. She at once took his dependency on her collaboration for exploitation and even extended that

to mean: "He doesn't love me; he merely finds me a convenience. Any other presentable woman would suit him as well."

(10) Another twist to this irrational conviction was more hidden and did not emerge until late in the treatment. She complained, "He didn't succeed on his own. I made him what he is, even if I never get the credit for it." With underlying feelings of this kind, how much chance for survival do any tender feelings toward her husband have?

(11) As the sessions continued and Patricia gained more confidence, she began to feel freer about discussing her sexual life. She confessed that she had never experienced any sexual pleasure in her entire life, neither before nor after marriage. Kissing or being stroked gave her no sensations whatsoever. From the beginning, intercourse was distasteful and often painful, though sometimes she took a little satisfaction from her husband's obvious pleasure from orgasm.

(12) The sexual life of this couple was at a standstill for nearly eight years. At most, intercourse occurred at three-month intervals. It was never spontaneous. She required her husband to make an appointment for a "date" several days before intercourse. She consented to such an affair only after she refused him several times and accumulated a great deal of guilt for so doing.

(13) From the moment she made the appointment, she became anxious, and this increased until dread filled her. Often she was forced to break the appointment and postpone it. As the time for the intercourse approached, she also experienced feelings of rage, repeated to herself over and over, "Why must I, why must I?"

In preparing for the act itself (putting her diaphragm in, inserting the jelly), she lingered for as much as an hour while her husband waited. She often found that her vaginal muscles contracted to such a degree that inserting the diaphragm was painful and difficult.

(14) With her misery increasing momently, she went to the marital bed as one might go to the executioner. Her husband's looks repelled her now; his nakedness seemed disgusting and offensive. She saw him as "skinny, white, and ugly, with an enormous penis. It was as if he were nothing but a big, disgusting sexual organ."

(15) She felt no tenderness or warmth—she could not even simulate it. She remained totally passive throughout the entire act. Later in happier times, she learned that her husband hurried as quickly as possible in response to her rejection.

(16) It is interesting that, despite her own inability to respond, Patricia complained bitterly that her husband's lovemaking was mechanical and hasty and that he never showed any tenderness. It had never occurred to her that he might be reacting to her clear aversion to the whole process. Indeed, she saw no justification for his shamefaced

approach to her until she was well on the road to sexual health. It is usual in such cases for the wife to blame the husband for her failures, no matter how glaringly unreasonable and untrue her accusation may be.

(17) After intercourse, Patricia was always depressed. She felt "dirty and used." Her husband's semen appeared to her to be disgusting. "All I want is to get to sleep fast and to forget the whole episode until the next ordeal becomes necessary," she said.

♥PRD: This case history presents a profile of "total sexual inhibitions" that lead to bitterness and blaming, both common problems with sex-denying spouses:

1. *The woman wanted help for her "nervous breakdowns."*
2. *She was unable to cope with social and family demands.*
3. *She was evasive and wanted easy solutions.*
4. *The facts finally began to emerge.*
5. *She was bitter and blamed her husband.*
6. *She quarreled over trifling matters and was bitter.*
7. *She thought her husband was extremely critical of her.*
8. *Her husband admired many things about his wife.*
9. *She didn't think her husband really loved her.*
10. *She thought her husband owed his success to her.*
11. *She never had any sexual response, even to kissing.*
12. *She required her husband to make appointments for sex.*
13. *She frequently broke appointments made days in advance.*
14. *She went to the marital bed like to an executioner.*
15. *She could not fake tenderness, so her husband hurried sex.*
16. *She blamed her husband for her sexual failures.*
17. *After sex, she was always depressed and felt dirty.*

Part 1 of this case history is extensive in exploring the wife's symptoms. Part 2 continues the story to analyze the causes. Although this case history is a woman, her symptoms are easily recognized in men as well. For example, totally sexually inhibited men and women are full of bitterness and easily blame the spouse for everything. Consequently, their bodies and minds are incapable of responding with love in even the smallest way.

Ways Men and Women Avoid Planned Intimacy

The Sexless Marriage Survey shows that sexually inhibited men and women frequently require their mate to make appointments for sex. Then they often break the appointment in creative ways to deflect blame from themselves. Notice how the survey participants answered the following questions:

Ways your companion sabotages sexual opportunities:

- *34% Picks fights with you*
- *31% Rants about what you do wrong*

- *22% Rants about work problems*
- *30% Finds reasons to be angry with you*
- *42% Finds reasons to be annoyed with you*
- *20% Picks at you until you get angry*
- *33% Blames you for the destroyed romantic mood*
- *31% Abandons you to deal with the anger he or she caused*
- *34% Abandons you to deal with the hurt feelings he or she caused*

Here are some of the comments:

- *During a sexual encounter, he complains that we do not have sex enough, which begins an argument and ends the mood.*
- *He doesn't typically destroy the mood, he avoids getting the mood going in the first place.*
- *Oh geez. That list looks more like me than it does him....*
- *He hides emotions, lies, refuses to have a relationship with me, picks fights extremely aggressively, berates me, then says "we" do not have enough of a relationship for treating me with affection as the Bible instructs, saying "women need to be close to have sex, you know...."*
- *Seems like Sunday night is her sex night. She initiates by asking if we are going to do something, then says hurry as she has to get up early. Knows I don't like feeling rushed or told I'm a chore, yet there we are.*

Do you destroy the mood with arguments or fights? If yes, explain.

- *If I have a resistance to intimacy (especially planned), I involuntarily start to get negative and look at everything through that lens. I even will consciously think to myself, "I want to have sex tonight! I hope my mood doesn't shift" or "I hope I don't sabotage things." Once again, I feel frozen with a lack of control over my emotions/desires.*
- *I think that I get too scared to get turned on sometimes because usually making out or touching doesn't lead to much. Sometimes I try to lead it to more before he's ready, and then he ends the mood. I'm afraid he will turn me on as a tease and then just stop. That happens almost all the time.*
- *Yes. I definitely do. I prefer him to jump through hoops to be near me. I get annoyed at him for snoring soon after we go to bed together (we have five kids, and I want to hang out with him in bed, and I want him to show me he wants me). But he gets tired (He has a reason to be tired. He works hard. We both do). But I let him know somehow that I'm usually annoyed.*
- *I walk on eggshells to try to do the right things so she won't get angry.*
- *Yes. I know where an evening out is going to lead: nowhere. And he starts making that evident before we even get home. Hard not to feel hurt/angry*

> *about that. I say things I've been STRUGGLING not to say...just blurt them out when I guess I just can't hold it in any longer.*

The survey makes it clear that both men and women can be totally sexually inhibited. And this chapter ends with a case history of a man who is totally sexually inhibited, just as Patricia was.♥

Case History—Part 2: The Causes of Total Sexual Inhibitions—Strong Father, Weak Mother

Now that we have seen a picture of the totally nonorgasmic woman, let us examine the causes for it. Every kind of sexual inhibition has a special cause. What was the cause in Patricia Agnew's case? To understand the origins of her problem, we will have to explore her earliest history, particularly her relationship with her father and mother. She was an only child, and her father was clearly the dominant figure in the household. He was extremely successful and lovable.

Her Description Was Unlikely from a Withdrawn Person

Her father abounded in all the virtues, was infinitely patient and loving with his little daughter. From her earliest times she considered him, physically speaking, "an enormously beautiful man," and in describing him she lingered lovingly over the details of his appearance—his "sculptured head," "wonderful deep kindly eyes," and "marvelously athletic figure." A psychiatrist pays close attention to such an ecstatic description, coming as it did from such an otherwise withdrawn person.

Never Consciously Had Strong Feelings About Her Mother

By way of contrast, she considered her mother "mousy" and, while she liked her in a general sense, she never consciously had any strong positive feelings about her.

As a "Daddy's Girl," Couldn't Transfer Love to Her Husband

Patricia clearly had been a "daddy's girl." Nothing is wrong with this under normal circumstances. Had she grown up to be sexually free and had she been able to transfer her early love feelings from her father to other men, this early attachment to the father would have been merely a phase in normal development.

The First Stage of Development Is Attraction to the Father

You will recall that in the first five years of life the child is a sensual little being. Patricia had been no exception in the beginning; she had transferred these feelings, in the normal course of events, to her father.

Her Father Overshadowed Her Mother

However, this powerful and charming man whose personality dominated the household and overshadowed his wife completely had been far too responsive (unwittingly, of course) to the little girl's erotic feelings. He dandled her and played with her endlessly, surrounded her with stimulating warmth, psychologically and physically. He showered her with kisses and hugs, compliments, and candy. He gave her anything and everything to express his devotion to her.

Her Father's Aggressive Forms of Love Overstimulated Her

The consequence? The strength of his love, its varied and aggressive forms, its unrelenting intensity, had a negative effect on the child. To put it most simply, his love overstimulated her budding sexuality. This man's love overwhelmed her. Her small ego could not handle such powerful feelings; they frightened her. To cope with such feelings, she had to repress them powerfully, deny their existence.

Children can do this, as you will remember from our discussion of the latency period of childhood. It is at the onset of this period, which occurs at about six years of age that infantile sexuality is pushed underground, to remain dormant until puberty.

Father's Love Sent Her Prematurely into Her Latency Period

Patricia, under the influence of her prematurely strong sexual response to her father, had been forced to enter her latency period, we were able to determine, at the far too early age of four.

She Continued to Worship Her Father and Win His Love

With sex out of the way, she was now able to indulge her worship of her father in complete "innocence." He was a man who believed passionately in success, and his ebullience, love of life, and high intelligence won him a great deal of it. His young daughter felt now that to win his love she must achieve and achieve, endlessly. From the first grade of school through her last year at college, therefore, she bent all her efforts into excelling mentally.

Father Was a Perfectionist Who Expected Top Performance

But her father was also a perfectionist; he expected top honors from himself and jeered at anything less in himself. Thoughtlessly he made the same demands on Patricia. Since she did not have his qualifications she was not always able to meet his standards in every field of endeavor; few could have equaled his demands. When she did not achieve top honors, she felt that she was not worthy of her father's love and indeed that he did not love her. He did nothing to correct this feeling.

She Was Arrested Emotionally and Sexually at a Young Age

If you will recall our normal stages of development for the growing child, you will easily see that when marriage time came around, Patricia Agnew had not touched first, second, or third base. She had appeared to be growing normally, excelling in schoolwork, playing the role of the dutiful daughter, and going out on dates. But in the emotional and sexual spheres, she had been arrested at an early stage.

Her Sexual Feelings Failed to Resurge in Puberty

So severe had been the repression of her childhood sexuality that when the glandular changes which usher in puberty occurred she failed to have the resurgence of sexual feeling and the development of psychological characteristics normal for that period.

She Lost the Adolescent Phase of Development

For that reason, she omitted her adolescent phase of development, the period of young love's long and lovely dream, which prepares the girl for the activities of love sexually and psychologically. How could she have had such a dream? It depends on the development of a true and normal sexuality. The door had been locked on her sexuality in infancy and the key thrown away.

Psychologically, She Was an Infant in the Latency Period

Psychologically, too, she was an infant. The need to excel, to master one's environment, is of course normal for the latency period. Nature has arranged this period, sagely put sex out of the way for a few years so the ego may have a chance to grow, to prepare itself for the sexual storms and stresses of puberty and adolescence. However, since in a real sense she could not pass through puberty and adolescence, she remained psychologically in the latency period, the non-sexual, competitive, father-worshiping childhood period.

Daddy Held Her Heart and Her Husband Couldn't Compete

Patricia had two distinct attitudes toward her husband. The first was expressed in her quarrelsomeness, her belief that he was selfish, unattractive, and unlovable. This attitude was based on the fact that, literally, her heart still belonged to Daddy. With her exaggerated childhood feelings toward her father, every other man suffered by comparison and seemed unworthy of her love.

Her Husband's Need for Her Love Filled Her with Rage

Her husband was an interloper who came between her and her ideal. Therefore, his normal need for her to love him, to be a good wife to him, seemed hateful to her and filled her with rage. Sex under such circumstances was a virtual rape of Lucrece, with the husband playing the role of the dark and frightening rapist. The father represented her true love for whom she must preserve her innocence and purity.

Her Husband Stood for Her Father and Was Sexually Taboo

More profound and more hidden, the second attitude was the exact opposite of the first one, indeed contradictory to it. In this aspect of her mind, her husband stood for her father. Thus sexual feelings toward such a person must be entirely taboo. She must repress them as she had in her earliest years, and she must keep them repressed. Too, she must excel in all the things her father wanted her to excel in.

She Must Excel in Her Wifely Functions to Her Husband

To her husband, she must primarily excel in her wifely functions, and this was the essential trap. For because she consciously knew she was not, and under the circumstances could not be, even a passable wife, she was constantly inundated by feelings of inadequacy and inferiority.

Her "Breakdowns" Were an Expression of Her Hopelessness

You can see then what a complete trap Patricia was in. Actually, unless she had been strongly motivated to seek help, she would never have found an exit from her difficulties. Her periodic "breakdowns" were a direct expression of the hopelessness of her situation. It was as if she were saying: "I am truly a helpless child. I can do nothing grown-up. I must be taken care of as a child is." She recovered her lost sexuality and her lost capacity for happiness. In a later chapter, we shall see how the Patricia Agnews of this life can achieve such an outcome.

This Case History Represents the Most Extreme Form

Patricia represents inhibited sexual desire and pleasure in its most extreme form, the type in which there is almost a total lack of sexual feeling. On our inhibitions scale, totally sexually inhibited would needle around zero. At the opposite end, a person would experience a great deal of sexual excitement before and during intercourse but would be unable to have an orgasm or it would be weak and unsatisfying. (Normalcy is more or less an absolute state and cannot be described in terms of degrees.) We rate this person near or at 10 on the inhibitions scale, meaning the person is close to normalcy. In between these extremes is every degree of sexual blocking.

♥PRD: *Case History: Totally Sexually Inhibited Male*

A 60-year-old respondent to my Sexless Marriages Survey identified himself as the one who withholds sex. During a 24-year marriage, he never initiated sex with his wife. He chose the code name "hopeless" to link his answers together because he's been through 40 years of professional and spiritual counseling without getting help. Below are his answers to relevant questions in the survey:

What is your story about your home of origin?

> *Full of abuse and neglect, including sexual by a neighbor. Coupled with the trauma I endured through 12 years of public school bullying (with no support from parents or anyone else for any of it), I am severely damaged goods.*

What is your story about your marriage or relationship?

> *Two atheist adult children of alcoholics who presented false images to each other and got married late in life (in our 30s) knowing nothing about marriage or each other's true self. Slowly dying marriage through years of sinful neglect (sins of omission) and broken vows.*

Do you withhold sex?

> *I prefer masturbation to sex with my wife; I never initiate sex; we have been 20 years without successful sex (some failed attempts); I have been impotent most of my adult life.*

Do you withhold emotions during sex?

> *Sex was mechanical and forced; I always kept eyes closed and lights off during sex; I was emotionally absent before/during/after sex; I didn't cuddle; I made her feel inadequate and unattractive.*

Do you destroy the mood with arguments or fights? If yes, explain.

> *I am never "in the mood." I am unable to feel or express love, joy, affection my entire adult life—only fear and anger.*

If you withhold sex, are you afraid you won't be able to learn how to enjoy the sexual embrace? If yes, explain why you have this fear.

> *I suffer from touch aversion. All physical affection and most sexual*

activity are unpleasant for me. I was able to go along with it when my wife initiated by pretending to enjoy it, but it kept me from being able to obtain or maintain erections.

If you withhold sex, before you married did you allow your future spouse to think that you would be a willing and eager sexual partner?

Yes. My wife always initiated relations, and I participated willingly (though often unsuccessfully). Three years after we married she stopped being willing to initiate. I've never been able to initiate relations (nor even conversation) with a woman my entire adult life.

If you withhold sex, what is your #1 most important challenge?

My uncertainty about whether I am regenerate or not. Within the marriage, it is the realization that I am without positive emotions due to suffering from adult attachment disorder (aversion style) (diagnosed by my last counselor). If I can't feel love or affection for my wife, I don't know how I can make affectionate or loving actions be real for her, never mind overcome my terror at the idea of being vulnerable at any level (emotional, physical, or spiritual) with her.

What other feelings do you have in dealing with a sexless marriage? Explain:

Despair at the failure of everything I've tried to improve things. Guilt that I've failed as a man/husband and hurt my wife deeply being unable to love her or show her affection in a way she feels is genuine.

The emotional damage done to this man in his home of origin is extreme. He has sexual anesthesia with his wife and any woman, although he was sometimes functional when his wife initiated. On Dr. Robinson's scale of degrees of sexual responsiveness, he would represent "absolute zero."

Men and Women Can Overcome Total Sexual Inhibitions

Total sexual inhibitions inflict devastating consequences on both men and women and their mates. The good news from Dr. Robinson's case history is that even the most severe form of inhibitions can be overcome. But total victory requires work in all four areas of one-flesh love—intellectual, emotional, sexual, and spiritual. God tells us:

2 Corinthians 13:5: "Test yourselves to see if you are in the faith; examine yourselves!"

Dr. Robinson's clinical experience provides unique insights into the scriptures and God's formula in 1 Timothy 4:1-10 for solving all marriage problems. The next section, "The Bridge to Love," explores these steps and processes for transforming your heart for loving your mate, children, and yourself.♥

13.

Partial and Other Sexual Inhibitions

In Chapter 5: "Five Common Types of Sexual Inhibitions" you learned that the severity of a sexual problem, or the lack of it, can be calculated in terms of the degree by three things:

1. The response to the mate's caresses
2. The frequency of satisfaction in intercourse
3. The quality of the orgasm itself

If the orgasm is weak and chronically leaves one with a feeling of dissatisfaction, a certain degree of inhibitions is present. In the previous chapter, you learned about Patricia Agnew, who was almost *totally* sexually inhibited with nearly zero sexual responsiveness on the inhibitions scale. She also displayed many personality problems related to her inhibitions. The main difference between Patricia and *partially* inhibited men and women is where they rank on the scale.

"Partial Inhibitions" Are Almost a Different Kind

The underlying structure of those with partial inhibitions is similar to Patricia's—too strong and too early erotic attachment to the parent of the opposite sex. This attachment has survived into adulthood. Depending on its original strength, this attachment causes a greater or lesser degree of sexual and interpersonal problems in the marriage.

However, as one goes up the scale toward greater sexual responsiveness, the *difference in degree* seems almost to become *a difference in kind*. From roughly just past the middle of the scale upward, the basic sexual problem has little to do with withdrawing from or hostility toward one's mate or feeling exploited sexually, such as Patricia displayed toward her husband.

Partial Inhibitions Result from Locked-Up Sexual Feelings

Partial inhibitions are more closely connected with direct sexual frustration and locked-up feelings. One is almost at one's goal of sexual fulfillment but cannot quite achieve it.

Case History:
Normal Parents and Close to Climaxing

Here is an example of what I mean. I shall call this patient Joan. She was 28 years old, a pretty woman, a generally carefree manner, and a pleased-with-life smile. She had been married for two years.

(1) During intercourse, Joan would become tremendously excited most of the time. It took little to stimulate her, and as the intercourse continued, she maintained a high level of excitement. But on most occasions, no matter how long lovemaking continued, she would reach no climax at all. She was left with a frustrated, almost frantic feeling.

(2) Occasionally, about one out of ten times, Joan achieved a climax of sorts during lovemaking. But it was weak and inconclusive and not by any means deeply satisfying to her, as it should have been and as she felt it could be. Here, however, is the most important point. Whenever Joan experienced this climax, she almost invariably woke the next morning with severe back pains, which lasted for two or three days and were clearly psychosomatic.

(3) After sex, she felt irritable and anxious. It was only on such days that she experienced personal difficulties with her husband. She quarreled with him about trifles, being generally cross and argumentive.

(4) "I should think," she said to me in puzzlement, "that it would be just the other way around; that I would be difficult with him when I didn't come to any climax and pleased and hopeful when I did, even if it wasn't the perfect orgasm." But Joan was merely logical in this assumption. The mind is not necessarily run by such rational considerations. When she understood the reasons behind the apparent anomaly of her backaches and her anxiety, she was close to being cured.

(5) Joan's problem was a mild one. Her relationship with her husband was sound. She thought him attractive physically and respected him. She enjoyed their social life and never felt exploited when he had to entertain business associates. Indeed, she had a great deal of fun playing the role of hostess to them. We could find no area where difficulty existed between Joan and her husband except in their sexual life.

(6) She resolved her sexual problem quickly, for she held it lightly in the soil of her personality. Yet in exploring it, we found it had precisely the same structure as Patricia Agnew's problem (previous chapter): *a basic, unresolved over-attachment to her father that occurred in early childhood.*

(7) The difference was that the attachment on Joan's part was much milder than Patricia's was. Therefore, while it did have a lingering aftereffect, it did not encompass Joan's entire personality, making it far easier to deal with.

(8) Joan's good relationship with her mother neutralized to a certain

extent the overstimulating effect of her father. It allowed her to identify with her own sex in a healthy manner. It gave her the feeling that it was acceptable to be a sweetheart, wife, and mother.

(9) Her sexual inhibitions were helped in a few sessions. One day she came to me upset. Her last intercourse was successful and culminated in the strongest orgasm she had up to that time. But, as usual, the next day she was anxious and had a severe backache.

(10) As she talked about it, she suddenly said, "I had the most amazing dream. I've just recalled it." She was on a swing in a playground, she told me, and her father pushed her. "I flew higher and higher," she said. "It was like flying. The sensations were delicious. I hoped he would never stop. Then suddenly I looked around, and he had turned into some kind of criminal or something. He seized me, and I screamed, but somehow I knew nobody could hear me. I suddenly remembered something a girlfriend told me in college when a group of us were discussing rape. She said that a woman might be killed if she resisted. And she said if it ever happened to her, she would just relax and try to enjoy it. I recalled this now, and the criminal in my dream did rape me, and I enjoyed it thoroughly. I came to a terrific climax, a kind I've never had in real life."

(11) She awakened at this point but then went back to sleep and had the following nightmare. "Women policemen were pursuing me for having committed some crime," she said. "They'd almost catch me, but I'd get away from them. Finally, one of them caught me, but when I looked in her face she was smiling at me tenderly, and she said, 'Don't worry. It's not so terrible after all.'"

(12) Knowing what you know already, it should not be too hard to see what Joan's dream means. The swinging with her father doing the pushing represented her early sexual feelings toward her father. When these became too direct, she disguised them by turning her father into a criminal rapist. Actually, she felt like a criminal because the police pursued her in her dream.

Significantly, they were policewomen, for the little girl felt strong guilt toward her mother because of the forbidden and taboo sexual feelings toward her father. The policewoman's forgiving attitude represented her excellent relationship with her mother and her inner readiness to get over the problem.

♥PRD: Following is an overview of Joan's inability to enjoy regular, robust orgasms although she liked sex and was close to success:

1. *She responded excitedly to sex, but seldom climaxed.*
2. *She experienced physical pain after occasionally climaxing.*
3. *She argued with her husband over trifles after orgasms.*

4. *She was disappointed she didn't feel loving after climaxing.*
5. *She enjoyed her husband and her marriage.*
6. *Her father-attachment was milder than Patricia's was.*
7. *Her problem was also an over-attachment to her father.♥*

Two Things Protected Joan from Severe Damage

Two things made Joan's relationship with her father less destructive than Patricia's had been.

- First, Joan's father was not so overpoweringly loving and attentive to the little girl during the first six years of her growth.
- Second, Joan's mother had a distinctive and strong personality of her own, and Joan enjoyed a good relationship with her all during her formative years.

♥PRD: The following steps trace Joan's healing as she finally began to enjoy orgasms with her husband:

8. *Her mother neutralized her father's overstimulating effect.*
9. *She experienced a pullback after her strongest yet orgasm.*
10. *She recalled a dream after her orgasm.*
11. *She had a nightmare about being chased by policewomen.*
12. *The dream reflected her relationship with her mother and healing.♥*

Recognizing the Basis of Her Fears Let Her Move Forward

Joan's experience is a perfect illustration of the whole theory of modern psychoanalysis. To her, at least, it was eminently clear. Her terror, expressed by her dream of policewomen pursuing her, disappeared before our session was over, and she stood ready to move into mature and satisfying sexuality with her husband.

With her conscious mind, Joan now knew that she had been frightened of complete sexual love because, in the highest reaches of passion, her feelings for her husband unconsciously reminded her of the "dangerous" feelings she once felt for her father. Thus she dared not indulge them to the utmost. *Understanding the irrational basis of her fears allowed her to dispense with them.*

♥PRD: Following God's Formula Works on Sexual Inhibitions

Both Patricia and Joan wanted to solve their problems of inhibited desire and pleasure. Patricia was reluctant to admit her "nervous breakdowns" were caused by a rejection of her femininity. In the end, she put the work in to overcome her difficulty. Both women followed psychology's version of God's formula in 1 Timothy 4:1-10 for solving all sexual problems:

1. *Receive God's plan for men and women with thankfulness.*
2. *Learn God's truth about the emotional nature of sex.*
3. *Go to God in an interview-type prayer to implement that truth.*

Dr. Robinson expands on these methods in "Section 4: The Bridge to Love," and I'll make specific comments about the formula then.

Case History: My Partial Inhibitions

This case history is my story of why I got such quick results when I read The Power of Sexual Surrender in 1973. Working on this commentary, I verified that I went through the four stages of development that Dr. Robinson described in "The Growth of Love" including the dreaming stage when I was dating my future husband.

My Mother Gave a Vague Answer to My Question About Sex

I took a detour in the fifth grade when I asked my mother how babies could look like the daddy when they came out of the mother. I was at the right age to learn about sex. But my mother didn't give me an honest answer. She said, "Because the mother and the daddy sleep together." In my young innocence, I took her words literally—you sleep with a man, you can get pregnant.

That summer my younger cousin and I went to the movie theater. It was a wartime movie where a female officer and a male officer spent the night in a vacant building during a severe rainstorm. That was in the days when movies left everything to your imagination.

Later, we learned the woman was pregnant. I leaned over to my cousin and whispered, "Do you know how she got pregnant?"

"No."

"They slept in the same room." I was proud of my knowledge about how babies looked like their daddy.

My Mother Hedging Made Me Terrified of Adult Men

The next year, I had my first male teacher, and I was terrified of him. I was afraid if I stood too close to him, I might get pregnant. I had no such fear of boys my age because, to me, daddies were grown men.

I Found a Medical Book that Gave Me Healthy Attitudes

Dr. Robinson warned in chapter 6, "for even the most prudishly feared child cannot be prevented from finding out the facts of life." On schedule, I found Drs. Willy, Vander, and Fisher's book The Illustrated Encyclopedia of Sex hidden in my mother's dresser and read it.

I reread parts of it while working on this update and am amazed that I stayed with it at that age. I learned two main things: (1) A wife should never tell her husband, "No," for sex because of his need to release the buildup of semen. (2) A woman's body is designed for her to enjoy sex too. In the chapter on the woman's orgasm, the doctors beautifully describe the vaginal orgasm. Then in the next chapter, "The Sexual Impulse," they describe the "cervical kiss":

> *In physically and mentally entirely normal women (unfortunately the minority today), the posterior part of the vagina is the most sensitive of these three main sources of excitation [clitoris, vagina, cervix]. We may therefore say that* ***the seat of female sexual satisfaction is the posterior part of the vagina*** *[emphasized by the doctors] (221).*

I promised myself that when I married, I would never tell my husband, "No," and I knew that I could and would enjoy sex. I wish I'd learned a third fact from this book—the emotional nature of sex for both men and women. Reading it this time, I recognized that the doctors frequently made that point.

I never asked my mother another question about sex. Fortunately, I didn't need to. I had multiple male teachers in both junior high and high school. I don't remember ever being afraid of any of them.

I Started Marriage Enjoying Sex

When I married, I enjoyed sex just as I expected to. But I hadn't comprehended vaginal orgasms when I read the book because I hadn't experienced sex and had nothing to compare the description to. I only knew that the description of lovemaking for a woman was beautiful. I didn't learn about vaginal orgasms until I read Dr. Robinson's book in 1973 and realized I was missing something even more enjoyable.

God's Formula in 1 Timothy 4 Taught Me How to Change

I recognized that Dr. Robinson's steps for overcoming inhibitions followed God's formula in 1 Timothy 4:1-10, and I put in the time to explore where my inhibitions came from. I discovered that although I intellectually knew that standing too close to a man couldn't make me pregnant and I no longer had that fear of men, I had not dealt with my sixth-grade terror of adult men that developed around my mother avoiding an honest conversation with me. She never attempted to have that conversation until I was engaged and planning my wedding. Then she took me to the drugstore to buy some supplies and answered my questions truthfully and frankly without embarrassment.

Once I was married, I thought of both my husband and myself as adults. I was "sleeping" with an adult man who could make me pregnant. Although I had educated my conscious brain about pregnancy, my emotions had stayed locked in youthful ignorance and terror about adult men. With this realization and praying to God, I quickly transitioned from clitoral orgasms to vaginal ones.

Sometimes Inhibitions Come from Misconceptions About Sex

My case history demonstrates that inhibitions don't always come from dysfunctional relationships with one's parents. They can also come from misconceptions about sex and pregnancy that we learned from our parents, friends, romance novels, porn, churches, and sex education in the schools.♥

Inhibited Men and Women Often Harbor Powerful Fantasies About Themselves

Women who are sexually inhibited often have, in addition to negative feelings toward the male sex, another marked characteristic. They are subject to fantasies, which are decisive factors in preventing their recovery of their lost sexuality and their psychological maturation.

These fantasies must be ruthlessly explored and exploded. If they are not, they often preserve the unhealthy conviction that one deserves a far better fate than that of being a beloved wife and mother.

Fantasies Are Often Half-Hidden from View

Such fantasies are often half-hidden from view, just as one's negative feelings about men are. They are daydreams leftover from adolescence or earlier. Their destructive power derives from the fact that:

1. The daydreamer still believes that the dreams are realizable.
2. Or that she could have achieved them if her husband and family had not prevented her from doing so.

It is amazing how powerful and persistent these fantasies can be. They generally spring from an early desire to become an actress, a dancer, or a concert artist. However, they may also express wishes to become a doctor, lawyer, athlete, diplomat, or whatever.

Daydreamers Ignore Reality to Hold on to Fantasies

I have had inhibited women of forty and even fifty, who just beneath the logical surface of their minds, still believed that someday (tomorrow perhaps, next year indeed) they would go to acting school and soon obtain leading roles in a Broadway drama. Or they thought they would resume piano lessons and become famous concert artists.

Inhibitions Don't Reflect Reality; They Glorify Fantasies

Such fantasies derive their power from the fact that the daydreamer feels unable to deal with reality. Since a woman who is sexually inhibited is coping with her real-life situation in an inadequate manner, it is not strange that she should hold onto such fantasies with passion.

The Fantasies Protect the Woman's Self-Image

The fantasies protect her from her feelings of inferiority. "What does it matter," says her unconscious mind, "if you are unable to love? What does it matter if your husband exploits you, attempts to misuse you? Tomorrow—someday, at any rate—you will show them all that you are beautiful, glamorous, a great performer, or a doctor, or a lawyer."

♥*PRD: Fantasies Can Be Part of Narcissism*

In Will I Ever Be Good Enough?, Dr. Karyl McBride exposes grandiose fantasies as a common characteristic of narcissistic mothers that affects the mother-daughter dynamic:

> *[The narcissistic personality] is preoccupied with fantasies of unlimited success, power, brilliance, beauty, or ideal love. For example, the mother who believes her career cleaning houses will bring her widespread recognition through the efforts of her famous clients. Mary's mother constantly talks about her "important" clients and how much they need her and appreciate her and how she believes she will be hired on a movie set with one of them soon (8-9).*

Other narcissistic characteristics that go along with fantasies that are common in both male and female sex-withholding spouses are:

1. *Flaunts grandiose sense of self-importance.*
2. *Believes is "special."*
3. *Requires excessive admiration.*
4. *Has a sense of entitlement.*
5. *Takes advantage of others to achieve personal goals.*
6. *Lacks empathy.*
7. *Shows arrogance, haughty attitudes.*

Narcissism Is the First Sin Listed with Being "Without Natural Affection"

Many of the characteristics of sexually inhibited men and women are typical of narcissists. Narcissism is a spectrum personality disorder, somewhat like high blood pressure. It can range from a little bit high to dangerously high.

"Lovers of themselves" is the first sin listed in 2 Timothy 3:1-5 that surround sin #9 "without natural affection for family," including the spouse and children. On the Sexless Marriages Survey, 90% of sexless Christians display narcissistic entitlement as they reject all forms of intimacy with their mates.

Case History: Man's Fantasies About His Work

One of the first women I worked with was married to a man with all kinds of fantasies. He was raised in an orphanage and didn't know what love looked, smelled, tasted, sounded, or felt like. He didn't know how to love himself, his wife, or his children. He met and charmed her while he was in the military. They married soon after his discharge.

He refused all kinds of jobs because he didn't want to work for a woman supervisor. Besides, he knew he could be a world-famous photographer. He rented a storefront and opened for business. His wife had to deal with creditors calling until he was evicted from the store property. His unrealistic fantasies and low view of women ended his marriage.♥

Approach Fantasies the Way You Do Negative Views of the Opposite Sex

The sexually inhibited man and woman should approach such fantasies in the same manner as they approach their negative feelings toward the opposite sex.

1. First, you should let the fantasy have full play. Allow yourself to imagine yourself as an actress, doctor, whatever fantastic dream your unconscious has fixated on. Let the daydream roll on and on.
2. Note the fantasy's magnitude, its grandiose quality, its glitter, and its glamour.
3. When you have experienced all the details of your fantasy, allow yourself to imagine what life would be like if you could never realize a single aspect of your daydream.
4. If you feel depressed by such a prospect, if the contemplation of life without the possibility of realizing such a dream of glory seems empty, you have had a meaningful experience. You have taken your fantasy full measure. You can now get some idea of what an important part it plays in your emotional life.

Do Not Fear the Depression and the Emptiness

Do not be afraid of the depression, the feelings of emptiness that will come with your first conscious attempts to free yourself of your fantasy. It can be the beginning of a far richer emotional life than any that depends on an unrealizable daydream.

Persist for a Few Days Imagining Not Living Your Fantasy

Persist for a few days in imagining what life will be like *if you do not ever realize your daydream*. Please notice that your depression does not go beyond a certain depth and that it is bearable. Also note that the feeling of deprivation is tolerable.

Deep-Seated Daydreams Are Like a Drug Addiction

I am not using auto-suggestion in these last remarks. A persistent daydream has certain characteristics in common with a drug or alcohol addiction. Over a long time, daydreamers have learned to handle reality in terms of their drug—their deep-seated daydream. Without realizing it, they have come to feel that life would be impossible without this psychological narcotic.

♥PRD: This is an amazingly insightful statement by Dr. Robinson that these "deep-seated daydreams are like a psychological narcotic."

Wikipedia says under Dr. Marie Nyswander [Robinson] that in 1955—four years before she published The Power of Sexual Surrender, she organized the Narcotic Addiction Research Project. It was the first program to accept patients who were still addicts. In 1956, three years before she wrote this book, she wrote The Drug Addict as a Patient. In 1963, four years after she wrote this book, she was recruited to help with drug research. In 1978 she received an award for her work related to drugs.

Thankfully, sandwiched in between all her work in drug rehabilitation, Dr. Robinson spent 15 years in private practice working with sexually inhibited women. This book that reflects her dedication to research has withstood the test of time.♥

Wean Yourself Gradually From Daydreams

In a real sense, you must wean yourself from your daydream, gradually realize that life without it is not nearly as dreary or difficult as you imagined it would be. The next step in the process is to explode the daydream entirely. You can do this with a few pinpricks of cold logic. Most people realize that such dreams, formed in the heat of youth, have no function in reality and have long ago given them up in favor of living as passionately as possible in the present. However, the sexually inhibited man and woman have a reason for keeping them alive and have never scrutinized their daydreams in the light of rationality.

Case History: Woman Who Dealt with Her Fantasy

I know one woman who, at the age of thirty-eight with three children under fifteen years of age, still felt she could become a dancer. As she looked more closely at this conviction, she became increasingly surprised at how seriously she took this fantasy. At length, when she felt ready to face sacrificing her lifelong dream, she wrote a list of facts and questions that I present here.

The Questions She Asked to Release Her Fantasy

1. To become a dancer, I would have to study the dance for a minimum of five years; during that time, I would have to practice dancing for about eight hours a day. Could I take this discipline?
2. If my mind were able to take such discipline, would my body be able to stand up under such arduous work?
3. If I could arrange it, would I be willing to give up my daily contact and relationship with my three children?
4. If I overcame every obstacle and became a well-known dancer, achieving my wildest dream of success, I would have to go on tour for at least eight months of the year; this would mean separation from my husband and children during that time. Do I want this? Even if I do, could I take it emotionally?

The answers to these questions were passionate ones. And the result of such a common-sense examination of the long-standing fantasy was, finally, freedom from it.

Ask the Case History Questions to Deal with Your Fantasy

It will not take much logical thought to dispose of your daydreams, thus clearing the way to a life in the passionate present rather than in a mythical future. Ask yourself the kinds of questions my patient did and give yourself honest answers.

When Professional Help Is Needed

Many men and women will find that they can conquer their sexual inhibitions with the methods prescribed in this book. However, some will find that though these techniques will help them, they cannot achieve their goal without outside help.

Indeed, one of my chief reasons for writing this book has been to open doors hitherto unknown to many men and women. If reading this book has but started you on the road to mature masculinity or femininity, its chief function has been accomplished.

How does one decide whether outside aid is indicated? No rule of thumb will cover all cases. Some men and women may decide they prefer to start and finish their work on this problem with a trained therapist. Others may start alone but find that self-exploration, the surfacing of painful emotions and attitudes and fantasies, is too difficult and confusing and decide to seek expert guidance. Still, others may find that though they can go a long distance alone, the final goal will elude them if they do not consult with a trained worker in the field.

A person who needs such outside help should feel no sense of shame about that fact nor hesitate to seek it.

♥*PRD:* Case Histories of Men with Partial and Other Sexual Inhibitions

I'm closing out this chapter by sharing the case histories of two men with sexual inhibitions. One solved his problems, and one didn't. The first is an excerpt from God's 11 Secrets of Sex, which gives an example of how sexual inhibitions can make a man susceptible to adultery:

Case History: Harold Never Learned How to Love a Woman

A husband, whom I'll call Harold, confided in me about why his wife divorced him after a decades-long sexless marriage. He said, "I never learned how to love a woman emotionally and sexually." He didn't say, "my wife." He said, "a woman." He didn't know how to love any woman.

He Grew Up Hearing His Father Ridicule His Mother

Harold grew up hearing his father make fun of his mother (the model for his future wife) every day at the dinner table. His dad disguised his ill-feelings toward his mother with humor. Harold and his siblings laughed at their dad's jokes. Even his mother laughed. Through deceptive, abusive humor, Harold was programmed to believe women are inferior to men and objects of ridicule.

When he tried to make fun of his wife as his father did his mother, she didn't laugh. She insisted he stop making her the brunt of his jokes. He stopped the public putdowns, but he continued to harbor negative attitudes toward women. This allowed him to justify withholding sexual and emotional love from his wife.

Sexless Marriages Are Not Adultery Proof

Harold's wife thought he was adultery proof since he wasn't interested in sex with her. How wrong she was as she discovered in their senior years that he had been unfaithful most of their marriage—perhaps even during courtship.

Sexual withholders experience stronger temptations for covert sexual sins than emotionally healthy spouses do. Sexual addictions along with mental and physical adulterous acts provide opportunities for secret sexual release with little intimate attachment to the object of their lust.

Harold neglected to unlearn his upbringing—to learn how masculine men honor feminine women. He got away with his secret cognitive distortions until his wife found evidence of his unfaithfulness and discovered he was not adultery proof after all. He chose divorce over learning how to love a woman.

Case History: Male Client Shares the Challenges of His Upbringing

A young millennial client wrote this second case history for me to share with you in this book. He worked hard to overcome the adverse treatment and messages he received from both his mother (his role model for his future wife) and his father (his role model for his masculinity). He wrote:

I grew up in a unique environment with parents who expressed masculinity and femininity in peculiar ways. My mother was intentional and had good intentions with my siblings and me. She struggled with a strong rejection of femininity and semi-quiet disdain for masculinity. This resulted in her having an expression of masculine behaviors and tendencies.

At times when I was younger, my mother would comfort me when I needed it. But more often than not, I went to my father or "self-soothed." This created unhealthy coping and problem-solving tendencies. I often self-soothed by daydreaming of creating better realities and escaping into my imagination.

Certain things that stand out to me growing up was my mother's aggressive nature toward life and others. She was competitive, dressed masculine and practical, and stayed away from feminine activities. She was always working from home in order to create a household income to "replace my father's income so he could come home and they could work together." It was almost as if she was trying to be a better version of a man.

Education was important to my mother so she introduced us kids to life very early. We had tons of books and magazines. Interestingly, we had lots of educational literature about reproduction and childbirth. These books and magazines had lots of thrilling pictures for a youngster.

He Experienced Negative Views of Men and Sex at an Early Age

From a young man on, I often heard her say, "all men are pigs." She made those comments around stories regarding sexual desires, intimacy, and male aggression expressed healthily or unhealthily. I remember thinking to myself around 8-9 years old that I don't feel like a pig, but I am a man. This also troubled me because I enjoyed looking at the pictures in all the books and magazines that were readily available. Unwarranted shame started creeping in for natural male desires and responses.

By 10 years old, my dad sat my older brother and me down and told us basic info about "how babies are made." He called it "sleeping together." Even with all the available reading material, I ignorantly replied to his explanation, "I thought the sperm jumped to her belly button." I was also confused by his explanation of sleeping together because it didn't seem like you could do that in your sleep. He then had to elaborate more.

That night my mother came into our room and asked if our father spoke to us about sex. We said yes, and she strangely laughed. I remember at that moment feeling extremely uncomfortable. It was as if we were now enlightened "pigs."

His Grandmother Perpetuated the Negative Views of Men and Sex

It was also around this time that my grandmother proceeded to tell me about her close friends' feminine struggles and how troublesome vaginas are. I felt uncomfortable and knew something was off. We saw her about once a month.

My mother and my grandmother were alike in lots of ways, but my grandmother was more feminine. She didn't want anything to do with anything masculine. She was also aggressive and wanted to be the main income earner.

They were alike in their attitudes toward men and sex. My grandmother openly voiced her irritations with and dislikes of men. She called my dad stupid. But she was independent, more feminist-minded. Just the opposite, my mom openly said men were better and wished she were one. My mother favored my brother and me. She had a harder time with her daughters.

By 13 (too old to go without a conversation), I had heard the term masturbation and asked my dad. He replied, "That's what gay men do." It was a series of unfortunate events as my grandmother in the same year told me the only reason someone would masturbate is if they had a demon. Now at 13 years old, I am told I am a pig, and if I masturbate, I'm gay and possessed by a demon.

His Personality Changed as a Result of the Negativity at Home

Over the years, I started taking on more passive behaviors at home to earn my mother's approval. My dad was focused and put his energy into my older brother, who was considered the "man's man." Of course, my dad cared about me and gave me attention, but not in the same way. My mother disapproved of male aggression and rewarded me for taking passive roles. This affected me deeply later in life. Early on, it was hard to identify or see anything wrong with being passive. It came with strong communication skills, ability to multitask, and I became overly intuitive for a man.

My mother was extremely body-conscious of herself and others. My sisters got the brunt of her body shaming and critical comments. She was always working out and dieting but was seldom content with any progress. She monitored my dad's fitness and eating obsessively. I remember hearing her snide comments to him and fearing that if I didn't meet her standards, she would turn on me.

As a young man, I was still seeking parental approval and comfort. She would make critical comments to my brother and me. She was highly fixated on making us healthy and removing blemishes. This became a challenge as all of us kids went through puberty. We could never hide a pimple from her. If she didn't say something, she would surely stare disapprovingly.

I became overly aggressive in public because I was taking a passive role at home. So I went and achieved a lot of accomplishments outside the home. I always got my parents' approval when I was accomplishing something.

My parents also had me take a public purity pledge and promise fidelity to my future wife. That was humiliating. I had a lot of work ahead of me to learn truth, and I didn't even know it. Between 13 and 17 years old, my sexuality was way off course, and my heart was aching for help. I remember praying and asking God to remove my sexual drive and get rid of my male response. I struggled with normal feelings and emotions, which I called "lust" because that's what I was taught.

He Left Home, Married, and Started a Better Life

At 17, I read a book by Brennen Manning, and by the grace of God, I was able to get on a healthy road. It was a tough journey to become independent from my parents, but I managed. I was out of the house by 18 and started my own life. I started coming alive and enjoying life apart from their ideology. My parents did not take kindly to my separation and becoming independent, but I had peace because I knew I needed to leave and cleave. That's just what I did.

I bought a house at 19 and married a loving "feminine" women at 20. My mom didn't support my dating and engagement time and spoke poorly about it. My parents felt they had "lost" me. I didn't care. I was in love and living life.

My wife and I had a wonderful honeymoon experience for about one year, and then all the old programming and bad belief systems started creeping in. Thankfully by God's grace, we recognized things were wrong with our belief systems early in our marriage and began the journey to healing. It took many years, tears, and pain, but we did get to the other side.

Years later, though things come up, we have the tools to handle them and enjoy passionate sex as God designed. We have young kids and a whole lot of love in our home. We are excited to teach our children what we learned and help them develop healthy attitudes toward God, men and women, and sex.

What He Wishes Was Different Growing Up

What would have helped me? Parents who got emotionally healthy! Parents who appreciated who God created them to be and appreciated each other for their differences. Healthy proactive conversations about sex and childbirth. Warm motherly affection toward my dad and us kids. Biblical instruction about sex. Support when leaving and cleaving. Choosing to love who their kids love.

This Couple Presents a Role Model for Healing

This client and his wife read my book God's 11 Secrets of Sex and Dr. Robinson's original book The Power of Sexual Surrender before contacting me. Their practice was to read everything together and discuss the points as they went. In addition to personality counseling, I assigned them chapters to read in Male and Female: God's Genius and God's People Make the Best Lovers.

The couple continued their practice of reading and discussing the text together. In evaluating that practice, the husband emailed, "To think sexuality is only the partner's responsibility is extremely shortsighted. Working together is hands down the most effective and soul-soothing way to grow."

Seeing how reading and discussing together helped this couple soulmate deeply caused me to start strongly recommending that others follow their example. It was evident that this practice not only accelerated their progress, but it also greatly increased the quality of sexual ecstasy for them both.

Changes in Thinking Releases Amazing Male Sensations

Although this client enjoyed lovemaking before he contacted me, he soon began delighting in sensations he didn't know were possible. He wrote the description of a #10 male orgasm that you read in chapter 2 on sharing vaginal orgasms. To put his description into the context of overcoming his negative childhood experiences and demonstrating the rewards of a couple working together to soulmate deeply, I'm ending this chapter by repeating his description:

As the sensation grows, it feels like I completely lose control and my body takes over. It feels extremely strong, first in the genitals then through my core, chest, and head. It feels deeply internal and ends on being on the verge of passing out but never actually do. Pure ecstasy. These types of orgasm are rarer, though not elusive. Every other orgasm is felt solely in the genitals (which are still extremely intense and pleasurable).

The key with the most intense orgasm is it happens when my mind is completely uninhibited. ***My attitude completely determines my level of pleasure.*** *My mind used to be messy with dishonesty, secrecy, doubt, and all the little things not communicated. Even when I wouldn't be conscious of situations/problems, my subconscious was aware, which kept me from experiencing supreme pleasure.*

Whether we are aware of it or not, we owe the truth its due, which is radical honesty and responsibility. Once that fell into place, my sexual sensations changed drastically. My refractory period significantly shortened (the recovery time after orgasm when it is physically impossible to have a second orgasm).♥

14.

Promiscuous Sexual Inhibitions

In the cases discussed up to now, we saw that a too-early sexual experience can lead to permanent repression of a child's entire sexual nature. Over-stimulation leads to anxiety, and anxiety leads to ruthless repression of sensuality by the little individual. *Basically, the sexual experience is felt as dangerous and unpleasant.*

The Promiscuously Inhibited React Differently

We see in our promiscuously inhibited type just the opposite kind of conscious reaction on the sexual level. Too early sexual stimulation causes a *pleasurable sensual response,* and the memory of this is held onto passionately. *However, the deep guilt that is generated in the small child causes a displaced psychological reaction of great intensity.*

Promiscuity Can Reflect a Desire to Be Awakened

The problem of sexual promiscuity in men and women suffering from inhibited sexual desire and pleasure is a common one. Generally, it comes from *a desire to be sexually awakened.* Men and women who seek a solution of this type feel that the next romantic interest will break through the barrier that separates them from true sexual satisfaction and real relatedness, which will restore them to their erotic birthright. They are doomed to disappointment because an exterior solution of any permanent kind of this interior problem does not exist.

Promiscuity Can Also Reflect Psychic Inhibitions

One form of promiscuity does not fit the above description. Basically, it is *not a search for the beloved but rather a deep, characterological tendency.* It is closely allied to a curious and seemingly contradictory form of sexual inhibitions. Men and women who suffer from this disorder we characterize as the "psychically" inhibited type. If sexual reactions alone determined our definition, we might consider them perfectly normal. Promiscuously inhibited men and women respond readily to sexual foreplay, and their orgasms are usually satisfying. At first, when we examine their reactions closely, we can find no aspect of them that indicates a sexual inhibition problem.

Promiscuously Inhibited Can't Form a Lasting Relationship

However, these men and women do have a severe problem. They are unable to form a close, enduring relationship. They are *devoted to an inner ideal of transiency in love.* Sometimes they are not conscious of the fact that short bursts of love are essential to them, but everything about their amorous career indicates this is so. They may select partners who are married or chronically hostile to the opposite sex and who always end up rejecting them. Or they may do the rejecting themselves. They are *usually faithful to their partner of the moment* and sometimes say they hope this time the love affair will last. But just below the surface of their awareness, they have no such wish.

Seduction Can Lead to Inability to Form a Lasting Bond

If the relationship shows any indication of moving toward permanency, they will create a reason for terminating it. And this is where their sexual problem shows: *if they could not end the relationship, they would inevitably become sexually inhibited with their partner.* In every case that I have treated, there was a profound sexual involvement. *Early and destructive sexual experiences (usually some form of seduction) led to a psychological inability to relate emotionally to another person.*

Case History: Seduction and Promiscuous Inhibitions

To understand the promiscuously inhibited personality more fully, let us look at a typical case. Molly, age 27, came to me because, as she stated it, she was scared. In the past two years, she had two abortions. Although she had made a commitment to change her ways, she was now living with an art student. A psychiatrist familiar with promiscuity considers the possibility of an early seduction. It had indeed occurred.

Molly was unwilling to discuss it at first. This was followed by her refusal to ascribe any particular significance to the event. She believed it was an isolated affair that had no permanent effect on her. As the matter unfolded, it became clear that it was the nucleus of her later difficulties.

(1) It happened when she was six. Three houses down from her lived a widowed man in his sixties. I shall call him Mr. Brown. Sometimes Molly played hopscotch outside Mr. Brown's house. One day he invited her in and gave her a piece of cake and ten cents. She was delighted. After that, he often had her in, always giving her something sweet to eat. He was pleasant and she loved him.

She did not remember the first time it happened, but soon sitting on his lap became an integral part of her now frequent visits. He would tell her a story, ruffle her hair, and touch her arms or hands. Gradually his touching extended to her legs and thighs. She liked the sensations and, being so young, she could not conceive of his doing anything wrong.

Mr. Brown did not confine his caresses to the little girl's clitoris. At length, he penetrated her hymen with his finger. She remembered it was painful, but the pleasurable sensations outweighed the pain. This seduction lasted for some time until Mr. Brown suddenly moved away.

If she had been a year or two older, Molly might have rejected the situation and reacted with shock or horror. It might have contributed to a different kind of sexual inhibitions, perhaps the anesthesia of total inhibitions.

However, it was clear she felt guilty about her reactions since she did not tell her parents—a clear indication of guilt feelings. Later she separated the seduction and its sensual pleasures from her conscious mind, made no connection between it and her later behavior. If she had not felt guilty, she would not have had to make any such separation.

(2) Although Molly had no other sexual experiences in her latency period, she began behaving differently from the other girls in her group very early. At twelve, she started to pet with a boy next door and was confident she would have had intercourse with him if her advances had not frightened him. At thirteen, she snuck out at night to meet one of several older boys. On one occasion, she had intercourse and went around with this boy for about a year.

When he graduated from high school and went away to college, Molly promptly started another sexual relationship with another high school senior. Sexual affairs followed one after the other through high school and college. The only concession Molly made to conventional morality was that she did not allow the relationships to overlap.

She had an upward of forty sexual affairs. None lasted more than a year, and some only one or two weeks. All were with men who were ineligible for marriage either because they were already married or were not emotionally capable of marrying.

(3) Despite some uneasiness of brief duration in college, she never seriously questioned the "rightness" of her sexual conduct. Each time she had an affair, she believed she was in love. When the current love relationship ended, she felt relieved. She experienced no conscious regrets or qualms of conscience as, year in, year out, she continued in this way of living, a mode so different from that of her parents. Her pride sustained her in what she called her "healthy animalistic nature."

Her animosity toward her parents did not diminish when she grew up, and at the time she came to see me, she had not visited them for two years. The consequences of Molly's early seduction were grave.

However, the psychological structure she developed to cope with this seduction is not hard to understand.

(4) Human beings are largely guided by the pleasure principle, which is clearly displayed in childhood. Molly received a lot of pleasure from her early sexual encounter, but she also experienced a great amount of guilt. When Mr. Brown departed, she entered her latency period. But with the reassertion of Molly's sexuality when puberty set in, the original sexual activity created a mold for her personality. She enjoyed and sought sex to an abnormal degree for her tender years.

(5) In her unconscious life, Molly felt guilty for her sexual feelings. Because of her highly developed sensuality, her problem was to get rid of the guilt feelings so she could indulge her sexuality. In childhood, this means getting rid of the parents because guilt of this kind is always associated with parental prohibition. She did this by denying that her parents had any importance to her. She repressed all warm feelings toward them and created a set of values in which they were, to use her words, "stupid," "loveless squares," and "without a drop of sensuality."

(6) As Molly and I continued examining her life and feelings, it became apparent that the erection of this defensive mechanism had cost a great deal in terms of her sexual pleasures. To be enjoyed, sex had to partake of the nature of the original seduction. It had to be a forbidden and guilty act with a person who was detestable to her parents. And it could not move into a permanent relationship, for if it did, it could no longer be considered forbidden and guilty.

For Molly, love could never lead to marriage or children and the joys these bring. If a man was respectable, "meant well by her and loved her," in her unconscious life, she would immediately associate him with her parents and their approval. This killed all her sexual feelings, and she became unresponsive to him. She experienced deep anxiety underneath her rebellion against a permanent relationship.

♥PRD: Overview of how Molly became promiscuously sexually inhibited:

1. *A neighbor slowly seduced Molly.*
2. *Molly became sexually promiscuous in puberty.*
3. *The seduction led to hatred toward her parents.*
4. *The development stage and pleasure led to Molly's promiscuity.*
5. *Guilt destroyed her relationship with her parents.*
6. *Sexual molestation took away the permanency of love.♥*

Molly Overcame Her Promiscuous Sexual Inhibitions

During our work together and after Molly began to see the implications of her problem, she started associating with men who were more eligible for a healthy relationship. A dream she had during her first attempt at a relationship with a young doctor shows the problem clearly.

In this dream, she is sitting in the backseat of a car, kissing a young man in an intern's uniform. She is excited as they kiss and decides to have intercourse with him. At this point, the young intern says, "Please marry me." She immediately begins to feel terrified, as though something awful is going to happen. She begins to tremble and wants to get out of the car and run, but she is so frightened she cannot move.

Suddenly she sees the face of a man outside the car. He has a large dollar sign on his hat. He points a gun at them and says, "Both of you must die." At that point, she woke up in an absolute panic.

The intern stands, of course, for the young doctor. The man with the dollar sign on his hat stands for her banker father. Sex is all right, and she wishes for it as long as it is sneaky. The moment sex becomes respectable ("Please marry me"), the hidden and guilty act will be made known, and her father will punish her in the most horrible possible way. She had never resolved her early guilt feelings about the childhood seduction. Molly had built her whole life around this early experience.

Her relationship with the doctor did not prosper. But she finally became engaged to an emotionally healthy man. On the basis of insights she gained from our work together, she decided to postpone intercourse with him until after marriage. She responded sexually when lovemaking began, but she became quite inhibited within weeks.

As in the case of the intern, this reaction represented her lifelong fear of emotional and sexual intimacy. Since she had faced up to her psychological inhibitions, she had stopped running away into meaningless relationships. Resolution of this problem was a matter of time, of "working through" the guilt she had never dared to face before.

♥*PRD:* *Male and Female Hormones Play a Role in All Promiscuity*

The following excerpt from God's 11 Secrets of Sex shows how hormones released during promiscuous sex hamper the ability to form a lasting, loving relationship:

The hormones of love are values-neutral. *In Hooked, New Science on How Casual Sex Is Affecting Our Children, doctors McIlhaney and Bush note that sex hormones don't care if the people are married to each other, cheating on a mate, or partying with a hookup. They don't care if the people love each other or are abusive. They don't care if the couple has just met or is celebrating their fiftieth anniversary. The hormones do their job by bonding the couple together.*

Having multiple sexual partners bonds men and women to every partner they have. *Their cycles of casual sex with one partner and then another limit their cranial response to only one kind of sexual experience. They get hooked or addicted to the immature dopamine rush of sex. They never allow their brains* *to experience the full benefits of the hormones of a long-term relationship.*

MRI and SPECT scans of couples who have been engaging in sex for a few months show that the hormones affect their brains. *Doctors McIlhaney and Bush state that with casual sex, "They risk damaging a vital, innate ability to develop the long-term emotional attachment that results from sex with the same person over and over."*

Having multiple sexual partners damages the bonding mechanism. *Concluding the section on the bonding similarities between oxytocin (female hormone) and vasopressin (male hormone), the doctors state that men and women lose their ability to bond after numerous sexual partners. They compare it to "tape that loses its stickiness after being applied and removed multiple times" (43).*

Adult brain plasticity allows men and women to overcome psychic sexual inhibitions. *Neuroscience continues to discover new ways that the brain never stops rewiring itself and growing. When we couple that fact with Dr. Robinson's successful treatment of Molly's psychic inhibitions, we find evidence that men and women have the power to become truly loving in long-term relationships.*

The brain has both ***structural*** *neuroplasticity (the ability to change its neuronal connections) and* ***functional*** *neuroplasticity (the ability to alter and adapt to new activities). This means if individuals educate their thinking about sex and modify their activity, they can change their responses to long-term partners.*

Case History: King Solomon Had Promiscuous Inhibitions

Interestingly, during his 40-year reign, King Solomon fits the profile of both forms of promiscuous sexual inhibitions. He married his first wife, the daughter of the Pharaoh of Egypt, when he was around 16. He quickly took a second wife and was introduced to polygamy (early sexual pleasure with multiple women).

Solomon married 1000 virgins in search of the perfect body to (1) "awaken" and satisfy his fetish for breasts (married promiscuity). No doubt, the bonding hormones played a role in his (2) "inability to form a lasting relationship" with any of his wives as he averaged spending about two weeks with each woman from courtship to marriage and on to the next.♥

Promiscuous Inhibitions Are Caused by Childhood Seduction

The form of promiscuous inhibitions represented by Molly's case has always, in my experience, been caused by a childhood seduction. The seduction usually takes place between the fourth and seventh year, and the child reacts to the experience with strong sensual pleasure accompanied by guilt. The guilt is handled by a withdrawal from the parents and from the values they represent. And the sensual pleasure becomes an end in itself, dissociated from a friendly, enduring relationship with another person. Sex must be furtive and indulged in with unlikely persons. Acute anxiety develops if it may lead to marriage.

♥*PRD: Promiscuous Inhibitions Explain Sin #6 "Disobedient to Parents"*

In 2 Timothy 3:1-5, "disobedient to their parents" is sin #6 in the list of escalating sins surrounding #9 "being without natural affection for family." "Disobedient" is the Greek compound word a (negative) + peitho (persuaded by evidence)." "Disobedient" isn't about rejecting the parents' authority. It's mentally refusing to accept the parents' beliefs and morals (Thayer 55, 497).

As Dr. Robinson has shown through Molly's case history, the child's rejection of the parents leads to the destruction of the adult child's ability to love his or her own family. No doubt, all forms of promiscuity reject the parents' moral teaching. The molestation of a child is a devastating way this can happen.

A positive example of peitho, "obedience," is the Shulammite maiden. In Song of Solomon 8:1-4, she explains that her mother "used to instruct her" regarding how to please a man sexually and enjoy lovemaking for herself. She heeded her mother's teaching and pleaded with the palace virgins not to force her to marry Solomon before they loved each other. When that never happened, she rebuked the King for his sensuous proposal to possess her body without love and commitment. Both her words and actions demonstrate her obedience to her mother's sexual teaching. She experienced a different love life than Molly had.

On the Sexless Marriages Survey, promiscuousness was a factor with 30% of the individuals who withhold sex from their mate. Here are two comments:

- *He was sexually abused at six by a girl cousin.*
- *He was sexually molested by his brother and his brother's girlfriend.*♥

Seeing Adults Having Sex Has the Effect of Seduction

I had a case where a single sight of grownups having sexual intercourse had the effect of seducing a child. In such a case, the pleasure reaction becomes associated with the early erotic feelings toward the opposite-sex parent. The suggestion in the child's mind is that the "evil" wishes can be granted if they are displaced onto another person. In later years this becomes the model for sexual behavior. Sexual desire is too closely associated with the parent's image, so the love object sought must be as different from the parent as possible.

♥*PRD: Case History: Man Developed Promiscuous Inhibitions*

At age 7, an acquaintance observed his older brother having sex with a girl he brought to the house when their mother was gone. The older brother encouraged him to have sex with his female cousin, who was about his age. The man grew up sexually active with many one-night stands, live-in girlfriends, and several marriages. He seemed to have a normal emotional relationship at first with his girlfriends and wives, all of whom considered him an excellent lover. However, the affairs lasted only a few years, at which time he would begin to withdraw sexually from his chosen companion. He then drove the woman away with unbridled anger over minor irritations. He immediately started looking for another girlfriend.

A woman participant in the Sexless Marriages Survey answered the question, "How did your sex-withholding companion learn about sex?" this way: "He hid as a child while he watched his grandfather sleep with strange women."

The two men in these examples were sexually seduced in their childhoods, which influenced and hampered their ability to bond sexually with their wives.♥

Nudity Within the Home Can Seduce Children

Sometimes parents seduce their children unwittingly. Not too long ago, it became the practice among certain intellectual families to indulge in nudism in the home. This practice was based on a misunderstanding of certain contributions of modern psychology, mainly the concept of inhibitions. The parents wished to prevent their children from being prudish about the human body. Such parents had no difficulty parading around nude in front of their sons and daughters of any age.

Parents who believe in this manner have rather elaborate rationales and present them convincingly. However, if some of my patients are any indication, I can testify that many children do not have the healthy reaction to nudism that the parents expect. To a 6-year-old girl, the sight of a naked father can be far too stimulating an experience for her to handle. She will react either with shock or excitement or both. The same is true of boys who are permitted to view their mothers in the nude.

We have seen that erotic fixation on parents constitutes a stage in the growth process. Whatever it may be in other societies, primitive or otherwise, nudity in our society is associated with lustful feelings. Family nudism, I firmly believe, tends to fixate children on parents permanently by causing unnecessary stimulation and hence strong guilt feelings. The result can be similar to a direct seduction of the child.

♥*PRD: Several participants in the Sexless Marriages Survey said their sex-withholding wives were taken to nude beaches in Europe as children.*♥

Situational Sexual Inhibitions Defined

Psychic inhibitions are often confused with a temporal emotional condition we call *situational inhibitions*. A man or a woman suffering from situational inhibitions has no basic sexual problem. Their responses have always been normal, and their orgasms are both frequent and satisfying. However, some severe reality problem has arisen in their life, which has caused a temporary eclipse of their sexual responsiveness.

Case History: Woman with Situational Inhibitions

On occasion, a woman may become disturbed by the fact that she can lose her sexual responsiveness. Let me give an example.

Anne was thirty-five. She had a happy marriage for ten years. In the first seven years, she had two children, both girls. She had no more fears of pregnancy and motherhood than she had of sex. Her upbringing had been, from a psychiatric standpoint, exemplary. In every determinable way, she was an excellent sweetheart, mother, and wife.

Six months before she came to see me, she gave birth to her third child, a boy. In a short time, it became clear that the child had a severe birth defect. When she came to see me, she had just learned that the child's medical problems would be fatal within two or three months.

When Anne resumed her sexual relationship with her husband after the child's birth, she had been unresponsive and disliked the whole act. This upset her. She thought this would pass in a week or two, but it did not. The fear that she may have lost her capacity to love her husband brought her to a psychiatrist.

Grief and Other Intense Emotions Can Inhibit Love

Anne could not have been more mistaken about the significance of her unresponsiveness. She had underestimated the depth of the blow the birth of an ill child can have on a mother. Grief and other profound emotions incapacitate the ability to love. One's entire confidence in oneself is shaken. It is perfectly normal under such circumstances to withdraw emotionally. In fact, it is desirable. Wounded feelings must heal, and emotionally immobilizing oneself is therapeutic.

Time Is Often Needed to Heal Emotional Pullbacks

Time is often the only cure for this kind of normal emotional pull-back. In this case, Anne's child died within two months, as had been predicted. Her so-called situational inhibitions lasted for three months after that and then disappeared entirely.

♥*PRD: The Bible Advocates Taking Limited Time for Healing*

The Apostle Paul regulated pulling back from lovemaking to heal emotionally:

> *1 Corinthians 7:5: "Stop depriving one another, except (1) by agreement for a time, so that you may (2) devote yourselves to prayer,*

and (3) come together again so that Satan will not tempt you because of your lack of self-control."

The word "time" refers to a "measure of fixed time" (Thayer 318). This "limited time" has three restrictions on it:

1. ***"Agreement"** means "mutual consent" (Thayer 598). In other words, whatever the issue is, it is out in the open. The couple is talking about the problem and agrees to give emotional support to the suffering spouse while abstaining from sexual contact.*

2. ***"Devote yourself to prayer"** means to "cease from labor, to give oneself to a thing" (Thayer 610). In this case, the hurting person "devotes" him or herself to praying to God for comfort and insight for solving the problem that is blocking their ability to enjoy passionate lovemaking.*

3. ***"Come back together again"** as it is your duty to love each other emotionally and sexually. Keep the bond strong between you so that neither one loses heart and is tempted to commit mental or physical adultery.*♥

Patience Is All that Is Needed for Situational Inhibitions

A wide variety of circumstances can cause temporary inhibitions that can last for a week to several months, depending on severity. Temporary inhibitions can be brought on by the death of a loved parent, the illness of a child (even a relatively slight illness), a husband's economic worries, and a difficult birth, to name a few. All one really has to know about situational inhibitions is that they aren't permanent. They are within the normal range of men's and women's delicately balanced sexual and emotional natures and will most certainly pass. The only therapy one needs is patience as one deals with the underlying problem.

One Solution Works with All These Sexual Inhibitions

The case histories in these three chapters represent the major types of sexual inhibitions. I presented them for three reasons.

1. It is important to understand what type of inhibition you have.
2. It can be helpful to see the individual characteristics of each kind.
3. Except for situational inhibitions, all sexual inhibitions (including psychic inhibitions) have certain basic characteristics in common.

This last fact allows us to approach each type with one basic solution. With this information in mind, we are now ready to turn our attention to the means by which sexual inhibitions can be resolved.

Section 4:

The Bridge to Love

15.

The Power of Love

We have now come to the last and most important part of our journey together, where we can examine how real love can be achieved. Let us start by examining what real love is, its role in life, and its components.

Inhibited Men and Women Turn Against Love Itself

Because of their problems in loving, many people arrive at a point where they turn against love itself. Having lost their hope of achieving love, they tend to depreciate it and minimize its importance.

Inhibited Statement:
"More Important Things Than Love"

One of the most common statements I hear from inhibited patients in the first interview goes something like this: "Well, it really doesn't matter, I suppose. There aren't many happy marriages anyway. And I suppose there are more important things than love."

♥PRD: *Case History: A Sexless Wife's Challenge to Her Husband*

Sexless spouses try to convince their mates that sex isn't required for a happy marriage. This serves as an excuse to not even try to learn how to love.

One sexless wife challenged her husband to name other couples in their circle of friends who were deeply in love. They could name only one couple. The wife rested her case that her husband should stop pushing her to change as the kind of love he wanted for their marriage was impossible for anyone to achieve.

Although the husband didn't believe it was an unattainable goal, his wife did. Consequently, she refused to put any effort into learning how to enjoy her husband and lovemaking for herself.♥

Love Is the Single Most Important Human Characteristic

Let us correct any tendency of this kind right here and now. Using the word in its widest sense, I would say that the ability to love is the single most important characteristic man has. It is the faculty upon which all the great actions, hopes, and aspirations of the world are founded. Without love, there could be no brotherhood among men, and therefore the basic concept of civilization as we understand it would be unknown, even unthinkable.

♥*PRD: Our Ability to Love Is a Major Way We Are in God's Image*

Love is also the most important characteristic of God. Our ability to love others is a major way God created us in his image. The Apostle Paul starts the great chapter on love this way:

> *1 Corinthians 13:1-3: "If I speak with the tongues of men and of angels, but do not have love, I have become a noisy gong or a clanging cymbal. If I have the gift of prophecy, and know all mysteries and all knowledge; and if I have all faith, so as to remove mountains, but do not have love, I am nothing. And if I give all my possessions to feed the poor, and if I surrender my body to be burned, but do not have love, it profits me nothing."*

Paul proceeds to name the qualities of love. However, nearly every single quality of love Paul names is missing in the heart of the inhibited man and woman. Thus I've bulleted them to help you stop and reflect on whether these are issues in your relationship:

- ✓ *Love is patient*
- ✓ *Love is kind*
- ✓ *Love is not jealous*
- ✓ *Love does not brag*
- ✓ *Love is not arrogant*
- ✓ *Love does not act unbecomingly*
- ✓ *Love does not seek its own*
- ✓ *Love is not provoked*
- ✓ *Love does not take into account wrongs*
- ✓ *Love does not rejoice in unrighteousness*
- ✓ *Love rejoices in truth*
- ✓ *Love bears all things*
- ✓ *Love believes all things*
- ✓ *Love hopes all things*
- ✓ *Love endures all things*
- ✓ *Love never fails*

Paul concludes by stating once again the great importance of love:

> *1 Corinthians 13:13: "But now faith, hope, love, abide these three; but the greatest of these is love."*

Male and Female: God's Genius concludes with a chapter devoted to understanding the mechanics of these characteristics of love.

Dr. Robinson wrote this book based on the science of her day, not on the Bible. From a human standpoint, she recognized how important love is for our world. Looking back over history, it's easy to observe that when hatred infiltrates the government and the citizenry, lawlessness and anarchy increase.

God's People Make the Best Lovers devotes the first four chapters to showing what happens to the world when people don't know how to love each other. Victorian morals evolved from false religious beliefs. Lovemaking was not a concept the early Christians understood as they limited sex to procreation. Extreme prudery became politically correct and medically supported due to ignorance about love and the human mind and body.

The feminist movement started when women rebelled against the disrespect shown to them by their Victorian government, doctors, and religion. They didn't recognize that what the world needed was authentic love. Instead of turning to love, they justified closing up their hearts to marital and parental love.

These mindsets live on in the Purity and Hookup Cultures that go from one extreme to the other. Both cultures destroy intellectual, emotional, sexual, and spiritual intimacy that God built into one-flesh love for husbands and wives.♥

Without Love, Terrible Loneliness Would Be Mankind's Lot

Men would be essentially isolated individuals whose personal drives, needs, and appetites would be the only realities to them. Aloneness, terrible loneliness, would be mankind's lot. Those who cannot love know what I mean.

♥*PRD: The Sexless Marriages Survey agrees with Dr. Robinson's statement that "those who cannot love know what I mean" about terrible loneliness. About 12% of the men and women who filled out the survey stated they were the ones who withheld emotional and sexual love. Although they rejected their mates' attempts to be affectionate, these sexually inhibited individuals frequently checked the following:*

- ✓ *Your feminine or masculine spirit has been crushed*
- ✓ *You're drowning*
- ✓ *You're fighting for emotional survival*
- ✓ *You can't think straight*
- ✓ *You don't know what's true anymore*
- ✓ *You're emotionally exhausted*
- ✓ *You're unlovable*

- ✓ *You hate yourself*
- ✓ *You're extremely lonely*

A husband who struggled to overcome his sexual inhibitions checked one additional item plus most of the ones above:

- ✓ *Your soul has been killed*

He wrote in the comments:

> *I am embarrassed and ashamed. I feel guilt also that it is my fault from past issues with having sex before marriage.*

A sex-withholding wife wrote:

> *I feel like I am missing out on a wonderful dimension of life. I feel like I am not being the kind of wife my husband deserves. I feel that in shutting myself off from intimacy and sex, I must be shutting myself off from other wonderful things in life as well.*

Another sexually inhibited wife wrote:

> *I am deeply saddened and feel a longing for wholeness.*♥

Love Is the Most Basic and Profound Urge We Have

In its deepest sense, love means union—the union between individuals, women and women, men and men, men and women. It is the most basic and profound urge we have, and its power for good is unlimited.

Love Unites the Child, the Neighbor, and the Sweetheart

In love, we make the good of our partner (whether our child, neighbor, or sweetheart) as important to us as our own good. In the union of love, we can experience the essential oneness of man and nature, to know that the universe is indeed our home and all men within it are members of our family. In this way, man learns through love that he is not alone. He is not condemned to the pain and anxiety that comes when he has nobody to share his mind, his heart, and his body.

♥*PRD: Second Greatest Commandment—Love Your Neighbor as Yourself*

When a lawyer asked Jesus what was the greatest commandment, Jesus replied:

> *Matthew 22:37-39: "'Love the Lord your God with all your heart and with all your soul and with all your mind.' This is the first and greatest commandment. And the second is like it: 'Love your neighbor as yourself.'"*

Being able to love others is what we have in common with God and is the basis of marriage and parenthood—love should guide our actions in every realm.♥

The Man and Woman Become One Flesh

The concept of this happy unity is most clearly seen in the love between men and women. The act of sexual love is a direct expression of it. Two individuals once unknown to each other, until recently total strangers, now nevertheless literally merge physically, know each other in the closest of physical embraces. They were miraculously made for this purpose, constructed for this union. The man leaves something of himself within the woman, his sperm. And a part of the woman joins this, merges with it. They have indeed become one flesh.

♥*PRD: God Said Husbands and Wives Would Become One Flesh*

After God created Adam, he had the man name all the animals and examine them to see if any would make a suitable companion. Even man's best friend the dog failed the test. Thus before God created the woman, he allowed the man to experience his great loneliness so he could appreciate the gift he was about to be given—a woman's love.

God put Adam to sleep while he made the woman, not according to man's wisdom, but designed solely on his divine insight into man's greatest needs. After God presented the woman to Adam, he declared:

> *Genesis 2:24: "For this reason a man shall leave his father and his mother, and be joined to his wife; and they shall become one flesh."*

*Before God created man, he pronounced each act of creation "**good**." After he created the man and the woman and the one-flesh relationship, God "saw all that he had made, and behold it was **very good**" (Genesis 1:31).*

The Four Parts of One-Flesh Love

*We often assume one flesh refers strictly to sex. However, sex is only **one-quarter** of being one flesh. If we neglect the other **three-quarters**, we doom ourselves to a make-do relationship. And the sex won't be all that great without the missing three parts. That's because all four parts of one flesh work together to create lasting, passionate intimacy that transforms lives and blesses children.*

*Ironically, although a child may result from combining the man's sperm with the woman's egg in the sexual act, the four times Genesis 2:24 is quoted in the New Testament to emphasize "one flesh," **none of them refer directly to procreation**. Following is a brief review of the four parts of one-flesh intimacy as revealed in the New Testament:*

1. ***Intellectual love** recognizes male and female: Intellectual love values one's*

own gender (masculinity or femininity) while appreciating and valuing the opposite sex (Matthew 19:4-5).

2. ***Emotional love** celebrates one in mind: Emotional love thrives on the husband's sacrificial love of his wife as himself and the wife's admiring love of her husband (Ephesians 5:31-33).*
3. ***Sexual love** honors one in body: Sexual love skillfully brings the male and the female bodies together to give both extreme ecstasy with the possibility of creating babies (1 Corinthians 6:16).*
4. ***Spiritual love** glorifies God joining them together: Spiritual love joins with the intellect, emotions, and bodies of the male and the female to create one-flesh love (Mark 10:6-9).*

At the creation,
God ordained passionate sex as the fulfillment of one-flesh love
to become the foundation of marriage and the family.

What a wonderful God we serve who created this amazing four-part way for husbands and wives to love each other and to serve him with their whole being!

All the attitudes found in one-flesh love are ones Dr. Robinson highlights as necessary for husbands and wives to manifest toward themselves and their mates if they are to step out of their inhibitions into glorious love.

The four parts of one-flesh love are taught throughout the Song of Solomon. For more information, see "Secret 4: Grow the 4 Parts of Intimacy and Love" and the appendix chapter, "The 4 Parts of One Flesh, Love, and Intimacy" in God's 11 Secrets of Sex.♥

Bodies Merge for the Creation of a Child

In addition to the joy and comfort it brings to each to join with the other as one, this merging can become a creative act. From the union, a child may be created. Thus we see that the profound result of the union which always characterizes love is productivity, creation.

Minds Merge to Form the Highest Form of Love

If this physical coupling were all there was, it would be miraculous still, though an experience shared by other forms of life. But man, as distinct from animals, has a mind. And minds also have the capacity to merge, the need to, and the profound joy in so doing. When the body and the mind of a man and a woman merge and become a unity, we see the highest expression of what we term love.

♥*PRD: Hormones of Love Glue the Husband and Wife Together*

In 1959 when Dr. Robinson wrote this book, science didn't know that the hormones released and mingled during sex affect the brains of both the man and the woman. Due to advances in MRI and SPECT imaging and volunteers who performed while being scanned, scientists now recognize that many hormones come into play during sex.

Although Dr. Robinson recognized the role of sex in making a man and a woman "one flesh," she didn't know that hormones released during lovemaking literally glue the man and the woman together emotionally. One can only imagine how she would have loved to have written about these hormones of love. Even with that handicap, her understanding of the emotional nature of sexual inhibitions is just as relevant and valuable today as it was in the 1960s.

I discussed the hormones of love in more detail in Chapter 2: "Vaginal Orgasms and Cervical Kisses." For additional information on hormones and how they affect husbands and wives, see "Secret 4: Grow the 4 Parts of Intimacy and Love" in God's 11 Secrets of Sex. Indeed, many of the secrets in the Song of Solomon take advantage of the hormones of love.♥

Lovers Achieve Their Own Potentials

When two people join as one in love, certain definite things happen to them as far as their minds are concerned. Each is able to come far closer to his or her own potentials. The merging that takes place in psychological love is essentially creative (just as its physical counterpart is), and so each lover comes closer and closer to his true self. All who have ever loved know of this inward blossoming, this inner fertilization through the love of the other. In work, in play, in all the inner and outer activities of life, the individual becomes far more vital and more productive than before when love reigns at home.

♥PRD: *Sexless Couples Never Rise to Their Full Potential*

The negative of Dr. Robinson's paragraph is seen in the Sexless Marriages Survey. Here are the frequently checked adverse results:

You feel like you never rise to your full potential as a:

- ✓ *Husband or wife*
- ✓ *Parent*
- ✓ *Employee or boss*
- ✓ *Christian*
- ✓ *Talented person*

In a sampling of the survey respondents, 81% of sex-starved Christians indicated they never rise to their full potential in all five of the above critical areas. In contrast, 100% of the ones who withheld sexual love said that they likewise never rise to their full potential in all five of the above areas. That leaves 19% who checked only one to four of the choices. Most men checked all five areas.

Here are some of their comments:

What other feelings do you have in dealing with a sexless marriage?

- *That I had to accept the sexless marriage because expecting sex from my husband was selfish.*
- *Guilty, deeply saddened, and a longing for wholeness.*
- *Disappointment. It could have been a good marriage.*
- *I feel abandoned. He does kiss me before he goes to work and when he comes home. It does seem like to me sometimes he doesn't like me very much although he says he loves me.*
- *I'm dying inside. I wasn't made to be celibate and I seem unable to live a goal-driven, overcoming, passionate life filled with accomplishments and achievements in one area of my life while a soul-crushing, mind-numbing, emotionally bankrupt intimate life. The two are incompatible and cannot both exist within me.*
- *I feel like my sexual desire and body are a waste. If we are supposed to be loyal, and God gave me a husband, why is a beautiful, horny woman in her twenties who is open to new things in the bedroom being left untouched?*
- *I feel stuck and depressed about the future. The thought of living in a marriage like this for the next 50+ years is awful.*

This small sample shows how the participants grieved the loss of productivity that the absence of emotional and sexual love in their homes created.♥

Lovers Do Not Struggle for Power

As I have said, the love partner becomes as important as oneself. This fact is why real love never leads to domination or a struggle for power between two people. Through the emersion of love, the uniqueness and individuality of the mate become precious, and hence all effort is made to guard the special qualities of the beloved. In love, we never encounter a man trampling on his wife's rights and needs or a woman competing with her husband. The value of the mate as he or she is and as he or she can grow to become the highest value in life.

♥*PRD: God Didn't Design Marriage to Be a Battle of the Wills*

Intellectual, emotional, sexual, and spiritual love is the foundation of the Bible's teaching regarding subjection and leadership. We see the elimination of the war of the sexes in the Apostle Paul's teaching in Ephesians 5. He begins the section by commanding, "Be subject to one another in the fear of Christ." Then he instructs wives to model their behavior after the church's admiring love and devotion to Christ, her spiritual husband. He holds up Christ as the example of self-sacrificing love for the husband to follow.

Paul concludes by going back to God's design in the creation for love to reign supreme in the home:

> *Ephesians 5:31-33: "For this reason a man will leave his father and mother and be united to his wife, and the two will become one flesh. This is a profound mystery—but I am talking about Christ and the church. However, each one of you also must love his wife as he loves himself, and the wife must respect [reverence—KJV] her husband."*

Male and Female: God's Genius devotes two chapters to proving that subjection was never a punishment for the woman in the creation and the fall. The rest of the book develops God's genius in designing the way husbands and wives balance, support, and love each other in the beauty of one-flesh intimacy.

Anyone who doesn't understand how much God loves passionate sex can't understand how true subjection and leadership foster self-sacrificing love on the parts of both husbands and wives. Passionate love is the foundation of all of marriage. Without the four parts of one-flesh love, the marriage may well deteriorate into a battle of the wills.♥

Lovers Soulmate Deeply

Because of the high-value husbands and wives place on their loved one, they make understanding their mate a priority. And this understanding furthers love, which in turn furthers understanding so that the process is a dynamic one. By gaining knowledge of their loved one, they ultimately go to the root of the loved one's personality, which makes possible an even deeper merging with the mate. Such understanding implies great sensitivity to all their reactions. It makes the mate inquire urgently (and creatively) into himself or herself, so no blocks to their deep psychological communion can develop.

♥*PRD: The Theme of the Song of Solomon and Sexual Surrender*

The theme of the Song of Solomon is "soulmate before lovemaking." The theme of The Power of Sexual Surrender is "take care of your soul so you can soulmate deeply to enjoy incredible lovemaking." Together, they are:

Take care of your soul so you can soulmate before lovemaking
to enjoy God's way of a man with a maid.♥

Lovers Know the Importance of Love

These are, then, some of the results of real love. I have listed them as a rebuttal of and a reminder to any who have, through repeated defeat become discouraged in their struggles to love and have tended to minimize love's importance. Nothing in life is as important as love. In fact, as one of my patients once said, looking back on the period when she was unable to love, "Without love, there is nothing in life."

Lovers Never Minimize Love

One cannot win the battle to love if one minimizes it. Above all, the inhibited man and woman must realize this and never give up their struggle. Indeed, complete awareness of how important love is can be a big step toward achieving the ability to love and to be loved.

♥*PRD: King Solomon Never Found Soulmating Love with 1000 Wives*

The Shulammite maiden's knowledge about the importance of love allowed her to see through King Solomon's empty substitutes of wealth and prestige for love. She chose true love with the Shepherd that soulmated before lovemaking. Fortunately, her mother had taught her how to liberate her soul for soulmating.

Solomon never understood the importance of love even though he spent a lifetime searching for happiness with 1000 wives. Not even his favorite wife—the daughter of the Pharaoh of Egypt whom he built a house for—could satisfy the loneliness in his heart. At the end of his life, rather than accept responsibility for his actions, he blamed his 1000 wives for his failure as a husband:

> *Ecclesiastes 7:27-29: "'Behold, I have discovered this,' says the Preacher [believed to be Solomon], 'adding one thing to another to find an explanation which I am still seeking but have not found. I have found one man among a thousand, but I have not found a woman [sometimes translated wife] among all these. Behold, I have found only this, that God made men upright, but they have sought out many devices.'"*

For more information on this verse and the three others in Ecclesiastes that comprise Solomon's confessions of not knowing how to love a woman, see God's 11 Secrets of Sex, "Solomon Never Had Great Sex with 1000 Virgins."♥

Lovers Esteem Each Other

Now if we summarize what was just said about love, what is its essential characteristic? This: the ability to see the mate as he or she is and to esteem the mate above everything else for his or her individual qualities, indeed to love the mate and want to merge with the mate for it.

Sexual Inhibitions Are the Opposite of Love

On the other hand, if we summarize all the case histories of the various forms of inhibitions that I have given and all the other pertinent facts I have adduced about the inability to enjoy orgasms, we would find the opposite of love and esteem. Inhibited men and women, of whatever variety they may be, never see the mate they want to love as the mate is:

1. The mate's individual and essential qualities are entirely unknown to the inhibited spouse and unknowable by him or her.
2. The mate is a series of projections from the inhibited spouse's past.
3. The mate is a composite of the fears, the misunderstandings, and the errors of the inhibited spouse's infancy and childhood.

Inhibitions Turn the Loving Spouse into a "Quasi-Monster"

The real union of love is therefore impossible with this "quasi-monster" the inhibited spouse has conjured up. about the spouse. ("Quasi" means "seemingly, apparently but not really, pseudo.")

♥PRD: *Wow! The Quasi-Monster Explains a Lot!*

One sentence from Dr. Robinson sums up the previous three sections of this book in her descriptions of the sexually inhibited spouse and the life of everyone married to a sex-denying man or woman. Transformation into a quasi-monster!

The Conjured Up Quasi-Monster

The inhibited husband and wife conjuring up a quasi-monster explains why they blame their spouse for everything that goes wrong. It helps us understand why they are so filled with anger and rage. This is why the anger turns to hatred as the marriage ages. The angry, bitter, mentally disruptive spouse doesn't live in God's world where love reigns and continues to grow in increased affection.

Instead, sex-withholding spouses live in a delusional, distorted inner-world where they have outfitted their loving mates with quasi-monster costumes. Only this isn't Disney World where children and adults laugh and play with Mickey and Minnie Mouse. This is their marriage, where instead of love reigning, they blame and hate their spouses irrationally. Consequently, their children grow up to make quasi-monster costumes for their own mates to scare the love right out of their children.

The Real Monster Is the Raging, Sex-Denying Spouse

When her marriage was ending, a wife asked her sex-withholding husband, "Why did you blame me for everything?"

He answered, "I was afraid if I looked at myself, I would see a monster."

Instead of Esteem, Bitterness and Anger Grow

Tragically, esteem for each other is missing in sexless marriages. Instead of appreciation and admiration, the Sexless Marriages Survey shows that bitterness and anger grow. The older the marriage, the more the anger turns to obvious hatred.

Here is how both male and female respondents answered three critical questions about hatred growing toward them by their sexless spouse:

63% Your gut tells you your spouse doesn't like you
39% Your spouse acts like he or she hates you
18% Your gut screams that you're in danger

Spouse abuse doesn't exist in marriages where love reigns and lovers cherish each other. In chapter 6, Dr. Robinson ascribes to inhibited husbands and wives the same bitterness and anger revealed in the Sexless Marriages Survey. She shows that it doesn't have to be this way as inhibited spouses can learn how to fill their hearts with love.♥

Step One: Give Up False Views of the Opposite Sex

Thus we see that the major task of the sexually inhibited man and woman is to rid themselves of the projections they make upon the opposite sex in general and upon their own spouse in particular. They must see through these negative attitudes and divest themselves of them, come to see the opposite sex in their true role, face-to-face with their mate in all their uniqueness and with all their potential. That is step one.

Step Two: Give Up False Views of Their Own Gender

When the man and the woman have given up their false views of their mate, there is another step they must take. The description of love I have given implies great security within oneself and acceptance of one's own uniqueness and essential masculinity or femininity. But the inhibited man and woman fears and rejects their masculinity or femininity, feeling it to be a dangerous trap. They must learn to alter this basic negative attitude entirely. They must see how childish and false, how utterly self-depriving this view of their gender is and give it up.

♥*PRD: Male and Female Are to Balance, Support, and Love Each Other*

Men and women can't give up their false views of the opposite sex until they rip off the quasi-monster costume they outfitted their mate with. God designed the male and the female to balance, to support, and to love each other. They can't see their true selves until they open their eyes to see their mates as they actually are, not who their childhood survival thoughts conjured them up to be.

Over and over, we see that God created the emotional and physical parts of sexuality in men and women to function in similar ways. What inhibits the female sexually also inhibits the male sexually. What releases the female to love the male also releases the male to love the female.♥

Open These Two Doors to Embrace Love

Thus we see that in inhibited sexual desire and pleasure the two main doors to psychological and sexual union—to love, in short—have been closed and locked. If these two doors can be opened again, the nonorgasmic woman and the non-ravished man will have resolved their sexual inhibitions.

Just these two doors? Is this not an oversimplification? To these two questions I can give unequivocal answers: yes to the first and no to the second. These are the two roots of the problem. Attack them, resolve them, and the major part of the task has been done.

♥*PRD: God instructs men and women to learn how to love the opposite sex in these excerpts from Male and Female: God's Genius:*

Masculinity in One Verse

The amazing verse below ties the husband's sexual love to his attitudes toward his wife's femininity:

> *1 Peter 3:7: "You husbands in the same way, live with [Latin—cohabito] your wives in an understanding way, as with someone weaker, since she is a woman; and show her honor as a fellow heir of the grace of life, so that your prayers will not be hindered."*

"Live with, "sunŏikĕō, pronounced soon-oy-keh'-o, is used only one time in the New Testament. It means "to dwell together (Latin—cohabito):—of the domestic association and intercourse of husband and wife" (Thayer 605).

Although the compound word is used only in 1 Peter 3:7 in the New Testament, it is used six times in the Greek-English Septuagint of the Old Testament. All six times refer to a married woman with one time referring to the widow of a dead brother. In every instance, the compound word implies sexual relations. It is translated to English as "married," "go in to her," "duty" for bearing seed for the dead brother, and "was given" (Isaiah 62:5; Genesis 20:3; Deuteronomy 22:13; 24:1; 25:5; and Judges 14:20).

The point? "Live with" in 1 Peter 3:7 ties "how the husband treats his wife sexually" and respects her femininity to God answering his prayers. The husband dwells with his wife sexually, not as a sex object, but by granting her honor as a weaker vessel while valuing her femininity and being joint-heirs.

This verse highlights the fact that sexuality is learned. If a man wants God to hear his prayers, he must put in the mental, emotional, and spiritual effort to "live with" his wife as a man of Proverbs 30:18-19 who knows "the way of a man with a maid."

Femininity in One Verse

Notice how Paul instructs the older women to teach the young women about love. This implies a responsibility on the part of the women to learn how to love their husbands:

> *Titus 2:3-5: "Older women likewise are to be reverent in their behavior, not malicious gossips, nor enslaved to much wine, teaching what is good, that they may encourage [teach to be sober—KJV] the young women to love their husbands, to love their children, to be sensible, pure, workers at home, kind, being subject to their own husbands, that the word of God may not be dishonored."*

Paul tells the older women, who are reverent, who have men, places, and things figured out, to teach the young women how to love (phileo, pronounced FILL-ee-uh) their husbands and children that the word of God may not be dishonored. Phileo is an emotional love that is physically expressed by hugging, patting, and kissing. This is significant for the sexual relationship because the Sexless Marriages Survey reveals that kissing, hugging, and touching are dead in sexless marriages as all forms of physical affection are withheld. In marriage, phileo encompasses sexual love from daytime flirting to nighttime passion.

The older women bring into play their sexual expertise per Proverbs 5:18-19, which portrays them as passionate lovers. This uniquely qualifies them to teach the young women how to ravish their husbands—how to overcome the influence of their dysfunctional homes origin. The other characteristics reflect the young women's femininity such as their sensibleness as opposed to distorted thinking and the raging of odious wives. Their purity, kindness, attention to making their homes a refuge, and working alongside their husbands, combine to honor God in whose mind ecstasy was created.

Husbands and Wives Must Put on Orgasmic Attitudes

To put on orgasmic attitudes, sexually inhibited men and women must (1) correct their distorted attitudes toward the opposite sex and (2) accept their own masculinity or femininity before they can truly love each other and themselves. When they complete these two steps, they can begin speaking God's beautiful language of love™ to each other.♥

16.

The Steps to Freedom From Sexual Inhibitions

The resolution of an emotional problem is a process, a process with a beginning, a middle, and an end. To put this process in motion and to maintain it, two distinct steps are necessary.

Step One: Grasp the Problem Objectively (Get the Facts About the Causes of Sexual Inhibitions)

The first step is to grasp the problem objectively, to understand its nature and implications, and learn all the outside facts about it. We have now taken this first all-important step. If you have read thus far, you now know a great many objective facts about sexual inhibitions.

What You Have Learned About Inhibitions Thus Far

You have learned what sexual inhibitions are and the toll they exact. You have seen why men and women are subject to sexual problems and how they originate in the individual, and the different forms they may take. You have seen how men and women have tried to eschew sex entirely. You have seen why their unhappy attempts can be successful, why they are inherent in biological and psychological possibilities.

Objective Understanding Frees One from False Solutions

This kind of objective understanding frees one from prejudice and prevents one from seeking false solutions (which abound). It brings one face to face with the real nature of the dilemma of sexual inhibitions, its basic psychological structure. And it uncovers the hidden area where personal responsibility lies.

♥*PRD: Christians Need to Learn God's Plan for Sexual Love*

In addition to understanding the psychological nature of sexual inhibitions, Christians need to understand God's design for lovemaking to bind the husband and wife together emotionally and to flood their bodies with the hormones of love. These surging hormones bless the children with a nurturing mother and father, which helps the children grow up into lovers who are good parents to their own children.♥

One Must Understand Inhibitions to Overcome Them

Without this kind of objective intellectual understanding, the individual man and woman could not come to direct grips with sexual inhibitions, for they would not know its nature.

♥*PRD: God's Formula Teaches the First Step of Objectivity*

When I read The Power of Sexual Surrender in 1973, this chapter opened my eyes to God's amazing truth in 1 Timothy 4:1-10. Prior to that time, I'd wondered how these scriptures applied to marriage. The truth? Dr. Robinson's 2-step process mirrors the formula the Apostle Paul gave over 2000 years ago for enjoying a passionate marriage for a lifetime.

Paul Warned About the Coming of False Sexual Teachings

Paul gave this formula in the context of warning that in later times, doctrines of demons would be taught regarding marriage—God's proudest institution. His prediction came true as some of the early Christians rejected God's blessings of sex by turning married lovemaking into an activity of shame (1 Timothy 4:1-3). Unfortunately, this disrespect for God's design for marital love continues among many religious groups today in various forms.

Step 1: Go to God's Word for the Truth About Sex

To protect Christians, Paul gave a simple process for recognizing and overcoming false religious teachings regarding sex and procreation. The first step in God's formula for solving all marriage problems, including sexual inhibitions, is going to God's word for the truth about lovemaking:

> *1 Timothy 4:4-5: "For everything created by God is good, and nothing is to be rejected if it is received with gratitude; for it is sanctified by means of (1) the word of God and (2) prayer."*

The sexual relationship is sanctified or "set apart to be better than what the world experiences" by two processes. Step one is to go to God's word for the truth about his design for loving marriages and the role of your attitudes in freeing your body for wonderful sensations.

The Bible teaches more about how to enjoy a passionate love life than any other area of marriage. Ecstatic love is the foundation of every aspect of marriage. If you miss it in the bedroom, you miss it everywhere.

False Teachings About Sex Abound

As Paul warned, many false teachings about God and the sexual relationship abound and keep Christians from enjoying wonderful, loving marriages. Here are a few of the false solutions that most current books and blogs promote:

1. *Asserting that the vaginal orgasm is a myth and insisting that clitoral and G-spot orgasms are the only ones women can achieve*
2. *Failing to realize that negative attitudes block sensations for sharing vaginal orgasms with cervical kisses*
3. *Teaching women to masturbate so they can discover what their husbands need to do to give them pleasure*
4. *Encouraging women to teach their husbands how to masturbate them to bring them to clitoral and G-spot orgasms*
5. *Believing the myth that men don't have sexual problems, that only women have sexual hang-ups*
6. *Disrespecting men's sexual needs by failure to realize that sex is more emotional for men than it is for women*
7. *Denying that men's sexual organs respond to their attitudes just as much as women's do and in the same way*

Studying God's word about the sexual relationship and what it means to enjoy a one-flesh relationship frees both men and women from these false beliefs and damaging practices.

Reading Together Completes Step One and Moves You Toward Step Two

Grasping the facts objectively about men and women and how they love each other is the goal of reading together this book and my other books in this series. As I've said before, reading together isn't for solving all your problems right now. Instead, you're focusing on fine-tuning your understanding of the scriptures about marriage and lovemaking. The rule is: You can't accuse your spouse of anything; you can only talk about what you're learning that you've misunderstood or are doing wrong.

My other books have questions at the end of each chapter to help you fine-tune your understanding of the scriptures and apply them to your daily life. As you go through the questions and hear your mate talk about his or her childhood, feelings, and attitudes, you will begin to see your spouse in a new light. You will start to develop sympathy and understanding for each other. It will become easier for you to support and love each other.

A young millennial husband who went through the books by reading and discussing them with his wife said, "Working together is hands down the most effective and soul-soothing way to grow into oneness."

This next step can be an emotional rollercoaster, but if you're reading and discussing God's word together, it helps keep you grounded and moving forward.♥

Step Two: Take a Subjective Approach (Check Your Attitudes and Emotions for Distorted Thinking)

Step one, objective knowledge, has carried us to the edge of the bridge for passing from a land of bitter deprivation to the richness that is your due. However, the individual man and woman must do more than merely understand inhibitions to cross it, which brings us to step two. The second and all-important step requires a subjective approach of self-examination. The husband and the wife must inquire into their attitudes and emotions that prevent them from crossing over into mature femininity and masculinity.

Inquiry into Attitudes and Emotions Gives Insight

The kind of knowledge one gains in this way we call insight. If one can get healthy insights into the attitudes and feelings upon which one's own inhibitions rest, one can resolve the problem entirely.

Inhibitions Are Like an Emotional Log Jam

Facing emotions and attitudes may seem hard and frightening. Everyone knows how complex emotions are, how difficult it is to understand them, and how multi-faceted every human being is. But I wish to tell you now that the whole approach can be kept simple. Sexual inhibitions are like a log jam on a narrow stream. If two or three logs jam together, all the other logs will pile up behind them, forming a complicated maze that stretches backward sometimes for miles.

Free Two or Three Logs to Release the Whole Jam

However, to release the jam, all one has to do is free the first two or three logs. Then the others will resume their unimpeded journey.

Attitudes About Masculinity and Femininity Jam Up the Logs

The emotional log jam we call sexual inhibitions is held in place by two disruptive attitudes:

1. A negative attitude toward the opposite sex
2. A negative attitude toward one's own sexuality

Insights Can Overcome Distorted Attitudes

We have seen these negative attitudes in every form of sexual inhibitions and have seen how they function. If the individual can come to grips with these two attitudes and dislodge them, the free flow of masculinity and femininity toward health and maturity will resume. Insight can dislodge these hindering attitudes and keep them dislodged.

♥PRD: Both men and women have problems with understanding and valuing masculinity and femininity. Male and Female: God's Genius explores male and female relationships and roles from the scriptures. Several chapters look at why God created men and women and their unique differences.

The chapters on subjection and leadership show how God requires both husbands and wives to practice sacrificial love toward each other. Leadership isn't a position of entitlement. It's a responsibility for service, as Jesus demonstrated when he washed the apostles' feet (John 13:1-17). Without the foundation of an ecstatic love life, it's impossible for Christians to get subjection and leadership right. As a result, resentment often abounds in the hearts of men and women toward each other. They fail to realize that God modeled the husband-wife team after his own relationship with Jesus and the Holy Spirit.♥

Give Yourself Alone Time Each Day at the Same Time

Let us start and see how sexually inhibited men and women can achieve insight into these harmful attitudes. The first thing you must do is very practical. At least at the beginning, you must give yourself a certain amount of time alone each day, *absolutely alone*. It might be for ten minutes or half an hour or an hour. But you must be alone, and you must regularly seek this time. It is most helpful to select a time when your mind is relatively free of worries and duties.

♥PRD: I encourage clients to follow this advice as much as possible to seek the "same time each day" for their alone time. When they do this, their subconscious begins to work with them and to look forward to this time of self-examination. Their subconscious will help them remember long-forgotten childhood incidents that they need to process as an adult. They will also experience moments of clarity as life events fall into place.♥

Feel Your Negative Emotions About Your Mate

What do you do to achieve insight at these junctures? On the simplest level possible, you start to let yourself feel your negative emotions about your mate. Your only aim is to let these negative feelings come to the surface, seek them out, and experience them to the fullest.

Choose a Recurring Irritation, the More Trifling, the Better

Pick out some small but recurrent irritation or annoyance your mate causes you; the more trifling, the better. Fixate on it, then dare to allow your emotions and thoughts about it to hold sway.

♥*PRD: God's Formula Teaches the Second Step of Subjectivity*

The following excerpt from Male and Female: God's Genius shows how the second step of God's formula for solving sexual problems addresses freeing up the log jam:

Pray an Interview-Type Prayer

> *1 Timothy 4:4-5: "For everything created by God is good, and nothing is to be rejected if it is received with gratitude; for it is sanctified by means of (1) the word of God and (2) prayer."*

"Prayer" (enteuxis) means "a falling in with, meeting with, an interview, coming together, for which an interview is held, a conference or conversation, a petition, supplication" (Thayer 218).

"Prayer" is not your usual word for prayer since it occurs as a noun in only this passage and 1 Timothy 2:2. The word is used only six times as a verb in the New Testament. Studying the verb form of enteuxis reveals exactly what this type of prayer involves.

*Two examples use the verb form of enteuxis in situations where something bad is reported about someone else: "Elijah . . . **pleads** with God against Israel" (Romans 11:2) and Festus told King Agrippa, "the Jews **appealed** to me, both at Jerusalem and here, loudly declaring that he [Paul] ought not to live any longer" (Acts 25:24).*

Once you learn God's truth about marriage and lovemaking, God wants you to go to him in an interview-type prayer and lay your emotions and thoughts bare before him—don't hold anything back. The interview is not like you do for a job where you present only your accomplishments and best qualities. In your interview with God, you discuss your faults and what you need to do to overcome them.

Examples of Interview-Type Prayers

If you're a woman, you might pray, "Dear Lord, I'm a daddy's girl, but my daddy neglected me. I've spent my life trying to earn his love. Help me face this and figure out the right attitudes to have toward my dad. Help me move beyond my childhood and learn how to love my husband from my heart. Help me not to fear my husband's masculinity, but to treasure him for it."

If you're a man, you might pray, "Dear God, I grew up hearing my dad make Mom the brunt of his jokes. He'd laugh great big, and us kids would too. Mom even laughed. He was impatient with her the rest of the time. He didn't show any respect for her. I have a low view of women because I've never been taught how to respect them. Help me value my wife's femininity, and love her for it."

Inhibited men and women nearly always have issues with their childhood that affect their ability to enjoy ecstasy with their mates. God's formula works for these husbands and wives. But they must be honest in examining themselves and with God in seeking his help and guidance in overcoming their faults.♥

Case History: Wife Enraged at Husband's Sloppy Habits

(1) Let me give you a single example from the case history of a sexually inhibited patient. Every morning this woman's husband dressed in the bathroom. He invariably left his razor on the sink and his pajamas in an untidy heap in a comer. His habits irritated her, and she had spoken to him about it several times. He would reform for a few days but then invariably fell back into his old ways.

(2) This information had been presented quite casually in the course of my first discussion with this patient. At that time, she spoke of her husband's offense as a minor annoyance. A bit later, she returned to the subject for the third time, each time expressing annoyance.

(3) I encouraged her to dwell on it, to let herself feel the full measure of her emotions about it. I told her that I suspected she had a good deal more in her feelings about this "trifling matter" than she hinted at because she had brought it up so many times.

(4) At first, she protested that the matter was too small to pay attention to, that she had more important things to consider. But with encouragement, she gradually allowed herself to pursue her true feelings. Underneath her commonplace protest was, as I had thought, an emotional cave-of-the-four-winds.

(5) Her husband's "sloppy actions," it turned out, did not merely "annoy" her; they "enraged" her. In her words, they signified his desire "to humiliate me." She asserted, "He thinks I have nothing to do but pick up after him, to wait on him hand and foot." Her anger became more and more explosive as she reflected on the matter, and it led quickly and directly to her underlying attitude toward men as a whole.

(6) Men wanted to do nothing more or less than to exploit women, to misuse them. They considered themselves a race apart, superior to women. All they wanted from a woman was sex or anything else they could get out of them. And they were powerful and thus dangerous. If a woman showed her hostility, they would use their physical strength against her. On and on went her stored-up rage. The hostile and frightened attitudes that lay just beneath the surface constituted the bricks and mortar of her sexual inhibitions.

♥PRD: Notice the steps Dr. Robinson took this woman through to help her discover her hidden beliefs about men:

1. *The wife was enraged at her husband's sloppy habits.*
2. *The wife brought up her "minor" irritation three times.*
3. *The wife was encouraged to dwell on her emotions.*
4. *She pursued her true feelings, which exposed an emotional cavern.*
5. *Her husband's actions enraged her about men in general.*
6. *She thought men wanted to misuse and exploit women.*

Fixating on a minor irritation—her husband's bathroom habits—allowed this wife to discover her subconscious beliefs about men that prevented her from enjoying a vaginal orgasm. Now Dr. Robinson will teach you how to apply this technique to your own negative inner thoughts.♥

The Step-Two Process for Getting the Insights

In pursuing this technique for getting at one's feelings, it is best always to select, as in the example quoted, one or more of the petty annoyances in everyday life.

How Does Your Mate Irritate You?

Does your mate's behavior in public embarrass you? Has your spouse an annoying habit? (Bathroom habits are fruitful sources for this kind of self-investigation.) Is your husband untidy? Does your wife's taste in clothes irritate you? Does your husband ignore the children? Does your wife pay too much attention to the children, ignoring you?

Explore Your Feelings Underneath the Complaint

You will know what has become the provocative agent in your life. Select it and explore the feelings underneath it to their limit.

You Move Quickly from Irritations to Broad Generalities

As you let your feeling come to the surface, please note how quickly you move from contemplating your mate's annoying characteristics to vast generalities about the opposite sex. In the case above, the woman moved almost at once from annoyance to rage to ascribing a hidden motive to all men—a desire to misuse women and exploit them. How can one love, in any real sense, a person one regards as a tyrant?

♥PRD: Men Who Harbor Hostility Toward Women

Sexually inhibited men harbor as many resentments toward women as nonorgasmic women do toward men. In fact, in 2005 Rabbi Shmuley Boteach wrote Hating Women: America's Hostile Campaign Against the Fairer Sex to expose the problem in modern society. As the father of five young daughters, he was alarmed by what he called the "woman-hating crisis among men."

His perspective as a Jewish rabbi is enlightening. He grew up in a culture where on the Sabbath, husbands quoted Proverbs 31:10-31 to praise their wives. That's the Woman of Great Price, whom we reviewed in Chapter 3: "The Not Impossible She" as the Bible's portrait of a wife with orgasmic attitudes and whose husband's heart safely trusts in her. His religion taught him that the woman reflects God's divine image more authentically than a man can (4).

In his Chapter 16: "Women as Nature's System of Checks and Balances," Rabbi Boteach states, "Women and the feminine energy are meant to serve as a counter to the aggressive male force. Any civilization that denies this natural balancing act will suffer the consequences for ignoring this most basic need." He praises the feminine-balancing touch in the home and also in politics. He warns, "Where femininity is undermined, subverted, corrupted, or marginalized, societies decay and often become scary places to live" (147-148).

Rabbi Boteach blames much of the disrespect for femininity on "the incessant male exposure to women as sex objects rather than thinking creatures" by the media, the Internet, and feminists (6). This is the exact opposite of the Victorian view of women as asexual. But the disrespect for women is the same.

The view of women today sounds like a modern description of King Solomon's sexual fetish for virgin breasts. He never treated the Shulammite maiden as a "thinking creature" who was his intellectual equal. Instead, he praised her body as the most gorgeous one he'd ever seen, saying all the other maidens were thorns compared to her (Song of Solomon 1:15; 2:1-2; 4:1-5; 6:4-12; 7:6-9a).

In contrast to the husband's admiration for his Proverbs 31 wife, here are some of the negative labels Rabbi Boteach says society and men apply to women:

1. *Gold Digger—marries for money*
2. *Publicity-Seeking Prostitute—will do anything for the camera*
3. *Cleaning Lady—cleans up the man's messes*
4. *Brainless Bimbo—entertains with crude comments*
5. *Catty Backstabber—fights other women over men (181, 197)*

Thus men must guard against viewing women as either a cold Victorian sexless shrew or society's empty-headed plaything.

Application of The Step-Two Process to Men

Dr. Robinson's process also works for husbands in examining their attitudes toward their wives' femininity.

1. *How does your wife irritate you? When you come home from work, do you notice everything that is out of place? Do you resent your wife staying home to take care of the children?*

2. *Explore your feelings underneath the complaint. Do you think your wife married you only because she wanted a paycheck?*
3. *You move quickly from irritations to broad generalities. All women want is a man to take care of them. Women have it easy in life.*

How can a man love and sexually enjoy, in any real sense, a woman he basically regards as inferior and a leech?♥

Let Your Generalities Give You Great Clarity

Pay attention to your generalities about the opposite sex. They will clarify how your underlying attitudes create an environment where real love and a productive marriage are virtually impossible. How can you love anyone in any real sense whom you basically regard as someone who exploits you?

Give Yourself Plenty of Time for This Emotional Inventory

Taking this highly emotional inventory cannot be a quick affair. During the first several sessions, you may find that no strong feelings or passionate generalizations will come up.

Negative Feelings Always Exist in Sexual Inhibitions

If you persevere, you will inevitably get to an area where the feelings are intense and negative indeed. We have found that such feelings always exist in sexual inhibitions. If hostile feelings did not exist, you would not have inhibitions.

♥PRD: As we saw in chapter 6: "Sexual Inhibitions Linked to Cognitive Distortions," anger and bitterness abound in the heart of the inhibited person. The man's and the woman's bodies cannot respond with glorious sensations as long as toxic emotions are allowed to exist in their subconscious and hearts.♥

The Inhibited Man and Woman Hide Their Feelings

The inhibited man and woman hide the intensity of such feelings from their conscious mind for two reasons. Knowing these reasons can help you and make you somewhat braver in your attempt to bring your feelings to the surface.

1. They Hide Feelings Because of Their Intensity

The first reason these emotions have remained hidden is their intensity. In the beginning, the feelings felt overwhelming. It was as if they proceeded from a bottomless well of emotions.

They Hide the Feelings Even from Themselves

And so, through the years, men and women learned to hide their feelings even from themselves. They hide their emotions from themselves by:

1. Minimizing negative feelings by fixating on trifles
2. Denying that, indeed, negative emotions exist at all

Defuse the Feelings by Becoming Aware of Them

Only by letting negative emotions up into their awareness can men and women experience the fact that the intensity of their feelings is not overwhelming. They will discover that their emotions have definite limits. Their negative feelings do not proceed from a bottomless well.

♥PRD: A client, who worked her way through many negative feelings, became discouraged when she kept fluctuating between sexual success and pullbacks. She described beginning to make real progress this way: "As I was expressing intense feelings to my husband that I just knew were true, I could see by the look on his face that I was in the midst of a 'cognitive distortion' meltdown."

She said, "It made me ask, 'What is really going on here?' I realized I was still trying to be perfect and keep my environment perfect so my perfectionist father would pay attention to me. Perfection is not my personality, and I was making myself and my husband miserable by continuing to live in that artificial space."

Once this client became aware of where her negative feelings were coming from, she began working on the real issues—her unresolved need for her father's love and appreciation.♥

Let Yourself Cry to Release Stored Emotions

In approaching this problem, I recall one woman who would not let herself weep over a strong underlying feeling of rejection by men she had become close to. "If I start crying, I'll never stop," she told me. She was not being dramatic either; that's the way she really felt. When she did let herself cry; however, the storm lasted for a mere thirty minutes or so—and then it was gone for good. She was relieved to find that the emotion, which seemed so boundless when unexpressed, had concrete limits. From then on, she was more at home with all of her feelings and not nearly so frightened of them.

♥PRD: God Catches Your Tears in His Bottle

Psalm 56:8:
"You [God] keep track of all my sorrows.

You have collected all my tears in your bottle.
You have recorded each one in your book."
(New Living Translation)

This psalm of David expressed his fear when the Philistines seized him in Gath. Read the definitions of the words and let them paint a visual picture in your mind of God's empathy and love for David and for you when you suffer from someone's mistreatment.

"Keep track" means "properly to score with a mark as a tally or record, i.e. (by implication) to inscribe, and also to enumerate; intensively to recount" (Strong 84).

"Sorrows" means "to nod [in agreement]; also (from shaking the head in sympathy), to console, mourn, take pity" (Strong 77).

"Tears" means "weeping:--tears" (Strong 31)."

"Bottle" comes from "a (skin or leather) bag (for fluids):--bottle" (Strong 75).

"Book" means "properly writing (the art or a document); by implication a book" (Strong 84).

In this psalm, David said God kept track of all his sorrows in two ways. First, in sympathy, God preserved his tears in a bottle so he could see David's pain.

God Records Your Tears in His Book

God didn't stop at just seeing David's pain. Second, he recorded David's pain in his book so he wouldn't forget it. In Malachi, God talks about recording good things about his people in his book:

> *Malachi 3:16: "Then those who feared the Lord spoke to one another, and the Lord gave attention and heard it, and a book of remembrance was written before Him for those who fear the Lord and who esteem His name."*

We know David "feared the Lord and esteemed His name." God recorded both David's acts of obedience and his sins in his book. The Apostle John refers to God's books:

> *Revelation 20:12: "And I saw the dead, the great and the small, standing before the throne, and books were opened; and another book was opened, which is the book of life; and the dead were judged from the things which were written in the books, according to their deeds.*

God knows how his people suffer at the hands of others, including their parents. And when adult children remain faithful, God catches their tears in his bottle and records their sorrows and faithfulness in his book. God knows what our lives are like here on earth, and he cares. He offers us comfort in our sorrows.

Handwrite Your Thoughts in a Journal

It's helpful to journal your thoughts. Many times your subconscious cycles over and over the same negative, anxious thoughts as if it's afraid you'll forget them. But when you write your thoughts down, your subconscious doesn't have to trust you to remember because the events and feelings are preserved on paper.

New research shows that you use a different part of your brain when you handwrite your thoughts than when you type your feelings. Many times journaling with pen and paper will lead to new insights. Clients who journal through unpleasant emotions make faster progress than those who don't.♥

2. They Hide Feelings Because They Fear They Are True

The second reason men and women fear to let their feelings come to the surface about their mate (and the opposite sex in general) is that they believe the things they feel are true. The feelings exist in their unconscious or partly conscious minds as profound convictions. They hold their emotions at bay because they do not wish to face how a part of their mind believes that their irrational feelings are based on reality.

Early Convictions Are Shaped Primarily by One's Parents

No matter how convinced a part of you is that your negative feelings represent reality, such is not the case. Your investigation is not going to prove that your hidden fears are valid. It is going to prove that they are invalid. These deep, hidden convictions are shaped early in men's and women's lives, primarily by their their parents.

♥*PRD: Your brain doesn't mature to solve problems until around 25 years old. Unfortunately, many men and women guide the rest of their lives based on conclusions they came to as children watching their parents interact with each other and them. They don't allow themselves to grow up emotionally and look at life with adult understanding.*♥

Fears Are Shaped Secondarily by One's Siblings

Convictions are shaped secondarily through one's relationships with one's brothers and sisters.

♥*PRD: Your siblings also had immature child minds when you were growing up together. It wouldn't be unusual for an older or younger brother or sister to say something that you believe subconsciously for the rest of your life unless you stop and examine it as an adult.*

Several questions on the Sexless Marriages Survey deal with your relationship with your siblings. Here are some of the negative experiences:

1. *Compared unfavorably to a sibling*
2. *Bullied by a sibling*
3. *Ridiculed by a sibling*
4. *Molested by a sibling*
5. *Engaged in verbal or physical fights with a sibling*
6. *Used as the family scapegoat*
7. *Became the little mother or the little father*
8. *Took on the job of being the peacemaker*
9. *Felt invisible in comparison to siblings*
10. *Expected to be the little mother or father*

Your relationship with your siblings is important because that's where you began to learn how to get along with other people. If you didn't get along with your siblings when growing up and still don't, you should expect marriage problems because you missed a vital life lesson.

One compliment the Shepherd paid the Shulammite in the Song of Solomon was to address her as "my sister, my bride." Loving siblings share confidences and secrets. They treasure each other as lifelong best friends. The Maiden was the Shepherd's "sister," in that they shared the emotional closeness that is common with emotionally healthy siblings.♥

Fears Are Irrational Defenses Against Childhood Abuses

Most of your complaints against your mate are irrational feelings erected as defenses against childhood misunderstandings, fears, and abuses. They have no real basis in truth. They do not pertain to your spouse as she or he is.

♥*PRD: The Apostle Paul Said It's Time to Grow Up into Love*

> *1 Corinthians 13:11: "When I was a child, I used to speak like a child, think like a child, reason like a child; when I became a man, I did away with childish things."*

Marriage forces you to grow up emotionally or to stay loyal to family and locked into childhood thinking. To enjoy incredible lovemaking, you have to put effort into soulmating. As a Christian, that means you must learn the truth about God's design for men and women and let go of your childhood prejudices through an interview-type prayer.

Case History: Brother Caused Man to Reject God at 4 Years Old

An older man tells the story of when he was 4 years old, his mother often sent him and his older brother to the barbershop together. The barber was a preacher who frequently spouted hell, fire, and brimstone scriptures while he worked.

The older brother always tried to get his hair cut first. When he finished, he baited the barber with a religious question. He took great glee in watching his younger brother's pain at being trapped in the barber's chair with religious fury bombarding his ears. The older brother laughed on the walk home.

The older brother's pranks led this man to reject God when he was only 4 years old. Now as a senior citizen, he immediately assumes that any individual who believes in the Bible or God is deceived. He refuses to examine his beliefs with his adult brain and stays locked into 4-year-old pain.

Lovemaking is for emotionally healthy adults—not for people acting out childhood emotions.♥

Convictions Are Only Feelings—Not Reality

When you begin to uncover your most secret convictions, it is essential to know this: *No matter how real these negative attitudes appear to be, they are only feelings, not reality.* As long as you keep this fact at the forefront of your mind, you will increasingly dare to let these feelings into your awareness and consciousness.

Do Not Stop—Press Onward and Inward Fearlessly

Men and women must be remorseless with themselves in this search for any negative feelings they might possess toward their mate and the opposite sex in general. Do not stop when you have seen one or two details that indicate feelings you had not known you possessed. Press onward and inward fearlessly until you have exposed every last hostile and irrational emotion and attitude.

♥*PRD: A Word of Caution About Pullbacks*

Dr. Robinson addresses pullbacks in detail in the next chapter. Many clients experience withdrawal from sexual pleasure during this time of inner searching. I warn them to expect emotional resistance throughout this process, so they don't become discouraged just as they begin to make progress.

Two Recovering Alcoholics Illustrate the Danger of Pullbacks

I tell clients the story of two recovering alcoholics I met at a codependency seminar back in 1986 when Melody Beattie came out with her book Codependent No More.

Both men had married "good-time gals" who were always ready to party with alcohol. But the wives joined Al-Anon and stopped supporting their husbands' drinking. Determined to force their wives back into supporting their alcohol addiction, the men made their wives' lives miserable. However, their wives refused to cave-in to their pressure.

The men said, "Finally, we knew we had two choices. We could give up our alcohol, or we could divorce our wives and find some new party gals."

I encourage my clients, "Think about your subconscious as being like these two alcoholics. Your subconscious is going to make your life miserable with some unbelievable pullbacks to try to make you go back to its emotional comfort zone, where you've lived since you were a child. But if you persevere, your subconscious will finally change after you've convinced it you're not going to."

Case History: Wife Stuffed Negative Emotions

One client who did not persevere sent me an email saying she wanted to move our session out a week. She explained that she'd just returned from a vacation and something came up with her husband that she needed to process emotionally.

When we finally talked, she explained that her husband had done something that triggered a lot of negative thoughts about him. She assured me, "I'm okay now, and I'm ready to proceed."

I asked, "What did you do with those negative thoughts about your husband? Did you stuff them?"

"Yes, I've got them where they're not bothering me anymore."

"Is the only reason they're not bothering you is because you've buried them where you don't have to think about them?"

"Yes."

This wife recognized that she was having an attack of negative emotions. But instead of pressing "onward and inward fearlessly," she avoided facing her feelings toward her husband. I could not help this client because every time she got close to identifying her issues, she canceled our appointment and hid until she buried the problem, which she then refused to discuss. It's impossible to help people who refuse to be honest with themselves.♥

Case History:
Woman's Negative Feelings Shaped by Childhood

One woman who came to me worked hard for five sessions on her negative feelings toward men. We started our joint investigation when she confessed that any slight irritability on her husband's part caused her extreme anxiety and often resulted in actual nausea.

(1) We pursued the matter and soon found a great store of antagonism toward men hidden just beneath the surface of a gentle person. She had the typical conviction that men wish to exploit women,

to bend them to their wills. She soon realized she had been interpreting many everyday happenings in the light of this belief.

(2) Her husband, an editor, sometimes worked at home in the evenings and would ask her to keep the television low until he finished. Though she knew his homework was exacting, she took this as an infringement of her "rights" and stored-up a great deal of rage about it. She also had hidden anger at commonplace duties such as taking his clothes to the cleaner, entertaining his business friends, and cleaning his "filthy" study.

(3) We explored them all, one by one. However, she and I both felt confident that something was eluding us. We persisted, and at last, the hidden feeling showed itself. Returning to her first complaint, I asked if her husband had physically struck her.

(4) "No," she replied, "but I often feel that he is going to strike me."

Knowing her husband to be a kind person, I pursued the matter. It soon developed that she had a strong unconscious conviction that men have no reluctance to use their superior strength against women to get what they want. She not only felt that men are hostile to women but that they also are potentially extremely violent.

(5) This was a bizarre conviction, and my patient soon understood its irrational nature. She had based her view of men on early memories of a sadistic father who had frequently struck her mother. When she realized the pervasive importance of this only slightly repressed fear of men, she was able to resume her psychological growth that had been severely inhibited from the earliest age.

(6) But the point I wish to emphasize is that she had to persist in her search for hidden attitudes. If she had assumed that she had gotten to the heart of her difficulty by uncovering the first few negative feelings, her self-investigation could not have succeeded.

(7) Please note that she did not feel she had come to the end of her emotional inventory until she had actually done so. If one is honest with oneself, one can sense when important attitudes still lie hidden within.

♥PRD: Review the steps Dr. Robinson took this woman through to deal with her negative feelings that were shaped by her childhood:

1. *She viewed her husband's actions through false beliefs about men.*
2. *Her rage extended to everything her husband did.*
3. *Dr. Robinson asked if her husband had ever struck her.*
4. *She thought men were hostile to women and could be violent.*
5. *She based Her views on her sadistic father who struck her mother.*
6. *She had to persist in her search for hidden attitudes.*
7. *She didn't feel she had come to the end of her journey until she had.*

This case history illustrates how intuitive a person can be in knowing they still have work to do.♥

Persist in Your Daily Sessions for Success

If you persist in your daily sessions with yourself, the time will come when you feel that you have exposed all of your angry feelings and negative attitudes toward the opposite sex. You will have uncovered the lees [sediment of wine in the barrel] of the emotions leftover from your childhood. You have now made a significant step toward recovery. You have removed the biggest log in the jam.

Expose Thoughts to Judgment, Reason, and Information

Why does this necessarily follow that freeing two or three logs will release the log jam? One of the major contributions of modern psychiatry is the fact that attitudes and feelings have the power to do lasting harm only when they are hidden from your awareness or half-hidden from it.

♥*PRD: After making substantial progress in dealing with negative attitudes from their homes of origin, several clients felt they hadn't completed the work of exposing their false beliefs and upsetting experiences. Although they knew they had made progress, a feeling deep inside told them they still had work to do. In every instance, doing the extra work yielded results.*

One woman said, "I can't believe how wonderful this last week has been. I finally feel like I've gotten to the bottom of my pullbacks. Sex has entered a whole new dimension for both of us. We are so unbelievably happy."♥

Youthful Errors of Thought Are Powerless When Exposed

The sexually inhibited man's and woman's troubling vestiges of youthful error automatically lose their power to do harm once they are made conscious. When they become known to the conscious mind, they are exposed to judgment, reason, and further information. They are seen to be fragile balloons of easily exploded ignorance.

♥PRD: *Exercise Naked for Complete Success*

Toward the end of God's formula for solving all marriage problems, Paul warned:

> *1 Timothy 4:7-8: "But have nothing to do with worldly fables fit only for old women. On the other hand, discipline [Greek gymnaze means—exercise naked] yourself for the purpose of godliness; for bodily discipline is only of little profit, but godliness is profitable for all things, since it holds promise for the present life and also for the life to come."*

Disciplining yourself or exercising naked expresses the idea of not letting tight clothing hinder you from getting the full benefit of physical exercise. In like manner, when engaging in mental exercise, you must fight the temptation to quit studying and being honest with yourself when you experience anguish and regret over believing worldly fables or myths about masculinity and femininity.

The gymnast experiences full, unhampered use of his body and mind only after long, diligent practice. Then the drills become second nature to him. The same is true when mentally exercising naked. In time, controlling your mindset and putting in due diligence will yield the reward you want. This kind of exercising naked frees your mind and body for ecstasy.♥

Exposure Releases You for Personality Growth and Health

Unblocking and exposing your hidden fears, rages, defenses, and false attitudes frees you for personality growth and health. When this negativity is released, your masculinity or femininity naturally begin moving toward health.

♥*PRD: Clients are amazed at how loving they become to their children and other people once they free their minds from inhibiting, false beliefs about masculinity and femininity and God's design for love. One husband, who had achieved a wonderful love life with his wife, said, "I have to be careful at work because it's second nature now to call everyone 'sweetie' and 'honey,' even my male coworkers. I have so much love in my heart, it comes out of my mouth without my even thinking about it."*♥

Expose Your Hidden Thoughts to Appreciate Your Mate

Men and women who achieve this are now prepared to understand their spouses and the opposite sex as they are. If you recall the previous chapter, that particular ability to comprehend and care about the mate's uniqueness is a chief prerequisite for love.

Hidden Feelings Override Truth for Overcoming Inhibitions

If the inhibited man and woman did not explore their irrational feelings in the manner I have described, any objective information about the opposite sex, learned from whatever source, would be useless. Their hidden feelings about the would still dominate.

♥PRD: *Case History: Husband Tried for 20 Years to Save Marriage*

I've witnessed several times that hidden feelings make truth useless. In one instance, the husband was extremely frustrated with living in a sexless marriage. He tried for over 20 years to get his wife to acknowledge their problem. He approached her by romancing her, referring to the scriptures, begging, crying, and even responding with anger—all to no avail.

Finally, he gave up and had an affair. He begged his wife to divorce him so he could marry a loving woman. She refused, promising she would change.

She came to see me. I asked what she thought when she read 1 Corinthians 7, where Paul told wives to lovingly satisfy their husband's sexual desires.

She replied, "I always had an excuse when I refused him, so I didn't think those verses applied to me," she said. "But my husband's adultery and my sexual coldness have been exposed to the whole congregation. I know I'm in sin, and I'm determined to change."

I met with her only one time as we were moving out of state. I gave her a copy of my two books, including God's People Make the Best Lovers. She called several times over the next months to ask questions and to give an update. She laughed when she told me she was enjoying being her husband's "sex slave." She indicated she'd completely changed her attitude and was enjoying lovemaking.

Several years later, I had a chance to ask her husband how they were doing. His wife had slipped back into her old ways of rejecting him. Learning the truth about how God created sex for women to enjoy equally with their husbands gave the wife insights for a little while. But she stopped her journey to learn how to love after her first few successes. She didn't put the mental effort into dealing with her hidden feelings. Consequently, her subconscious negative attitudes slowly came back to rob her and her husband of the joy they shared temporarily. Sadly, I've witnessed this pattern several times.♥

Get Hidden Feelings Out to Learn About the Opposite Sex

Now with the hidden feelings exposed, men and women are ready to hear more about the true nature of the opposite sex, to contrast the reality with their projection upon it.

♥PRD: This is why studying the scriptures about the differences between men and women is so important. What God says about the value of both husbands and wives and how their differences complement each other has a powerful impact upon their intellect and emotions—more so than some human counselor's opinion or experience of the same thing. At this point, I've observed that many couples are ready to study Male and Female: God's Genius. They learn how God designed men and women to balance, support, and love each other with intellectual, emotional, sexual, and spiritual intimacy.♥

How Much of Your Past Must You Uncover?

In giving the case histories of women suffering from the various forms and degrees of sexual inhibitions, I have described the early origins of their problems. I should now like to raise the question of just how much knowledge of one's early, often buried, experiences men and women must uncover to achieve maturity.

One Does Not Have to Reveal Much of the Past

In my opinion, most men and women suffering from inhibited desire and pleasure do not need to go into the matter of their childhood experiences to any extent at all. The evidence that their life was traumatic to some degree is contained in the fact that they do have problems in the present. It is always the immediate problem with which people develop their most profound and strongest emotions.

Present Emotions and Feelings Reveal the Past

The technique of "feeling" one's way through one's problem works with sexual inhibitions. It is one's present emotions, therefore, that constitute the major material of self-examination. Understanding present feelings and attitudes reveals the past, for it was in the past that these attitudes were established. They have changed little since their inception.

Knowledge of Inhibitions Makes It Easier to Face Problems

Why, then, did I go into the detailed childhood development of inhibitions in my case histories? For the same reason, I gave all the other objective facts about inhibitions before approaching this section. The more conscious knowledge one has of the entire problem of inhibited sexual desire and pleasure, the more one dares to face up to the responsibility for one's own problem—and the more one can face up to it. Knowledge can free one of the ignorance and superstition upon which resistance to achieving psychic maturity is based.

Understanding Your Feelings May Be Helpful with Rape

On the other hand, I am not holding any fundamental objection to the scrutiny of early experiences or helpful speculation about them. For example, sometimes, as in the case of an early seduction or a rape that is remembered, it can be helpful to remember those early details to throw a therapeutic light on one's present feelings.

You Do Not Always Need All the Details to Find Freedom

However, the numerous details that go into the formation of one's personality while growing up can be confusing if one tries to understand them all without an expert guide's help. In most cases of inhibited sexual desire, it is not required for recovery to understand them all.

♥*PRD: Jesus and the Apostles Did Not Pursue Gory Details*

Jesus and the apostles didn't spend time quizzing people about their past. They dealt with the present—what the person needed to do right to solve their problem. Working with couples for half a century now, I found that I don't need to know all the gory details. I just need to know enough to get to the gist of the problem. While the details vary, the core problems fall into classic categories.

Case History: Husband Visited Prostitutes

One wife who called for an appointment had discovered her husband had visited prostitutes. It was not the first time he'd done it. I emailed her material on 1 Timothy 4:1-10—God's formula for solving all problems.

When we sat down at my dining-room table with our Bibles, she asked, "Where do you want me to start?"

I replied, "When your husband committed adultery before, did you follow God's formula for dealing with it?"

"No, not at all."

"Okay. You need to learn how to deal with this instance the right way. I'm going to give you some reading assignments and some homework to do before we meet again."

It turned out that both she and her husband needed to do some mental housecleaning to fully appreciate each other and make their marriage be what God desires.♥

"Feel Through" Your Present Negative Emotions

If self-examination of one's early experiences does not seem to be immediately helpful, abandon it entirely. Confine yourself to "feeling through" your present problem, undoing the harm the childhood attitudes are still causing in the here and now.

Healing Can Occur Rather Naturally

The steps for achieving insight into one's negative emotions, which I recommend here, are the most difficult steps one has to take on the road to maturity. If you can take them, the most challenging part will be over. The remaining part of the process of recovery occurs naturally:

1. Acquire more information.
2. Allow new feelings to grow.
3. Expand inside yourself.

4. Accept guidance past a few possible pitfalls.

You will see what I mean as we continue in the following chapters.

♥*PRD:* God's Step Three: Approach Problems with Thankfulness

In 1 Timothy 4, we looked at the first two steps for solving all marriage problems, including sexual issues. However, the Apostle Paul takes God's formula beyond Dr. Robinson's two steps to begin and end with an important third step—thankfulness.

> *1 Timothy 4:3-5: "[Some] who forbid marriage and advocate abstaining from foods which God has created to be **gratefully shared in** by those who believe and know the truth. For everything created by God is good, and nothing is to be rejected if it is **received with gratitude**; for it is sanctified by means of the word of God and prayer."*

What are Christian couples to "gratefully share in" amid sexual inhibitions? And what are they to "receive with gratitude"? Their marriages! Paul said God created both marriage and food to be "gratefully shared in" and to be "received with gratitude" by those "who believe and know the truth."

To solve complex marriage problems, a person must approach (1) learning God's truth and (2) meeting him in interview-type prayer with thankfulness. Gratitude enables a person to replace negative subconscious thinking, teaching, and myths about men, women, and sex with heartfelt love. A spirit of gratitude makes the journey to overcome inhibitions easier and is required for lovemaking success.

Sexless Marriages Sin #7—Ungratefulness

The opposite of gratitude is "ungrateful," which is #7 in the list of 18 sins surrounding #9, "without natural affection," in 2 Timothy 3:1-5. The responses to my Sexless Marriages Survey show that of sex-withholding Christians:

70% are ungrateful for the things their mates do, and many look down on the opposite sex.

61% seldom give a genuine compliment regarding their mate's character, habits, accomplishments, etc.

Here are some of the comments the respondents made that reveal the severity of the problem:

- *I do not appreciate my husband enough because of resentments. I seldom give genuine compliments and criticize the opposite sex in general, but not to him.*
- *He barked at me today because when I put his tools away from a project he*

is working on, I placed the battery on the charger. It turns out the charger was broken even though I pointed out it was flashing when I left it on the shelf. My husband said he knows it's broken but just never threw it away. I was trying to be helpful.

- *Yes. I tend to lose sight of the things I'm thankful for in my spouse and begin "looping" negative thoughts.*

3 Ways Gratitude Can Help Transform a Sexless Heart

1. *It replaces the negative with the positive in your brain.*
2. *It focuses on what you can change—praying to God with thankfulness.*
3. *It prepares your mind to love others.*

Sample Prayer of Thanksgiving to Get You Started

Dear Lord, I accept your gifts of femininity to balance my husband's masculinity and a wonderful love life along with the laughter, smells, and insights that you've given me. Thank you for setting me free through your word to enjoy your love and blessings of marriage. In Jesus' name, I pray and thank you. Amen.

Your Thankfulness Notebook

If you haven't started your "Thankfulness Notebook" that was suggested at the end of chapter 1, it's not too late to begin to reap the benefits of a grateful heart. Answer the following four questions for each of the final chapters in this book beginning with this one:

1. *What Bible verse especially spoke to your needs now? Why?*
2. *What things did you learn about to thank God for as gifts from him?*
3. *What do you need to ask God to help you with in your life?*
4. *How can you change your routine to make it happen?*

Review of God's Three-Part Formula for Solving Marriage Problems

1. *Learn God's truth about the differences in male and female and one-flesh love.*

2. *Go to God in an interview-type prayer to apply what you learned to your specific problems.*

3. *Receive God's teaching about marriage with thankfulness for God's creation of men and women and the way they relate to each other in one-flesh love.*

What an incredible, life-changing formula for overcoming childhood-imposed sexual inhibitions and developing orgasmic attitudes toward one's mate and oneself! Thank you, Dr. Robinson, for opening up these amazing scriptures on how to solve all marriage problems. To God be the glory forever and ever!♥

17.

The Nature and Danger of Pullbacks

For many men and women, the ability to surrender physically comes rather swiftly. To others, it is a gradual process, as though the unconscious mind needed to build up a reserve of reassurances before it felt secure. In either case, but particularly in the latter, *they need to be forewarned of one crucial thing: sexual thaw will not proceed uninterruptedly. There is no straight line from inhibitions to real adulthood.* I should like to explain this more fully.

The Man and the Woman May Experience Pullbacks

In the sexual embrace, as the man and the woman allow themselves to experience more pleasure and as their physical sensations increase, a part of their unconscious mind frequently takes alarm. This causes them to draw back from any further immediate advance.

♥PRD: *Men and Women May Backslide from Previous Gains*

I've witnessed men and women backsliding many times: they go forward, regress a little bit, learn more and go forward more, regress a little bit, and learn more to go forward once again. The cycle may continue for a while. They may even experience an enormous regression that might make them fear all is lost. But it isn't. It's just part of the normal process of learning and making adjustments.♥

Childhood Feelings of Fear or Guilt Reassert Themselves

If you stop to ponder this point, you will find it readily understandable in terms of our former discussions. The experiences and relationships upon which an inability to orgasm vaginally is based took place a long time ago, often in early childhood. They occasioned fear in the child, fear of sexuality, fear of surrender to one's sensual impulses, or powerful guilt. *Now, as one starts to move toward a resumption of one's sensuality, it is almost certain that these irrational, buried fears will try to reassert themselves.*

♥PRD: *Male Examples of Childhood Pain to Overcome*

A male client remembers his mother frequently saying, "All men are pigs," beginning at 4 years old, continuing throughout his childhood, and even now that he's left home and married.

A male Sexless Marriages Survey respondent wrote: "In my family of origin, I received unconditional love from my mother, but only blame from my father. I learned to deny myself in my family of origin. What I wanted was not important to my father. He never came to a baseball game I played in or to any award ceremonies at school or awards at Cub or Boy Scouts. So I believe I do not see my need for sexual closeness as a high priority. My sin is not putting my wife's needs as a high priority in our marriage.♥

Not Necessary to Uncover Childhood Incidents

In most cases, it is not necessary to uncover the childhood incidents these fears are based on. If one will insist on pursuing the techniques for inner change I describe in the previous chapter and the next two, these fears will finally become inoperative in the sexual area. It is, however, necessary to know that you are experiencing such fears.

Failure to Realize that Great Sex Causes Alarm

Generally speaking, the pullbacks do not show themselves directly. Husbands and wives will not say to themselves, "That new sensual experience I had last night is causing me alarm."

♥PRD: *Case History: Man Didn't Realize Significance of Great Sex*

Looking back over several decades of unsatisfying sex with his vaginally orgasming wife, a husband realized he had been living through one massive pullback. Although he preferred the ease of self-masturbation to the necessary emotional connection with his wife for penetration, he agreed to sex on a somewhat regular basis to keep her from complaining.

Only one time in his marriage had he enjoyed intercourse more than pleasuring himself. A year earlier, their first son was born, an unexpected event that brought joy to the whole family. About a year later, he and his wife left the kids with the grandparents and took an extended vacation. After days of soulmating and sightseeing, he made real love to his wife.

He said, "Not only did my wife experience the most powerful orgasms ever, but my orgasm was so sensational that I asked myself, 'What was that all about? Why did that happen?' When we got home, and I went back to work, everything returned to normal with sex with my wife being boring."

He continued, "I never forgot that experience, and from time to time, I wondered what caused it. I never made the connection between my masturbating and mentally criticizing my wife all the time with being bored with sex with her except for that one time when we were so happy and connected as new parents."♥

Uncover the Old Quarrelsome, Critical Feelings of Inferiority

The fear separates itself from the sensual experience and expresses itself indirectly. Husbands and wives may find themselves once again becoming quarrelsome, critical of their mate. Old feelings of deprivation or inferiority may reassert themselves with apparently new vigor. And the new sensual capacity may retire once more from view. *The reason: the old defenses are protecting one against the new masculinity or femininity.*

♥*PRD:* *Case History: Wife Has Frequent Sex Then Pulls Back*

A male participant in The Sexless Marriages Survey, who was the one deprived of sex, wrote: "I do not feel I withhold sex, however after years of rejection, I no longer try to initiate it that often because of being rejected so many times. When we do have sex, we normally will have sex frequently for 1-2 weeks several times a week. However, something will happen (a fight or sickness), and then it will be months before it happens again. The last time we had sex was on her birthday."♥

Be Aware that the Anxiety Comes from the New Sensuality

Such anxiety reactions, I wish to make clear, should not give any cause for concern. Indeed, one does not have to analyze or investigate them. One merely has to be aware that they result from the new advance in sensuality, the new ability to surrender oneself a bit more completely than before. *Advance of this kind is never lost in any final sense.*

Case History: Woman's Pullbacks

(1) Let me give you an example of a typical reaction to such an advance. The patient was of the type I call the clitoral woman. Her orgasm had been exclusively clitoral. Together we covered the ground that I have presented in this section. She was able to air her feelings about men and women's lot. She corrected her view of men and, in a real way, began to view her husband with the eyes of a loving woman.

(2) One day, she came to me in great excitement. It was unmistakable, she told me; during last night's lovemaking, she felt for the first time distinctly pleasurable vaginal sensations.

(3) But in the next session, her attitude was entirely different. She

had quarreled with her husband over some trivial matter, and she forthwith launched into the kind of tirade against men I had not heard from her for several sessions.

(4) After letting her air her feelings, I pointed out to her the possible connection between her new sensual experience and her regression to her old defenses. She was unconvinced and remained so.

(5) Then, a week later, the episode repeated itself in its entirety: vaginal sensations and delight, followed quickly by a quarrel and ill feelings toward her husband.

(6) Forewarned, she was now on guard for such negative reactions. When they appeared, she knew their significance and was able to handle them. She successfully prevented herself from acting out her irrational feelings and avoided quarreling with her husband.

♥*PRD:* Recognizing the Pattern Can Change the Outcome

Dr. Robinson's case history shows how pullbacks can wreak havoc until the person sees through them. Notice the sequence of going forward and then backward:

1. *Aired her grievances against men and mistreatment of women*
2. *Excited she'd had her first orgasm*
3. *Quarreled with her husband and launched a tirade against men*
4. *Unconvinced her bad attitudes came from sexual success*
5. *Repeated the episode a week later, success followed by a quarrel*
6. *Handled future ones and avoided acting out distorted feelings*

It's helpful for the mate of an inhibited husband or wife to watch for this pattern. As you can see, it isn't about you. It's about your spouse's reaction to the fears and traumas of their upbringing.

Many Sex-Withholding Spouses Fight Dirty

As sympathetic as you might be to your spouse's dysfunctional childhood home, it's never right for your spouse to perpetuate the sin of his or her parents onto you and your children. You need to draw boundaries and stop listening to harangues. If you need help with this, you can pick up the free handout for my class "How to Fight Fair and Face Anger" at my website on the Book Shelf page. You'll learn how to stop verbal abuses such as the following:

1. *Name-calling*
2. *Yelling and screaming*
3. *Interrupting and talking over you*
4. *Judging your motives with extreme accusations*
5. *Comparing you to despicable people*

Sadly, many sexually inhibited spouses are dirty fighters. But loving mates have tremendous power to change the course of arguments. You may have to teach your spouse how to fight fair before you can begin to address the problems his or her inhibitions and distorted thinking create in your home.

You can read "Stacey's Story" at the end of each of the chapters in God's 11 Secrets of Sex to learn how she taught her husband to fight fair. Being able to talk about the sensitive topic of sex created the opportunity for them to start reading about God's design for sexual love. They realized neither one of them had grown up in a home where true marital love was portrayed. Today Stacey and her husband Joe enjoy a sexually loving marriage.♥

Great Sex May Be Followed with Negative Reactions

In making the point that pullbacks may occur, I do not wish to be misunderstood or thought to be contradicting myself. I am not advising one to fixate obsessively on one's new sexual sensations. However, noticing such new experiences will be unavoidable. I am merely saying that it is helpful to know that minor regressions may follow orgasms with cognitive distortions.

♥PRD: *Ask for Hugs to Break the Power of Pullbacks*

The key is to recognize the pullbacks without yielding to the negative emotions. Rather than starting a quarrel, go to your spouse and say, "I enjoyed last night with you, but today I'm experiencing a pullback. I hate thinking these thoughts. I need a hug." But your negative feelings may make this seem impossible because the last thing you may want to do is touch your mate.

Don't let your parents' ignorance and neglect of you cheat you out of a sympathetic hug with your spouse. You're worth it. If you need to cry, let the tears flow as they release the tension in your body and thoughts.♥

WARNING!
A Crisis Pullback Can Endanger the Marriage

The above observations lead me to a related matter, which is of central importance. In the move toward masculinity and femininity, most cases reach a juncture called "the danger point." When men and women are working with a therapist, the danger point is minimized by the therapist's awareness of the problem and the ability to help handle it when it arises. However, if husbands and wives tackle the problem by themselves, they should be forewarned of a potential adverse reaction.

The First Orgasm May Lead to Regression

This danger point generally comes when one who has suffered from sexual inhibitions has, at last, allowed oneself to experience a magnificent orgasm for the first time. The immediate reaction is tremendous relief. But this is almost always followed by the same kind of regression I described previously; only this time, the pull-back from one's own advance and the mate is far more powerful.

The Pullback May Endanger the Marriage

In some of the case histories in the last section, we saw just how dangerous this period can be to the relationship. Indeed at this point, the husband or the wife may precipitate a crisis of such severity that the marriage itself is threatened.

The Pullback May Take One of Several Forms

The form the difficulty takes is always individual. It is usually an exaggerated version of a particular man's or woman's most typical cognitive distortion:

1. If one is argumentative, one is apt to start a fight of proportions heretofore undreamed of.
2. If one's tendency is to become depressed, the melancholy can become profound indeed.
3. If one is critical and carping, one can make Craig's wife appear to be a normal, healthy woman.

♥PRD: Craig's Wife was a 1936 film about a domineering wife. It was based on the Pulitzer Prize-winning 1925 Broadway play of the same name by George Kelly. At least three movies were made from the play.♥

The Danger to the Marriage Is Not Exaggerated

I am not exaggerating. It is possible that many divorces are caused by husbands and wives who, by the natural reassurance that marriage to a tender mate often brings, have moved close to their true natures all unwittingly. They share a wonderful vaginal orgasm, and then, without the benefit of any insight, an intense anxiety reaction sets in, causing a powerful desire to flee from the frightening situation.

♥PRD: Clients Report Experiencing Dangerous Pullbacks

Men and women, who are working on their own to become loving, need to be forewarned about this danger. Several clients contacted me because they had read the original The Power of Sexual Surrender and were enjoying some success. Then suddenly, the deeply inhibited spouse was in such a terrible state, they thought their marriage would end.

This sounds frightening, and it is. But these couples quickly realized their feelings weren't reliable. They were in the midst of a major pullback. That realization didn't make the overwhelming feelings go away, but it pointed the couples toward gaining additional information. That's when they contacted me.

The Scriptures Transform Lives when Human Words Don't

In addition to our work to take off their childhood personality masks, I assigned the couples specific chapters to read in my books as dictated by the distorted accusations. It was most helpful for the pair to read the chapters aloud together and then stop and discuss points that caught their attention. Listening to the loving mate's views dispelled many of the inhibited spouse's judgments about the mate's motives. Likewise, the loving mate benefitted from hearing how the sexually withholding spouse was working to overcome a lifetime of negative thinking about the opposite sex and his or her own gender.

The Rule: You Can't Say "You…."

I stress the following rule to my clients: "You cannot accuse your mate of anything. You cannot say, 'You always….' Or 'You never….' You can only talk about what you learned that you need to do differently. At this point, you do not know enough about God's word regarding men and women and sex to accuse anyone of anything. Your job right now is to fine-tune your knowledge and understanding of God's word and how he desires for you to enjoy passionate sex with your mate."

Replacing the negative thoughts with the positives in God's word made a difference for these marriages. However, the couples continued to experience pullbacks of decreasing frequency for several months. Interestingly, the sexual withdrawals varied in intensity.♥

The Danger Is Not Knowing "Success Can Lead to Danger"

The worsening of early fears brought on by the orgasmic experience causes the pullback. But again, I must emphasize that the chief danger during this period of reaction lies in the fact that husbands and wives see no connection between their emotional upset and the successful sexual experience they just achieved. Why should they see such a connection? Orgasm and powerful sensations are what they have been consciously waiting for, has it not? It would only be surprising if they did see a relationship between the two experiences.

Emotional Outbursts Represent an Inner Panic

The emotional outbursts represent an inner panic. Consider this: In growing up, it took these men and women years to construct a defensive system against masculine or feminine sensuality, which the person had learned was dangerous or wicked. Through this defense system, the inhibitions and psychological rejection of the opposite sex, etc., deprived them of much. It had at least allowed them to feel secure in some deep manner. The defenses were maintained to hold onto the feelings of unconscious security.

Sexual Inhibitions Offer Security Against Growing Up

And now, with orgasm and heightened sensations, they feel all these defenses swept away in a moment. They feel exposed, guilty, and naked to their imaginary enemy—their mate. And now they are tempted to surrender to their mate completely. In their panic, they forget the advance they have made, the revaluation of their attitudes toward men, women, and children.

Inhibited husbands and wives cannot admit the irrational nature of their unconscious fear, even to themselves. So they repress it and create an exterior diversion. Real trouble is always an excellent defense against personal insight.

♥*PRD: Remember the Apostle Paul's Words About Growing Up*

It is easier to blame your mate for your own lack of tenderness than admit your life is broken and fix it. To move forward, you must keep the process going.

> *1 Corinthians 13:11, 13: "When I was a child, I used to speak like a child, think like a child, reason like a child; when I became a man, I did away with childish things.... But now faith, hope, love, abide these three; but the greatest of these is love."*

The Sexless Marriages Survey shows that the marriage is either growing in love or growing in anger and hatred. Only 11% of the respondents' sex-withholding spouses were willing to read and study to overcome their problems. That means 89% refused to talk or read about how to bring love into their marriage. And 79% of sexless spouses fought dirty to stop any accountability for their distorted rants against their mates.

The marriage won't change as long as the love-withholding spouse stays locked into immature, childish ways of dealing with childhood fears, stress, and anxiety. The withholding spouse deprives him or herself and their family of the greatest characteristic of being a Christian—love.♥

Pullbacks Can Take Harmful Paths

When husbands and wives do not understand the nature of their actions in such cases, the flight can take a potentially harmful direction.

1. I have known some who "fall in love" with another person at this juncture.
2. Others feel that they have finally discovered just how incompatible their mates are and think seriously of divorce.
3. Still, others develop somatic difficulties, sometimes serious ones. I know two women who had tuberculosis during adolescence and who both broke down again during this "danger point." In both cases, their disease was considered arrested.

Do Not Act on the Pullbacks

I realize such reactions sound alarming to a reader. However, my intention in stating the facts is not to frighten but to forewarn. You have nothing to be alarmed about. Feelings are not reality. But men and women must be certain they do not act upon their emotions. The only danger is that they might.

The Pullbacks Will Pass on Their Own

How can one cope with such fears, fears so deep one does not even dare to let them into the conscious mind? Generally, the answer is that you do not have to cope with them in any active way. They will pass. All you have to do is wait without taking action. The unconscious will, in short order (a week, a month), calm down.

♥*PRD: Tips for Speeding Up the Healing Process*

Our brains don't operate in a vacuum. We can't just eliminate the negative thoughts without replacing them with positive ones. The following suggestions help fill the void with constructive ideas:

1. *Journal your feelings toward your parents and how they raised you to help stop the same thoughts from cycling repeatedly.*
2. *Start a thankfulness journal to replace the negative thoughts with positive ones. Work in it daily. Include thanks for all your family members and non-personal items such as the weather, good smells, a tasty meal, etc.*
3. *Set up two chairs facing each other. Mentally set your parents or a parent down across from you and discuss how you wish you had raised "you." Replace the negative with the positive by telling them what you are striving to do differently with your children.*
4. *Write your parents or parent a letter sharing the hurts you suffered during*

your childhood. Tell them how you are healing and changing the family dynamics. Burn or bury the letter as a symbol of freeing your emotions from those experiences so you can create new happy ones.

5. *Buy a helium-filled balloon. Tape a picture of yourself at a difficult age to the balloon. With a felt-tip marker, write some words of encouragement or love to yourself. Then ceremoniously set your child free of those painful influences.*
6. *Take Dr. Karyl McBride's Healing the Daughters of Narcissistic Mothers Virtual Workshop. This course is also suitable for men who are the sons of narcissistic mothers and fathers. Dr. McBride is the author of* <u>*Will I Ever Be Good Enough?*</u> *She guides participants through coming to terms with harmful parenting and shows them how to continue to deal with that parent in a less stressful way.*
7. *Pack away or get rid of items that were given to you by a narcissistic parent or friend. Continually seeing these items can create a subliminal effect on your subconscious as a reminder of that person's negativity and putdowns.*

Start with two or three projects to see how they affect your inner thoughts. For example, 1) journaling your thoughts about your parents and problems and 2) starting a thankfulness journal are good foundational exercises for a lifetime of solving the normal difficulties of life. If your mind still refuses to give you peace, move to 3) and mentally set your parents down for a heart-to-heart talk. Let your tears flow. Tell them you're sorry you can't help them understand your feelings and pain. If anguish continues to torment you, consider 6) taking Dr. McBride's class. Continue to add and mix activities as needed.

Case History: Wife Mentally Talking to Her Dad Offers Healing

A client was dealing with pullbacks related to rejection from her father starting at about 7 years old. I emailed her, "Consider mentally talking with your dad sitting in a chair opposite you. Discuss his upbringing and how that affected him. Explore how he didn't have an opportunity to learn better. In other words, work on understanding how he did the best he knew how with what he had, which is what you and your husband were doing (the best you could) before you started studying. Find a way to extend grace and mercy to your dad."♥

Continuing with the Plan Disarms the Cognitive Distortions

Reality, a good reality, can prove to the infantile unconscious that it has nothing to fear. When one has quieted again and resumed the straight line of progress one had been pursuing, orgasm will occur again. This time the reaction of alarm is generally far less. By the third and fourth times, it has become virtually nonexistent. The distortive, defensive portion of one's mind has then been disarmed.

♥PRD: The circumstances of life are always changing, such as births, illnesses, deaths, job changes, empty nesting, and retirement. These can trigger regression. However, keeping the soulmating going with honesty between the couple and frequent lovemaking helps keep these setbacks to a minimum. The Apostle Paul told Christians not to let life keep them from loving each other:

> *1 Corinthians 7:5: "Stop depriving one another, except by agreement for a time, so that you may devote yourselves to prayer, and come together again so that Satan will not tempt you because of your lack of self-control."*

Paul's instructions require the sexually inhibited spouse to discuss pullbacks openly with the mate and to make short work of them with prayer and deliberate effort to limit their impact.♥

Review of the Sexual Maturity Process

I have called the steps by which men and women move from inhibitions to emotional and sexual maturity a "process." Once started, it tends, almost by inertia, to complete itself. It needs only a kind of minimal guidance from their intelligence and a few specific facts. For the sake of clarity, then, let us review what the steps in this process are.

Step One: Replace the Negatives with Positives

Step one is launched by the surfacing of negative emotions and fantasies from which the inhibited man and woman have been hiding. These thoughts reflect underlying attitudes toward the opposite sex, which come from childhood fears and misunderstandings that seriously limit one's ability to love. As the emotions are exposed to full view, they lose their power for harm. It is only when emotions are partially or totally hidden from oneself that their primitive force is dangerous. When emotions are exposed to the light of intelligence and judgment, their power over one can at first be greatly reduced and finally disposed of entirely.

♥PRD: God's Formula for Solving All Marriage Problems

Dr. Robinson's instructions correspond with God's formula in 1 Timothy 4:1-10:

1. *Go to God's word to learn the truth about femininity, masculinity, and love.*
2. *Go to God in an interview-type prayer for help in replacing the negative emotions and fantasies with God's positive truth.*
3. *Maintain a spirit of thankfulness for God's creation of male and female and the way of a man with a maid.♥*

Step Two: Revaluate the Mate

When all or most of one's negative daydreams and emotions have been exposed, step two can be taken. This is a revaluation of the mate in terms of his or her real nature and goals.

The Wife Revaluates Her Husband

We saw that the man's real nature is naturally aggressive, and one of his chief aims in life is to put this aggression to work for his wife and family. Viewed from this standpoint, the man's differences from the woman are seen in their true light. The sexually inhibited woman, from this revaluation, learns that she can now let down her defenses, knowing that her husband, far from being hostile or wishing to misuse or exploit her, is her loving ally. She sees that his once-feared aggression is the very thing that makes it safe for her to be a woman.

♥*PRD: The Husband Revaluates His Wife*

The man learns that his wife's innate emotion is one of desiring to love her husband and children. Rather than wanting to use the man, her greatest joy comes in creating love and tranquility within the home. He appreciates that she is not inferior to him, but his peer with a different set of talents for helping him subdue the earth, fill it with people, and glorify God. Soulmating with her frees him to be his most creative, productive self, and for this, he is eternally grateful.♥

Step Three: Tranquility and Surrender

From this realization, on a deep level of their personalities and acceptance of the other's masculinity or femininity, the next step follows naturally. They first achieve a tranquility and then a serenity they have not known before. This is followed by an acceptance of and a surrender to their real roles—loving and wise companions who glory in their functions and shared love.

♥*PRD: The Three-Step Process Simplified*

1. *Expose the negative.*
2. *Replace with the positive.*
3. *Practice thankfulness.*

It's that simple. Going to God's word to expose the negative and replace it with the positive helps speed up the healing process. Practicing thankfulness also promotes healing and helps keep the negative out.♥

Pullbacks Can Come with Step Three

The last step is sharing vaginal orgasms as a natural sequel to psychological maturation. This part of the process can be attended by a resurgence of early anxiety when powerful sensations finally occur. This anxiety can cause a desire to flee from the newly acquired ability to love. However, the only danger at this juncture is the possibility that anxious men or women might act upon their fears. Forewarned, they are forearmed. *By seeking further insights and waiting out the anxiety, the pullback will gradually subside completely.* These general steps outline the process that can lead to recovery. I can add little to them. This method has worked for many people, and I know of no other that will.

♥*PRD: More Tips for Dealing with Pullbacks*

1. *Spread your raw feelings before God in an interview-type prayer. Ask him to have Jesus and the Holy Spirit make intercession for you. Thank him for the progress you've made so far and for your mate and your children. Thank him for the chance to remember your upbringing and the opportunity to purge faulty thinking from your soul.*
2. *When intense emotions appear, sit with them and allow them to wash over you. Know that they will pass. You are dealing with a lifetime of experiences and feelings. You may need to feel and process your emotional pain more than once. Each time you relive your emotions, their strength weakens until the moment comes when they no longer need to be expressed.*
3. *Try to do something that requires concentration to give your brain a chance to rest from being anxious about lovemaking. You might refinish a piece of furniture you've been meaning to or spring clean that room where you put everything you don't know what to do with.*

Case History: Wife Kisses Husband Publically

You may find that when you give your mind a break from the hard work, your subconscious will take this opportunity to process the new positives you've been feeding it and give you some breakthrough insights. As one client was driving to her husband's office to take him his lunch, her subconscious reminded her of all kinds of positives about her man.

Her husband saw her drive up and went to greet her. Without thinking, she got out of the car and met him with a prolonged kiss—something she had never done. Then she was concerned some of his coworkers might have seen her and would embarrass her husband. Her surprised husband assured her that he would never be embarrassed by her public display of affection. Even with this great victory, she continued to experience very real, but weakening pullbacks. Such seems to be the nature of overcoming a less-than-loving childhood.

Tap on Your Bones to Change Your Heart to Overcome Pullbacks

I teach my clients how to tap with their fingertips on acupuncture points to help expose and replace their negative emotions with positive ones. Tapping, also known as EFT or Emotional Freedom Technique, is an effective method of overcoming pullbacks. If you're not familiar with this powerful technique, watch "How to Tap with Jessica Ortner" on YouTube to learn how to do it. You'll find information about what it is including how Harvard Medical School verified that stress and fear can be lessened by stimulating certain points with acupuncture or acupressure at https://www.thetappingsolution.com/what-is-eft-tapping/.

Acupuncture (needle) and acupressure (tapping) recognize the power of emotions on bodily responses. The impact of emotions on various body parts is taught throughout the Old Testament. For example, notice the tonic effect of happiness on the heart compared to depression's crushing impact on the bones:

Proverbs 17:22:
"A merry heart doeth good like a medicine:
but a broken spirit drieth the bones."

The Bible uses both "heart" and "bones" in "an anatomical sense" and also as "a seat of emotions." The Theological Wordbook *lists the following dispositions along with scriptures as part of the spectrum of temperaments these body parts respond to: comfort, grief, sadness, regret, broken, contempt, envy, anger, fear, courage, thought functions such as mind, wisdom, and understanding, along with the will, generosity, pride, and faith" (466-467, 690).*

Nick Ortner explains in The Tapping Solution for Pain Relief *how that using sophisticated CT imaging, two studies confirmed the existence of three anatomical anomalies at acupuncture points. The scientists found "[1] a distinct bone structure, [2] a higher density of micro-vessels that are larger than those in nonacupuncture points, and [3] a higher partial oxygen pressure than nonacupuncture points" (Ortner 5). Our God, who designed blood vessels, oxygen pressure, and how bones are formed in the womb, built into our bodies a brilliant health network:*

> *Ecclesiastes 11:5 "Just as you do not know the path of the wind and how bones are formed in the womb of the pregnant woman, so you do not know the activity of God who makes all things."*

We serve an amazing and loving God in the way he designed our bodies! Science is only beginning to understand many of God's ingenious mysteries.

Tapping Script to Overcome Pullbacks

I wrote the following tapping script for a client who enjoyed many sexual successes but also endured frequent pullbacks. The tapping sequence helped her identify triggers and move out of upsetting anger into more expressive love.

First, you tap on the acupuncture points to acknowledge your negative thoughts. Finally, you do additional rounds to tap into the positive changes you want to make. Change the words below to fit your feelings and needs.

Side of the Hand: Even though my attitude toward sex is not what I want,
I deeply and completely love and accept myself and how I feel.

Side of the Hand: Even though my attitude toward lovemaking is not healthy,
I deeply and completely love and accept myself and how I feel.

Side of the Hand: Even though my attitude toward my marriage is not happy,
I deeply and completely love and accept myself and how I feel.

Eyebrow: I don't understand why I keep having pullbacks.
Side of the Eye: I'm ready for sex and even initiate it,
Under the Eye: I don't know why pullbacks are happening.
Under the Nose: Now I'm worried that I don't have the right attitude.
Under the Chin: Am I holding onto resentments?
Collarbone: Am I afraid that I won't respond right?
Under the Arm: Do I think I have to be perfect every time?
Top of the Head: Do I still need to work through old beliefs?

Eyebrow: Why do I keep having pullbacks?
Side of the Eye: If I respond with love, it's okay no matter what.
Under the Eye: I don't have to figure it all out right now.
Under the Nose: I have time to figure it out later.
Under the Chin: Right now, I can enjoy this moment with my mate.
Collarbone: I can enjoy the hormones flooding my body.
Under the Arm: Life is full of surprises, and I might just be tired.
Top of the Head: Even then, I know I'll enjoy connecting with my mate.

Eyebrow: It's okay to have pullbacks as they show I'm moving forward.
Side of the Eye: It's okay to give a voice to what is worrying me.
Under the Eye: It's okay to enjoy small orgasms.
Under the Nose: They still give me pleasure and loving hormones.
Under the Chin: All orgasms are good, and I sleep better.
Collarbone: Even when I don't have a lot of energy,
Under the Arm: Lovemaking soothes my nerves and attitudes.
Top of the Head: I enjoy different kinds of orgasms, and that's okay.

Eyebrow: I'm on a lifelong journey of growing in love,
Side of the Eye: I choose to relax and feel safe on this journey.
Under the Eye: I'm growing in faith as I'm growing in love.
Under the Nose: I'm growing in my ability to forgive others.
Under the Chin: I'm growing in love for myself and my femininity or masculinity.
Collarbone: My heart is filling with love for my mate and my family,
Under the Arm: My heart is filling with greater love for God and his word.
Top of the Head: I accept God's loving design of sex for myself and my mate.

Repeat your script as many times as you need until you feel clarity. Take a deep breath and place your hands over your heart. Say a prayer of thankfulness to God for creating the way of a man with a maid. Ask him to continue to open your mind and your heart to greater love for him, your mate, and your family.♥

Patience and Faith Lead to Emotional Maturity

Patience and faith are the prime requisites for emotional maturation. Nobody can name the time it will take for any given individual to cross the bridge to adulthood and love. But that most men and women can cross it, there can be no doubt. Those who have gone before make that point ultimately clear.

♥*PRD: Case History: Young Wife Works Through Pullbacks*

A client had worked through a couple of significant issues with her father that led to numerous pullbacks. Afterward, she continued to face smaller pullbacks. After nearly four months of diligence, she said, "Sex has become so wonderful, I don't have the words to describe it. We are both so incredibly happy. It makes dealing with any future pullbacks worth it because I know that when I get on the other side of them, sex will be just that much more exciting."

Case History: Older Wife Begins Craving Her Husband

I received this letter from a former client who was raised with a lot of sexual shaming when she was a teenager:

> *I was just thanking God for you this week! We were in Mexico, just my husband and I, for 5 days, and it was fantastic! We are doing so great! I can't quite put into words the peace we're living in. I started craving him, and loving sex, and hounding him for it. Ha! Internal, vaginal orgasms make me laugh uncontrollably. He has broken out of many of his anxiety behaviors, and that hugely played into my breakthroughs. A lot of fear-based spiritual beliefs were broken, and I believe that relieved the pressure!*

Even after this success, the client continued to deal with pullbacks for a while. But she and her husband understood what was happening and worked their way through them.

Pullbacks Signal the End of Inhibitions and the Beginning of Love

The above two clients persevered through their pullbacks to reap sexual ecstasy they didn't even know was possible. And God reserves the same results for you when you understand the nature and the danger of pullbacks and work through your personal setbacks. You stand on the edge of a tomorrow filled with love. What is your choice for today?♥

18.

The Nature of Emotional Surrender

When the sexually inhibited man and woman, using the methods described in this section, have:

1. Divested themselves of the destructive fears and false convictions that have been leftover from their childhood.
2. In all honesty, view their mate with new eyes, knowing the mate to be the hard-beset but loving human being the mate is.
3. Rejected the quasi-monster, they had conjured up in the mate's image.

When these things are achieved, a profound change begins to take place within the man and the woman.

Changing Attitudes Creates Emotional Richness in Men and Women

This change is not a direct product of the man's and the woman's conscious will. Forces with the character of a tide are suddenly freed of long-standing barricades and now begin to move irresistibly within them. They feel new potential inside, intimations of an emotional richness they had not dared dream could exist. When such a process is loosed within a man and a woman, they are ready to surrender. Indeed, surrender has already started within them. What does this mean?

They Are Ready to Glory in Their Gender and Love

In the broadest sense, it means that the man and the woman are prepared to become loving at long last. It means:

1. They are ready, indeed anxious, to yield to their biological and psychological destiny.
2. They have ceased to fear their real role, mentally, emotionally, spiritually, and physically.
3. They have ceased to resist their role and ceased to resent it.

4. They are ready to glory in their masculinity or femininity.
5. They are ready to love.

This Ultimate Change Is Natural to a Man and a Woman

When a man and a woman are ready for this final step, they no longer need any urging, any coaxing or coaching. Since this ultimate surrender to their true natures is so natural to them, they are often not entirely conscious of its varied manifestations. It is slow, cellular, tidal, and certainly not subject to the conscious will.

But the Changes in the Subconscious Can Be Frightening

Though change is now going on mainly outside their awareness, I should like to emphasize that this phase is a part of the process that was initiated with the first two steps:

1. Airing their emotions and fantasies
2. Reevaluating their mates

The More Men and Women Understand, The Faster Healing Occurs

For a man and a woman whose mind and body are finally taking the path nature intended, it is wise for them to be conscious of the process going on within them. Many feelings are new and powerful. They run counter to much of what they have experienced and believed in before. New convictions, new insights, and new prospects open up before them. This novel proliferation may be confusing or even frightening. *Therefore, the more a man and a woman understand the nature of their brave new inner world, the more thoroughly and swiftly they can claim it for their own.*

Continue with the Daily Private Time

Because of all these new experiences, I urge the man and woman to continue the regular daily sessions I mentioned at the beginning. Much of the mental activity in these sessions with oneself will be a matter of watching the process unfold and celebrating the unconscious advances.

♥PRD: Take time to think deliberately back over how you were a year ago, then six months ago, and finally today. How have you changed? Although you may feel like you still have work to do, celebrate your victories. Then continue with your daily private time until you intuitively know you've uncovered all the issues affecting your subconscious way of thinking and acting.♥

Don't Abandon the Learning Process too Soon

In this role of constant observer, the conscious mind can also be ready for more aggressive activity. Watch for any tendencies of the old pattern to reassert itself. Waves of anger, fears, and fantasies can come out in new guises. They can thus be noted and dispensed with before they can do any real damage. Such pullbacks are not only possible but usual, and it is well not to abandon the sessions with oneself until the withdrawals have disappeared entirely—or as much as they're going to.

♥PRD: It's not possible to overemphasize the necessity of being aware of pullbacks. They can be relentless in trying to pull you back into the survival mode of your childhood. Many people give up when they are on the threshold of victory.♥

The Inner-Growth Process Emerges in a Given Order

The inner-growth process that follows when a man and a woman are ready to surrender to their real nature traces a relatively straightforward pattern. Some of the new feelings overlap, but mostly they emerge in a given order. Each unfolds separately but related to the other as petals to a bud. Let us take them in the usual order of their coming.

As the man and the woman who have suffered from sexual inhibitions explode their groundless fears, one by one, they explore new attitudes toward:

1. The opposite sex
2. Love
3. Parenthood
4. The mate

♥PRD: Overview of the Two Steps for Developing Orgasmic Attitudes

In Chapter 15: "The Power of Love," Dr. Robinson taught the two steps that sexually inhibited men and women must go through to develop orgasmic attitudes. "Orgasmic attitudes" are the thoughts and beliefs that allow husbands and wives to share vaginal orgasms with cervical kisses. Now she has listed the specific thoughts that makeup orgasmic attitudes in the order they occur. For ease of reference, I've overviewed the two steps with the attitudes.

The Woman and Orgasmic Thoughts

Step One: Rid Herself of False Projections of Masculinity:

1. *Toward men*

Step Two: Give Up False Views of Femininity:

2. *Toward love and sex*
3. *Toward motherhood*
4. *Feel new esteem for her husband*

These two steps mirror God's formula for solving all marriage problems in 1 Timothy 4:1-10. (1) Go to God's word to learn the truth about masculinity and femininity and how they respond in love and sex and parenthood. (2) Go to God in an interview-type prayer to implement that truth into your life. (3) God adds a third step of practicing thankfulness for his creation of marriage.

The Man and Orgasmic Thoughts

Step One: Rid Himself of False Projections of Femininity:

1. *Toward women*

Step Two: Give Up False Views of Masculinity:

2. *Toward love and sex*
3. *Toward fatherhood*
4. *Feel new esteem for his wife*

Inhibited men and women must correct their attitudes toward the opposite sex before they can genuinely love and accept their own masculinity or femininity.♥

The Woman Experiences Feminine and Spiritual Tranquility

As all these things happen, her lifelong restlessness begins to depart. For the first time, she realizes just how restless she has been, how unsatisfied; she feels how precariously balanced her life, inwardly and outwardly, has always felt. Now something deep within her relaxes, lets down. When this happens, she is beginning to experience the essential attribute of truly feminine, spiritual tranquility.

New Emotions Permit the Full Flowering of Her Femininity

Tranquility arrives as the result of the woman allowing herself to trust her husband in a profound sense. She finally realizes that she no longer has to fear or oppose his strength. She can now rely on it to protect her and give her the security necessary for the full flowering of her femininity.

♥PRD: The Proverbs 31 Woman Portrays Feminine Tranquility

The description of the Woman of Great Price in Proverbs 31:10-31 sounds amazingly like the woman who lives in feminine tranquility:

Proverbs 31:25-26:
"Strength and dignity are her clothing,
And she smiles at the future.
She opens her mouth in wisdom,
And the teaching of kindness is on her tongue."

This wife is the opposite of the nonorgasmic woman who is quick to anger and blames her husband for everything, although her irritations come from her childhood.♥

Feminine Tranquility of Spirit Is a Grace and a Beauty

Feminine tranquility of spirit is a grace and a beauty of the first order. It is the psychological cornerstone of a happy family. Based on an abiding faith in the goodness and loyalty of her husband, tranquility emanates from a woman who has found herself. Peace envelops those about her, giving them unity and strength. The children of such a mother are strong against the anxious restlessness of these difficult times. The husband of such a wife returns home to an oasis and redoubles his loving efforts to make her even more secure.

♥*PRD: The Proverbs 31 Woman Portrays the Strength of Femininity*

The Proverbs 31 woman's husband and children agreed with Dr. Robinson's description of a loving wife and mother:

Proverbs 31:28-29:
"Her children rise up and bless her;
Her husband also, and he praises her, saying:
'Many daughters have done nobly,
But you excel them all.'"

Feminine tranquility of spirit is a grace and a beauty of the first order that blesses the loving woman's husband and children. And her family rise up to praise her.♥

The Inhibited Woman Presents a Difficult, Frenetic Quality

Because she can trust no man, the sexually inhibited woman's approach to the tasks of life has a difficult, painful, frenetic quality:

1. She feels responsible for everything, guiltily responsible.
2. Details and trivia overwhelm her.
3. She has no unity.

4. She fights herself, her resentment, and her self-rejection to get the simplest things done.
5. Her household work, planning the dinner, carrying and fetching the children—everything looms.

♥PRD: Inhibited Women Identify with the Difficult, Frenetic Quality

One wife who made the journey from sexual inhibitions to femininity said this description describes how she was in the early years of marriage. Now she enjoys tranquility and the grace and beauty that comes with it. She said, "I'm amazed at how quickly I make decisions now compared to how I was before. My daily life is totally different. And now I even have more children than when I was so frustrated—but now I have so much more peace."

The nonorgasmic woman's lack of trust forces her to do everything herself while her resentment and anger mount. Instead of coming home to an oasis, her husband enters, perhaps a spotless house, only to be greeted with his wife's condemnation of all the wrongs she's imagined he has done against her. This is the opposite of what the husband of the Woman of Great Price experienced:

Proverbs 31:10-12:
"An excellent wife, who can find?
For her worth is far above jewels.
The heart of her husband trusts in her,
And he will have no lack of gain.
She does him good and not evil
All the days of her life."

Interestingly, "excellent" refers to "the strength of an army." She is not some weak-willed woman, but a strong woman who has taken charge of her life and allowed herself to love and cherish her husband. Her husband's heart trusts in her. His home is truly an oasis for both of them.

Inhibited Men Experience Panic and Neurosis

A marriage and family therapist said he saw all human reaction in light of a relationship. Regarding men, he specified:

> *The degree to which men worry about their jobs is highly interactive with the level of trust and support they get from their closest of allies. Assuming the spouse is the nearest and strongest bond they have, it is my experience in Clinical Marriage and Family Therapy settings that men can be relatively stress-free from life's burdens providing their marriage is secure. To me, secure does not mean "Roses and Violins," of course.*
>
> *I can say for sure the opposite is true; men who feel threatened in*

keeping a close connection with a spouse or other intimate partner seem to be on the verge of panic or some level of neurosis most of the time.

Read again Proverbs 31:10-12 and this time apply it to the contented husband. The husband and wife who have learned how to share intellectual, emotional, sexual, and spiritual love enjoy tranquility in their hearts and their marriage that escapes those who harbor sexual inhibitions.♥

The Feminine Woman Now Enjoys the Irksome Qualities

With the development of the new quality of tranquility, those details of life that once seemed so difficult become simple. And because they are feminine tasks, household work, planning or getting dinners, keeping the children busy or inline—whatever life demands—soon lose their irksome and irritating quality and become easy, even joyful.

The Feminine Woman Treasures the Miracle of Childbirth

As tranquility moves over to serenity and becomes more and more a part of her psychic character, a woman begins to realize what a miraculous and wonderful thing womanhood is. Frequently, this realization is ushered in by a sudden awareness of the miracle that her body is able to perform: the miracle of childbirth.

♥*PRD: Teenagers and Pregnant Women Need to Remember*

During pregnancy and childbirth, a whole new dimension of pullbacks can arise—even for women who have never experienced a serious problem with inhibitions or pullbacks. Pullbacks can happen because God built hormones into teenagers and pregnant women to make them examine their childhood.

Now they look at everything Mom and Dad did with a critical eye. What do they want to do differently as an adult from their parents? They no longer believe everything their parents say "just because Mom and Dad said it." They must examine their home-of-origin experiences and come to their own opinions about life and parenthood.

Although this remembering can frustrate both teenagers and pregnant women, it is good. The danger comes when they focus only on the negatives. Teens may need their parents to share picture albums and remind them of special events and happy family times. While they are trying to move away from parental love into romantic love, young people continue to need words and physical displays of love from their parents.

Likewise, during a woman's pregnancies, her hormones cause her to examine her parents' childrearing techniques. The new mother often determines to do some things differently. Many prospective mothers choose to become the kind of parent they wish they'd had. Teenagers and pregnant women give each new generation a chance to deliberately reject the mistakes and sins of their parents and grandparents.

An Inhibited Mother Usually Has an Inhibited Daughter

> *Ezekiel 16:44-46: "The Lord said, 'People will use this proverb about you, Jerusalem: "Like mother, like daughter." You really are your mother's daughter. She detested her husband and her children. You are like your sisters, who hated their husbands and their children. You and your sister cities had a Hittite mother and an Amorite father.'"*

God draws a metaphor from real-life—children often grow up to be like their parents. In this case, an unloving mother can't teach her daughter how to love her husband and children. The sin of narcissistic sexual inhibitions is passed down through the generations until someone rises up and says, "Enough! I'm going to treat my family differently."

Through remembering, the pregnant woman who has embraced her femininity enjoys an opportunity to break the cycle of the past and start a new family tradition of love.♥

The Inhibited Woman Fears Pregnancy, Frets, and Rages

In her frightened heart, the sexually inhibited woman has always detested and feared her capacity to become pregnant. To her, this faculty has seemed onerous and burdensome, a curse. In pregnancy, she feels trapped, sick at heart and in body during it, increasingly frightened of delivery as the day of confinement approaches. She views all this as a woman's burden. Men, those enviable creatures, are free of such a frightening duty. Indeed, she has heard that men use pregnancy as a way of keeping women subject to them! Thus she frets and rages and trembles, rejecting her destiny.

♥*PRD: The Mothers' Complaints Live on in Their Daughters*

A client worked her way through her inhibited attitudes that stemmed primarily from emotional neglect from her father. Her mother had given birth to several children at home with a midwife. The daughter witnessed the birth of her last sibling. The experience was so positive, when she had her children, she successfully followed her mother's example and gave birth at home.

However, each time the mother was pregnant, she frequently said, "I hate being pregnant." She was always nauseous and lethargic during the first trimester. Even after her children grew up and left home, the mother continued to talk about hating being pregnant. When her daughter got pregnant, that gave the mother a new opportunity to voice her frustrations.

After transitioning to enjoying wonderful orgasms with her husband, the daughter was excited to become pregnant and looked forward to enjoying every aspect of her pregnancy. She was upset when her mother's negative words about pregnancy started echoing in her head and creating major pullbacks. Not only was the daughter extremely nauseous herself, but the old negative feelings toward her husband returned.

She recognized immediately what was happening, and wouldn't have taken the pullbacks seriously except her morning sickness was lasting all day. She felt it was primarily the result of her mother's words.

As mentioned in the section above, God gives pregnant women and teenagers hormones to make them remember their homes of origin to plan their future lives—what they want to do differently from what their parents did. Here's how I advised this client to take advantage of those hormones:

1. *Let go of your mom and dad's marriage and childraising habits. That's past history and not much new to discover there. Dr. Robinson advises that you don't have to dredge everything up.*

2. *Your hormones make you remember for one reason: To figure out what you are going to do differently. That's your job right now. That's the conversation you and your husband need to be having. What are you going to do differently? It's not just differently from yours and his parents (because the pregnant wife's hormones also make the husband's home of origin an issue), but also differently from what you did with your first babies. How are you going to change course as parents for your family here on out?*

3. *The key is to replace the negative from both of your parents with positive plans for how you and your husband will do things differently for your family.*

4. *To help you make positive plans read some books on pregnancy, childbirth, and nursing. You've already read some of these books with your first babies. But you are at a different place emotionally and intellectually than you were then. You'll pick up new concepts. Especially notice the loving, happy attitudes the books promote.*

5. *Along this line, you might want to read some books on orgasmic birthing. A large number of women, even ones who give birth in a hospital with a traditional doctor, are promoting entering a state of orgasm while giving birth.*

   Orgasmic births make sense because the woman's birth canal from beginning to ending is where she receives her greatest pleasure from her husband—from their shared vaginal orgasms with cervical kisses. Indeed, sometimes toward the end of a woman's series of orgasms, she clamps down around her husband's organ of love with a tremendous Kegel squeeze that brings her upper body forward, almost into a birthing position.

The Israelite Women Enjoyed Easy Births

The Israelite women, who had healthy attitudes toward femininity and sexual love, were known for their easy births. Frequent lovemaking strengthens the pelvic floor and helps prepare women for childbirth. God refers to this phenomenon in describing his relationship with Israel:

Isaiah 66:7-9:
"Before she travailed, she brought forth;
Before her pain came, she gave birth to a boy.
Who has heard such a thing? Who has seen such things?
Can a land be born in one day?
Can a nation be brought forth all at once?
As soon as Zion travailed, she also brought forth her sons.
Shall I bring to the point of birth and not give delivery?" says the Lord.
"Or shall I who gives delivery shut the womb?" says your God."

For the feminine woman who "treasures the miracle of childbirth," many wonderful and amazing options await her.

Siblings Experienced the Same Negative Influence

Interestingly, this woman's younger sister endured some of the same experiences with sexual inhibitions as my client from both the father's and the mother's influence. But she also had a positive experience with home births.

The two sisters' experiences demonstrate how powerful the mother's and father's influence is over their sons and daughters. When the mother enjoyed and promoted home births, her daughters followed her example. But when she complained about morning sickness and hating pregnancy, that also negatively influenced her daughters.

Friend's Mother Created a Negative Home Birth Experience

The client had a friend whose mother also practiced home births, but not with a positive attitude. She told her 10-year-old daughter, "I want you to watch my home birth because that's about the best birth-control I can give you." The mother deliberately set out to terrify her daughter of pregnancy and childbirth. Her daughter suffered greatly from the emotional assault.

Fortunately, these three young women are working to free their minds and bodies from the negative attitudes they inherited from their parents as they make plans to do things differently.♥

Motherhood Awes the Feminine Woman

With a new evaluation of her husband, a deepening sense of security, and the growth of tranquility, the woman embraces her femininity. Her childish, frightened protest against the miracle of motherhood washes away. Now the scales fall from her eyes, and she feels the full meaning and majesty of what it means to be a woman.

What a privilege it is, she realizes, to be the carrier of the race, the agent of its immortality. No fate could be richer, more beautiful, more filled with wonder and awe than motherhood.

The Madonna Paintings Revere Femininity

I am not exaggerating the importance of this realization. Pride and joy in it are the most central characteristics of the feminine woman. To me, its highest expression is in the Madonna paintings, which the great Renaissance artists took, over and over again, as a frequent subject. The Alba Madonna by Raphael catches the essential quality of femininity, expresses it for all to see and revere.

The Feminine Woman Loses Her Envy of the Male's Role

With this realization, the last vestiges of her envy of the male and of his role in life disappear. With this marvelous, unmatched capability of hers, she may wonder how she could ever have depreciated the woman's role and wanted what men have.

♥PRD: *Case History: Husband Changes View of His Job*

A man said he used to think he had the most important job providing for his family. Then he realized that if his wife messed up taking care of the children, it didn't matter how much money he earned. It was for naught. His new attitude became that his wife had the most critical job in caring for the children, and it was his duty to provide everything she needed to fulfill her destiny—to serve her. That was the attitude of a man who gloried in his masculinity.♥

The Woman Can Make Pregnancy Beautiful or Miserable

Around this juncture, a woman begins to feel her full power that comes to her for surrendering to her destiny. She realizes that, far from being in a weak position with the man, her position is so strong that she must be careful not to exploit it. One of man's deepest and strongest psychological needs is his poignant desire for immortality through his children. She can deny him this, or she can make his life miserable while granting it to him. Or she can make it the most beautiful and meaningful thing in her life and his.

♥*PRD: God Used a Mother to Describe His Love*

God used the portrait of a loving mother nursing her child, carrying him on her hip, and bouncing the child on her knee to illustrate his love for the Israelites:

Isaiah 66:10-13:
"'Be joyful with Jerusalem and rejoice for her, all you who love her;
Be exceedingly glad with her, all you who mourn over her,
That you may nurse and be satisfied with her comforting breasts,
That you may suck and be delighted with her bountiful bosom.'
For thus says the Lord, 'Behold, I extend peace to her like a river,
And the glory of the nations like an overflowing stream;
And you will be nursed, you will be carried on the hip and fondled on the knees.
As one whom his mother comforts, so I will comfort you;
And you will be comforted in Jerusalem.'"

The peace God gives the loving mother corresponds to the feminine woman's tranquility as she loves and cares for her family.♥

Case History:
Woman Realizes the Power of Femininity

A letter I received from a former patient stated beautifully what this new realization means to a woman. We were able to work for only two weeks on her problem, for she came from a different section of the country and could spend only that amount of time in New York City. We worked quickly to expose the hostilities to and misapprehensions about men that plagued her grownup life. I gave her a thumbnail sketch of the problems and changes she might encounter within herself in the future—much as I describe them here.

(1) Within six months, I received a letter from her. It described the step-by-step process I have depicted: the change in her feelings toward her husband, the incredibly swift growth within her of the new and wonderful serenity. And then she realized in her whole emotional being the miraculous nature of the female body and the feeling of power and glory it gave her.

(2) But this feeling of power was quickly followed by intense humility. She wrote, "I thought of how I held within me, within my body, the ability to bring my husband the greatest of joys or to deprive him of it. I realized the terrible thing it would be to misuse this power. And now I felt, for the first time, despite my former lip service to the idea, the reason why marriage must be considered sacramental."

(3) The relationship between husband and wife, which results in the unsolvable mystery of birth, goes far beyond human understanding. To participate in this mystery requires a consecration by both. Any lesser

attitude toward it is like the laughter of mockery in a holy place.

♥PRD: After this woman exposed her hostilities toward men that had plagued her, she naturally moved toward femininity and understanding of her destiny for motherhood. She shared her progress through these natural stages with Dr. Robinson in her letter:

1. *She recognized the miraculous nature of her female body.*
2. *She determined not to abuse her power over her husband.*
3. *The mystery of birth led to consecration with her husband.*

At this point, her feelings were genuine, not lip service as they were before.♥

The Other's Welfare Becomes the Dearest of All Things

With this kind of acceptance of her central role, changes now come rapidly to a woman. As she feels the unity of need and goal between her husband and herself, any remaining contentiousness leaves her. In the marriage, consensus now becomes her aim. She is no longer afraid of losing an argument or fearful that she will be forced to do something disgusting or humiliating. She realizes her welfare is the dearest of all things to her husband. And, conversely, his happiness and peace of mind become her first desire.

"Essential Female Altruism"—Woman's Capacity to Give

She taps in on the greatest psychological joy of a woman—her capacity to give. In an earlier chapter, we called this a characteristic rooted in every woman's biological nature. Women who are secure in themselves and their roles have an inexhaustible store of this altruism.

Inhibited Women Fear Men Will Exploit Their Desire to Give

Nonorgasmic women fear this fundamental characteristic, feeling as they do that men will exploit and abuse their desire to give.

♥PRD: Inhibited Men Fear Women Marry Only for a Paycheck

Many men state on the Sexless Marriages Survey that their wives actively pursued them in courtship, with some saying, "She couldn't keep her hands off me." They were shocked to discover that the person they dated was not the same as the person they married. The change often happened on the honeymoon.

Amazingly, a large percentage of the wives told their husbands that if they earned more money, they could have more sex. Unfortunately, the spouse who withholds love is not emotionally healthy and may have ulterior motives for marrying.

Ironically, the Sexless Marriages Survey indicates that sex-withholding spouses are more likely to harbor ulterior motives for marrying than are sex-deprived mates—the exact opposite of the inhibited person's distorted views of their mate! In real life, as opposed to distorted life, exploiting the wife's desire to give and using the husband as a paycheck is rare among loving mates.

Many participants in the survey asked their sexless spouse, "Why did you marry me?" Here are some of the answers from both male and female deprivers:

- *You cook better than my girlfriend.*
- *You had a college education, so I knew you could get a high-paying job, and I want a lot of things.*
- *My dad said he would disinherit me if I didn't get married.*
- *I wanted children.*
- *I wanted someone to cook and clean so I could pursue my hobbies.*
- *I thought you'd make a good parent for my children.*

As you can see, the sexually inhibited spouse may have similar unloving motives for pursuing the marriage, not the other way around.

I Recommend Using My Books to Work Through Distorted Issues

Anyone trying to overcome sexual inhibitions is usually clueless about what a loving person is really like. The loving mate's thinking and motives are totally different from the sexless spouse's mental processing. For this reason, I highly recommend to my readers and clients that as a couple, they go through my books (Male and Female: God's Genius, God's People Make the Best Lovers, and God's 11 Secrets of Sex). Reading these books together often gives four benefits, which can make a major difference in your marriage:

1. *You are fine-tuning your understanding of God's word, which carries more authority than Dr. Robinson's experience or mine.*
2. *You are hearing each other express wonder at God's love for you and experiencing each other's thinking and behavior changes.*
3. *You are witnessing the other's confessions of ignorance and sin along with the determination to do better in the future.*
4. *You are soulmating on a deep and personal level that must happen before your love life can transform.*

The rule? You cannot talk about anything the other person does wrong. You can only talk about what you are doing wrong or have done wrong in the past. A time may come when you need to talk about what the other does wrong, but at this time, you don't know enough about God's word to have that conversation intelligently. You need to do a lot of fine-tuning before that happens. Here's two options that work:

1. *Read the chapters separately and then discuss your answers to the exercises.*

2. *Read the chapters aloud together. Stop and talk about various points as needed.*

The survey indicates that the longer sexless marriages go on, the more likely the loving spouse will start fighting sin with sin. That never works. Consequently, both parties may need to adjust their thinking to enjoy a loving marriage.♥

The Body Changes in Response to Love

As men and women reap the rewards of their new capacity to give themselves generously and fearlessly to their mates and children, their appearances often change. Drawn expressions relax, anxious forehead wrinkles disappear, and thin-lipped mouths soften. Indeed, their bodies take on the looks associated with femininity and masculinity as they receive compliments as being a "cute couple."

Physical Difficulties Disappear in Response to Love

Physical difficulties often disappear. I have known women who were plagued with intense pre-menstrual and menstrual pains all their lives to lose such symptoms in a matter of weeks. I have known women whose irregular periods became regular. And I have known women with complicated pregnancies behind them who, becoming pregnant again, went through the entire nine months without discomfort and with a highly accelerated feeling of pleasure and well-being.

♥*PRD: The Husband's Semen Benefits His Wife*

- *Regulate her hormones, including ones that cause monthly cramps.*
- *Relieves her headaches better than aspirin without the side effects.*
- *Decreases her depression and helping to prevent suicide.*
- *Stimulates her immune system to help prevent colds.*

When everyone in the family is sick, the wife usually takes care of everyone. According to psychologists at Wilkes University, she can do this easier if she has an active sex life. She gets more health protection from her husband's semen than antibiotics with none of the side effects. Frequent sex also helps prevent incontinence for senior women by strengthening their pelvic floor muscles.

The Wife's Hormones Benefit Her Husband

Statista.com states that prescription sales of testosterone are expected to reach 3.8 billion dollars by 2018. This figure doesn't include over the counter testosterone. Yet regular sexual activity and exposure to the wife's estrogen increase a man's testosterone, which regulates his:

- *Bone density*
- *Muscle strength*
- *Fat distribution*
- *Red blood cell production*

The Boston University of Public Health found that the more men ejaculate, the greater their protection against prostate cancer and painful urination later on. Irish and Swedish studies found that the earlier a man ceased to have sex, the earlier he died from all causes.

The Heart Thrives on Robust Sex

A 30-year study at Duke University revealed that men having sex two times a week or more reduces their death rate from a heart attack by 50%. Frequent lovemaking benefits women the same way. But more than frequency, women need quality sex with a husband who knows how to share orgasms with them. The truth is, medical science doesn't have any...

- *Treatment*
- *Health program*
- *Prescription drug*

...that has proven to be as effective as regular passionate lovemaking to prevent and treat heart attacks for both men and women.

New York Times bestselling author of Love and Survival and world-renowned heart-research specialist who was the first to prove the reversal of heart disease by changing lifestyle, Dr. Dean Ornish, wrote, "I am not aware of any other factor in medicine that has a greater impact on our survival than the healing power of love and intimacy. Not diet, not smoking, not exercise, not stress, not genetics, not drugs, not surgery" (book backcover).

This is just a small sampling of some of the health benefits God packed into passionate lovemaking.♥

Surrender All to Find Encompassing Love

These are some of the results that a man and a woman may expect when they give up the missteps of their childhood and yield to their true self. Their return on such an investment of self is enormous. It is paid in the coinage of love returned for love given; love from one's mate and children, love from friends, new and old, attracted by the endless benevolence of the man and the woman who have surrendered all to find all.

19.

The Nature of Sexual Surrender

The ability to share vaginal orgasms can be called the physical counterpart of psychological surrender. In most inhibited sexual desire cases, "sexual surrender" follows the release of the man's and the woman's rebellious and infantile attitudes as day follows night. It signals that they have given up their resistance to masculinity or femininity and have embraced adulthood with their souls and bodies.

Orgasm Is the Last Step in Growing Up

Usually, the sharing of vaginal orgasms is the last step in the process of growing up. If one reviews in one's mind the actual orgasmic experience, it is not difficult to see why this is so.

Orgasm Requires Absolute Trust in One's Partner

For both men and women, sharing vaginal orgasms requires absolute trust in their partner. In sexual intercourse, as in life, the man is the actor, the woman the passive one, the receiver, the acted upon. Giving oneself up in this manner to another human being, making oneself a willing partner to such seismic physical experiences, means one must have complete faith in the other person. In the sexual embrace, any trace of buried hostility toward the other or fear of one's role will show clearly and unmistakably in numbed sensations.

Orgasm Requires Physical Eagerness for Ecstasy

But the psychic state necessary for orgasm requires more than faith in one's partner and readiness to surrender. Sensual eagerness to surrender must exist. In the shared vaginal orgasm, *the excitement comes from the act of surrendering to love.* A tremendous surge of physical ecstasy occurs in the yielding itself—in the uniting of two hearts and two bodies.

♥*PRD: Nighttime Pullbacks Start During the Day*

A client, who had worked hard to overcome negative attitudes toward her husband, said she often started the day thinking about enjoying lovemaking

that evening. But by nighttime, her feelings had changed. Instead of looking forward to lovemaking, she was in the midst of a pullback.

Leaning into the Daily Twinges Builds Nighttime Sexual Desire

I explained that part of the joy of lovemaking is looking forward to it all day and preparing emotionally to share love. One way to do this is to lean into the tingling twinges of sexual desire that a loving person's body emits all day long.

However, the inhibited person often ignores or doesn't even notice these signals. Becoming aware of these natural love twinges lets a person prepare emotionally throughout the day for love. Additionally, the twinges nudge a person toward flirting with the mate, which also increases nighttime ecstasy.

At our next session, the wife said that just knowing about the twinges had let her recognize them. Once she began allowing herself to feel the desire they generated, the nighttime pullbacks disappeared.

Sex-Denied Spouses Don't Feel Safe to Yield to Sexual Twinges

Unfortunately, husbands and wives, who are married to an inhibited person, also shut down their twinges as they become a source of frustration. Sexually deprived mates know that if they allow themselves to look forward to sex or try to initiate lovemaking, their inhibited spouse will reject them. Noticing the daily twinges makes the rejection more devastating.

As sexually inhibited men and women heal, they need to accept responsibility for their past rejection of their mate and the emotional and sexual pain they caused. They can show true repentance by sharing these twinges with their mates and flirting during the day.

But if the flirting only leads to another opportunity to reject the mate, inhibited spouses need to examine their motives. Have they crossed over into the addiction Dr. Douglas Weiss speaks of where intimacy anorexics get pleasure from causing pain for their mate. In that case, they need to go back to the beginning and continue to purge faulty ways of viewing the opposite sex along with the rejection of their own sexuality.♥

The Whole Being Is Swept Up in the Experience

There can be no reservations in such surrender. As one thinks of it, one can undoubtedly feel why, of all the steps in the process of yielding, of surrendering, the orgasm should be last. To those who are moving toward it, the experience is often elusive for a time because of its totality. It uncompromisingly demands that the whole being be swept up in the experience, which remains somewhat frightening.

♥PRD: *Take the "Hand Love Test" to Check Your Emotions*

Orgasms flee from negative feelings, anger, resentment, or bitterness against one's mate or against one's own masculinity or femininity.

A simple test proves this true: The hand, while not thought of as a sexual organ, responds sexually to the attitudes and feelings of the mind. Look at your hand. How did it feel the last time you indulged in anger toward your mate? What did your hand do when your mate touched your hand? Did your hand automatically squeeze your mate's hand in return, or did you fight the urge to jerk it away?

Now remember the last time you thought loving and adoring thoughts about your mate. What happened when your mate touched your hand? Did the electrical charge race up your arm, do a leaping somersault to the pit of your stomach only to dance back up along your spine, and sparkle out your eyes to fondly caress your mate? Or did you only experience that tingle of excitement during courtship when your minds truly enjoyed each other's company?

And all that with a body part not designed primarily for love! The sensitive organs of love respond even more dramatically to a mind filled with God's principles of daily living and loving standards. Learning the sexual truths of the Bible unlocks the power of the mind to provide genuinely fulfilling and enjoyable lovemaking for God's people.

You can view my video on "The Hand Love Test" on my YouTube channel, my website, or on my author's page on Amazon for a demonstration of how this works.♥

The Difference Between the Emotional and the Physical

Orgasm, as I have said, is the physical aspect of surrendering. However, important differences exist between the physical and the psychological experience as well as similarities.

Orgasms Come from a Change in Emotions and Attitudes

The difference is that sharing vaginal orgasms cannot be sought entirely rationally. *They will arrive when they will arrive, as the end process of a total change in the man's and the woman's deepest psychological attitudes.* Vaginal orgasms cannot be sought separately or as an end in themselves. Indeed, to seek them directly, to wait upon them, to try to force them is the surest way of postponing their arrival.

Orgasms Cannot Be Forced to Mask Bad Attitudes

The idea that the vaginal orgasm can be forced is typical thinking of a person with inhibited desire and pleasure. We have seen that, because the person is frightened and mistrusts the mate's love and his masculinity or her femininity, *the person has to feel "in control"* all the time. The trouble with that view is that in real orgasm, *a person must be out of control*; must willfully, delightedly desire to be entirely so.

♥*PRD: Bad Attitudes Show Up in the Bedroom*

Respondents to the Sexless Marriages Survey checked the following ways that inhibited sexual attitudes come out during sex:

Ways your companion withholds emotions during sex:

66% Sex is mechanical and routine.
74% Sex lacks joy and laughter.
59% Never compliments you sexually.
51% Emotionally absent before, during, and after sex.
49% Does the minimum to get the job done.
52% Makes you feel sexually unattractive.

One husband wrote: "She professes love and says the things she thinks she is supposed to say as a way of checking off a list of duties while remaining emotionally distant. She provides minimal physical demonstrations of affection, and even then, she does it in mechanical ways, and in ways that limit any possibility that the physical affection might develop any further than the minimal step she initiated."♥

Physical Techniques Can't Make Up for Inhibited Attitudes

The delusion that the vaginal orgasm can or should be sought as an end in itself and not as the result of a deep inner change of the kind discussed in the preceding chapters of this section has been fostered by many of the books which have dealt with the problem of inhibited desire and pleasure or with the role or responsibility of the woman in marriage.

One recent book counseled the conscious contraction of certain muscles during intercourse, holding that this would heighten sexual pleasure. Other books emphasize the importance of position during intercourse. Their tacit or stated contention is that orgiastic potency can be achieved by mechanical means.

♥*PRD: Most Thought-Leaders Don't Know About the Power of the Mind*

Most blogs and podcasts continue to promote techniques and clitoral orgasms over orgasmic attitudes, although some recognize that attitudes make the techniques more pleasurable. It's rare to find a sexuality author or thought-leader who teaches the power of the mind for sharing vaginal orgasms and cervical kisses. To them, the vaginal orgasm is still a myth.♥

Focusing on Sensations Destroys Real Sexual Passion

The fact is that concentrating on one's sensations during intercourse and wondering if one is feeling the "right" feeling can destroy sexual passion more completely than any technique. We know this from scores of patients. Such a clinical and objective attitude toward local sexual sensations reflects *the inhibited person's need to control* a situation and fear of surrendering to the mate. This obsessive scrutiny of their sexual reactions creates an even more frustrating experience than usual.

What Attitude Is Helpful?

Is there an attitude one can take toward orgasm and rapture before one has achieved it? Yes. This attitude may be summarized in this fashion: *If one has genuinely pursued the goal of self-surrender, uprooting and exposing attitudes leftover from childhood and youth, the ability to achieve orgasm must inevitably arrive.* Until that time, and particularly during intercourse, one must put the matter out of one's mind entirely and *yield emotionally to the moment.*

Each's Pleasure Increases the Other's Pleasure

The growth of one's ability to share a vaginal orgasm is natural. Distorted attitudes have impeded it; it resumes its development when these attitudes change. It is as natural a move as the move from winter to spring. Gradually, one finds oneself allowing new tenderness and concern for the mate to become a part of the meaning of the sexual embrace.

One sees and feels the pleasure one's sexual thawing brings the mate, and this process becomes circular, the mate's increased pleasure giving one even more pleasure. And with the mate's pleasure in mind, one now seeks out more and more those things that please the mate. This exploration leads inevitably to the discovery that what pleases the mate most, outside of one's own sensations, provides the greatest pleasure.

Ends in Total Surrender to the Delights Love Can Bring

This mutual spiraling of feeling ultimately climaxes in an unconscious decision to give the mate the greatest emotional pleasure of all, one's total surrender to the delights the mate brings to the act of love.

♥*PRD: Excerpt from God's 11 Secrets of Sex:*

Why Men Love Vaginal Orgasms and Women Should, Too

Three husbands tell how sharing vaginal orgasms with their wives brings joy to their wives and them.

1. Women Get More Enjoyment from Sex Than Men Do

"I've always thought sex is more for women than men because my wife has many orgasms while I can only have one. After I've come and we're still connected, she deliberately squeezes her PC muscle around me. She doesn't stop until she's had several more small orgasms. When she relaxes, we both laugh out loud."

2. The Husband Goes Deeper When His Wife Orgasms

"I hear men say, 'I can't tell if she's faking it.' I know they've never been with a woman having a vaginal orgasm because when my wife has hers, her vagina opens up, and I go deeper. We both enjoy a whole new range of sensations. You can't fake that."

3. The Husband's Greatest Joy Is His Wife's Pleasure

"It's very satisfying watching my wife orgasm multiple times and knowing I'm the cause of all that pleasure."

Nestled tenderly in each other's arms, with their bodies, souls, and minds, they say, "Thank you, My Lord, for creating the way of a man with a maid. To You be the glory forever and ever for your profound love for men and women. Amen."

Dear Reader,

Thank you for reading and sharing your time with me. I pray that your amazement at God's love for you and your marriage has grown. I hope that Dr. Robinson's text that mirrors God's divine wisdom has touched your heart as it did mine in 1973 and again as I updated and added scriptures to her wisdom.

If you benefitted from this study, please consider leaving an honest review of this book on Amazon and Goodreads. A short, honest review of a couple of sentences along with your rating works great. Your words help other book lovers decide what to read.

If you don't want to write anything, you can just leave a rating.

May God bless you on your journey of love,
Patsy Rae Dawson♥

20.

The Lore of Love and Sexual Positions

In this book, I have taken a firm stand against any mechanical approach to love or lovemaking. This represents the psychiatric view of love and is based on the premise that inhibited sexual desire and pleasure is psychological. Therefore, the resolution of sexual inhibitions must be a psychological one.

Once Emotionally Healed, Lovemaking Becomes an Art

The mechanical approach is based on the premise that lovemaking is an art or even a science that can be learned, as piano or chemistry can be learned. From the psychiatric view, the so-called art of love is instinctual. The perfectly free person, if he loved and were loved in return, would soon become a sophisticated practitioner of this art with the barest of preparation.

Free spirits are relatively rare in our society. Usually, more instruction is needed. Taboos against sexuality have characterized Western civilization. The art of love seems to be primarily the art of getting over societal induced ignorance, superstition, and inhibition.

Suggestions Are for Couples Sharing Vaginal Orgasms

When through the methods employed in this book or through therapy, one has achieved psychological maturity, and vaginal orgasm is no longer blocked, examining some of the technical information about lovemaking can be helpful. Before that point, such lore tends to lead to inhibiting self-consciousness.

Don't Lose the Spontaneity and Magic of Lovemaking

Students of the matter generally agree that spontaneity in sexual relations must never be lost. Married life tends to impose a relatively rigid pattern in all areas. Such routine is a necessity if the world's work is to get done. For example, for most people, it becomes necessary to breakfast every day at the same time, in the same place, and in the same manner. If one allows this to happen to sexuality, one is imprisoning the unicorn and exposing lovemaking to the loss of its magic.

Variety Is the Spice that Married Love Needs

Variety is the spice that married love often needs, and it takes no great effort to practice variety in lovemaking. It takes only a sense of its importance and the knowledge of a few minimal facts.

Don't Make Love the Same Time Every Time

One method of preserving spontaneity is to prevent lovemaking from always occurring at the same time. Evenings in most homes tend to follow a pattern. Supper must be cooked, dishes must be done, children must be put to bed. And then there's television or guests. I have had many men and women defend the proposition that, since lovemaking tends to make them sleepy, the last moments of the day are by necessity the time for love.

But this is making convenience a necessity. And love is too beautiful, too centrally important to be domesticated so. If love can laugh at locksmiths, it can also laugh behind locked doors once every week or two. Children have homework to do or a television program to watch, and anyhow, it is good for them to realize that Mother and Father spend some time alone and love to.

Make Love at Non-Routine Times

Desire often arises unbidden and for no apparent rational reason. Men are more subject to outside stimuli than women and are perhaps more uninhibited. So the inception of lovemaking at non-routine times may frequently originate with men.

Women Can Initiate Sex, Too

When they feel the urge, women should realize that they can initiate a passionate interlude. It is proper and good that a woman do this. And her husband will love it. I am assuming the partners in such delightful off-hour trysts are sensitive to each other's responses.

Refuse Sex in a Gentle Way

Every man and woman must realize that it is perfectly all right to say no if one is tired or preoccupied. But the nay-saying must be gentle, and if it is so and the partner who makes the advance is hurt, he or she must examine the rejected feeling, take full responsibility for it, and dispose of it. Holding onto such feelings causes one to fear making advances, and this will deprive the relationship of one of the best techniques for maintaining spontaneity.

It is insensitive and unloving to force a partner by sulking or other forms of psychological blackmail to satisfy a need. It is far easier for the ardent one to wait as the time will come soon enough. The fact that you have announced your desire has a delayed reaction on your loved one.

Some Women Love Waking to Middle-of-the-Night Sex

Waking in the middle of the night, many men find themselves prepared for lovemaking, the penis firmly erect. Many women love awakening to find themselves mistily, dreamily in the embrace of love. The body on waking is often highly sensual.

Changing the Time for Love Can Renew Excitement

Changing the time for love can happen in various ways, and it is advisable to look for opportunities. Not too much effort is necessary as the hour at the end of the day when preparing for sleep will remain the primary time for intercourse. But an occasional switch in time can keep this romantic hour from losing its quality of ever-renewed excitement.

Vary the Position for Spontaneity

An even more basic technique for preserving the spontaneity of sex is that of varying the position used during intercourse. In most relationships, one preferred position generally evolves. If this position is always adopted, the feeling of a monotonous repetitiveness can enter the love situation, and this must be guarded against. This fact has been recognized from the earliest times, and efforts to combat it have given rise through the centuries to many books on the subject.

Most Position Books Come from Ancient Sources

Hindu, Greek, Roman, and Persian literature record hundreds of sexual positions. If one has a library of erotica and is sufficiently curious, these positions may be studied. However, such a proliferation of detail can become exhausting and even morbid and absurd—though perhaps gaily ridiculous. Most of the modern books that dispense direct sexual advice obtain their material from these ancient sources.

Only Five Basic Positions Have Real Relevance

Only five basic positions have real relevance to most couples. I will describe them so that when you encounter them or wish to change from your usual position, you will not feel that they are strange, awkward, or so exotic or suffer feelings of shyness, embarrassment, or guilt.

1a. Ventro-Ventral (or Face to Face) Position

The first position is the ventro-ventral (or face to face) position, with the man on top and the woman on the bottom with her knees up. This is the classical "missionary" sexual position used in our society.

If used properly, it is perhaps the best position for sexual union. It allows for deep penetration of the vagina by the penis, and because it leaves the pelvic regions of both partners free, it allows for variety in sexual movement, though the man has more freedom of movement in this position than the woman.

There's an old but apt joke about this position. A young chorus girl asks an older one what her definition of a gentleman is. The older one promptly replies: "One who leans on his elbows." Men should remember that this fact can be pertinent. The full weight of the heavy man can be tiring even to a passionate woman.

1b. Pillow Ventro-Ventral (or Face to Face) Position

A pleasant variant of this position can be achieved by placing a pillow under the woman's buttocks before intercourse. If it is placed a little toward the small of the back, women who receive preliminary pleasure from friction between the clitoris and the penis will find the contact easier to effect. If it is placed a bit forward, it will be exciting to those who get a great deal of sensation from the pressure of the penis against the posterior walls of the vagina.

Generally, in this classical position, the woman spreads her legs and raises them (lying with the legs straight down makes vaginal entrance difficult for the male). Those who enjoy stimulation of the posterior vaginal wall may lock their legs around their partner's hips. Those who in the initial stages of intercourse are most aroused by clitoral stimulation may close their legs; in this position, the man is half kneeling, straddling his partner's hips. This latter position is not too comfortable for the man if it is maintained for long.

A less arduous position for the man is achieved if he straddles one of his partner's legs and enters the vagina at a slightly oblique angle. This allows the woman to close the leg that is free, which gives maximum contact of all portions of the vulva with the penis.

2. The Reversal of the Top-Bottom Roles Position

The next major position reverses the top-bottom roles. In this variant, the woman is on the top, the man on the bottom.

This position is adopted either as a spontaneous change for variety's sake or because the woman may be feeling more energetic than the man as the partner on top does a significant portion of the moving. This position can express tenderness on the woman's part. If her husband feels sensual but fatigued, she can give him pleasure without making it necessary for him to develop the usual amount of male aggressiveness. Such a passive role can be exciting to a man on occasion, and he should allow himself to indulge in his wife's love. This position is also useful if the woman is physically small, and the man is large and heavy.

In this position, the woman may straddle her husband's hips, which facilitates deep penetration and may be incredibly pleasurable. Since she is in charge, she may feel freer to exert more than the usual pressure of the penis against the cervix. In this position, she may lie on top of her husband, her legs supported by his, or she may lie between his legs. In these two latter positions, the clitoris can be brought into close contact with the penis, and this is extremely pleasant for some women.

3. The Face-to-Face and Sideways Position

Another alternative for lovemaking is the face to face and sideways position. In this position, since the woman is generally the lighter of the two, one of her legs is placed over the man's hips; this allows him to insert his penis at a slightly oblique angle. Pillows for head and shoulder are usually necessary if this position is maintained the entire time.

4. The Dorso-Ventral Position

The next position is the dorso-ventral position, where the man's penis enters the woman's vagina from the back. If the entire intercourse is performed while lying sideways, this is perhaps the most "restful" of all positions. For obvious reasons, it is sometimes the preferred form for intercourse during pregnancy.

This position is often extremely exciting to a man. I do not know why this is so, though it is suggested that the position suggests the "animality" of pure lust. I must emphasize, however, that this idea is merely speculative.

The dorso-ventral position can also be assumed with the woman kneeling, or standing up and bending over, supporting herself against a chair or wall with her hands. It can be achieved less athletically if the man sits on a chair, and his partner sits on his lap, although this allows for less movement by both.

5. The Standing Position

The last general position I shall describe here is the standing position. It is a particularly arduous position for the male; he generally must bend his knees slightly to enter and must hold onto his partner's buttocks to maintain entrance.

Most Positions Are Based on These Five Basic Ones

I think these are the major sexual positions relevant to know and adopt when the mood is upon one. Most of the "hundreds" of others described in antiquity literature are subtle variations of these and have no particular application to a modern couple's lovemaking. Indeed, it is apparent that any excessive preoccupation with such nuances could indicate morbidity, may be a confession that the person, far from having achieved sexual maturity, is in some profound way impotent.

Generally, Men Can Orgasm in Any Position, Women Can't

I should like to make one further point about these positions. While men can usually have an orgasm in any position, many women achieve it most completely and satisfyingly in one favorite position. This is entirely compatible with full psychological and sexual maturity, and one should in no wise feel the slightest bit embarrassed about it. It is advisable to make this fact known to one's partner in love. He will, if you are both feeling positionally experimental, return to the position you prefer when you are ready to have your climax.

Frequency of Intercourse

The frequency of intercourse is entirely an individual matter. The only important criterion is that both partners feel completely satisfied with the amount of lovemaking. If one of the partners is dissatisfied, the subject should be discussed in a frank manner. No cause for feelings of rejection by a partner should be allowed to develop in silence. The rate of intercourse in any marriage may slow down or stop for a while due to circumstances such as pregnancy, business worries, sickness, etc.

Length of Intercourse

This is entirely an individual matter. It varies with each couple and often with each intercourse. Indeed, this variability in time can add to the spontaneity factor in lovemaking.

Orgasm in unison is widely held to be desirable. However, I have had many people of both sexes report that they prefer to reach climax immediately before or after their partners. Some say they are distracted by the other's movements at this juncture. Others say they profoundly enjoy the partner's excitement and prefer to have a small amount of ego left to experience it more completely.

Part 2:

Insights from Patsy Rae Dawson

21.

31 Surprises About Sex from the *Sexless Marriages Survey*

I launched the *Sexless Marriages Survey: With Self-Assessment Checklists* July 12, 2016, through my newsletter *Embarrass the Alligator* and website. During those first five years, 322 Christians participated anonymously—185 women and 137 men ranging in age from 24 to 80. Of those, 38 were the ones who withheld sex. Single men and women wanting to learn how to avoid Mr. or Ms. Wrong totaled 8.

The Most Shocking Fact

The most shocking fact I learned from the participants' answers is that sex is much more emotional for men than it is for women. That is not to discount women's emotions or their pain of sexual rejection. It's just that over and over and over, the men checked many more items of emotional pain than the women did. Rejection also affected the men's ability to function in everyday life more than it did the women.

Rather than an animalistic release of pent-up semen, for a sexually healthy man, sex is primarily an emotional expression of love. Unfortunately, society gets it exactly backward.

I had an opportunity to make that statement twice at professional meetings of both men and women when I was quizzed publicly about what I do. Both times, as I was sharing this shocking fact, the men were shaking their heads, "Yes, finally someone gets it."

When I started the survey, I had no expectation of learning as much as I have. After all, I had been the confidante of both men and women for 45 years. In thinking about the fifth anniversary of launching the survey, I reviewed the newsletters I wrote about it. Of the 31 surprises about sex, I wrote articles on about half of them.

One of my critique partners said, "The survey turned you into even more of an expert than you were before. No one knows this material like you do."

I am sharing with you a list of the 31 surprises that I hope are self-explanatory even though I'm not giving details. The surprises are categorized according to the checklists in the survey that they correspond with. Those checklists are based upon 2 Timothy 3:1-5 and follow the escalating order of the 19 sins common in sexless marriages.

How 2 Timothy 3:1-5 Applies to Sexless Marriages

When Paul was in prison, he wrote the young evangelist Timothy to defend the faith in dangerous times. He warned that people would lose their natural love for their family, and they would become involved in all kinds of family-destroying sins:

> *2 Timothy 3:1-5: "But mark this: There will be terrible times in the last days. People will be lovers of themselves, lovers of money, boastful, proud, abusive, disobedient to their parents, ungrateful, unholy,* ***without love [without natural affection—KJV]****, unforgiving, slanderous, without self-control, brutal, not lovers of the good, treacherous, rash, conceited, lovers of pleasure rather than lovers of God—having a form of godliness but denying its power. Have nothing to do with such people" (NIV).*

"Without natural affection," a compound word, is used only two times in the New Testament (2 Timothy 3:3 and Romans 1:31). It comes from the Greek *a* (negative) plus *storge* (pronounced stor-JAY). The negative means "without natural love for family" (Thayer 82).

A positive form of *storge*, also a compound word, is used one time:

> *Romans 12:10: "Be devoted [philos plus storge] to one another in brotherly love [philos plus delphos--brother]; give preference to one another in honor."*

The compound word "devoted" comes from *philos* (affectionate love) plus *storge* (love of family). It refers to "the mutual love of parents and children; also of husbands and wives, loving affection, prone to love, loving tenderly; used chiefly of the reciprocal tenderness of parents and children; love of the brethren tenderly affectioned one to another, Romans 12:10" (Thayer 655).

The devotion we are to manifest toward other Christians should mirror *storge*—the natural love between parents and their children and between husbands and wives. In contrast, the list of 19 sins including the negative of *storge*, the absence of parental and marital love, in 2 Timothy 3:1-5 reflects the usual 24/7 conduct of unloving spouses.

Do 19 sins common in sexless marriages sound extreme? Sadly, my *Sexless Marriages Survey* verifies that these sins against the mate abound in sexless marriages. The longer the marriage continues in a sexless state, the more pronounced the 19 love-defying sins become. Sin never stagnates, but always grows, often secretively.

Sexless Marriages Are About Character

Sexless marriages aren't simply about sexual inhibitions and naivety about sex. They are about the withholder's whole character, soul, and lack of intimacy with the mate. God calls it the sin of being unloving—without natural affection for family.

At the end of the verses, Paul told Timothy, "Have nothing to do with such people." God doesn't want us to tolerate the sin of being unloving in our homes or in our congregations. He expects us to imitate him and be loving toward our family, brethren, and neighbors.

Solomon Was The King of Sexless Marriages

Toward the end of Solomon's life, God condemned him as a sinner without natural affection. As The King of Sexless Marriages, he displayed many facets of intimacy anorexia including all 12 classic characteristics that Dr. Douglas Weiss identified in his book *Intimacy Anorexia.* In *God's 11 Secrets of Sex,* the chapter "Secret 8: Avoid the 12 Love-Defying Traits of a Sexless Spouse" exposes Solomon's love defects. You'll probably come away from that study with a different view of Solomon than you had before.

Here are the surprises as they correspond to the scriptures:

Profile of Sex-Starved Marriage Partners

Christians who stay married to sexless spouses often share these common characteristics:

1. 81% of sex-starved Christians lack confidence in spiritual leaders or got bad advice from them.
2. Men need emotional intimacy more than women do, and society has this exactly backward.
3. 81% of sex-starved Christians don't rise to their full human potential with men suffering the most.
4. 63% of sex-starved mates grew up in a narcissistic home and don't know what true love looks like.
5. 50% of sex-starved mates grew up in an alcoholic home and didn't enjoy a loving experience.
6. 77% of sex-starved mates grew up with one or both parents screaming at them and didn't experience parental love.
7. 45% of sex-starved mates bury their feelings instead of facing the

spouse's sin, and nothing changes.

Level 1 Profile: Naivety About the Bible and Sex

Jude discusses three levels that sin progresses through. They require three different levels of intervention to get the sinner's attention to begin working on overcoming the sin. These three levels of sins correspond with the stages sexless marriages progress through and follow the escalating order of sins in 2 Timothy 3:1-5.

> *Jude 22-23: "[**Level 1**] And have mercy on some, who are doubting; [Level 2] save others, snatching them out of the fire; and [Level 3] on some have mercy with fear, hating even the garment polluted by the flesh."*

All three levels share ignorance regarding God's teaching on sex in the Bible. The simple naivety of Level 1 is easy to overcome. Many individuals respond with joy to learning God's truths about male and female, marriage and sex, and God's plans for men and women to subdue the earth, fill it with people, and glorify him.

8. 11% of sexless Christians are willing to learn how to overcome their sexual inhibitions.
9. 70% of sexless Christians lived with an alcoholic parent and suffered emotional and physical abuse.
10. 77% of sexless Christians grew up in a narcissistic home and don't know what true love acts like.
11. 50% of sexless Christians grew up with one or both parents screaming at them and didn't experience parental love.
12. Sexless men and women treat their mates the same, and you can't recognize their gender by their actions.
13. Sexless marriages damage children emotionally, which often doesn't show up until they marry.
14. Kissing and touching are dead in sexless marriages as all forms of physical affection are withheld.
15. 66% of sexless spouses respond to sex in a mechanical and routine manner.

Level 2 Profile: Flirting with Character Sins

In Levels 2 and 3, the survey exposes the full-spectrum of sins revolving around being "without natural love for family" as found in 2 Timothy 3:1-5. The survey verifies that these sins thrive at the core of sexless marriages with the first 9 sins comprising Level 2:

*2 Timothy 3:1-3a: "But mark this: There will be terrible times in the last days. People will be **[Level 2]** [1] lovers of themselves, [2] lovers of money, [3] boastful, [4] proud, [5] abusive, [6] disobedient to their parents, [7] ungrateful, [8] unholy, **[9] without love [without natural affection—KJV]**,..." (NIV).*

As Jude warned, Level 2 love sins are harder to deal with than the simple ignorance of the scriptures regarding lovemaking of Level 1.

Jude 23a: "...save others, snatching them out of the fire;...."

"Snatching them out of the fire" implies that it is hard to get the attention of Level 2 sexless spouses that they even have a problem. The majority refuse to study and work on their marriage, blame the spouse for all problems, and fight dirty to avoid accountability.

"Save others" implies that these individuals can be helped and that they can become loving. God devotes a lot of space in the Bible to teaching them how to put on love.

16. 90% of sexless Christians flaunt narcissistic entitlement as they reject intimacy with the mate.
17. 87% of sexless Christians misuse money to control their mate, which gets worse as time goes on.
18. 30% of sexless spouses are affected by promiscuously created sexual inhibitions.
19. 89% of sexless Christians refuse to talk or read about sex and refuse to learn about becoming loving.
20. 70% of sexless Christians are ungrateful for the things their mates do and look down on the opposite sex.
21. 83% of sexless Christians blame the spouse, although their sexual issues existed before the marriage.
22. Sexless marriages are not about the absence of sex, but about 24/7 character faults and sins.
23. Statistics show sexless spouses pretend to be loving for pictures and company and at worship services.
24. 79% of sexless Christians fight dirty to avoid accountability and to shift blame to the loving spouse.
25. 28% of sexless Christians are "weasel-word liars" who tell a little bit of truth to give a false impression.
26. Sexlessness revolves around being "without natural love for family," including the children who suffer greatly.

Level 3 Profile: Moving Deeper into Morally Polluted Sins

The 19 sins clustered around being "without natural affection" for family occur in escalating order. Below are the Level 3 sins:

> *2 Timothy 3:3b-5: "**[Level 3]** [10] unforgiving, [11] slanderous, [12] without self-control, [13] brutal, [14] not lovers of the good, [15] treacherous, [16] rash, [17] conceited, [18] lovers of pleasure rather than lovers of God – [19] having a form of godliness but denying its power. Have nothing to do with such people" (NIV).*

As you would expect with Level 3, it's extremely hard to get the attention of these sexless spouses, because the sin is becoming addictive. They require more effort to convict them of sin, and Jude warns about personal danger. One danger is that the loving spouse will withdraw emotionally and begin fighting sin with sin. Another danger is not calling the sin out so that the abuse grows unhindered.

> *Jude 23b: "...on some have mercy with fear, hating even the garment polluted by the flesh."*

27. 87% of sexless Christians used bait and switch in courtship by feigning desire for married passion.
28. Statistics show sexless marriages get worse over time as withholding turns into blaming and hatred.
29. 62% of deprived mates are surprised sexless mates enjoy causing pain as their withholding addiction deepens.
30. Sin in sexless marriages never stagnates but always grows, often secretly until it becomes openly addictive.
31. 61% of sex-deprived Christians consider divorce but don't know when they can scripturally severe the relationship.

Obviously, in most sexless marriages, you're not dealing with someone "who is perfect except for sex." You're trying to get along with someone who may be involved in Level 1 naivety sins, Level 2 character sins, or Level 3 moral sins.

You can take the *Sexless Marriages Survey: With Self-Assessment Checklists* at PatsyRaeDawson.com to learn more about the character and moral flaws that often thrive 24/7 in a sexless spouse's life. The survey helps you determine the level of sin in your marriage. And the free eReport you receive when you finish gives a procedure for tackling the love sins you discover based on the level of sin in your marriage.

22.

The Bible Teaches Nine Stages of Sexual Development

Instead of being prudish and sexually inhibited, the Bible teaches nine stages of sexual development that a person's life goes through. A lack of respect for these stages often results in inhibited sexual desire and pleasure. Indeed, "sexless marriages" is the #1 marriage problem googled with women making only slightly less than 50% of the inquires.

Responsibility for Each Sexual Stage

The first four stages of sexual growth are our parents' responsibility. The three most important ones occur before sex education in the schools begins. We share responsibility with our parents for the fifth stage. The last four stages are our personal responsibility regardless of whether we grew up in a loving or a dysfunctional home.

Parental Responsibility for the Child's Sexual Development

1. Gestation
2. Infancy
3. Childhood
4. Adolescence

Overlapping Parental and Personal Responsibility

5. Courtship

Personal Responsibility for Sexual Growth

6. Honeymoon Year
7. Middle Years
8. Senior Years

Overlapping Senior and Personal Responsibility

9. Next Generation

Sadly, we fail during nearly every one of these nine stages to teach our children and to learn for ourselves about God's marvelous design for sharing love in our homes. Notice the Bible's teaching:

God Uses the First Three Stages to Describe His Love

God uses the portrait of a loving mother to illustrate his own love for the Israelites, which illustrates the first three stages.

1. Gestation

Isaiah 66:7-9:
"'Before she travailed, she brought forth;
Before her pain came, she gave birth to a boy.
Who has heard such a thing? Who has seen such things?
Can a land be born in one day?
Can a nation be brought forth all at once?
As soon as Zion travailed, she also brought forth her sons.
Shall I bring to the point of birth and not give delivery?' says the LORD.
'Or shall I who gives delivery shut the womb?' says your God."

Science now knows that sexual activity during pregnancy floods both the mother and her unborn child with hormones of love. Many mothers-to-be who have never enjoyed an orgasm do so during pregnancy due to surging hormonal feelings of love for their unborn child and the father. Additionally, pregnant sex exercises and strengthens the woman's pelvic floor and muscles, which helped the Israelite woman give birth "before she travailed" (verse 7). Indeed, Jewish women were known for their easy deliveries.

2. Infancy and 3. Childhood

After the child was born, began developing, and growing, God continued comparing his love to that of a mother for her child:

Isaiah 66:10-13:
"'Be joyful with Jerusalem and rejoice for her, all you who love her;
Be exceedingly glad with her, all you who mourn over her,
That you may nurse and be satisfied with her comforting breasts,
That you may suck and be delighted with her bountiful bosom.'
For thus says the LORD, 'Behold, I extend peace to her like a river,
And the glory of the nations like an overflowing stream;
And you will be nursed, you will be carried on the hip and fondled on the knees.
As one whom his mother comforts, so I will comfort you;
And you will be comforted in Jerusalem.'"

In conception, during the pregnancy and the birth process, and then when nursing and playing with the child, the mother and baby are bathed in God's bonding hormones of love and tranquility.

Touching Teaches the Babe and the Child How to Love

Ashley Montagu, in his book *Touching: The Human Significance of the Skin,* explains in chapter 6, "Skin and Sex," how touching the babe and young child prepares them for the skin-to-skin contact of married love:

> The enormous variety of meanings which sex may have for different individuals, a language which has the kinds of things to say to the other that can be said in no other way, an exchange of love, a means of hurting or exploiting others, a mode of defense, a bargaining point, a way of self-denial or self-assertion, an affirmation or a rejection of masculinity or femininity, and so on, not to mention the abnormal or pathological expressions which sex may take, all, more or less, are influenced by early tactile experience (219).

What a blessing that God illustrated "touch" in Isaiah 66 as an example of maternal love that described his divine love for his people.

The Song of Solomon Teaches the First Five Stages

God preserved the Song of Solomon to teach parents how to oversee the first five stages of sexual development. Teaching children how to love is the overriding theme of the captivating story.

Through parental sex education and example, the Shulammite maiden escaped a disastrous unloving marriage to an emotionally and sexually defective man—King Solomon. She said both she and her shepherd boyfriend began learning about love and preparing for a wonderful marriage as babies sucking their mother's breasts:

Song of Solomon 8:1:
"Oh that you were like a brother to me
Who nursed at my mother's breasts."

4. Adolescence and 5. Courtship

The Maiden credited her mother with teaching her about sexual love and preparing her for marriage. Because of her mother's words and example, she looked forward to married lovemaking. Thus the love that began as a baby offered protection through adolescence and courtship:

Song of Solomon 8:2-3:
"I would lead you and bring you
Into the house of my mother, who used to instruct me;
I would give you spiced wine to drink from the juice of my pomegranates.
'Let his left hand be under my head
And his right hand embrace me.'"

The Shulammite repeated the theme a third time to the palace virgins. She begged them to learn the lesson her mother taught her—not to force love, but to allow a true intellectual and emotional bond to develop between her and the king before marrying:

Song of Solomon 8:4:
"I want you to swear, O daughters of Jerusalem,
Do not arouse or awaken my love
Until she pleases."

The Song of Solomon climaxes by applying the theme to the parents of future generations of children—to you and me. At the wedding, the maiden's brothers asked how to protect their baby sister from falling in love with a dysfunctional male:

Song of Solomon 8:8:
"We have a little sister,
And she has no breasts;
What shall we do for our sister
On the day when she is spoken for?"

You can learn more about what God wants parents to teach and exemplify for their children in "Secret 11: Pay Passionate Love Forward" in *God's 11 Secrets of Sex.*

God Commands Us to Become Better Married Lovers

At every stage of life, from conception to death, God instructs us to be continually learning how to more fully love our mate intellectually, emotionally, sexually, and spiritually. Notice the responsibilities God gives us when we marry to practice and work at becoming better lovers:

6. Honeymoon Year

God commanded bridegrooms to stay home for a year making love to their bride, being playful, experimentive, and joyful.

> *Deuteronomy 24:5: "When a man takes a new wife, he shall not go out with the army nor be charged with any duty; he shall be free at home one year and shall give happiness to his wife whom he has taken."*

A year of passionate lovemaking strengthens a couple's emotional and physical intimacy. They begin to learn how to relish the hormones of love before they start their family and get caught up in the trials of life. *As eager, new lovers,* they are well on their way to *becoming excellent lovers.*

7. Middle Years

During midlife, frequent lovemaking continues to grow the couple's love for each other:

Ecclesiastes 9:9: "Enjoy life with the woman whom you love [literally sexually or otherwise] all the days of your fleeting life which He has given to you under the sun; for this is your reward in life, and in your toil in which you have labored under the sun."

As excellent lovers, the couple continues to strengthen their emotional bond. Rejoicing in each other's arms helps them reduce the stress of working hard to make a living and raise their children.

8. Senior Years

God reserves the best sex for older couples. What's the difference between honeymoon and midlife sex with lovemaking in the golden years? Young adults are first aroused, and then they make love. Older couples start the process, and then they're aroused to the most tender, emotional sex of their life *as expert lovers.*

Proverbs 5:18-19:
"Let your fountain be blessed,
And rejoice in the wife of your youth.
As a loving hind and a graceful doe,
Let her breasts satisfy you at all times;
Be exhilarated always with her love."

Dr. Bernie Zilbergeld, in his interviews with 145 men and women aged 45 to 87, noticed that women in their 70s who had figured out the emotional and physical part of sex could "out orgasm" the average 20-year-old woman. He also learned that older couples often enjoy fantastic lovemaking even when dealing with age-related medical problems.

God Wants Older Lovers to Teach New Lovers

The first five stages demonstrate that God wants children to grow up with parents who passionately love each other. God, the Father, set the example for his earthly children to love each other and their children, as we saw in the first stages development. But if we didn't learn how to love others as children, God instituted a way for us to learn as adults.

9. Next Generation

The parents loving each other and their children is so essential for the healthy development of the child's personality and sexuality that God commands older women to teach the next generation of young wives how to love their husbands and children with the caresses of love:

Titus 2:3-5: "Older women likewise are to be reverent in their behavior,

> *not malicious gossips nor enslaved to much wine, teaching what is good, so that they may encourage the young women to love their husbands, to love their children, to be sensible, pure, workers at home, kind, being subject to their own husbands, so that the word of God will not be dishonored.*

The word "love" that a woman gives her husband and children comes from the Greek word *phileo.* It conveys emotional affection that is expressed physically, such as hugging, patting, and kissing the object of one's *phileo.* Thus, if a mother didn't learn how to love her family in her home of origin, God instructs the older women to teach her. The fact that God gave this command implies that an adult can learn how to love their mate and family. We never get too old to embrace love.

The young women have the responsibility of being willing to learn from the older women. In some instances, the older women will need to almost re-raise the young women.

Paul began Titus 2 with a similar command for older husbands:

> *Titus 2:1-2: "But as for you, speak the things which are fitting for sound doctrine. Older men are to be temperate, dignified, sensible, sound in faith, in love, in perseverance."*

Just as older women are to be reverent in demeanor (have men, places, and things figured out) and teach what is sensible, older men are also to be sensible. "Sensible" implies that the older men have figured out life, just as the older women have. They don't engage in cognitively distorted thinking or spew out anger and extreme accusations. These older husbands know how to love their wives as they are sound in faith, love, and perseverance. "Love" is the Greek word *agape,* which describes the sacrificial love a husband is to show for his wife as he models Christ in his marriage (Ephesians 5:25-31).

Young men share the same responsibility as young women:

> *Titus 2:6: "Likewise urge the young men to be sensible…."*

"Urge" means to beg and plead with the young men to be sensible. If they are sensible, they don't engage in the cognitive distortions, anger, and blame that plague sex-withholding spouses. They follow the example of the sensible, loving older men to become passionate lovers with their wives.

God's Nine Stages Lead to a More Loving World

When men and women follow God's instructions for the nine stages of emotional and sexual development, they put on love for each other and their children. Everyone benefits as the world becomes more loving.

23.

Radical Epiphany on Awakening Male-Female Sexuality

In Chapter 7: "Various Traumas Lead to Sexual Inhibitions," Dr. Robinson said, "One of my colleagues summed up the difference [in male and female orgasms] in this way: 'To express it in a purely biological sense, [for propagating the species] the male orgasm is a necessity. The female orgasm is a luxury.'"

No! The Female Orgasm Is Never a Luxury!

God designed the female orgasm as a necessity! He foretold the glory of orgasmic love when he created Adam and Eve and declared, "And they shall become one flesh." To help make that happen, God set processes in place and gave men and women commandments to help propel the wife toward exciting orgasms in the arms of her husband.

The Three Reasons God Created Men and Women

Genesis 1:27: "God created man in His own image, in the image of God He created him; male and female He created them."

The male-female differences originated in the mind of God. He made the man for a different reason, from different material, and with different hormones and abilities from the woman to qualify him for special jobs. He equipped the female with different expert talents for giving comfort and sustenance to her husband and their children.

1. To Fill the Earth with People

Genesis 1:28a: "And God blessed them; and God said to them 'Be fruitful and multiply, and fill the earth...."

After God made them "male" and "female," he commanded, "Be fruitful and multiply, and replenish the earth." To ensure obedience, God created a strong sexual drive in both men and women. Sex is so crucial in God's design that he devotes more space in the Bible to teach husbands and wives how to love each other than to any other area of marriage.

The command to "be fruitful and multiply, and fill the earth" doesn't stop with the sexual act, which creates a new life, but begins with procreation. God gives parents the responsibility to raise their children to adulthood and help them rise to their full potential. Just as God created men and women in his image, God desires for them to fill the earth with like beings—children in the image of God.

2. To Subdue a Hostile Earth

Genesis 1:28b: "...and subdue it; and rule over the fish of the sea and over the birds of the sky, and over every living thing that moves on the earth.'"

God's command to Adam and Eve to subdue the earth shows he intended for them to work and use the earth and its products along with the animals to make a living. The word "subdue" carries the idea of coercing a hostile environment into submission. It shows God expected men and women to *work hard* for their food, clothing, and shelter.

3. To Glorify God in the Process of Subduing and Filling

Isaiah 43:7: "Everyone who is called by My name, and whom I have created for My glory, whom I have formed even whom I have made."

God not only designed men and women to bear children and to work, but God also created them to glorify him. "Glorify" means to cause someone to be well spoken of by others. By their earthly lives, men and women either cause God to be well spoken of or blasphemed.

How Those Jobs Translate to Men and Women

1. God designed the man as the primary subduer and gave him a masculine spirit of aggression.
2. God designed the woman as the family's love specialist and gave her a feminine spirit of nurturing.
3. God surveyed the man and the woman—his self-providing and self-propagating creation and declared it "very good."

Discounting the Female's Orgasm as a Luxury Is Harmful

The ability to enjoy an orgasm is so emotion-based that the woman can become pregnant when neither the man nor the woman enjoys the process. But mutual pleasure is paramount for the one-flesh relationship and for accomplishing the work God gave men and women. Modern science supports the Bible's emphasis that good sex is a requirement for women as the guardians of love and the family's emotional health.

The Stages of Sexuality and Personality Growth

Dr. Robinson states that a person's sexuality and personality develop side by side, beginning at birth. If something disrupts either the child's sexuality or personality development, both are damaged. See my chapters "The Connection Between Personality and Sexuality" and "The Bible Teaches 9 Stages of Sexual Growth" for insights into this process. For this chapter, review the following stages of development:

The Girl's Stages of Sexual Growth

In Chapter 10: "The Growth of Love," Dr. Robinson traces a girl's sexual and personality development through the two stages that culminate in a successful marriage:

1. First stage has two 5-year parts
    1) Infantile Period—Ages 1 to 5—Sexuality developing alongside personality
    2) Latency Period—Ages 6 to 10—Sexuality goes underground
2. Second stage has two parts
    1) Puberty Period—ages 10 to 13, 14, or 15—Sexuality is awakened as the body begins to change, and she learns the facts of life.
    2) Adolescence Period—ages 13, 14, or 15 to Maturity—Sexuality goes back underground for the Daydreaming Stage about motherhood.
3. Marriage—The husband awakens the mature woman's desire for vaginal lovemaking.

The Teenage Boy Prepares to Awaken His Future Wife

While the teenage girl is a sleeping beauty daydreaming about all the different aspects of becoming a mother, the adolescent boy is on his own sexual journey preparing for fatherhood. His sexuality is wide awake on the outside of his body, demanding his attention. His dreams are a different kind than the girl has. His nocturnal wet dreams release the buildup of old semen to make way for fresh sperm.

Wet Dreams Highlight the Teen's Orgasmic Abilities

In the cleanliness laws of the Old Testament, God declared these dreams "unclean." This meant that after a wet dream, the young man had to isolate himself and not associate with other people. The law discouraged masturbation and pushed men toward marriage.

Epiphany on Awakening Male-Female Sexuality

1. God gives the husband the job of being a lover who awakens and sustains his wife's sexual pleasure, but it isn't clitoris or G-spot manipulations as taught in most books, blogs, and videos.

2. The woman's vaginal orgasms help her fulfill her role of motherhood as they release the hormones of emotional love that protect the woman, her husband, and her children as they serve God on a hostile planet.

3. The husband cannot fulfill his God-given role as a lover IF...his wife refuses to awaken to ecstasy—to her God-given role as the guardian of love and emotional health in the home.

The Husband's Job Is to "Awaken" His Wife's Sexuality

From the time they are born, God begins preparing the man and the woman for their roles in filling the earth with people. In the Song of Solomon, the Maiden tells the Shepherd that she knows they will enjoy a passionate marriage because they were raised in loving homes:

Song of Solomon 8:1-3:
"Oh that you were like a brother to me
Who nursed at my mother's breasts.
If I found you outdoors, I would kiss you;
No one would despise me, either.
I would lead you and bring you
Into the house of my mother, who used to instruct me;
I would give you spiced wine to drink from the juice of my pomegranates.
Let his left hand be under my head
And his right hand embrace me."

The Shulammite recognizes that when parents provide an example of affection through marital and parental love, their children reap the natural blessings of the parents' sexual love. This foundation begins to form in infancy as the mother nurses, cuddles, plays with, and talks to her children. As the children mature, emotional warmth builds through the free rein of love in the home. As the parents flirt, kiss, and hug each other, their love overflows to envelop their children.

The Daydreaming Stage Is About Preparing for Motherhood

The girl doesn't have wet dreams about sex as the young man does. Instead, Dr. Robinson said she daydreams about being pregnant, nursing a baby, and nurturing her children to adulthood. Although even prudish preteens learn about sex during the previous puberty stage, the young girl's sexual thoughts go underground as she focuses on motherhood.

Dr. Robinson describes how this happens:

> Gradually, puberty merges into adolescence. This is the last stage before maturity. I call this whole period the "daydream stage." It is a period of almost literal *waking* dreams on the part of the young lady. She is still held lightly by the long preparatory sleep of childhood and early youth, but she is ready to *wake*....
>
> The satisfaction of her now nearly mature maternal and sexual impulses through such dreams is clear. But they serve another function, which is perhaps a bit more obscure. She is not quite ready for real love yet. She still has one foot in childhood and one foot in adulthood. She is reluctant to give herself wholly to the realities of adulthood. She needs to hang upon the tree, so to speak, for a few more years, to ripen a bit (85).

Sex won't become important to the developing girl until it is "awakened" in marriage unless she engages in teenage sexual activity. Such early experimenting can damage her sleeping sexuality. Indeed, the *Sexless Marriages Survey* reveals that many sexless wives were sexually active before marriage, only to become sexual deprivers with their husbands. They must frequently expend effort to overcome this harm.

Dr. Robinson explains how the man "awakens" the woman:

> It is essential to know that it is the man who ultimately *awakens* the sleeping beauty sexually. Until she is ready for intercourse and all it implies in a relationship, she is conscious of no particularly urgent vaginal sensations of a sexual nature. The man *awakens* these for the first time in the act of love (85).

The Husband "Awakens the Wife's Sexuality" in Marriage

Dr. Robinson concludes chapter 10 with the beautiful promise of the young girl's sexual "awakening" in the arms of her new husband:

> With her first intercourse, she finds a whole continent of sensations whose existence she had only heard about secondhand. While her clitoral sensations may still be quite pleasurable in the period of foreplay, her whole body now, in excitement, soon learns to yearn for the penetration of her lover's penis, the unspeakable delight of the now vaginally centered sensations he can give her.
>
> She has little or no block to these sensations; there may be a period of adjustment for a few weeks or months until they become totally unfettered from childhood inhibitions and fears, but the months will be short. Now true orgasm is hers at

virtually every sexual encounter with her husband, and in mutual delight, their relationship will prosper and deepen (86).

The Song of Solomon Uses Forms of "Awake" Nine Times

What a thrill it was to realize Dr. Robinson used the same word—"awaken"—that the Bible used 3000 years ago in the Song of Solomon to describe the necessity of "awakening" love before lovemaking.

Each of the nine times that a form of "awake" is used in the story shows an adolescent 13-year-old maiden being awakened emotionally as she prepares to be awakened sexually in marriage. The story reveals that her mother guided her successfully through the infantile, latency, and puberty stages. Now she stands on the edge of full maturity, ready to embrace a lifetime of passionate lovemaking when she marries.

The Song of Solomon takes place over three whirlwind days as King Solomon woos a young country maiden in an effort to add her to his harem of 140 wives. If she marries the King, it will be like winning the lottery as she and her family will go live in the palace.

But she loves the Shepherd and had planned to marry him that spring before Solomon arrived from Jerusalem with his proposals and gifts. As the Maiden listens to the King's sensuous pleas to possess her body, she compares his practiced speech to the Shepherd's humble declarations of love.

In trying to decide whom to marry, she takes us on an amazing journey of awakening her love. Notice the nine times "awake" occurs in the Song of Solomon:

"Awake" in the Song of Solomon

1 & 2: In the theme, the Maiden uses two forms of awake as she pleads with the palace virgins "do not *arouse* or *awaken* my love until it pleases" by forcing her to marry Solomon before they love each other (Song 2:7).

3 & 4: The Shulammite repeats the theme to the palace virgins with the same two forms of awake, "[do] not *arouse* or *awaken* my love" (Song 3:5).

5: The Shulammite prayed "*Awake,* O north wind," as she beseeched God to make her sexual maturity known (Song 4:16a).

6: The Shulammite's "heart was *awake*" when she had a wet dream that was the turning point of her affections (Song 5:2).

7 & 8: The Maiden repeats the theme to the palace virgins with the same two forms of awake, "do not *arouse* or *awaken* my love" (Song 8:4).

9: The Shulammite "*awakened*" the Shepherd's affections for her under the apple tree (Song 8:5).

"Sexual Awakening" Is the Theme of the Song of Solomon

Song of Solomon 2:7:
"I adjure you, O daughters of Jerusalem,
By the gazelles [male] or by the hinds [female] of the field,
That you will not ***arouse*** *or* ***awaken*** *my love,*
Until she [it—NASB footnote] pleases."

The Shulammite tells Solomon's palace virgins not to force her to marry the King before they learn to love each other. She repeats this plea two more times, representing the theme of the Song of Solomon: soulmate before lovemaking. The Maiden describes the same process of awakening love that Dr. Robinson teaches.

In the three occurrences of the theme, "arouse" is used three times and "awaken" is also used three times (Song 2:7, 3:5, 8:4). Both arouse and awaken come from the same root word, which means "(through the idea of opening the eyes), to wake (literally or figuratively" (Strong 86).

"Love" is the same word used for the Shepherd's banner of love over her (Song 2:4). It means "to have affection for (sexually or otherwise)" (Strong 9).

Gary Martin, a Hebrew scholar, explains the Shulammite's play on words by using two similar ones of different intensities. "Arouse" carries the idea of waking from sleep either mentally or physically. "Awaken" also indicates to "stir up," but is probably more intense than the first word. He concludes:

> Both words carry the idea of "arouse" in the sense of inciting to (some kind of) action. Thus, to "arouse" or "stir up" love would mean to incite it to action, to "wake it up" from its sleeping, resting state, and set it into motion (72-73).

The gazelles and the hinds, like most animals, instinctively understand enough about mating and love not to force themselves on each other. They go through a courting period of getting acquainted before they breed. The males perform elaborate rituals to display their beautiful colors. They dance, fight, or snuggle to impress the chosen female. Sex takes place only after the male has sufficiently "aroused" or "awakened" the female's emotions to accept him.

As a country girl, the Shulammite understands the way of animals and the importance of courtship for "waking up" and then "stirring up" a woman's affections. She begs the palace virgins, "By the example of nature, don't force me to marry the king before love has a chance to develop between us." She continues, "I know what it's like to be emotionally intimate with a man for I love the Shepherd. I don't want to settle for a loveless marriage—even if the man is King Solomon."

The Shulammite Asks God to Bless Her "Sexual Awakening"

Song of Solomon 4:16:
*"**Awake**, O north wind,*
And come, wind of the south.
Make [Blow on—NIV,] my garden breathe out fragrance,
Let its spices [balsam odors—NASB footnote] be wafted [streams] abroad.

As she is waking up sexually, the Maiden calls to the north and south winds to "wake up" as well. It's time for action and to let everyone know she has matured and is ready for love. The verb "wafted abroad" is used 16 times in the Old Testament and figuratively refers to something coming from God (Psalms 147:18).

Emotionally alone in Solomon's garden, the Shulammite bares her soul to God after remembering the Shepherd's proposal. He had used a metaphor of her sexual favors as a spiritual garden with a life-giving stream flowing with love for him and their children (Song 4:12-15). All four lines of her prayer invoke God's favor to bless her as she seeks to be a ravishing wife and a loving mother.

She beseeches God to blow on her garden of love to scatter the fragrance of her multi-faceted sexual favors. Now, in the fourth line, she asks God to open up her love in marriage by appealing to the metaphor of the multi-useful balsam bushes that thrive in her sexual garden to bless both her future husband and children. As the God-given hormones released during lovemaking join her stream of love, her soul will overflow with life-giving tenderness for her family.

The Shulammite Plans to Satisfy Her Husband's Needs

Song of Solomon 5:1a:
My sister, my bride, I have entered my garden;
I am gathering my myrrh and my spices [balsam – NASB];
I am eating my honeycomb along with my honey;
I am drinking my wine as well as my milk (CJB).

The Maiden hears in her thoughts the satisfaction the Shepherd will find with her. The Shepherd says, "I have come into my garden." When he proposed, he described her as a locked sexual garden (Song 4:12-15). Now he speaks as if he has already tasted the first fruits from her park-like paradise.

Essentially, the Shepherd says, "I'm getting ready to talk about making love with you when we marry." The Shepherd sends beautiful, erotic, poetic words flowing over the Shulammite. (For an in-depth discussion of this verse, see *God's 11 Secrets of Sex*.)

God Says, "Get Married and Get Drunk on Lovemaking"

Song of Solomon 5:1b:
"Eat, friends;
Drink and imbibe deeply, O lovers
[and drink, until you are drunk with love!—CJB]"

In the second half of the verse, God responds and tells the Shulammite to marry the Shepherd and get drunk on lovemaking. A student observed, "It takes a lot of wine to get drunk."

Now you're figuring out God's message for awakening sexual love in marriage. A wonderful sex life is so important to God that he made sure the Israelite man accepted his duty to awaken his wife's sexuality.

God Commanded a 1-Year Honeymoon for the Israelites

> *Deuteronomy 24:5: "When a man takes a new wife, he shall not go out with the army, nor be charged with any duty; he shall be free at home one year and shall give happiness to his wife whom he has taken."*

"Give happiness" means "to brighten up, make blithe or gleesome, cheer up, make glad, joyful, and merry, cause to rejoice" (Strong 118).

What a beautiful concept of God commanding the groom to awaken his bride's sleeping sexuality by devoting himself to "giving her happiness" for a whole year! Every wife should be so lucky.

Through the Law of Moses, God instructed the bridegroom to "be free at home," to spend the first year of his marriage "giving happiness" to his bride. It takes time and practice to lay a solid foundation for a lifetime of loving and sharing the problems of life in each other's arms.

For this reason, God told the new husband not to leave with the army, or to take on work responsibilities such as a traveling job or extra duties in the camp. God commanded the bridegroom to stay home for a year making love to his bride, being playful, experimental, and joyful. A year of frequent passionate lovemaking strengthens their emotional bond and awakens their physical intimacy.

A Wet Dream "Wakes Up" the Shulammite's Heart

Song of Solomon 5:2:
*"I was asleep but my heart was **awake**.*
A voice! My beloved was knocking:
'Open to me, my sister, my darling,
My dove, my perfect one!
For my head is drenched with dew,
My locks with the damp of the night.'"

All nine times "awake" is used in the story, it refers to a call to action. Earlier, the Shulammite called to God saying, "Awake, O north wind" (Song 4:15). She pleaded for God to wake up and act as he hears her urgent prayer. She is in the midst of a dilemma, trying to decide whom to marry. She asked for God's blessing as she works to present herself as a sexually healthy bride to her husband. Then she beseeched God to help her choose a husband capable of giving and receiving love.

Now she tries to sleep; tomorrow she meets Solomon's 140 queens. But her heart "wakes her up" demanding action on her part. Her wet dream pleads with her to choose soulmating love before she marries the King, and it's too late.

First thing that morning the Maiden sends the palace virgins to find her true beloved—the Shepherd. "Bring him to me quickly," she pleads. "Tell him I am sick with love for him."

When the Shepherd arrives, they begin the long walk home, her ordeal with Solomon is over. And on the journey, she tells the Shepherd why she chose him over the King.

The Shulammite "Awakened" the Shepherd's Love for Her

Song of Solomon 8:5b:
"Beneath the apple tree I ***awakened*** *you.*
There your mother was in labor with you,
There she was in labor and gave you birth."

"Awakened" is the same word used in the theme of the book (Song 2:7, 3:5, 8:4). Now the Shulammite applies the theme to the Shepherd showing how they had been soulmating for some time. Their emotional bond has prepared her to be awakened in his arms when they marry.

She says, "Remember how I awoke your love for me under the apple tree?" She turns to face him as her soft brown eyes caress him. "I came to your house often and you came to mine. We spent lots of time together getting to know each other...and our siblings and parents."

She laughs at the sweet memories. "I remember the first time you called me, 'my sister.' We do get along well, don't we? We can talk about anything. I dearly love that I can tell you my deepest fears and you won't think less of me. And I can share my faults with you, and you give me such wonderful emotional support instead of rebuking me."

She continues, "I love that old apple tree. Your mother gave birth to you there and all the neighbor women and relatives welcomed you into this world with kisses. I paid attention to how your mother and father talk to each other and how they treat each other. I love the way they tease and flirt. I want the same kind of home for us and our children."

The Shulammite claims she's the one who awakened and nurtured the Shepherd's love for her. She said, "No," to sex and, "Yes," to spending time together in each other's homes. Because she was a frequent visitor in the Shepherd's home, she observed firsthand how he grew up in a loving home like her own. Thus, she's confident that they will both bring emotional and sexual love to their marriage.

God Created the Man to Be an Excellent Lover

Proverbs 30:18-19:
There are three things which are too wonderful for me,
Four which I do not understand:
The way of an eagle in the sky,
The way of a serpent on a rock,
The way of a ship in the middle of the sea,
And the way of a man with a maid.

Mankind learned from the eagle how to fly in the sky, from the serpent how to scale the highest mountains, and from ships how to map the shipping lanes. These three wonders are brilliant. But God declares that his fourth invention is the most magnificent of all: "Ecstatic lovemaking is my crowning act of creation!"

God expertly designed the man with everything he needs to awaken his sleeping beauty to all of God's wonders awaiting her as she experiences sexual love.

God Gave the Woman Three Supporting Orgasms

A woman's three orgasms are the man's playground for pleasuring her. Her sexual canal is orgasmic from beginning to end. She's capable of three kinds of orgasms. They all work together, but not in the way described by people who assert the clitoris is the secret of the woman's orgasm. She has three orgasms:

1. Clitoral
2. Vaginal
3. Cervical

I disagree with Dr. Robinson's statement that the clitoral orgasm is "immature." Sure, it's the first orgasm a woman experiences. And yes, she can get stuck and never experience anything more profound. She doesn't even have to love her husband or know a one-night-stand's name to enjoy it. But I'm unwilling to call it immature. It's part of her sexual repertoire.

More importantly, the clitoral orgasm is only one-third of the pleasure God designed for the woman. If a woman stays there, she's stopped short of enjoying the whole package God gives her for love and pleasure. The woman's three orgasms work together for both her and her husband's delight.

Sex is like a three-course meal for the woman. First, the chef serves her a tantalizing soup—the clitoral orgasm. Next, he provides for her enjoyment a sensational entrée—the vaginal orgasm. And when she thinks the meal couldn't get any better, the chef dishes up a scrumptious dessert by going deeper to kiss her cervix with his warm, velvet-tipped penis. That orgasmic dessert is the most delicious of all for them both.

The clitoral woman sits down to eat and gets up after the first course. And maybe both the vaginal woman and the chef stop after the main course, not knowing more is waiting to tease their taste buds. But for the chef and the woman who maintain orgasmic attitudes, not chocolate kisses, but cervical kisses provide the most delicious, satisfying culinary experience.

The Aphrodisiac of Love Opens the Gate to Ecstasy

A couple must heed the Shulammite's theme in the Song of Solomon to experience all three orgasms—soulmate before lovemaking. Love is the greatest aphrodisiac of all that opens up a woman's sexual canal to unbelievable thrills. Love also primes the man's penis for wonderful sensations that evade men who leave love out of sex.

The Husband Explores All Three Orgasms Together

The woman's body opens up as she has a vaginal orgasm, and her husband goes deeper to kiss her cervix with his penis. Or he may withdraw so that he can stroke her clitoris with his penis as he slips back in. His blood-gorged penis is hot to the touch as it brushes against her clitoris. The sensation is delicious as he moves inside her.

He plays her like a fine musical instrument, slipping in and out to their own rhythm. He brings her to the point of a vaginal orgasm and then teases by slowing her down. Then he turns up the volume to their song once again. And when he thinks she's ready, he kisses her cervix with his warm, velvet-tipped penis. And oh, such indescribable joy and pleasure that flood her being.

God's three things that are too wonderful for man can't compare. The eagle soars in the sky with breathtaking views. The snake climbs high rocks to sun in the midst of God's majestic scenery. And the cruise ships travel the shipping lanes to take honeymooners to exotic places.

But the fourth wonder is the most mysterious of all—the way of a man with his maid. Truly, we serve an amazing and loving God to create such an unspeakable private language of love for husbands and wives.

24.

The Wife Needs Passion to Be a Wonderful Mother

Sexless individuals often try to convince themselves and their love-starved mate that sex is not essential for a good or happy marriage. But without love reigning supreme in their homes, they are heaping tremendous harm upon themselves, their spouses, and their children.

The Parents' Love Life Affects Their Daughter's Love Life

Dr. Robinson's case histories show how the different forms of inhibitions develop during the four growth stages of a girl's personality and sexuality. The major contributing factor to sexual inhibitions is her relationship with her father or her mother or both. The father either ignores the little girl or gives her too much attention. The mother is either wimpy or has an angry or complaining relationship with the father. Or the child is trapped between two love-deficient parents.

Passionate lovemaking protects the parents' relationship with each other because it requires them both to grow up emotionally and sexually. Only then can their love for each other spill over to nurture their daughter. This enables them to give the right kind and amount of attention to her. Open affection between the parents provides their child with an example of healthy marital love for her to seek in her own marriage as she imitates her mother and looks for a mate like her father.

Sexual Inhibitions Lead to Maladjustment in All Areas

Dr. Robinson defines "sexual inhibitions" as "an inability to enjoy sexual love to its fullest potentiality. This means, purely and simply, the inability to have an orgasm of the type described in Chapter 2 [vaginal with cervical kisses] in *The Power of Sexual Surrender*. But the matter is more complicated than that, for there are degrees of sexual inhibitions." She states:

> It is these psychological repercussions that make the problem of sexual inhibitions a serious one for the individual

and society. The inhibited woman's often grossly distorted psychological traits are raising havoc with our marital institution in the form of:

1. Unhappiness
2. Divorce
3. Maladjustment in the children

I must emphasize the fact again and again that the reason sexual inhibitions present a problem that must be solved is that it has harmful repercussions on the woman and on those close to her. It causes acute misery to her, causes personality damage to the children, and tends to destroy her marriage (43).

The Bible Defines Sexual Inhibitions as "Without Natural Affection"

When he was in prison, Paul wrote the young evangelist Timothy to come assist him. He encouraged Timothy to defend the faith in dangerous times. He warned that people would lose their natural love for their family, and they would become involved in all kinds of family-destroying sins:

> *2 Timothy 3:2-5: "But mark this: There will be terrible times in the last days. People will be lovers of themselves, lovers of money, boastful, proud, abusive, disobedient to their parents, ungrateful, unholy,* ***without love [unloving]****, unforgiving, slanderous, without self-control, brutal, not lovers of the good, treacherous, rash, conceited, lovers of pleasure rather than lovers of God—having a form of godliness but denying its power. Have nothing to do with such people" (NIV).*

"Unloving," a compound word, is used only two times in the New Testament (2 Timothy 3:3 and Romans 1:31). It comes from the Greek *a* (negative) plus *storge* (pronounced stor-JAY). The negative in these two passages means "without natural love for family" (Thayer 82).

A positive form of *storge*, also a compound word, is used one time:

> *Romans 12:10: "Be* ***devoted [philos plus storge]*** *to one another in brotherly love [philos plus delphos--brother]; give preference to one another in honor."*

The compound word "devoted" comes from *philos* (affectionate love) plus *storge* (love of family). It refers to "the mutual love of parents and children; also of husbands and wives, loving affection, prone to love, loving tenderly; used chiefly of the reciprocal tenderness of parents and children; love of the brethren tenderly affectioned one to another,

Romans 12:10" (Thayer 655).

The devotion we are to manifest toward other Christians should mirror *storge*—the natural love between parents and their children and between husbands and wives. In contrast, the list of 18 sins clustered around the negative of *a* + *storge,* the absence of parental and marital love, in 2 Timothy 3:1-5 reflects the usual 24/7 conduct of unloving spouses.

Do 19 sins common in sexless marriages sound extreme to you? Sadly, my *Sexless Marriages Survey* verifies that these sins against the family abound in sexless marriages. The longer the marriage continues in a sexless state, the more pronounced the 19 love-defying sins become. Sin never stagnates but always grows, often secretively.

Sexless marriages aren't simply about one person's sexual dysfunction. They are about the sex-denying spouse's whole character, soul, and lack of intimacy with the mate. Intimacy anorexia is an addiction of deliberately withholding intellectual, emotional, sexual, and spiritual love from the spouse to create a sexless marriage.

God calls it the sin of being unloving—without natural affection for family. At the end of the verses, Paul told Timothy, "Have nothing to do with such people." God doesn't want us to tolerate the sin of being unloving in our homes or in our congregations.

God's Portrait of a Loving Mother with Her Child

We learn from extremes, and the Bible preserves the extremes of two mothers—one loving and the other full of hate for her husband. In both examples, God is the husband.

In the following description of the loving mother, God begins with her pregnancy and childbirth and continues through nursing, cuddling, and playing with her child. These are natural feminine responses, behaviors, and activities of a loving and loved woman. And God chose her to illustrate his own love for his people.

Isaiah 66:7-13:
"Before she travailed, she brought forth;
Before her pain came, she gave birth to a boy.
Who has heard such a thing? Who has seen such things?
Can a land be born in one day?
Can a nation be brought forth all at once?
As soon as Zion travailed, she also brought forth her sons.
Shall I bring to the point of birth and not give delivery?" says the LORD.
"Or shall I who gives delivery shut the womb?" says your God.
"Be joyful with Jerusalem and rejoice for her, all you who love her;
Be exceedingly glad with her, all you who mourn over her,
That you may nurse and be satisfied with her comforting breasts,

That you may suck and be delighted with her bountiful bosom."
For thus says the LORD, *"Behold, I extend peace to her like a river,*
And the glory of the nations like an overflowing stream;
And you will be nursed, you will be carried on the hip and fondled on the knees.
"As one whom his mother comforts, so I will comfort you;
And you will be comforted in Jerusalem."

God uses the portrait of a mother experiencing an easy delivery and then nursing, carrying her child on her hip, and fondling the child on her knee to illustrate his own love for the Israelites.

Science now knows that sexual activity during pregnancy floods both the mother and her unborn child with hormones of love. Many mothers-to-be who have never enjoyed an orgasm do so during pregnancy due to surging hormonal feelings of love for their unborn child and its father.

Additionally, pregnant sex exercises and strengthens the woman's pelvic floor and muscles, which helped the Israelite woman give birth "before she travailed" (verse 7). Indeed, Jewish women were known for their easy deliveries.

From conception, throughout the pregnancy and the birth process, and then when nursing, both the mother and her baby are bathed in God's special hormones of love and tranquility. God's genius shows in designing passionate lovemaking to ensure women rise to their full potential as loving mothers and to protect their children in the womb and while nursing and growing up. Passionate lovemaking between fathers and mothers may affect mood swings during pregnancy and ease of delivery. It also might even transform those teenage years into joy for everyone. These hormones of love show God's love for women in helping them be the most loving mothers possible. The effect of passionate lovemaking on the whole family is phenomenal.

Dr. Robinson's Description of the Loving Woman Agrees

> Feminine tranquility of spirit is a grace and a beauty of the first order. It is the psychological cornerstone of the happy family. Based on an abiding faith in the goodness and loyalty of her husband, tranquility emanates from a woman who has found herself and peace envelops those about her, giving them unity and strength. The children of such a mother are strong against the disruptive restlessness of these difficult times. The husband of a wife who has achieved such tranquility returns from his work to his home as to an oasis, redoubles his loving efforts to make her ever more secure.

God's Portrait of an Unloving Mother and Her Daughters

Ezekiel 16:44-46: "The LORD said, 'People will use this proverb about you, Jerusalem: "Like mother, like daughter." You really are your mother's daughter. She detested her husband and her children. You are like your sisters, who hated their husbands and their children. You and your sister cities had a Hittite mother and an Amorite father.'"

"Detested" means "detest; by implication to reject:—abhor, loathe, cast away, fail" (Strong).

God refers to his marriage relationship with Jerusalem to condemn the way the Israelites rejected him, a husband who loved and provided for them. King Solomon built altars to the pagan god's of his foreign wives on the high places in the countryside. From this influence, the Israelites began to sacrifice their own children to the detestable idol Moloch. Some commentators wonder if the reason the scriptures don't record more children for Solomon is because his wives offered them to their idols. Thus, the Israelites rejected God as their husband and imitated the sexually ignorant religions of the pagan nations around them as a daughter would follow in the steps of her unloving mother.

Dr. Robinson's case histories mirror God's statement about the daughter following her mother's example of hating her own husband. In this case, all the women in the family are sexually inhibited and unable to love their husband. The unloving mother can't teach her daughter how to love her own husband and children because she hasn't learned how. The sin of narcissistic self-love over the love of family is passed down through the generations until someone says, "Enough! I'm going to treat my family differently than my mother treated us."

Dr. Robinson's Description of the Inhibited Woman Agrees

> To put it plainly, sexual inhibitions are generally a product of cognitive distortions. And, importantly, the inhibited woman's distorted behavior is in direct proportion to the degree of her inhibitions. I have found it to be true that the more sexually inhibited a woman is, the more distorted her behavior becomes, the more detrimental to her own good and the good of her family.

The Song of Solomon Riddle Protects Young Daughters

Song of Solomon 8:8:
"We have a little sister,
And she has no breasts;
What shall we do for our sister

On the day when she is spoken for?
If she is a wall,
We shall build on her a battlement of silver.
But if she is a door,
We shall barricade her with planks of cedar."

I'm convinced the primary way God expects us to learn is from hindsight. He allows us to be tested in various ways. Then he expects us to meditate on our life and figure out what we could have done better, so we can do differently in the future. The past illuminates the present and the future.

The Song of Solomon didn't end with the Shulammite's pledge of undying love for the Shepherd and them living happily ever after as we know they did (Song 8:7). Instead, verse 8 continues with what authors call an epilogue, playwrights call ACT THREE, and inspirational writers call the takeaway. It's the most important part of the story.

Solomon taking the young vineyard keeper to Jerusalem and her coming back with the Shepherd was a news-breaking event in Shunem. For the last four months, the Shulammite, the Shepherd, her family, and the townsfolk have talked about little else. They've drawn some powerful conclusions. Now at her wedding, they are ready to share their hindsight. It's God's grand finale.

The Bible reveals that Israelite brothers were usually extremely protective of their sisters' chastity and honor (Genesis 34; 2 Samuel 13:22-33). The Shulammite's brothers are no different. They use the custom of asking a wedding riddle to show how seriously they take their responsibility to protect their sisters.

Her oldest brother says what's been on everyone's mind, "Hey! Sweet Missy, we're thrilled you're marrying the Shepherd. But you're leaving home, and our baby sister is growing up way too fast. Right now, baby sister doesn't care anything about boys. But one day her hormones will start to develop her breasts, and she'll start thinking about boys."

Her middle brother chimes in, "Yeah, Sis. We want to know, how can we protect our baby sister from making a terrible mistake...like you almost did?"

The Song of Solomon is all about teaching courting couples how to soulmate for marriage and lovemaking so they can enjoy a lifetime of passion. And why is a lifetime of passion important? To create a loving home environment for the next generation to grow and thrive in to pay forward God's blessing of a wonderful love life.

25.

The Sin of Judging Motives to Be "Bad" or "Good"

The bitterness, anger, and distorted thinking that Dr. Marie N. Robinson says is common among sexually inhibited men and women often find expression by judging the loving mate's motives to be "bad." On the opposite end, sex-deprived mates frequently try to emotionally survive by judging the sex-withholding spouse's motives to be "good." God condemns judging other people's motives to be either bad or good. Judging motives encourages sin and makes all marriage problems worse.

Judging Motives to Be Bad or Good Is a Sin Against God

The Apostle Paul forbids us to judge anyone's motives for bad or good. Only God can judge hearts.

> *1 Corinthians 2:11: "For who among men knows the thoughts of a man except the spirit of the man which is in him? Even so the thoughts of God no one knows except the Spirit of God."*

> *1 Corinthians 4:5: "Therefore do not go on passing judgment before the time, but wait until the Lord comes who will both bring to light the things hidden in the darkness and disclose the motives of men's hearts [bad motives]; and then each man's praise will come to him from God [good motives]."*

The only way we know what our companion thinks is if our spouse tells us. And the only way our companion knows what we think is if we tell him or her. If we want to know what someone's motives are, the only way we can know is to ask and for the person to tell us. Judging someone's motives is assuming a characteristic that belongs only to God.

The *Sexless Marriages Survey* Addresses Judging Motives

In the list of 19 sins surrounding being "without natural affection" in 2 Timothy 3:1-5, survey questions address judging motives in the sins of reviler, unholy, irreconcilable, and malicious gossiper. At least one-third of the respondents to the *Sexless Marriages Survey* indicated their sex-withholding spouse judges their motives to be evil:

33% Judges your motives to be evil.
4% Judges the children's motives to be evil.
14% Tells you what you're thinking and then criticizes you for it.
17% Makes wild accusations against you.
15% Accuses you of having a dirty mind when you ask about questionable behavior.

Blaming the mate for everything bad is another way people judge motives that isn't easily recognized. Dr. Robinson frequently describes bitter-based and cognitively distorted blame in her case histories. The survey shows that those who withhold sexual love are prone to invent ways to blame their spouse for their own inhibitions:

83% Blame the spouse for their refusing sex, although their sexual issues existed before the marriage

Judging Motives to Be Bad Increases Problems

Having your spouse blame you and judge your motives to be bad unleashes resentment and anger in the spouse that you cannot appease. In my "How to Fight Fair" MP3 class in *Challenges in Marriage*, I advise students to not even try to answer these extreme accusations. Generally, the more a person introduces reason into the discussion, the more the accuser modifies the charges to justify blaming you. Truth never wins.

Instead, I encourage students to focus on the sin of judging motives by saying something such as, "You don't know that. You are judging my motives, and that's a sin. Only God knows what my true motives are." Repeat over and over as often as necessary without answering the accusations. Until the person you're arguing with begins to fight fair, nothing will ever be solved. You can read the "How to Fight Fair and Face Anger Handouts" at PatsyRaeDawson.com in the Book Shelf.

Judging Motives to Be Good Increases Problems

One of the free eReports for completing the survey, *Which Are You? Codependent Enabler, Narcissistic Abuser, or Passionate Lover,* addresses motive judging and some of the consequences. Notice them in the checklist for you and your companion:

√	The Codependent Enabler	√	The Narcissistic Abuser
	Judges motives to be good to make excuses for the bad		Judges motives to be evil and blames for everything
	Overlooks mistreatment of self		Keeps lists of perceived slights of self

	Gullible		Vindictive
	Emotionally exhausted		Emotionally energized
	Rescues others		Expects others to make happy

When you judge your companion's motives to be good, you essentially make excuses for the bad behavior—a classic practice of codependents. Excuse-making prevents you from holding your companion accountable for his or her harmful actions or words. When a person is not held responsible for mistreating others, they are emboldened to continue the sin, which allows the problem to get worse:

Ecclesiastes 8:11: "Because the sentence against an evil deed is not executed quickly, therefore the hearts of the sons of men among them are given fully to do evil.

Chapter 21: "31 Surprises About Sex from the Sexless Marriages Survey" shows the progression of sin from Type 1: Sexually Naive to Type 2: Fire Flirting and finally to Type 3: Morally Polluted (Jude 22-23). When the sins in sexless marriages aren't dealt with, the relationship will continue to deteriorate. Sin seldom stagnates or gets better on its own. In long-term marriages, the sins of anger and bitterness frequently turn to hatred. And the loving spouse often begins to "fight sin with sin."

Make Judgments Based on the Person's Actions—Fruit

However, God and Jesus want us to make judgments about others to determine how we need to respond to them. We are to make judgments based on how others *act* and *talk*. Jesus warned:

Matthew 7:15-17: "Beware of the false prophets, who come to you in sheep's clothing, but inwardly are ravenous wolves. You will know them by their fruits. Grapes are not gathered from thorn bushes nor figs from thistles, are they? So every good tree bears good fruit, but the bad tree bears bad fruit."

Dr. Douglas Weiss says the same thing as Jesus about making judgments based on a person's actions. He says many times in *Intimacy Anorexia: Healing the Hidden Addiction in Your Marriage* that he can see noticeable improvements in sexless marriages within 90 days. That is, *if* the companion, or both partners, who need to overcome flaws in their thinking and actions are completing the necessary marital homework and want to make changes.

Weiss defines "intimacy addicts" as being addicted to withholding sex and causing emotional and sexual pain. He warns that they "can talk a really good game. They have what I call *verbal reality*. If they say it, it is true; if they say it with emotional vibrato, it is really true. However, they don't feel obligated to follow through." He emphasizes that addicts of all kinds (alcoholics, druggies, hoarders, and intimacy anorexics) "do exactly what they want to do even if it is self-destructive. Nobody can stop the addict" from doing what the addict wants to do.

Consequently, you can't believe anything addicts say. You can only believe their actions—make judgments according to their "fruit" as Jesus tells us. Weiss says to watch for actions that show the companion is working the program and genuinely trying.

On the other hand, if the spouse blames others and avoids responsibility for his or her actions, believe the actions—not the manipulative words of appeasement. The actions demonstrate if your companion is trying to change or is simply negotiating or stalling for as little change as possible. Weiss cautions us to believe the spouse's behavior, not what the spouse says (161-164).

The Survey Indicates Sin Gets Worse

Here are the percentages of checks in the survey under "Irreconcilable—Can't Persuade to Honor Marriage Vows: Arguments over lack of sex":

66% Going on for years
40% Going on for decades
51% Gets better and then goes back to the way it was
60% Sexual neglect slowly gets worse over time
57% Have given up having a loving marriage
26% Hormones slowed down and you no longer fight over sex
71% But you are more emotionally lonely than ever

Instead of Judging Motives, Study Together

Throughout Dr. Robinson's book, I've emphasized the benefits of husbands and wives reading this book and my other books aloud and discussing the points together. In addition to learning God's amazing truths about one-flesh love, this exercise gives an added benefit of letting the couple hear each other's thinking. In other words, they allow each other to reveal their own motives rather than guessing about them.

I frequently hear, "We both realized that neither one of us grew up in a loving home, and neither one of us knew as much about sex as we thought we did. And we're committed to teaching our children what we wish we'd learned from our parents."

Compassionate studying together is the key to opening each other's hearts and bodies to wonderful ecstasy. It's the beginning of *speaking God's beautiful language of love*™ for a lifetime of passion.

26.

The Connection Between Personality and Sexuality

Nearly all sexless marriages involve at least one person who is not living in their genetic personality strengths. Instead, they're functioning in their survival weaknesses from their childhood. This inhibits their ability to love themselves, their mates, and their children.

Why is understanding personality important for overcoming sexless marriages?

The Bible Links Our Personality to Our Sexuality

Briefly, Proverbs 7 preserves a portrait of the personalities of both the sexually inhibited wife and the sexually naive young man who frolics with her. The Woman of Great Price in Proverbs 31:10-31 reveals the personality and character of a woman who knows how to love her husband and enjoy sex for herself. The sexually fulfilled man's personality is showcased in 1 Peter 3:7 and Ephesians 5:23-33.

God's People Make the Best Lovers devotes four chapters to discussing these verses and their relationship to our personality and sexuality.

Our Sexuality Develops Side-by-Side with Our Personality

Dr. Marie N. Robinson explains in *The Power of Sexual Surrender* the relationship between a child's developing personality and sexuality:

> When all goes well in the development of the young girl, both her personality and her sexual passions will flower, she will achieve a beautiful and integrated maturity. But if, as so often happens, thwarting or blighting experiences take place, the development of her personality and her sexuality will be frozen at their sources, and maturity will remain a never-never land whose very existence she will come to doubt (17).

As the above paragraph shows, Dr. Robinson's practice involved women. Research about men that supports her view of thwarted development are as follows: Drs. Douglas Weiss (*Beyond the Bedroom*), Bernie Zilbergeld (*Male Sexuality*), Archibald D. Hart (*The Sexual Man*), Kenneth Adams (*Silently Seduced*), and Patrick Carnes (*Sexual Anorexia*).

Children's developing personality and sexuality support and balance each other. However, growing up with inattentive or narcissistic parents or experiencing bullying or sexual abuse can block their emerging personality and sexuality. As adults, they may lack the capacity to feel even the beginnings of sexual excitement (Robinson 11).

How Freezing the Personality and Sexuality Occurs

Our personality is 60% genetics and 40% nurturing or learned. But as Dr. Robinson explained, toxic nurturing and relationships can overwhelm and hide our genetic personality and loving nature.

Often children and adults in an unloving home suppress their natural personality to walk on eggshells. They may even adopt the personality of the abuser to keep the peace. Frequently, abusers try to change the codependent child or mate into a clone of themselves. This pressure to change intensifies the harm done to a person's genetic personality, which affects their budding sexuality.

Overview of the Brain's Quadrants with Corresponding Personality Squares

The four genetic personality types correspond to the four quadrants of our brain. Although we use all four parts of our brain, we have a dominant way of thinking and doing.

You've heard of left brain versus right brain. Our personality is more complicated than that. In addition to our dominant way of thinking, we also utilize a connecting secondary mode.

We might be all left brain (logical, analytical, and objective) or all right brain (intuitive, thoughtful, and subjective). Or we might blend our left and right brains to be all frontal or all basal thinking.

The Brain's Quadrants Line Up with the Personality Squares

- Frontal left is the *choleric leader*. This analytical extrovert specializes in analysis, logic, priorities, mathematics, negotiation, finances, and debate.
- Frontal right is the *sanguine creative*. This intuitive extrovert succeeds with breakthrough thinking, innovation, humor, expressiveness, and sees the big picture.
- Basal left is the *melancholy perfectionist*. This organizing introvert

excels at detailing and monitoring procedures, routines, schedules, and efficiency.

- Basal right is the *phlegmatic peacekeeper*. This harmonizing introvert soothes with nurturing, spirituality, intuitive wisdom, and one-liners to break the tension.

Not Living in Genetic Personality Is Difficult and Exhausting

Dr. Richard Haier, who pioneered the use of neuroimaging to study intelligence in 1988, says:

> We prefer one mode [of thinking] because our brain is naturally more efficient in that mode. He emphasized: When we aren't thinking or working in our primary mode, we use 100 times more oxygen and energy than we require to function in our genetic personality. Consequently, not living in our authentic personality is difficult and exhausting.

Case History: Unmasking Stuart's Personality Changed His Life

Stuart (not his real name) grew up with both parents abusing alcohol and drugs, as did his wife's parents. He contacted me for help when his wife said she wanted a divorce because of his sexual issues. Additionally, after seeming to enjoy sex, his wife would pull back and reject all future sex except on special occasions. See Chapter 17: "The Nature and Danger of Pullbacks" for information about pullbacks.

Spouses who are denied an active sexual life with a loving mate frequently develop sexual hang-ups of their own. They miss out on the opportunity to grow into a mature, passionate lover. Plus the emotional and physical pain of constant rejection by someone they love damages their personality.

Stuart and I began with an in-depth personality reveal over several weeks. This work takes out a lot of the guesswork, and many issues resolve organically. It accelerates sexual understanding and healing as the reasons for being masked are usually the same experiences that inhibit a person's sexuality. It speeds up progress by highlighting and enhancing the person's genetic-emotional needs and inherent way of addressing problems and stress.

A program at work had tested Stuart as a perfect melancholy and peaceful phlegmatic blend. Unfortunately, most personality programs give results for how you're acting at the time and don't look for ways you're masked.

Stuart had carried his childhood survival mask of avoiding

problems into his work and marriage. He hated confrontations and withdrew emotionally when his wife complained. The more passive he became, the louder she screamed, trying to get a reaction out of him.

We discovered Stuart is a genetic take-charge choleric and happy sanguine blend of left and right frontal-brain thinking. He was totally masked. He walked on eggshells with his wife as a pseudo perfectionist/phlegmatic instead of exercising his choleric's natural leadership qualities. He clamped down on his happy, loving sanguine side because his wife protested that she didn't want to be the bad parent while he was the fun parent.

Too many times, we think of a leader as domineering and enforcing mindless obedience. But a leader doesn't boss others around. A true leader leads and inspires. We combined the assets of Stuart's genetics with the how to fight fair rules in *Challenges in Marriage: What to Do When Sin Inhibits Love.*

Stuart developed his genetic choleric/sanguine personality into a natural loving leadership style. The frequent arguments began to change as his wife responded to her new, authentic husband. His sense of humor returned, and he initiated discussions of problems instead of withdrawing. Plus he was able to foresee potential conflicts and head them off with insightful leadership.

We combined the personality work with studying my marriage books to address Stuart's sexual issues. Once he was no longer draining his emotional energy by functioning as someone he wasn't, he applied the resulting vitality to facing his sexual problems. His logical choleric thinking responded to the wisdom of the scriptures to transform his sexual views and responses.

After several months of working together, Stuart excitedly reported that his wife said, "We've been in a bad place in our relationship for a long time. But I want you to know that I want a good marriage, and I want it with you. I'd like for us to start reading together some of those marriage books you've been studying."

Stuart asked, "Where do you suggest we start?"

I said, "Read *God's 11 Secrets of Sex for a Lifetime of Passion: Embrace the Song of Solomon's Soulmating and Lovemaking Guide* together in bed."

Disclaimer: Everyone has different homes of origin and personality and sexual issues. They may not respond in the same manner Stuart and his wife did. Some problems may resolve quickly, while others may require more time or professional psychological intervention. The Bible does not guarantee that all marriages can be saved.

27.

Why Don't Sexless Spouses Kiss, Hug, and Touch?

The Song of Solomon begins with the Shulammite maiden yearning for a passionate kiss with her shepherd boyfriend. King Solomon had brought her to his tent to court her as an addition to his growing harem of 140 wives. She tells the palace virgins that she longs to escape with the Shepherd:

Song of Solomon 1:2-4
"May he kiss me with the kisses of his mouth!
For your love is better than wine.
Your oils have a pleasing fragrance,
Your name is like purified oil;
Therefore the maidens love you.
Draw me after you and let us run together!
The king has brought me into his chambers."

But instead of leaving, she stays. And the King begins three days of a whirlwind courtship with expensive jewelry and gourmet dining, complete with risqué words to make any maiden swoon (Song 1:9-12). When she continues to resist by telling him she needs time to think, he takes her to Jerusalem to dazzle her with his wealth (Song 3:6-11).

Fortunately, her mother had taught her about the emotional foundation of marriage and sex (Song 2:7; 3:5; 8:1-4). Solomon makes a final sensuous plea saying he wants to fondle her breasts and taste her with deep kisses.

She rejects him stating she can't stand the thought of his lips on hers. Then she has the audacity to tell him lovemaking will flow gently through her lips, caressing the Shepherd's as they fall asleep in each other's arms:

Song of Solomon 7:9b
"It goes down smoothly for my beloved,
Flowing gently through the lips of those who fall asleep."

What a beautiful, romantic true story of emotional kissing the way God designed it to be. But kissing in marriage is not always God's way.

Kissing and Touching Are Dead In Sexless Marriages

I was surprised to discover in my *Sexless Marriages Survey* that most sexless spouses not only don't like sex, but they also don't like kissing or touching. Here are the statistics on how 284 *sex-deprived* men and women answered the question:

Ways your companion withholds demonstrations of love:

51% Gives the silent treatment
50% Doesn't initiate hugs
53% Hugs are stiff—not caressing or back rubbing
18% Doesn't return hugs
68% Doesn't initiate kisses
56% Kisses are stiff-lipped
39% Doesn't return kisses
76% Doesn't initiate touching
46% Doesn't return touching
19% Calls touching groping
81% Doesn't touch your face
80% Doesn't touch your hair
58% Eyes don't sparkle when looks at you
46% Avoids looking at you

Here are some of the answers the 30 *sex-withholding* men and women gave to the follow-up question:

Do you withhold demonstrations of love? Review the above list and explain:

- *Yes, I am not affectionate. I don't feel like touching, kissing, or sex.*
- *Yes, when I feel unsafe, I become an ice cube. Basically, all on the list except I withdraw from everyone, all friends as well as him.*
- *I freeze up when my husband touches me in a hug, kiss, or any sexual way.*
- *Yes, no hugging, no kissing, no touching, no I love you.*
- *I don't initiate hugs, kisses, intimacy.*
- *Yes, I give the silent treatment when I'm angry. I don't initiate hugs, kisses, or touching often because I don't want it to lead to sex…because I NEVER orgasm, so sex feels like a chore.*

Why Do Sexless Spouses Dislike Kissing and Touching?

I didn't know why sexless spouses don't like kissing and touching, so I consulted Dr. Marie N. Robinson's book *The Power of Sexual Surrender*. She saw this problem frequently in the 1950s when she was treating women she labeled "frigid." She referred to kissing and touching as "secondary erotic zones."

She explained that the primary issue is that inhibited individuals lack sensuous feelings in their lips and skin, just as they also don't have intense sensations in their sexual organs. In Chapter 5, "Five Common Types of Sexual Inhibitions," *Dr. Robinsons calls this condition sexual anesthesia or total sexual inhibitions.* For sex-withholding spouses, the secondary areas for expressing love and generating passion along with their genitals are often home to varying degrees of numbness (40-41).

The First 5 Years Are Extremely Important for the Child

Dr. Robinson stated that during the first 5 years, the infantile period, "The whole personality takes shape and develops the characteristics that will distinguish it from that time on" (78).

A person's personality is 60% genetic and 40% nurturing. However, the nurturing can be so defective that it totally covers up the genetics. An abusive marriage can also change the dynamics of one's personality.

As a Certified Advanced Personality Trainer, when working with individuals who are obviously not living in their genetic characteristics, my clients and I try to go back to this early time to gather clues before their personality was damaged. We look at old pictures, and if the parents are still living, we ask them to complete a short survey of the child at different ages. If something traumatic happened to the child, such as the death of a parent or some other major adverse event, this analysis often shows a personality shift.

Additionally, Ashley Montagu, in *Touching: The Human Significance of the Skin,* said:

> The mother's holding and cuddling of the child plays a very effective and important role in the child's subsequent sexual development. A mother who loves her child enfolds it. She draws the child to her in a close embrace and, male or female, this is what as adults they will later want and be able to do with anyone they love. Children who have been inadequately held and fondled will suffer, as adolescents and adults, from an affect-hunger for such attention (207).

The First 10-12 Years Require Parental Tactical Support

Mantagu quoted researcher Lawrence Frank who said that from about 4 or 5 years to about 12 that girls, and especially boys, seek less physical contact with their parents (218).

However, during this time, the child forms an important relationship with both parents, which affects their ability to enjoy a healthy bond with the opposite sex (Robinson 78-79).

Caresses Can't Sensualize Numb Body Parts

Dr. Robinson explained that a husband "manipulating or caressing his wife for X minutes in Y number of erotic zones" won't sensualize numb body parts. The change must take place in the woman's mind:

> Any failure of a woman to respond adequately in the marital bed was always supposed to be due to faulty technique on the husband's part. This is simply not true. Caressing or manipulating the genitalia or secondary erotic zones of certain types of frigid women would only result in exacerbated nerves or in a condition of inwardly screaming protest (15).

Only in romance novels do techniques turn a sexually inhibited person into a passionate lover. That's why Dr. Robinson's instructions revolve around changing the sexless person's mindset and dealing with false childhood notions and myths about the opposite gender.

The Sexless Wives of Titus 2:3-5

After reviewing Dr. Robinson's material, I asked, "Why do I love deep kissing, and why does it turn me on, and sexually inhibited women avoid it, and it turns them off? How do I help my clients get past their aversion to simple little acts of love so they can enjoy the grand finales?"

Older Women Qualified to Teach Aren't Sexless

The words of Titus 2:3-5 that I studied 50 years ago for my first classes came to mind. I realized Dr. Robinson was once again opening up another one of God's amazing scriptures for me. I missed the application to sex-withholding wives until the statistics on withholding kisses, hugs, and touches caught my attention.

> *Titus 2:3-5: "Older women likewise are to be reverent in their behavior, not malicious gossips nor enslaved to much wine, teaching what is good, so that they may encourage [teach to be sober – KJV] the young women to love their husbands, to love their children, to be sensible, pure, workers at home, kind, being subject to their own husbands, so that the word of God will not be dishonored."*

In the following discussion of this verse, notice how some of Dr. Robinson's chapters expand on the Apostle Paul's instructions to Titus:

"Reverent" means "befitting men, places, actions or things sacred to God, reverent" (Thayer 299).

Having men, places, and things figured out for pleasing God means the older women possess the two *orgasmic attitudes* that Dr. Robinson describes as necessary for men and women to avoid the mental log jams that make them sexually inhibited. These two attitudes free the body for wonderful orgasms:

1. A positive attitude toward the opposite sex
2. A positive attitude toward one's own sexuality

Of necessity, they aren't controlled by "cognitive distortions" that frequently spew out of sexually inhibited people as anger and extreme accusations (chapters 6 and 16).

Older Women Teach Young Women to Be Sensible

"Teaching what is good" or "teach to be sober" *(sophronidosi)* means "to restore one to his senses, to moderate, control, curb, discipline, to hold one to his duty, admonish, to exhort earnestly" (Thayer 613).

In other words, the older women help the young women overcome distorted thinking (chapters 5-11). Dr. Robinson says in Chapter 18: "The Nature of Emotional Surrender":

> Some of the new feelings overlap, but mostly they emerge in a given order, each unfolding separately but related to the other as petals to a bud. Let us take them in the usual order of their coming.
>
> 1. The opposite sex [liking men in general]
> 2. Love [loving their husbands emotionally and sexually]
> 3. Parenthood [loving their children emotionally]
> 4. The mate [bonding with one-flesh love]

These are the same healthy attitudes the older women are commanded to teach the young women to develop. Essentially, Dr. Robinson wrote a whole book as a commentary on Titus 2:3-5. Notice the emphasis on these attitudes of love in the older women's teaching:

To Love Their Husbands

"Love" comes from the Greek word *phileo* attached to *anēr,* the word for husband, and means "1. to love, to be friendly to one, to love, i.e., delight in, long for; 2. to kiss" (Thayer 653).

The Septuagint, the Greek translation of the Hebrew Old Testament, uses *phileo* to describe sexual love between an older husband and his older wife (the woman he married in his youth) in Proverbs 5:19:

Proverbs 5:18-20:
"Let your fountain be blessed,
And rejoice in the wife of your youth.
As a loving hind and a graceful doe,
Let her breasts satisfy you at all times;
Be exhilarated always with her love [phileo – Septuagint].
For why should you, my son, be exhilarated with an adulteress
And embrace the bosom of a foreigner?

Thus these qualified older women in Titus display the orgasmic attitudes of the older wife in Proverbs who can out orgasm women in their 20s. That's why they can teach the young women about expressing affectionate, emotional love all day long to their husbands with *phileo* kissing, hugging, and patting. If the older women aren't passionate lovers, they aren't reverent in their behavior and can't teach the young women the nuances of loving their husbands (chapters 1-4).

Although I taught the kissing part of Titus 2:3-5 for over 50 years, I didn't make the sexual connection until the survey demonstrated that kissing one's husband is related to flirting and enjoying lovemaking with him. God designed kissing and sex to go together. If the older women and the young women obey Titus to learn how to intellectually and emotionally love their husbands, they will instinctively transition into bedroom ecstasy (chapters 14-19).

The older women are to give the same kind of teaching to the young women that the Shulammite maiden's mother gave her (Song 8:1-2). The theme of the Song of Solomon is about cultivating emotional love so your body can respond gloriously in the bedroom.

To Love Their Children

"To love their children" comes from the same Greek word *phileo* for loving the husband only this time it's attached to *tiktō* (meaning "to give birth to, bear, produce"). The compound word means "loving one's offspring or children, i.e. maternal:--love their children" (Thayer 655).

God commands the older women to teach the young women to love their children—to kiss, hug, and pat them—to shower them with affection. This speaks directly to the first two reasons Dr. Robinson gives as to why men and women become sexually inhibited in chapters 7-8:

1. Orgasm is subject to various traumas.
2. Orgasm disappears with fear of parenthood.

The various traumas that Dr. Robinson gives examples of come from the child's home of origin as demonstrated in Chapter 11: "Dangers on the Road to Adulthood." Likewise, fear of childbirth and resentment of motherhood often stem from mothers and older women telling horror stories about birthing and ridiculing men and the sexual relationship.

God gives older women the responsibility to teach the young women how to love their husbands. Then they are to show them how to cherish and protect their children from physical and emotional harm. This helps prepare their children to enjoy wonderful love lives.

To Be Sensible

Twice, the older women are urged to teach the young women to be "sensible." As mentioned in the first use of "teaching to be sensible," this speaks directly to Dr. Robinson's Section 2: "The Psychology of Sexual Inhibitions" (chapters 5-11). These chapters address the distorted thinking, anger, and extreme accusations against the mate that are common among sex-withholding wives and husbands.

The Sexless Husbands of Titus 2

Dr. Robinson didn't write about the sexual hang-ups of husbands because, back then, no one thought men had problems. Now we know differently. Nearly 50% of the people googling and complaining about a dead bedroom are wives. Additionally, the survey shows that both sexless husbands and wives withhold kisses, hugs, and touches. In fact, men and women mistreat their mates in similar ways.

Obedient Older Men Aren't Sexless

Paul began Titus 2 with a command for older husbands:

> *Titus 2:1-2: "But as for you, speak the things which are fitting for sound doctrine. Older men are to be temperate, dignified, sensible, sound in faith, in love, in perseverance."*

Just as older women are to be reverent in demeanor and teach what is sensible, older husbands are to also be sensible. This implies that the older men have figured out life, just as the older women have. They don't engage in cognitively distorted thinking or spew out anger and extreme accusations. They don't blame their wives for their own emotional and sexual inhibitions.

These older husbands know how to love their wives as they are sound in faith, love, and perseverance. "Love" is the Greek word *agape,* which describes the sacrificial love a husband is to show for his wife as he models Christ in his marriage (Ephesians 5:25-31).

Obedient Young Men Aren't Sexless

Titus 2:6: "Likewise urge the young men to be sensible…."

"Urge" means to beg and plead with the young men to be sensible. If they are sensible, they don't engage in cognitive distortions or the anger and blame that goes with that faulting way of thinking.

"Sensible" has now been used four times in Titus 2:1-6:

Verse 2: *Older men* are to be "sensible."
Verse 4: *Older women* are to "teach to be sensible."
Verse 5: *Young women* are to learn to be "sensible."
Verse 6: *Young men* are exhorted to be "sensible."

No one gets to indulge in distorted thinking, anger, or blame. God holds older husbands and wives responsible for setting the example of "sensible" thinking and acting. Young wives are responsible for learning the fundamental characteristics of loving their husbands and children while being sensible. Young husbands are accountable for obeying the plea to be sensible by exercising mental self-control in their relationships.

The Formula for Growing Up into Love

Dr. Robinson used three steps to help men and women overcome their aversion to kissing, touching, and lovemaking:

1. Learn about the opposite sex so you can replace faulty childhood assumptions and myths with the mate's true nature and real goals.
2. Spend time alone each day to search one's inner thoughts and to release the negative ones.
3. Embrace vaginal orgasms with cervical kisses realizing that some pullbacks will likely occur on the journey to love (168-169).

The steps that worked for Dr. Robinson's patients mirror the Bible's 3-part formula in 1 Timothy 4:1-10 for solving all marriage problems and enhancing love:

1. Learn God's word regarding men, women, marriage, and sex.
2. Go to God in frequent interview-type prayer to implement his word and throw out the distorted emotional log jams.
3. Do all with thankfulness for God's genius in creating male and female to free your body for *speaking God's beautiful language of love*™.

Case Histories of Applying the Formula

In *God's 11 Secrets of Sex,* I started "Secret 10: Face Your Past to Get

Fired Up About Sexual Love" with the case histories of two of my first students. The examples start this way:

Someone always asks during class about how to overcome a sexual past. The obvious question is, "I've done things I'm not proud of. How do I overcome a sexual past so I can have a great marriage now?"

The not so intuitive question is, "I was raised in the Virginity Culture (or I come from a hell, fire, and brimstone environment). How do I overcome my shame and fear of sex?"

In the first classes I taught on the Song of Solomon, two young women asked each version of this question, one married with a promiscuous past and the other single and scared witless of married sex.

The Promiscuous Wife

The young wife, I'll call her Judy, had been married three years. She stayed after class to talk about her problems and said, "When I went to college, this boy told me, 'If you love me, you'll prove it.' I loved him, so I proved it. Then he dropped me. I was so upset, I slept with any boy who came along. I went from bad to worse until I married my husband."

Every time her husband made love to her, all she could do was lay there and cry from the pain. She knew nothing was wrong physically, that the pain came from guilty feelings over her past. She said, "After I was baptized, I knew my sins were forgiven and washed away. Our sex life is better. I enjoy the sexual relationship more, but I still have pain. It isn't what it should be."

Judy came to the classes regularly and listened. She often said, "That makes sense. I agree with that." But when she went home, she wouldn't study her Bible or look at the class handouts. She refused to do the homework. She made no effort to help herself except to come to class. She wanted her marriage to become wonderful without any action on her part other than just talking about it. It never happened.

The Perpetual Virgin

The single girl, I'll call her April, attended the same classes. One night she stayed after class. She said, "This class has torn me up and upset me."

I asked, "Why would the Song of Solomon upset you?"

"This boy wants to marry me. I love him, and I want to marry him, but I'm scared of sex. My father raped my older sister, and he tried to rape me. I made up my mind he'd have to kill me first. My mother was extremely Victorian and harped about the evils of sex. Our father tried to make us loving by raping us."

She began to cry softly, "I was caught in the middle. Sex just looks like a horrible, nasty relationship—men are just beasts who think about nothing but sex. I told this boy about my feelings and why I feel like I do. He is understanding and says he won't push me. He's willing to wait up to three weeks after we get married to have sex."

I said, "My husband is going to be out of town for a week. Why don't you come over some evening for supper? We can talk all night long if we want to."

April came over. She had already been through the classes on Victorian morals and turned in the homework. But she had not been able to change her attitudes about men and marital sex. As we talked, she shared specific things her mother and father said and how they distorted her views of men, marriage, and sex. Then we examined the scriptures that applied to each one. That night April cleaned her mental house and deliberately threw out many false impressions from her upbringing. She only needed someone to help her apply the scriptures to her situation.

Soon afterward, April married the young man, and we invited the new couple over. She gushed, "Marriage is so great! And I'm married to the most wonderful man there ever was!"

My husband teased her, "That offends me. My wife says I'm the most wonderful man there ever was, and you think your husband is that man. We can't both be that man."

April averted the potential for a tragic sexless marriage by doing the homework and then asking for help to apply the principles to her traumatic upbringing. She put in the mental effort to free her mind from all the inhibiting beliefs she accumulated while growing up and dealing with two unloving parents.

As a result, she became a happily married wife who thoroughly enjoyed lovemaking. She also delighted in fulfilling her husband's deepest needs for sharing emotional and sexual love.

God's Love-Enhancing Formula Works

Yes, sexless husbands and wives don't like kissing, hugging, and touching due to their distorted thinking about the opposite sex and their own sexuality. But God's love-enhancing formula works. He teaches more about enjoying a loving sexual relationship than any other area of marriage. He designed ecstatic lovemaking as the foundation of all of marriage. He expects husbands and wives to face their parents' neglect and their own childhood ignorance and to learn and do better.

If older men and women, along with young wives and husbands, obeyed Titus 2:2-6, we wouldn't need Dr. Robinson's book. And we would live in a kinder and more loving world because of our influence on our children and neighbors.

28.

Pullbacks and Terrified, Angry, Truth-Telling Child-Adults

I worked with a husband and wife for 16 weeks. They made tremendous progress with a couple of major pullbacks along the way. Now the wife suffered a pullback that eclipsed all the others. It started a couple of weeks earlier after the best sex ever for both of them, followed a couple of days later with great sex. Dr. Robinson explains that this often triggers a pullback as the subconscious tries to hang onto the safe alternate reality it created.

After building for nearly two weeks, the pullback erupted into a full-blown temper tantrum using some "bad words," breaking a cup and saying things she wished she hadn't. These actions were out of character for my client.

On our Zoom call, I could see and feel the pain that clouded both the wife's and the husband's faces. The husband said his wife's extreme accusations made him feel like he had to answer every one of them.

I said, "You never answer extreme accusations. It's not about you, so you can never satisfy the person hurling putdowns at you."

"But it feels like it's about me."

"I know. But it's not about you—it's about her parents and their failures—not yours. And when you can accept that, then you can back away emotionally and begin to get some clarity."

Then it hit me. I addressed the wife, "And it's not about you either. It's about your parents and the way they treated you when you were growing up." Her face relaxed.

The Terror and the Anger Began to Make Sense

I learned in the 1970s from Maxwell Maltz's book *Psycho-Cybernetics,* one of the greatest, top-selling self-help books of all time, that when we give our brain a problem and do something automatic, such as driving, washing dishes, or raking leaves, it begins to clean our mental house. It files away our activities, trying one category and then another in our mental filing cabinet of past events. Searching to find the right topic to file our thoughts in is one reason we often wake up with insights—two opposing ideas that connect brilliantly—that our conscious brain might never recognize.

The next morning after our call, I woke up understanding better why my client's meltdown was not about her. About 9 years ago when I started my journey to heal childhood abuses, I didn't have temper tantrums, because I was dealing with a different kind of emotional flashback—terror.

I would wake up biting my bottom lip to stifle crying. I could feel the fear swelling in my chest, "Please don't let Mother hear me!" Her coming would be worse than the emotional pain I felt as she would pinch and twist my 6-year-old shoulder as she leaned down inches from my face.

I could still see and feel her hot putrid breath as she hissed through gritted teeth, "I wish you were never born!" My mother's caustic bitterness came from birthing too many children and not enough maternal love.

My client also grew up with a mother who was burdened with too many babies. But still, love was there, just not enough to spread around as needed. A dysfunctional marriage added to the lack of attention to the young children.

My client's emotional reaction to her upbringing was not terror as I experienced, but anger at being neglected. Her anger mirrored Dr. Robinson's case histories. In the recounts of emotional neglect, her patients responded as adults with distorted anger. They bristled at the slightest irritation coming from their husbands and children. It's cognitive distortion because their rage is directed toward the wrong people—the husbands and children instead of the parents.

Who Are Truth-Telling Children?

I recognized my client and myself in Dr. Ramani Durvasula's discussion of truth-telling children in her YouTube video, "What Do Narcissists Do to Truth Tellers?" A licensed clinical psychologist, "Dr. Ramani" said:

> The truth-telling child at an early age has grasped the reality that significant players in their lives, people who are supposed to keep them safe and love them unconditionally, didn't. And that recognition is painful whether or not you're a truth-teller child. Yes, there's freedom and wisdom in being the truth-teller. But there is also a permanent sort of a sense of grief that can pervade the person who is the truth-teller—recognition that you don't really have a safe space, feeling like you don't

really have a family. And that kind of loneliness and isolation can, very devastatingly, potentially impact adult relationships.

I recommend you listen to Dr. Ramani's 15-minute video and see if it increases your understanding of yourself and perhaps your spouse.

Silencing the Truth-Telling Child

Dr. Ramani explains how truth-telling children often learn to silence themselves:

> The truth-teller will usually have their truth-telling silenced before long. The truth-teller will come to understand as a child that calling out a narcissistic parent or sibling or another family member is potentially a disaster. So over time, they may keep their truth to themselves. In fact, by dent of them being a truth-teller, they also run the risk of becoming the scapegoat really fast. With age and time, the truth-teller will also become the sort of proverbial black sheep, often the one who sees the family dynamic with clarity. They know something is not right, will witness the triangulation, enabling, the gaslighting, the codependency, the trauma bonding. And even without any of that vocabulary, the truth-telling child knows all of it is wrong. The truth-telling child is the one who is biding their time waiting for the chance to get out of this dysfunctional system.

Back to my story of crying in terror, I learned early that it wasn't safe to challenge the way my mother treated my brothers and me. Still, I spoke up, "I wish we had a different mother." Every time I voiced my truth, I was slapped, ridiculed, shamed, or sent to stand with my nose in the corner. Until I married, I continued to climb out of the emotional hole my mother pushed me down into as retaliation, to call out her bitter rejection.

After I married, my mother confessed that she had been angry for four years after the birth of my fourth brother, saying, "I had just gotten you older kids big enough to take care of yourselves, and then I was saddled with another baby. I didn't get over it until your brother got big enough to hug my leg and say, 'I love you, Mama.'"

Now I wonder if her confession was her way of apologizing. I remember thinking, "I know, Mom. I was your target during my three years of high school." I married and missed her fourth year of anger. Although I then understood some of why my mother treated me the way she did, my child's terror and pain still hid in my subconscious, waiting to be relived and released.

As my client described her unusual response of using "bad"

language and breaking a cup, I realized she was detailing a child's temper tantrum. She was bringing to life the emotions of her childhood in much the same way I sobbed in the early morning hours. Only her parents weren't there for her to rage against them. Even if they had been, her child-adult's emotions that suppressed her child's truth would probably have prevented the outburst. But her husband was there. And she heaped all her child-adult fury onto him with extreme accusations that were beyond answerable because they weren't about him.

What Can the Truth-Telling Child Do to Move on?

In thinking about previous clients, I recognize that many of them were truth-telling children. I don't know how universal that observation is. But it makes me wonder if many of Dr. Robinson's patients were also truth-telling children. I wonder if that's why they were receptive to getting help. Were they truth-tellers not only with their parents but also with themselves?

Truth-Teller Tips for Finding Peace and Freedom to Love

Here are some suggestions to help child-adults find peace and free themselves to love in the fullness of God's image and design:

1. *Journal the upsetting events.* When I woke up crying, the trick was realizing I was releasing emotions that I had buried over 60 years earlier. I would immediately journal them, so they didn't need to keep cycling over and over. Journaling is also one of the activities my client found helpful in previous smaller pullbacks.
2. *Talk to your parent in an empty chair.* Both my client and I sat two chairs facing each other. Then we discussed with our imaginary parents the things we needed to say.
3. *Talk to your young self in an empty chair.* It's also effective to comfort your young self. Move the second chair beside you and put your arm across the back around your young shoulders. Listen as your child tells you how the hurts affected him or her. Tell your child that you're older now and understand life better. Give your child the support and love you needed growing up. Dr. Karyl McBride suggests getting a doll that looks somewhat like you and giving the doll the love and attention you missed.
4. *Check the flashback time.* Editing this chapter, I realized that the flashbacks occurred at about the same time of day that they happened in real life for both my client and me. For example, I woke up in the early hours of the morning terrorized and biting my lower lip to suppress crying out loud—the same time, I would have been trying

hard not to wake my mother with my emotional distress. Knowing I was reliving childhood events kept me focused on the incidents that caused the flashbacks.

The neglect my client experienced occurred during the daytime with her mother and when her father was home. Although this is just two people's experience, I suspect that the time pullbacks occur for others may also be roughly about the same time of day or night that the original events happened.

Truth-Tellers Need to Release Their Suppressed Emotions

Sexually inhibited men and women need to release their stored-up negative feelings. They need to acknowledge that *they are reliving the emotions of their childhood just as they felt them*. Anger is often a healthy response. And in my client's case, it was probably a good reaction for her as a child.

When she learned her mother was pregnant with her last sibling, she confronted her dad. "Mom doesn't need to have any more children. She can't take care of the ones she already has."

Her dad laughed at his 7-year-old choleric take-charge daughter, who was already assuming lots of the responsibilities for her younger siblings.

The neglect she suffered didn't turn her into a narcissist, as happens to so many not-loved-enough children. Her truth-telling qualities protected her sense of self. Like Dr. Robinson's patients, she asked for help, spoke her truth, and made adjustments to grow her love for her husband and children.

Truth-Tellers Need to Release Their Silenced Voices

Dr. Ramani explains what happens to the truth-teller:

> It's painful to watch how the truth-teller learns to slowly silence themselves. When I say they get it, what the truth-teller really sees is, "This isn't okay. It's not okay to gaslight. It's not okay to invalidate. It's not okay to treat my siblings this way. It's not okay to treat me or my other parent, or other people, or the guy at the gas station this way. It's not okay."
>
> You see that kid wide-eyed, taking it all in. Truth-tellers can often go on to do some great things. Truth-tellers can do quite well going into healing professions for example. They become good therapists because they are willing to call things out. They tend not to be enablers so much when they grow up because they are willing to call things out.

Understanding what is going on allows truth-tellers to let their frustrations out as *righteous anger* directed toward the *right people,* the parents, rather than making false accusations against the mate. Some counselors promote punching bags or even beating on pillows. Journaling and talking to the empty chair involves mental and emotional processes more directly that offers relief.

My Prayer for Truth-Telling Child-Adults

In Ephesians 5, the Apostle Paul tells us to be submissive to each other, husbands to love their wives sacrificially, and wives to love their husbands with admiration. But he introduced those instructions regarding marriage in chapter 4 by commanding us to put away (1) bitterness, (2) wrath, (3) anger, (4) clamor, (5) slander, and (6) malice:

> *Ephesians 4:32: "Let all bitterness and wrath and anger and clamor and slander be put away from you, along with all malice. Be kind to one another, tender-hearted, forgiving each other, just as God in Christ also has forgiven you."*

These six attributes of anger are part of the 19 sins surrounding being "without natural affection" in 2 Timothy 3:1-5. They are also part of the cognitive distortions that Dr. Robinson says are common in men and women with sexual inhibitions.

Paul says to replace the negatives with the positive features of love that include (1) kindness and being (2) tenderhearted and (3) forgiving.

"Tender-hearted" is a compound word that adds "well" or "good" to "compassion" or "sympathy" that is felt in our bowels (the seat of affection) to "position one well" toward "tender affection" (Thayer 262).

"Forgiving" means "to do something pleasant...bestow a favor unconditionally" and is used of both divine and human forgiveness in this passage—forgiving others as God has forgiven us. As you can see, forgiveness isn't based on someone deserving it—it's "unconditional" and an expression of kindness coming from a tender heart (Thayer 665).

When we can practice kindness and forgiveness that we feel in our bowels, we begin to transition from being a child-adult to an adult-child who is becoming healed and wiser about the ways of the world. Best of all, we can grasp how important it is to love our mate and our children unconditionally according to God's image of love living in us.

My prayer for all truth-telling child-adults and myself is that once our eyes open to where the anger or terror comes from, we can find a healthy way to release it. Then we can open our hearts to kindness, compassion, and forgiveness for our parents and ourselves.

29.

Marital Duty Requires Orgasmic Attitudes

God designed husbands and wives to become excellent lovers. Beginning with chapter 1, I've referenced several times God bragging about inventing the "way of a man with a maid" as the fourth and best wonder of all of his creations:

Proverbs 30:18-19:
There are three things which are too wonderful for me,
Four which I do not understand:
The way of an eagle in the sky,
The way of a serpent on a rock,
The way of a ship in the middle of the sea,
And the way of a man with a maid.

Mankind learned from the eagle how to fly in the sky, from the serpent how to scale the highest mountains, and from ships how to map the shipping lanes. These three wonders are brilliant. But God declares that his fourth invention is the most magnificent of all: "Ecstatic lovemaking is my crowning act of creation!"

The Duty to Provide Each Other with Orgasms

After seeing God's fourth wonder of the "way of a man with a maid," talking about one's "sexual duty" in 1 Corinthians 7:3-5 seems like a letdown because of the way men and women abuse the passage.

> *1 Corinthians 7:3-5: "The husband must fulfill his duty to his wife, and likewise also the wife to her husband. The wife does not have authority over her own body, but the husband does; and likewise also the husband does not have authority over his own body, but the wife does. Stop depriving one another, except by agreement for a time, so that you may devote yourselves to prayer, and come together again so that Satan will not tempt you because of your lack of self-control."*

"Authority over" means "to have power or authority, use power; to be master of any one, exercise authority over one, to be brought under the power of any one" (Thayer 225).

"Exercise Authority" Doesn't Mean What Many Assume

Often husbands and wives selfishly use this passage on each other by saying, "Your body belongs to me, and I have the right to say what happens sexually. I have authority to use your body for my pleasure." This attitude conveys the opposite of what the verse says.

This verse contains two ellipses—two "not-but" constructions with a common verb. An ellipsis, a common Greek word combination, shows a relationship between two things that are both true, but it places the emphasis on the second over the first. In other words, the wife has authority over her own body, but the husband exercises greater authority over her body than she does.

The Husband Exercises Authority Over His Wife

Yet the husband's authority isn't to tell his wife what to do with her body. Instead, the husband exercises his power *by giving his wife's body orgasms* in keeping with the context of the passage "because of your lack of self-control."

The wife possesses some authority or ability to satisfy her own sexual desires through masturbation. However, this passage emphasizes the husband's ability to satisfy his wife compared to her own ability. As we saw in Proverbs 30:18-19, the husband exerts the ability to give her earth-shaking vaginal orgasms with cervical kisses. He has the power to be the fourth and most exhilarating wonder in all of God's creation.

Once a woman starts enjoying vaginal orgasms, masturbation seems empty. It takes a husband to satisfy a wife's deepest feminine needs.

The Wife Exercises Authority Over Her Husband

The woman wields the same power over her husband as he does over her. The husband, likewise, exercises limited ability to relieve his sexual urges compared to his wife's ability. The *Redbook* survey of 40,000 men found that the most happily married men didn't enjoy masturbation nearly as much as making love with their wives (Tavris 197).

Why would a man who has kissed his wife's cervix ever think masturbating with computer graphics was satisfying? Consequently, a husband doesn't possess the necessary body parts to *satisfy himself fully*—only his wife can give him the best sexual thrills.

Although both the husband and the wife depend on the other for true sexual pleasure, both also find their greatest delight in experiencing the other's ecstasy. The wife delights in seeing her husband's response to her charms. The husband finds great pleasure in his ability to give supreme delight to his wife. Many of the men in the *Redbook* survey said the best lovemaking occurred for them when their wives obviously experienced their best times (Tavris 195).

God's People Make the Best Lovers devotes a chapter to a verse-by-verse study of 1 Corinthians 7:1-5, God's amazing law of compatibility.

The Creation Calls for Orgasmic Attitudes

Four times the New Testament quotes the creation account to teach us something about one-flesh love and orgasm. Ephesians highlights the orgasmic attitudes that ecstasy requires:

> *Ephesians 5:28-33: "So husbands ought also to love their own wives as their own bodies. He who loves his own wife loves himself; for no one ever hated his own flesh, but nourishes and cherishes it, just as Christ also does the church, because we are members of His body. FOR THIS REASON A MAN SHALL LEAVE HIS FATHER AND MOTHER AND SHALL BE JOINED TO HIS WIFE, AND THE TWO SHALL BECOME ONE FLESH. This mystery is great; but I am speaking with reference to Christ and the church. Nevertheless, each individual among you also is to love his own wife even as himself, and the wife must see to it that she respects her husband."*

Just as Christ focuses on supplying the church's needs, so the husband "ought" or "owes a debt" of nourishing and cherishing his wife—surrounding her with self-sacrificing *agape* love that does what is best for her. Just as the church loves and admires Jesus, her husband, the wife is to see to it that she admires her husband exceedingly.

The Apostle Paul appeals to God's creation and his declaration of one-flesh love as the reasoning behind the debt of love the husband and the wife owe each other. Then he commands the husband and wife to fill their hearts with the orgasmic attitudes that will release their bodies to share powerful vaginal orgasms that climax with cervical kisses.

The Husband Surrounds His Wife with Sacrificial Love

The husband surrounds his wife with unselfish love day in and day out, no matter what the hostile earth throws his way. As he fulfills her need for love and protection, he frees her to rise to her full potential as a feminine woman, a wife, and a mother.

And when he's giving his wife orgasms and kissing her deeply, he's also loving himself and easing the stresses of life on both himself and her. Not only is he receiving in his own body unimaginable pleasures, but he's also bonding emotionally with the love of his life. His magnified adoration for her spills over onto their children.

The Wife Showers Her Husband with Admiring Love

The wife heaps heartfelt admiration upon her husband who sacrifices all for her and gives her such soul-touching pleasure. She admires his masculinity and his strength as she enjoys safety in his love and protection. As she obeys God with her reverence, she supplies the emotional support her husband needs to rise to his full potential as a man, a husband, and a father.

She pays him the highest compliment possible when she surrenders sexually and welcomes him into her inner chamber to share indescribable pleasures. She validates her femininity and his masculinity. She thrills to one of the chief purposes behind God's design of the man and his organ of love—to flood her with peace and love for God, him, and their children.

Together They Celebrate One-Flesh Love

In each other's arms, husband and wife come together as intellectual, emotional, sexual, and spiritual lovers whose union defies words. So it is that God put in place sexual laws for the husband to awaken and sustain his wife's powerful orgasms of love. Those same laws require the woman to allow herself to awaken to God's fourth and most amazing wonder of the creation. Although God designed sexual love for pleasure, the woman's orgasm is necessary for her to fulfill her destiny of motherhood to the degree of expertise that God instilled within her—the embodiment of his own love for his people.

God's hormones of sex fill husbands and wives with peace and increasing love for each other and their children. Not only do they grow into emotionally healthy, mature lovers and parents, but they also spread mental health to their families. When men and women reject orgasmic attitudes, Dr. Robinson says they replace them with harmful cognitive distortions for themselves, their mates, and their children.

Case History: Orgasmic Attitudes Changed a Whole Family

In *God's 11 Secrets of Sex*, I share an overview of the escalating effect of emotional love through frequent lovemaking in Charla Muller's book *365 Nights, A Memoir of Intimacy*. She writes with humor and transparency as she talks about wanting to give her husband Brad something extra special for his fortieth birthday. Like many couples, they argued from time to time about her lack of interest in lovemaking. Brad tried to adjust by telling himself, "Quality is more important than quantity." They both knew that was a lie.

She explains, "The year our daughter was born, I think my husband could count on his fingers and toes (or perhaps just his fingers) the number of times we even had sex at all.... It was good when we had it; we just didn't have it all that much."

So for his fortieth birthday Charla offered him a "knock-your-socks-off, the-stuff-that-dreams-are-made-of-fantastic" gift that no one else could give him. The idea of "The Gift" of intimacy for 365 nights was born—no strings attached.

Because of their "fairly abysmal" sex life, Brad was reluctant to accept her birthday present. He didn't want to be set up for disappointment. When she assured him she would keep her pledge, The Gift began (8-14).

After a month, she wrote, "I don't know if anyone noticed a change in me.... But *I* noticed something. Brad and I flowed better as a couple. We were happier (yes, I was happier having sex every day, but it was only July). Our house ran better because we were both more agreeable, more helpful, more solicitous to each other" (33).

Seven months into her gift, she titled three sections "Our Gift Was Making Me Healthier," "Sex Was Making Me Happier," and "Our Intimate Moments Were Making Me Feel Younger" (142-6). But soon Charla did a major backslide in attitude. She struggled for months to gift herself emotionally while she continued to give her body to Brad. Overcoming her lack of enthusiasm, when their year was up she declared, "There is no denying that this might be the best year of our marriage...yet" (256).

I was fortunate to watch Oprah interview Charla and Brad soon after the book came out. Oprah asked about the effect on their children. Charla said that once she and Brad started having sex every day, the whole family became more loving and touching. The children responded to living with happier, more affectionate parents by being more loving to each other and their parents. The children developed the sibling intimacy we explored previously when the Shepherd calls the Shulammite "my sister."

Charla Muller's book is a good read for both husbands and wives who are dealing with a sexless marriage. Her candid approach will help open your eyes to faulty excuses and produce some weighty topics for honest conversation and self-examination. Hopefully reading *365 Nights* alongside the study of *The Power of Sexual Surrender for Christians* will assist in bringing more love into your home.

Yes! Charla and Brad's story demonstrates that love can change the whole family. What an amazing God we serve. He not only loves us, but he also teaches us how to love others, especially our mates and children.

To God be the glory forever and ever. Amen.

30.

Resources for Speaking God's Beautiful Language of Love

The Sexless Marriages Survey—With Self-Assessment Checklists: The intensely personal, simple questions in these checklists help you analyze the core issues in your relationship so you can begin to solve the real, hidden problems. Free at PatsyRaeDawson.com.

The Power of Sexual Surrender for Christians—Awaken Orgasmic Attitudes to Overcome Inhibited Sexual Desire and Pleasure: In this book, learn the formula for changing your mindset to release your body for sexual ecstasy by overcoming childhood trauma, survival techniques, and inhibitions.

God's 11 Secrets of Sex for a Lifetime of Passion—Embrace the Song of Solomon's Soulmating and Lovemaking Guide: This book's verse-by-verse study serves as the foundation of marriage as it portrays the 4-parts of one-flesh love—intellectual, emotional, sexual, and spiritual intimacy.

Male and Female: God's Genius—Soulmate to Fall in Love All Over Again: This book emphasizes how men and women soulmate. Beginning with the creation, it promotes love and admiration for the opposite sex and oneself.

God's People Make the Best Lovers—Thrill to God's Way of a Man with a Maid: This book studies the mechanics of love necessary for enjoying vaginal orgasms and cervical kisses. It exposes the Victorian and feminist mindsets that still harm couples today.

Everyone in a Sexless Marriage Is an Adult Child—Learn Why God Doesn't Tell Children to Love Their Parents but Tells Them to Leave Their Parents: This eReport reveals the three responsibilities God gives parents and the three he gives adult children. It is free when you participate in the *Sexless Marriages Survey.*

Challenges in Marriage—What to Do When Sin Inhibits Love: These free YouTube classes teach how to fight fair, how sin progresses, and how to deal with sin in the home, including the family of origin.

The Song of Solomon—God's Sex Education for Ages 11 to 99: These free YouTube classes provide a quick and easy way to grasp the Song of Solomon and start your journey of learning how to love. They are excellent for family time.

31.

The 5 Love Languages Versus The Sexless Marriages Survey

I conducted a survey to help answer 3 questions about sexless marriages vs. the 5 love languages that Dr. Gary Chapman promotes:

1. Are "acts of service" a love language or a symptom of inhibitions?
2. Or can "acts of service" be either one depending on the person's general ability to give love?
3. Are "words of affirmation" one-sided in unloving marriages?

I asked specifically about 3 of Dr. Chapman's love languages that are commanded of both husbands and wives in the Bible. They are also expressions of the 4 parts of one flesh love, with the scriptures adding a fourth love language that Dr. Chapman omits.

1. Acts of Service—Intellectual Love
2. Words of Affirmation—Emotional Love
3. Touch—Sexual Love

The Bible's addition:

4. Thankfulness—Spiritual Love

The remaining 2 love languages, "gifts" and "quality time," are often byproducts of the first 3 love languages. Although a small number of people participated (17), the results between the couples in loving marriages vs. the ones in sexless marriages were consistent with the answers of over 300 participants in my Sexless Marriages Survey.

A Surprising Result

People in emotionally healthy marriages rarely fill out my Sexless Marriages Survey. However, a little more than half of the participants in the 5 Love Languages Survey were in good marriages. I was pleasantly surprised to discover that most of the happy participants practice all, or nearly all, of the 5 love languages and don't limit the way they express love to their spouses. Their spouses were also good at giving love.

The surprising result? *The happier the marriage, the more love languages practiced by both partners.*

Participants in Loving Marriages

The 9 satisfied respondents ranged in age from 27 to 75 years old and had been married from 6 to 51 years, with 4 of them married over 40 years. I left the ages off to help protect their identities. Notice the wisdom they share.

1. A husband, married 37 years, practices 4 love languages, and leaves out gift giving. His wife shows love with only acts of service. However, the love languages she wants to be spoken to her are quality time and receiving gifts. Although she is the only one in the good marriages who does not show love with "touch," he indicated that she does not withhold affection and is not bitter or angry. She wants help with her projects and a listening ear. He said, "The love languages are an excellent starting point to build upon." Perhaps by looking over his answers and the other successful marriages, he will start to give gifts as an expression of his love since that is one way his wife receives love.

2. A husband, married 21 years, practices 3 love languages and leaves out words of affirmation. His wife practices 4 love languages and leaves out acts of service. Thus, they are both missing 1 of the commanded love languages, but both practice touch. About how his love languages have changed over the years, he wrote, "Words of affirmation: I don't seem to get much out of 'words of affirmation' and aren't likely to give out any, but I do encourage my children verbally. This is a great disappointment to my wife. Even though I have read countless books on words of affirmation, it's like a foreign language I just don't get!" He concluded, "We have distance between us much of the time, i.e., lack of intimacy. We struggle to talk about important things, such as where to live, income earning, sex. She seems to have an undercurrent of anger, which I'd rather avoid. So I don't talk with her much or reveal much about myself to her." However, they both show love with touch and acts of service. About touch, he said, "I come from a non-huggy family, yet my wife is very huggy with hers and with me. I do desire more sexual touch and time with my wife than she desires, such I tend to avoid touching a lot of the time. She gets really angry if I 'grope' first, then 'touch' second."

   TIP: An easy way to give words of affirmation is to listen. If you really listen, your spouse will tell you what they are proud of and what they want you to notice. And so will your children. You will learn a lot about your family from just listening and expressing genuine appreciation for what they have done.

3. A husband and wife, married 40 years, practice 4 love languages, including the 3 commanded ones. The husband wrote that their love languages have changed over the years by becoming more frequent and more heartfelt. He added that they affected their marriage "in a positive way, but the (my) inhibition in our sex life remains. I think you have helped me discover that the acts of service may be covering up my uncomfortable approach to having more intimacy in my sexual relationship with my wife, whom I love dearly."

4. A husband, married 6 years, who practices all 5 love languages as does his wife, wrote, "I have always felt that the love language book is a way to justify bad attitudes and neurosis. I've seen firsthand in family and a couple of friends that they won't give or receive love because it's 'not my love language.' I've seen a spouse not give a gift to her husband on his birthday because she gives love by spending 'quality time,' not by giving gifts. I've also heard a friend say 'physical touch' isn't his wife's love language, so they don't have a lot of sex. From my experience with my wife, we are both equally able to give and receive love in all forms."

5. A husband, married 21 years, practices 3 of the love languages leaving out acts of service. His wife practices 4 of the love languages, including all 3 of the commanded ones. Their love languages have changed over the years as he has "learned to provide quality time and words of affirmation since she responds so well to them." About words of appreciation, he wrote, "We have added a layer of extra protection in our marriage even though it is not one of our top three love languages. The love languages have had an incredibly positive effect on our marriage as we learn to speak each other's languages."

6. A husband, married 43 years, practices all 5 love languages. His wife practices 2 of the love languages, acts of service and touch. She has no anger. When asked how their love languages changed over the years, he said, "Having her tell me how she loves and respects me. Her desire to be physical with me. We tell each other how we feel every day. She is very domestic. She cleans, cooks, and takes care of our home. She always tries to look good when I get home."

7. A man, married 51 years, practices 3 of the love languages. He leaves out acts of service and practices quality time. His wife shows love with the same 3 love languages. They do not practice anger or blaming.

8. A man, married 46 years, practices all 5 love languages, as does his wife. He said, "Understanding the love languages helped enhance our connection/bond."

9. A woman, married 45 years, practices all 5 love languages, and her husband practices 4. The husband leaves out "quality time." She said their love languages have changed over the years as, "The more I learned about my husband, and the more I knew when and what 'language' to use. Learning the unique differences between men and women and not expecting him to think like me helped me dig deeper into what his 'take' is in the current situation." She added, "I can only assume my words of affirmation are effective for he performs acts of service and gives me physical touch. The comfort and refuge that I provide in our home ease the burden of his workload. Sometimes he surprises me by doing some of my chores. Working at appreciating his acts of service and physical touch helps me not obsess on some unclear or undefined levels of 'quality time.' Quality time ends up being redefined by unexpected snatches of time, not necessarily an event. Friends and lovers are what we are."

Conclusion About the Non-Withholding Marriages

In satisfying marriages, both partners put effort into giving love in multiple ways—not just how they prefer to receive affection. Good marriages are not about how the partners *receive love*, but about how they *give love.* They avoid the problems of the unsatisfying marriages, where the ones *withholding love* focus on how they *receive love.*

Participants Married to a Withholder

The 8 sexually deprived participants ranged in age from 41 to 56 and have been married from 4.5 to 33 years, with 4 of them married over 30 years. Their responses reveal one-sided marriages:

1. A man, married 18 years, practices 4 love languages, but not acts of service. His wife practices only acts of service. She blames him for everything, complains about what he does or doesn't do, when he masters one area, she moves on to another to complain about. He can never provide enough acts of service to make her happy. She wants him to help around the house and with her projects.

2. A man, married 19 years, practices all 3 commanded love languages. His wife practices 0 love languages. He said, "My wife doesn't seem to fit any of these (or at least that is what she says), so I feel like I am unable to serve her in any way because I do not know how. She does not show love in any of the 5 ways." She is angry and impossible to please. She says, "If you loved me, you would know what to do to please me." She wants him to "earn more money" as an act of service.

3. A woman, married 33 years, practices all 5 love languages. Her husband practices only gift giving. She checked 6 of the negatives

attitudes for him, including blaming, bitterness, anger, complaining, impossible to please, and moving on to another area when she masters one. He requires her to help with his projects.

4. A man, married 31 years, practices 4 love languages, including all 3 commanded ones. His wife practices only 1 love language, quality time. He said, "I give, but I never receive." She gets angry, and moves on to another one to complain when he masters one area. She wants him to help with her projects and requires him to do any and all work at home. She does no acts of service for him. He said, "I feel unloved and in a platonic relationship."

5. A woman, married 28 years, practices 3 of the love languages, which include only touch of the commanded love languages. She shows love with quality time and gifts. Her husband uses only acts of service. He complains about what she does and doesn't do, moves on to another area to complain about when she masters one, and is impossible to please. She said, "I quit giving words of affirmation because I don't feel loved in return." He wants her to help around the house more and do things without being asked or reminded. He shows love by keeping the gas tank full without being asked.

6. A woman, married 30 years, practices all 5 love languages. Her husband wants acts of service and quality time, but his only demonstration of love is acts of service. He shows bitterness toward her and wants her to do more around the house and spend more time with his family. She said, "He cares for the house, but no nurturing for my heart."

7. A man, married 33 years, practices 4 love languages, including the 3 commanded ones, plus giving gifts. His wife uses only acts of service to show love. Although she wants to receive words of affirmation, and he praises her, he is unable to provide enough to make her happy. He said, "My spouse is a taker, not a giver." Likewise, he is not able to provide enough acts of service to satisfy her. She wants help with her projects and "sometimes" will provide acts of service for him. He concluded, "I believe my primary love language is physical touch, and I get VERY LITTLE." On blaming and anger, he checked, "My companion doesn't do any of these things."

8. A woman, married 4.5 years, practices 3 love languages: words of affirmation, quality time, and gifts. She said, "I didn't realize that physical touch was important to me until it seemed to be lacking." Her husband wants words of affirmation, and she doesn't know what else. He uses quality time, gifts, and acts of service to express love. He blames her for everything, gets angry, and complains about what she does or doesn't do. He wants her to help around the house more.

Overview of the Withholding Marriages

All the participants would like to practice "touch" with their spouse who is a withholder. The survey shows that the ones being deprived are trying much harder to show love in their marriages than the deprivers are, with 1 of the deprivers not even giving the appearance of trying. Only 1 person checked that the withholding spouse was not involved in any of the negative qualities such as blaming, anger, and bitterness.

However, the second husband in the not-deprived group said his wife had an "undercurrent of anger" that he tried to avoid. They did not enjoy the same intimacy that the other couples in that group did.

Both Dr. Douglas Weiss and Dr. Marie N. Robinson expose these anger-related character flaws as typical of intimacy anorexia and sexual inhibitions. In chapter 6, Dr. Robinson describes them as "cognitive distortions" based on negative attitudes toward the opposite sex, one's own sex, and lovemaking.

Both doctors demonstrate that withholding love is not the fault of the one being deprived. Withholding affection is frequently a holdover from a dysfunctional home of origin. The child adopts defective survival mechanisms and refuses to grow out of the behaviors as an adult.

Answers to the 3 Questions

1. *Are "acts of service" a love language or a symptom of inhibitions?* For emotionally healthy, loving spouses, acts of service are a natural love language with many of them giving service when it was not one of their primary love languages. Of the withholders, 5 said acts of service was their love language, 1 claimed quality time, 1 gave gifts, and the remaining 1 practiced 0 love languages. The withholders were given to various forms of anger and being hard to please. For deprivers, acts of service provide an excuse for heaping distorted blame and anger upon their mates.

2. *Or can "acts of service" be either one depending on the person's general ability to give love?* Acts of service can be either good or bad depending on whether it is given freely or angrily demanded.

3. *Are "words of affirmation" one-sided in unloving marriages?* Yes! None of the deprivers even tried to give words of affirmation. Instead, they found ways to blame, criticize, and reject their mates.

For in-depth information on the Bible's teaching regarding the 3 commanded love languages, plus God's fourth one, thanksgiving, see my book, *Male and Female: God's Genius, Soulmate to Fall in Love All Over Again.* These 4 love languages correspond with the 4 parts of one-flesh love that God instituted in the Garden of Eden and are commanded of both husbands and wives.

32.

When Your Spouse Chooses Inhibitions Over Passion

The greatest spiritual challenges occur when sin enters the home—they don't come from the ungodly outside Christ. The most common marital sin I've encountered in over 50 years of working with husbands and wives is one spouse withholding sexual love from the mate.

Dr. Marie Robinson exposed that inhibited spouses often choose distorted anger and blaming over love and passion. Dr. Douglas Weiss observed that many of them use anger or silence with a vengeance "to push away, punish, or control" their mates. Thus deprivers add more sins to withholding sex. Paul warned that character faults thrive among the 18 sins that surround being "without natural affection":

> *2 Timothy 3:1-5: "But mark this: There will be terrible times in the last days. People will be lovers of themselves, lovers of money, boastful, proud,* ***abusive****, disobedient to their parents, ungrateful,* ***unholy, without love [without natural affection—KJV], unforgiving, slanderous****, without self-control, brutal, not lovers of the good, treacherous, rash, conceited,* ***lovers of pleasure rather than lovers of God—having a form of godliness but denying its power.*** *Have nothing to do with such people (NIV)."*

No one chooses inhibitions. However, sexually depriving the mate becomes a sin when a person refuses to work at overcoming his or her childhood influence. It's like being raised in a family of thieves and continuing to rob others. As adults, everyone chooses for themselves if they will be love thieves or love promoters—a sinner or a lover.

Yes, the greatest spiritual challenges occur in our homes. Along with the sin of withholding sexual love, the sins of anger, blame, and the silent treatment regularly crowd out love for God and godliness as well.

A Spiritual Battle Must Be Fought in the Home

God inspired the Song of Solomon to overcome these hateful sins that destroy marriages and damage children for a lifetime. So what can you do when your spouse refuses to learn how to soulmate for glorious lovemaking? In Ephesians 5:22-33, Paul told couples to practice sacrificial love for each other and to model their marriage after Christ and the church. But first, he warned about sin in the home.

Let No One Deceive You with Empty Words

> *Ephesians 5:6-10: "Let no one deceive you with empty [vain – KJV] words, for because of these things the wrath of God comes upon the sons of disobedience. Therefore do not be partakers with them; for you were formerly darkness, but now you are Light in the Lord; walk as children of Light (for the fruit of the Light consists in all goodness and righteousness and truth), trying to learn what is pleasing to the Lord."*

"Deceive" means "to cheat, deceive, beguile." It's the same kind of deceit Satan used to trick Eve into eating the forbidden fruit in Genesis 3:13 and is referenced in 1 Timothy 2:14 with this same word (Thayer 55).

"Empty" is used "of places, vessels, [words], etc., which contain nothing; a metaphor for empty, vain; devoid of truth" (Thayer 343).

In sexless marriages, the deceit of empty words often surfaces as distorted anger and blame ("words devoid of truth") are heaped upon the sex-deprived mate. *Dr. Robinson shows that the unbridled anger and twisted blame are not about the loving mate.* Chapter 6: "Sexual Inhibitions Linked to Cognitive Distortions" and Chapter 28: "Pullbacks and Terrified, Angry, Truth-Telling Child-Adults" develop this point.

You get deceived with empty words when you allow your inhibited spouse's distorted reasoning to intimidate you into accepting responsibility for his or her behavior. When you become codependent with your spouse's love sins, all progress toward healing the marriage stops. Get my free "How to Fight Fair and Face Anger" report at PatsyRaeDawson.com to learn how to disarm angry, empty, vain words.

Expose and Reprove the Sin in Your Home

> *Ephesians 5:11: "Do not participate in the unfruitful deeds of darkness, but instead even expose [or reprove – NASB footnote] them;...."*

Notice how strong a word "expose" or "reprove" is and that it includes convicting the person of sin by both word and deed. "It means "1. to convict, refute, confute, generally with a suggestion of the shame of the person convicted, by conviction to bring to light, to expose. 2. to find fault with, correct; **a. by word;** to reprehend severely, chide, admonish, reprove; to call to account, show one his fault, demand an explanation; **b. by deed;** to chasten, punish" (Thayer 202-203).

Both husbands who love their wives as their own body and wives who submit to their husbands have the responsibility to expose and reprove their spouses' sins. Love and subjection never cover up sin in the home. Paul warned that when you don't deal with the sin in your marriage, "you participate in the unfruitful deeds of darkness." Indeed, you demonstrate and teach the debilitating inhibitions to your children.

The best advice I can give is, "Get the sin out into the open and deal with it—don't hide it." However, often the sinful spouse objects to the mate seeking outside help as Paul advised in Galatians 6:1–2 with "bear one another's burdens." The resistance usually comes from the spouse not wanting anyone to know about his or her behavior. Jesus said:

> *John 3:20: "For everyone who does evil hates the light, and does not come to the light, lest his deeds should be exposed."*

One wife said every time she threatened to talk to the preacher, her husband, who verbally abused her daily, acted better for several weeks. Then he always went back to his old behavior. They didn't solve the problem because she never followed through on getting help.

Another wife, who flaunted her mental adultery before her husband, quickly left the congregation when she learned her husband was getting ready to ask other Christians to talk to her. Her husband didn't realize that withdrawing one's membership is a common way to avoid public exposure. He falsely thought he couldn't ask other Christians to admonish his wife since she was no longer a member.

Sin Thrives on Secrecy

> *Ephesians 5:12-13: "...for it is disgraceful even to speak of the things which are done by them in secret. But all things become visible when they are exposed [or reproved—NASB footnote] by the light, for everything that becomes visible is light."*

Sometimes loving husbands and wives resist exposing the sin and getting help because of their own shame regarding what is happening in their marriage. Or they may believe and be embarrassed by the distorted blame heaped upon them for the spouse's ungodly behavior. As the sinner is, they also are afraid of the light. By husbands or wives accepting the shame and blame rather than bringing the problem into the "light," they buy into the sinner's need for secrecy.

The Sexless Marriages Survey and experience show that when sin in the home is not exposed to the light, it will get worse over the years. Secrecy that covers up sin ultimately destroys the marriage and harms everyone it touches—especially the children.

Sin thrives on secrecy. Sin never stagnates. Sin always grows.

Getting the sinful behavior out into the open is hard and

embarrassing, but it can also be a relief to talk about it to others and get help. If your spouse refuses to work at overcoming his or her sexual inhibitions, don't hide it or make excuses. Get the problem out into the open and deal with it as sin because your mate is not justified before God. You will be the best friend your spouse has by insisting that he or she deal with the sin. Treat the issue as grievous, impenitent sin.

If you don't face the problem now, be assured that when your children grow up, they will blame you for not protecting them from their unloving parent. Most will move across the country to get away from both parents who failed to love each other and them.

Don't Be Deceived by Pious Faces at Church

Ephesians 5:14-16: "For this reason it [or He – NASB footnote] says,
"Awake, sleeper,
And arise from the dead,
And Christ will shine on you."
Therefore be careful how you walk, not as unwise men [fools – KJV] but as wise, making the most [literally redeeming the time – NASB footnote] of your time, because the days are evil."

Many angry, blaming, silent, and inhibited husbands and wives put on deceitful faces of piety when attending worship or serving in the congregation. In the Old Testament, God stated what he thinks of "the wicked" quoting scriptures in service to him:

Psalm 50:16-21
"But to the wicked God says,
'What right have you to tell of My statutes
And to take My covenant in your mouth?
'For you hate discipline,
And you cast My words behind you.
'When you see a thief, you are pleased with him,
And you associate with adulterers.
'You let your mouth loose in evil
And your tongue frames deceit.
'You sit and speak against your brother;
You slander your own mother's son.
'These things you have done and I kept silence;
You thought that I was just like you;
I will reprove you and state the case in order before your eyes.'"

Likewise, Peter said that God doesn't hear husbands' prayers when they mistreat their wives, no matter how long or beautifully prayed:

1 Peter 3:7: "You husbands in the same way, live with your wives in an understanding way, as with someone weaker, since she is a woman; and show her honor as a fellow heir of the grace of life, so that your prayers will not be hindered."

Part of getting the sin out into the open should be insisting that the inhibited spouse be removed from all congregational duties because God doesn't accept their service or hear their prayers. When wives watch their husbands assume leadership positions in the church and hide the sins in the home, they partake of their husbands' sins. That includes husbands who serve as elders or deacons, preach or teach, or offer prayers and lead singing. The example of Ananias and Sapphira in Acts 5 shows God's attitude toward wives who cover up their husbands' sins.

Husbands also bear responsibility when they cover up their wives' sins and don't object to their congregational duties, no matter how significant or minor they might be. One mother screamed at her teenage children continually as she drove them to Sunday morning worship. Only when she parked the car did the verbal abuse stop as she hopped out and ran in to teach a children's Bible class. One of her daughters imitates her by regularly haranguing her husband when he drives the family to services. When they get out of the car, she criticizes him for walking into the building with a frown on his face. How outrageous!

Such mockery against God takes place in many congregations due to the cooperation of husbands and wives who know what is going on in secret, yet remain silent. Even when the congregational members are fooled by the smiling faces, the children see the hypocrisy. Many adult children become agnostics or atheists because of growing up surrounded by love sins at home while witnessing their parents' feigned love for each other and them at religious services.

Study and Prepare for a Spiritual Battle in Your Home

Ephesians 5:17: "So then do not be foolish [unwise—KJV], but understand what the will of the Lord is."

"Foolish" means "senseless, foolish, stupid, without reflection or intelligence, acting rashly" (Thayer 90).

"Understand" means "to comprehend and act accordingly" (Thayer 605).

Regardless of what your inhibited spouse chooses to do, study for yourself so you can deal wisely with the sin and protect your children. Comprehending the will of the Lord helps you identify areas where you may be codependent and submissive to sin, which makes you a partaker in your companion's abuse. Learning God's truths allows you to reject your spouse's foolishness so you can make healthy decisions for your family. May God bless you with understanding on your journey of love.

Works Cited

Works Cited by Dr. Marie N. Robinson

Benedek, Therese. *Psychosexual Functions in Women.* New York, NY: Ronald Press, 1952.
Bonaparte, Marie. *Female Sexuality.* New York, NY: International Universities Press, 1953.
Davis, K. B. *Factors in the Sex Life of Twenty-Two Hundred Women.* New York, NY: Harper, 1929.
Deutsch, Helen. *The Psychology of Women,* Vols. 1 and 2. New York, NY: Grune and Stratton, 1944-45.
Ditzion, Sidney. *Marriage, Morals and Sex in America.* New York, NY: Bookman Associates, 1953.
Fromm, Erich. *The Art of Loving.* New York, NY: Harper, 1956.
Lundberg and Farnham. *Modern Woman – The Lost Sex.* New York, NY: Harper, 1947.
Reik, Theodor. *Psychology of Sex Relations.* New York, NY: Rinehart, 1945.
Piper, Otto. *The Christian Interpretation of Sex.* New York, NY: Scribner, 1941).
Stone, Hannah and Abraham. *A Marriage Manual.* New York, NY: Simon and Schuster, 1952.

Works Cited by Patsy Rae Dawson

Anderson, Dianna E. "Taking the Lead in Developing New Sexual Ethics." Rachel Held Evans Blog, 2/4/2015. Web.

Anderson, Ryan T. *Truth Overruled: The Future of Marriage and Religious Freedom.* Washington, DC: Regnery Publishing, 2015

Berman, Jennifer and Laura Berman. *For Women Only, A Revolutionary Guide to Overcoming Sexual Dysfunction and Reclaiming Your Sex Life.* New York, NY: Henry Holt and Company, 2001.

Brennan, Dan. "Signs of a Sex Addict." WebMD, 12/02/2020.

Boteach, Shmuley. *Hating Women: America's Hostile Campaign Against the Fairer Sex.* New York, NY: ReganBooks, 2006.

Carnes, Patrick J. *Out of the Shadows: Understanding Sexual Addiction.* Center City, MN: Hazelden Educational Materials, 1992.

Davis, Maxine. *The Sexual Responsibility of Woman.* New York, NY: Dial Press, 1956. As quoted by Hastings, Donald W., M.D. *A Doctor Speaks on Sexual Expression in Marriage.* Boston, NY: Little, Brown and Co., 1971 Second Edition.

Dawson, Patsy Rae. *Challenges in Marriage: What to Do When Sin Inhibits Love.* Amarillo, TX: Patsy Rae Dawson LLC, 2015.

---. *God's 11 Secrets of Sex for a Lifetime of Passion.* Seagoville, TX: Marriage: A Taste of Heaven Media, 2020.

---. *God's People Make the Best Lovers, Thrill to God's Way of a Man with a Maid.* Seagoville, TX: Marriage: A Taste of Heaven Media, 2021.

---. *Male and Female: God's Genius, Soulmate to Fall in Love All Over Again.* Seagoville, TX: Marriage: A Taste of Heaven Media, 2021.

---. *Sexless Marriages Survey: With Self-Assessment Checklists,* Amarillo, TX: Patsy Rae Dawson LLC, 2016.

Deutsch, Ronald M. *The Key to Feminine Response in Marriage.* New York, NY: Random House, 1968.

Diefendorf, Sarah. "After the Wedding Night: Sexual Abstinence and Masculinities Over the Life Course." Unpublished doctorate paper at the University of Washington. Used by permission. Published *Gender & Society,* Vol. XX No. X, Month, IIII, 15 July 2015. Sociologists for Women in Society. Web.

D'Souza, Dinesh. "Feminists Are Re-evaluating 'the Movement.' " *Seattle Post-Intelligencer* (March 30, 1986).

Durvasula, Ramani S. "What Do Narcissists Do to Truth Tellers?" YouTube Video, July 14, 2020.

"FDA Approves First Treatment for Sexual Desire Disorder, Addyi Approved to Treat Premenopausal Women." FDA News Release 8/18/2015. Silver Spring, MD: U.S. Food and Drug Administration

Frank, Lawrence. "The Psychosocial Approach in Sex Research." *Social Problems,* 1, 1954.

Harris, R. Laird, Archer, Gleason L. Jr. and Waltke, Bruce K. *Theological Wordbook of the Old Testament* (TWOT). Chicago, IL: Moody Press, 1980.

Hart, Archibald D. *The Sexual Man: Masculinity Without Guilt.* Dallas, TX: Word Publishing, 1994.
Henry, Matthew. *Matthew Henry's Commentary on the Whole Bible, Vol. III.* New York, NY: Fleming H. Revell Co., 1710.
Jasper, William F. "Teaching the Perversions." *The New American*, 1/19/87.
Kaplin, Helen Singer. *New Sex Therapy, Active Treatment of Sexual Dysfunctions.* New York, NY: Routledge, Taylor & Francis Group, 1974.
---. *The Sexual Desire Disorders, Dysfunctional Regulation of Sexual Motivation.* New York, Routledge, Taylor & Francis Group, 1995.
LaHaye, Tim and Beverly. *The Act of Marriage.* Grand Rapids, MI: The Zondervan Corporation, 1976. Used by permission.
Linden, David. *Touch: The Science of Hand, Heart, and Mind.* New York, NY: Penguin Books, 2015.
McBride, Karyl. *Will I Ever Be Good Enough?* New York, NY: Atria Paperback, 2008.
McIlhaney, Joe E. Jr. and Freda McKissic Bush. *Hooked, New Science on How Casual Sex Is Affecting Our Children.* Chicago, IL: Northfield Publishing, 2008.
Montagu, Ashley. *Touching: The Human Significance of the Skin (Third Edition).* New York, NY: Harper & Row, Publishers, 1986.
Muller, Charla with Betsy Thorpe. *365 Nights, A Memoir of Intimacy.* New York, NY: Berkley Books, 2008. Used by permission.
Murphey, Cecil. *When a Man Yu Love Was Abused: A Woman's Guide to Helping Him Overcome Childhood Sexual Molestation.* Grand Rapids, MI: Kregel Publications, 2010.
Murray, Linda. "Why Women [or Men] Lose Interest in Sex." *McCall's* (February 1984).
O'Connor, Anahad. "Bernie Zilbergeld, 62, Dies; Expert on Male Sexuality." *The New York Times* (June 21, 2002).
Ornish, Dean. *Love and Survival.* New York, NY: HarperCollins Publishers, Inc., 1998.
Ortner, Jessica. "How to Tap with Jessica Ortner." YouTube (April 11, 2013). Web.
Ortner, Nick. *The Tapping Solution for Pain Relief.* Carlsbad, California: Hay House Publishing, 2015.
Piper, Otto. *The Christian Interpretation of Sex.* New York, NY: Scribner, 1941).
"Premature Ejaculation, Erectile Dysfunction, and Lower Urinary Tract Symptoms Were Associated with Low Sexual Desire." National Library of Medicine (July 16, 2019). PubMed.gov.
Reik, Theodor. *Psychology of Sex Relations.* New York, NY: Rinehart, 1945.
Robinson, Marie N. *The Power of Sexual Surrender.* New York, NY: Signet Book, 1959.
Rueben, David. *Any Woman Can.* New York, NY: David McKay Co., 1974. Quoted by LaHaye in *The Act of Marriage.* Grand Rapids, MI: The Zondervan Corporation, 1976. Used by permission.
---. *Everything You Always Wanted to Know About Sex But Were Afraid to Ask.* New York, NY: Bantam Books, 1969.
Sarrel, Lorna and Philip. "What Men Need from the Women Who Love Them." *Redbook* (April 1977).
Schafer, Jack. "Odd Facts About Kissing." *Psychology Today.* 12/2012.
Stump, Jane Barr. *What's the Difference? How Men and Women Compare.* New York, NY: William Morrow and Company, 1985.
Tavris, Carol. "40,000 Men Tell About Their Sexual Behavior, Their Fantasies, Their Ideal Women and Their Wives." *Redbook* (Feb. 1978).
---. "The Sex Lives of Happy Men." *Redbook* (March 1978).
Taylor, Arlene Ph.D. and Katherine Benziger. "The Physiological Foundations of Falsification of Type and PASS," 1999.
Thayer, Joseph Henry, D.D. *Thayer's Greek-English Lexicon of the New Testament.* Grand Rapids, MI: Associated Publishers and Authors Inc., n.d.
TWOT. See Harris, R. Laird, Archer, Gleason L. Jr., Waltke, Bruce K. *Theological Wordbook of the Old Testament.*
Walton, Alice G. "Male Sexuality: Not so Simple." Web: TheDoctorWillSeeYouNow.com.
Weiss, Douglas. "#43 To Masturbate or Not to Masturbate." *Love & Sex Today* YouTube Podcast, 10/31/2018.
---. *Intimacy Anorexia: Healing the Hidden Addiction in Your Marriage.* Colorado Springs, CO: Discovery Press, 2010.
---. *Sex, Men and God.* Lake Mary, FL: Siloam Press, 2002.
Whiteman, Honor. "Worldwide Obesity Rates See 'Startling' Increase Over Past 3 Decades." *MedicalNewsToday* (May 29, 2014).
Willy, A and L. Vander, and O. Fisher. *The Illustrated Encyclopedia of Sex.* New York, NY: Cadillac Publishing Co., Inc., 1950-1955.
Yetman, Daniel. "Is Erectile Dysfunction Common? Stats, Causes, and Treatment." *Healthline* (March 5, 2020).
Zilbergeld, Bernie. *Male Sexuality.* New York, NY: Bantam, 1978.

Marie N. Robinson MD

Marie Nyswander Robinson was born in Nevada and educated at Sarah Lawrence College and Cornell University Medical School. She was a graduate of the Flower and Fifth Avenue Hospitals' Psychoanalytical Institute, a Diplomate of the American Board of Psychiatry and Neurology, and a Fellow of the American Psychiatric Association. In addition to her private practice, Dr. Robinson was very active in community mental-health projects. She contributed frequently to professional and technical journals and wrote many magazine articles for general readers.

In 1955 she helped found the Narcotic Addiction Research Project, a program for treating drug addicts using psychotherapy. Through the 1950s and 1960s she continued to treat addicts in two programs. During this time she wrote *The Drug Addict as a Patient* (1956). She also worked with women in private practice for fifteen years in New York before writing *The Power of Sexual Surrender (1959).* In the early 1960s, she left private practice and devoted the rest of her life to narcotic addiction research. She founded several programs for addicts and won awards with her third husband on drug research. She was known for developing and popularizing the use of methadone to treat heroin addiction.

Dr. Robinson was an adjunct professor at The Rockefeller University from 1964 to 1986. She died of cancer in 1986. Her book *The Power of Sexual Surrender* is in the public domain where digital copies are available. (Wikipedia, Marie Nyswander. 1965 Staff picture from The Rockefeller University, digital commons.)

The Way to Sexual Maturity

In this important book, a leading psychiatrist examines a problem that endangers the stability of marriage and threatens the happiness of four out of ten American husbands and wives—sexual inhibitions. Through the use of actual case histories, she considers vital aspects of the problem: its cause, degree, and treatment. She details the roles that husband and wife must play if the couple is to effect a cure and achieve sexual fulfillment through the mature power of sexual surrender.

—1959 SIGNET BOOK Back Cover

Patsy Rae Dawson

Patsy Rae got her start studying and teaching about marriage as a young bride when an abusive husband baited her: "If a husband tells his wife to eat beans 7 days a week, don't you think she should eat beans 7 days a week?" She knew only a Bible answer would stop the man from trying to get her to say something he could use against his wife.

Believing the Bible didn't say much about being a woman and marriage, Patsy Rae was shocked to discover the Bible is full of marital wisdom. She has been studying, teaching, writing, and mentoring both women and men ever since—**for half a century.** She's fascinated by the power of the scriptures to transform lives—yours and hers.

As an overcomer of a 46-year sexless marriage, Patsy Rae says:

> *I could not know the things I do if I had not lived the life I did. It gave me insights you can't find in any book or class. I thank God for what he has done for me and for allowing me to share his love and his marvelous sexual secrets with you. What a wonderful life of service he's given me!"*

Sexless Marriages Survey, Self-Assessment Checklists Administrator

Patsy Rae designed a comprehensive set of checklists of intensely personal questions. They help participants recognize the common 24/7 love sins in their sexless marriage so they can work on the real issues.

Sexuality & Personality Breakthrough Christian Coach

Certified as an Advanced Personality Trainer, Patsy Rae specializes in helping clients move out of childhood survival mode into their loving genetics. This skill helps her get quickly to the core issues of clients who have a variety of sexual problems.

Embarrass the Alligator Newsletter Editor and Author

Patsy Rae shares surprising facts and trends from her survey checklists in her newsletter. Due to participants asking for more information, she's working on books related to the survey. She's the author of *Male and Female: God's Genius, God's People Make the Best Lovers, God's 11 Secrets of Sex for a Lifetime of Passion,* and the MP3 *Challenges in Marriage: What to Do When Sin Inhibits Love.*

You can contact Patsy Rae and learn more at PatsyRaeDawson.com.

Made in the USA
Middletown, DE
26 September 2023

39457936R00215